The Kogod Library of Judaic Studies
7

Mysticism and Madness

The Religious Thought
of Rabbi Nachman of Bratslav

By

Zvi Mark

מכון שלום הרטמן
SHALOM HARTMAN INSTITUTE

continuum

Published by Continuum
The Tower Building, 11 York Road, London SE1 7NX
80 Maiden Lane, Suite 704, New York, NY 10038

www.continuumbooks.com

British Library Cataloguing-in-Publication Data
A catalogue record for this book is available from the British Library

Typeset by Free Range Book Design & Production
Printed on acid-free paper in Great Britain by CPI Antony Rowe

ISBN   HB: 0–8264-4516–0
        PB: 0–8264-4144–0
        HB: 978–0-8264–4516-2
        PB: 978–0-8264–4144-7

Contents

Dedicated in profound appreciation and friendship to Prof. Moshe Idel

Introduction

When the winds of general education blew through the Jewish world, and the light of knowledge and wisdom captivated the hearts of many, a young man, who spent much time in seclusion in the forests and cruised by himself in tempestuous rivers, began a stubborn struggle, replete with song and poetry, against the philosophy and the *Haskalah* that placed knowledge at the head of its values. The *niggun* (melody), the story, Torah study, and prayer served him as tools in the presentation of a world of faith and innocence as an alternative to that of wisdom and intellect.

The demonstrative lack of faith in the ability of the intellect to show man the way to serve the Lord and the call to 'cast off' the intellect are the outstanding characteristics of the spiritual world introduced by R. Nachman of Bratslav. A study of the place of madness and the acts of madness, which starkly symbolize life and deeds not in harmony with knowledge and intellect, is an examination of the foundations of the teachings of R. Nachman and an inquiry into their unique nature. The attitude toward acts of madness, to fools, and to the spirit of folly are the conspicuous tip of a comprehensive and magnificently constructed worldview that stresses that knowledge and the intellect are but a single channel for the life flow of man, and not necessarily the main or most exalted such stream. There is a rich and diverse conscious life that occurs specifically when the mind and knowledge are absent, life that cannot be attained by the regular consciousness of knowledge. This study clearly shows that the alternative consciousness proposed by R. Nachman is a plainly mystical consciousness. The casting off of the intellect and the struggle against its despotic rule constitute a way and means to enable the creation and development of mystical states of consciousness.

One of the conclusions emerging from this work is that the previous explanations and descriptions offered for R. Nachman's teachings, concepts, and practices that neglected the mystical goal at the center of his worldview missed the significance of the latter, and the resulting picture does not reflect the world of R. Nachman. This is the first comprehensive study that clarifies and analyzes the thought of R. Nachman of Bratslav as mystical thought, both in its theoretical aspects and in the practical realm, with its actual practices.

Chapter 1 discusses the cardinal role of the imagination in the human experience and in man's worship of God. The centrality of the imagination in belief and in prophecy restricted and bound the place of the intellect. This limitation constitutes the ideational underpinning for the religious service of the 'casting off of the intellect.'

Chapter 2 examines in greater detail the place and role of the withdrawal of the intellect in the various mystical experiences, both as a preparatory phase for the mystical experience, and as a characteristic of the state of consciousness during this experience. The unique state of the post-mystical consciousness is also studied.

Chapter 3 shifts from the theoretical teachings to their consequences for everyday religious activity. The discussion centers on the theological and existential significance of those practices and religious labors fashioned by R. Nachman and characteristic of Bratslav Hasidism. Here as well, the opposition between the intellect and its withdrawal is of central importance.

Chapter 4 is devoted to R. Nachman's interpretation of the kabbalistic *tzimtzum* and the vacant space. The faith required in the face of the vacant space has two components, silence and *niggun* (melody). Silence represents the renunciation of the intellect, and is parallel to the 'casting off of the intellect,' but it is only an interim stage toward the attainment of the mystical perception expressed by *niggun* and song.

Chapter 5 discusses the Land of Israel, portrayed as the land of the imagination and prophecy. These activities are performed by the imaginative force, and not by the intellect; the path to the Land entails the casting off and withdrawal of the intellect, which removes its presence from the consciousness and enables the granting of primacy and dominance to the activity of the imaginative force. This conception casts new light on the strange behavior of R. Nachman on his way to the Land of Israel, and imparts additional meaning to the states of forgetfulness, the 'I do not know,' and the acts of foolishness that characterized his *aliyah* (immigration) to the Land.

Chapter 6 describes the cluster of elements belonging to the states of consciousness known as 'smallness [*katnut*]' that R. Nachman developed from their roots in Lurianic Kabbalism. Our analysis teaches that *katnut* is a state located on the fringes of normal, adult and mature existence. The descent to 'smallness' is, mainly, a return to the first stages of the development of life, and it encompasses, both in terms of terminology and in essence, a return to a fetal state that is to be understood as a pre-life existence, and not only as one preceding the intellect. The descent to 'smallness' and the ascent from it are understood by R. Nachman as a process of death and rebirth.

The existence of the mythos of death and rebirth in relation to the world of the Godhead in the Kabbalah of the Ari leads to a highly interesting analogy between the description of the processes of death and rebirth of the god-king in ancient cultures and their Christian metamorphosis in the Messiah-king who dies and is resurrected, on the one hand, and, on the other, the depiction of the world of the Godhead in Lurianic Kabbalah as having a periodicity of death ('the death of the king') and rebirth.

Chapter 7 examines the aphorism 'the ultimate knowledge is that we do not know,'and the manner in which R. Nachman develops it in accordance with his mystical worldview.

Chapter 8, concluding the book, contains a comprehensive analysis of R. Nachman's 'Story of the Humble King,' which presents different meanings of the inability to know God. The philosophical lack of knowledge, the mystical lack of knowledge, the sensation of the sublime, and standing before the total otherness of God all join together in the story into a single vector leading to the mystical experience of the revelation of the countenance of God as Nothingness.

An analysis of this tale and additional sources in the thought of R. Nachman indicates that the world of Torah and commandments, and in prominent fashion the Temple service, are a sort of play that man presents, a play that contains a complete system of actions, props, cast, and audience, all the while disregarding the fact that this is not a 'real' system, with the understanding that everything that is done is a joke in comparison with the greatness of God, and that everything is only 'seemingly.' The entire religious system is presented as essentially refuted. What motivates the entire system are not acts of malicious deception, but the tremendous motivation ensuing from the desire to draw closer to God. The observance of the commandments is the outburst of man's desire-love for his God, and the commandments are to be regarded more as love toys than as purposeful actions and the 'service of the King.'

The 'Story of the Humble King' and the accompanying discourses present in keenly-honed fashion the powerlessness of the intellect to impart meaning to the world of Torah and commandments. Only love, will, and longings lead man to exceed the rules of the intellect, and only they are capable of giving reason and meaning to the worship of God. The lack of intellect in the worship of God is not denigrated here, but rather praised, and is a beneficent example of such a lack. Not only is worship not founded on the intellect, rather, its entire underpinnings and possible existence are based on the willingness to cast off the intellect and waive knowledge. The observance of the Torah and the commandments is madness, in the sense that it demands of man the constant willingness to act as a buffoon and madman in the worship of the Lord. It is only the understanding that the latter are the follies of love that imparts to the Torah and commandments, not logic, but meaning, significance and supreme value.

ONE

Imagination, Prophecy and Faith: The Role of the Imagination in Religious Life, and the Character of Bratslavian Faith

In the world of R. Nachman of Bratslav, the imagination occupies a central position, and receives in-depth, extended attention regarding its purpose in human existence and in the service of God. The principal role given to the imagination inevitably narrows and limits the role of the intellect, both in respect to the worship of God and the attainment of religious insight.[1] The intellect is understood as, on the one hand, a restraining force, whose purpose is to clarify and purify the imagination and, on the other, as a force that competes with and limits the imagination; consequently, the intellect may function as an impediment to worship and religious fulfillment. It is R. Nachman's deep relationship with the unrestrained nature of the imagination that characterizes his entire creative output, and warrants the prominence attributed to the imagination within his *Weltanschauung*.

In this opening section, I hope to clarify the role of the 'imaginative faculty' in its various manifestations – e.g., prophecy, madness, faith, joy and the evil inclination. Afterward, I shall examine R. Nachman's directive to 'cast away the rational mind' in its relation to religious worship, as assisted by the 'imaginative faculty.'

I. Imagination, Prophecy and Madness

The role of the imagination in prophecy has long occupied Jewish thinkers, going back to medieval times; many philosophers and kabbalists regarded the 'imaginative faculty' as a fundamental element[2] in the prophetic experience. Maimonides' *Guide of the Perplexed* is often cited[3] as a source, by both philosophers and kabbalists,[4] and as an opening point for argumentation in their consideration of the role of the 'imaginative faculty' in prophecy and prophetic dreams.[5] Similarly, R. Nachman's consideration of the role of the 'imaginative faculty' in many ways echoes the *Guide of the Perplexed* in its treatment of prophecy and dreams, as well as in its identification of the imagination with the evil inclination. It may be inferred that the same foundational principles as developed by Maimonides were influential for R. Nachman. These principles, though, were integrated into a system of values and religious outlook radically unfamiliar to the *weltanschauung* of the *Guide of the Perplexed*.

In the kabbalistic tradition, the imagination shifts, in certain Jewish thinkers, from operating as a mere component in a theoretical discussion on the understanding of prophecy to a vital mechanism that assists the kabbalist in the attainment of divine inspiration and prophecy. And indeed, in kabalistic literature, one finds explicit descriptions of mystical practices of worship involving the imagination.[6] In this context, it is appropriate to mention R. Pinchas Eliyahu of Vilna's *Sefer Habrit*, characterized as a continuation and expansion of part 3 of R.Chaim Vital's, *Shaarei Kedushah*, which deals with the 'attainment of divine inspiration.'[7] In this framework R. Pinchas Eliyahu devotes much attention to both theoretical considerations and practical applications[8] concerning the imagination. And since we know that R. Nachman was familiar with *Sefer Habrit*, and that traces of that work appear in his writings,[9] we must recognize the centrality of focus R. Pinchas devotes in *Sefer Habrit* to the imagination as background to understanding the decisive role ascribed to it by R. Nachman.[10]

1. Song, Prophecy and Madness

In his teaching, *Akrokta*,[11] R. Nachman asserts that melody is drawn from the place of prophecy, and that therefore a relationship exists between a cantor (*chazan*) who sings melodies and prophetic vision (*chazon*).[12] 'That is why the musician is called a *chazan*, from the word *chazon* – which is a reference to prophecy – or he takes the tune from the same place which prophets draw from.' However, R. Nachman goes on to explain that at present God's Kingdom and 'consciousness' are in exile; therefore melody is drawn down without 'consciousness' (*da'at*), and because of this cantors are foolish:

> [...] At present, there is a widespread folk-saying that cantors are fools and lack sense, because the Holy Kingdom is in exile, and therefore the melodies which are drawn from the place of the prophets, coming from the aspect of 'mind' (*mochin*) and 'consciousness' (*da'at*) of the Holy Kingdom, which is at present in exile, the melodies are damaged, and as a result, the cantors lack mindfulness, since they presently do not possess the ability to draw melody from its source in holiness, which is the aspect of 'mind' and 'consciousness' of the Holy Kingdom. [...] But in the future days, when the Holy Kingdom will rise and 'God will be King over all the land,' then melody will rise and be *perfected* in the aspect of the mindfulness of the Holy Kingdom, from which melody is derived, 'for the King of all the earth is God; sing a wise tune.'[13] At that time, when God will be King over all the earth and the Holy Kingdom will be elevated, then 'sing a wise tune' – i.e., the cantors who sing will do so with 'mindfulness' and intelligence, since the Holy Kingdom will be elevated and they will receive

melody from its source in holiness, which is the aspect of 'consciousness' and 'mindfulness' of the Holy Kingdom.

The connection between *melody* and *prophecy*, as well as *madness* and *prophecy* is extensively developed in much greater detail in his teaching, '*Vayihi-Miketz*':[14] 'That is the nature of musical instruments played with the hand, which cause prophecy to rest upon the prophets. As the verse states, "Take for me a musician....".'[15] In this teaching, R. Nachman describes the two ways in which a spirit may rest upon a person: in one case the spirit of *prophecy*, and in the other the spirit of *foolishness* and *madness*.

> There is a spirit of sadness, a broken spirit, an evil spirit, as the verse states of Saul, 'An evil spirit misled him.'[16] And then there is a good spirit, as the verse states, 'Let your good spirit guide me in a straight land,'[17] and this latter corresponds to a spirit of prophecy, a holy spirit. But, when a person is a mixture of good and evil, he cannot receive true prophecies. And so the verse states about Saul 'and he prophesied ... and he fell down naked,'[18] which Rashi understands to mean that he was 'possessed with madness', since he had become knotted within a foolish spirit – a spirit of depression.

Following Rashi, R. Nachman describes various states of prophecy. Regarding, for example, 'Saul prophesied,' it's written that Saul was in a state of madness. It is important to understand also that madness, the evil spirit, is a spirit of God, as the biblical narrative states, 'an evil spirit drove him away from God; and Saul's servants said to him, Behold, an evil spirit from God is terrifying you ... an evil spirit of God is upon you. ...'[19] This being the case, R. Nachman understands certain states of divine inspiration to be states of madness. Saul was susceptible to bouts of madness because a spirit of God seized him, an evil spirit, a spirit of foolishness, and it terrified him.[20]

2. Conditions for Prophecy that is not Madness

The ability to prophesy without succumbing to a state of madness is dependent, according to R. Nachman, on the extent to which the 'instrument is perfected' and the capacity of the individual 'to know the melody.' 'Perfection of the instrument' means that a person has the ability to take in and reproduce music that has been clarified from the cacophony of spirits that rest upon him. 'Knowing melody,' in this context, indicates the ability to differentiate 'voices' while under inspiration and maintain distinctions in the realm of the imagination.

It is 'consciousness' (*da'at*) that develops the facility to differentiate[21] between an evil spirit and a good spirit, between a holy spirit and a spirit of foolishness. This faculty is characterized by R. Nachman as the 'subjugation of the imagination' by one's consciousness (*da'at*).

> When the prophet hears a tune from a person who knows melody, he receives a spirit of prophecy from him [...] and this is the meaning of the verse, 'When the musician played, the hand of God rested upon him.' From this, we learn that when a person plays upon a musical instrument with his hand, he separates the good spirit from the evil spirit. This corresponds to the spirit of prophecy mentioned earlier, and all of this corresponds to the 'subjugation of the imagination' – that it is the quality of the evil spirit, the spirit of foolishness, which desires to damage and confuse the good spirit, the spirit of prophecy [...] Because if the instrument is not *perfected* or if a person does not know how to make melody and does not know how to rise and descend with his hand, separating the good spirit from the evil spirit, then 'the fool brings forth all of his spirit'[22] – i.e., he brings forth all of the spirit at once. Then the melody is certainly not well-constructed, for the essence of a tune's pleasantness is created when the spirit (i.e., the sound traveling through the air, as is known to musical authorities) is refined, which is the essence of the melody. And this is accomplished through the separation of the spirit of good from the evil spirit. However, when the spirit is discharged at once, it goes forth with good and evil mixed together. Then the melody and the joy are not properly constructed, and the imagination is not subjugated.[23]

The difference between madness and prophecy owes, therefore, not to any distinction in the character of the spirits or the essential nature of the divine inspiration that rests on the imagination, but rather in the ability to subjugate the power of imagination,[24] command it and with its help to bring out the desired melody from the experience of divine inspiration. The prophet subjugates the imaginative faculty and creates order within it through the aid of his 'consciousness (*da'at*),[25] discerning between the different spirits (voices, agencies) that rest upon his imagination, thus creating a melody of joy, holy spirit and prophecy. In contradistinction, in the madman's prophecy, the imaginations dominate, making him a medium for every spirit that comes upon him without the necessary process of clarification or the ability to cultivate the experience. In such instances, the spirit that rests upon a person becomes a spirit of foolishness and madness.

We thus see that R. Nachman's words in his lesson, *Akrokta*, correlating cantor, vision and prophecy, are clarified by his lesson, *Vayihi*.[26] Melody, the fruit of inspiration and of the spirit resting upon a person, results not through intellectual attainment but via the faculty of the imagination. It draws its source from 'the place which the prophets draw (receive),' possessing a dimension of prophecy and vision. However, if this state of divine inspiration is not mediated by 'consciousness' and is not able to maintain a connection to the world of 'mindfulness and consciousness,' it becomes madness. Cantors who sing melodies are indeed inspired and possess vision (*chazon*) from which melodies come; but since their actions are (at present) divorced from the mindfulness that subjugates and directs the imagination, the spirit that rests upon them causes cantors to be fools.

3. Dreams: Demon or Angel?

R. Nachman's attitude towards dreams parallels, and is indeed informed by, his complex attitude towards the faculty of the imagination. Dreams can be the elevated realization of an internal 'image of God,' and at such moments, appear to a person as 'true and correct dreams,'[27] dreams on the level of prophecy. Or, on the contrary, the dream might express a person's animal nature that leads him towards spiritual pollution. In both instances, dreams are an inspiration from above; the question, however, is whether the inspiration comes about through the agency of an angel or a demon.[28]

> There is the aspect of man and the aspect of beast – that being, the aspect of a dream that comes through an angel and the aspect of a dream that comes though a demon. A dream that comes through an angel is (the aspect of) man, the aspect of, 'Let us make man in our form, like our image' (*Genesis* 1:26). 'Like our image' means the faculty of the imagination – and that faculty 'in our image,' is the aspect of dream that comes through an angel. When a person sleeps, his rational ability leaves, and all that is left is the faculty of the imagination. And when a person's rational mind is pure, then the remaining faculty of the imagination is angelic – 'in our form, like our image' – because the power of the faculty of the imagination 'in our image,' is the aspect of angelic. A dream that comes through an angel has the aspect of human – 'Let us make man, etc.' But a dream that comes about through a demon has the aspect of an animal – 'a demon brings the animal nature to life.'[29] [...] Then the person's 'imagination is compared to a beast.'[30] His imaginative faculty has fallen to the aspect of beast, the quality of a dream that comes about through a demon, which is the level of a beast.[31]

R. Nachman understands *dream* as the mixture of two fonts of agency that come upon a person as one: the angelic and the demonic. A person with a purified mind filters the dream via the angelic faculty and, in using it, brings

his imaginative power to the realm of the godly, while a person on an animalistic level receives the dream through a demon. It is clear from R. Nachman's
subsequent words in this teaching that he does not view dreams as deriving
from two entirely separate 'spiritual' tracks, i.e., that an angel comes to the
righteous and a demon to the wicked. Rather, angel and demon simultaneously rest upon every individual, and within every dream each individual, in
accordance with the purity of his mind and his imaginative faculty, clarifies
the manner in which he will receive the dream. As R. Nachman explains: 'the
word *chalim is the meaning of chalom (dream)...* is related to the idea of
connection,[32] because the *chalom* (the dream) is composed by two powers:
the angelic and the demonic.'[33] Therefore, a person is responsible for
purifying his imagination and thus receiving the angelic influence as he filters
out the demonic element.[34]

   In addition, R. Nachman postulates an equivalence between dream and
prophecy in regard to the polarities inherent within each – i.e., a dream can
be true or bestial, and a prophecy can be true or mad. The means that
R. Nachman proposes to attain true dreams and true prophecy presents
another parallel: the central technique for strengthening the *angelic* and
weakening the *demonic* is joy.

> We strengthen the angelic through joy [...] Thus, the realm of the
> angels is called *sehakim*, which is related to the word *sehok*, laughter and
> joy. This is because the main method of strengthening the angel is
> through joy. Therefore, if a person had a dream that was not good,
> his rectification comes about through fasting.[35] This is because fasting
> is in the category of joy. As the verse states, 'Give us joy as in the days
> of our fasting.'[36] Fasting leads to joy. With that, we strengthen the angel
> and we rectify and subdue the evil dream, a dream that came about
> through a demon because the angel was not strong. And so when a
> person does not intend to fast because of a dream he has had, his well-
> wishers tell him, 'Go, eat your bread with joy.'[37] His eating should be
> joyful, as a result of which he will strengthen the angel and subdue the
> demons who damaged the dream [...][38]

In a similar vein, in his teaching, *Vayihi Miketz*, when R. Nachman discusses
the need to cultivate the imaginative faculty so that it will lead to true
prophecy and not to an evil spirit and madness, he proposes 'joy' as an
indispensable means and methodology.[39] Joy leads to prophecy, whereas
sadness leads to an evil spirit and madness. Joy, which our Talmudic sages
define as a condition for prophecy,[40] is understood by R. Nachman in the
following specific sense: not as the determining condition by which a spirit
rests upon a person – because a spirit rests upon a person even when he is

depressed – rather, joy assures the subjugation of the imaginative faculty so that entering a prophetic, inspired state leads to prophecy and a good spirit, not to madness and an evil spirit.[41]

4. Joy, Imagination and Prophecy

Joy plays a central role in the worship of a Bratslav hasid. R. Nachman's battle against sadness and his proclamation that 'it is a great mitzvah to be constantly joyful'[42] develop and continue the Baal Shem Tov's emphasis on cultivating joy and eschewing sadness.[43] R. Nachman's prescription for joy is not exclusively applicable to a 'spiritual aristocracy' grooming itself for prophecy and holiness, but is incumbent on every individual and is thus part of a standard and widespread Hasidic tradition.[44] The importance of joy is explained by R. Nachman in various and original ways; however, in this instance, his particular concern is to emphasize its significant influence on the imaginative faculty. On this matter R. Nachman engaged in an ongoing and hidden dialogue[45] with Maimonides' thought, which provides additional background to understanding R. Nachman's transformation of the topic of 'joy' to prominence in the world of Hasidism

A certain similarity exists between R. Nachman and Maimonides in their understanding of the relationship between joy and prophecy. Both see in the 'imaginative faculty' the essential component connecting joy with prophecy. In Maimonides' view, all prophecy (except that of Moses) passes through the imaginative faculty, and therefore 'the perfecting' of the imaginative faculty is a fundamental condition for prophecy. According to Maimonides, joy physiologically influences the imagination, which is a physical faculty, and enables the imagination to function properly.[46] R. Nachman also maintains that the imagination possesses a physiological aspect. In his teaching *Lifamim*,[47] R. Nachman describes the fantasies of the evil inclination as flowing 'from the turbidity of the blood and from the turbidity and confusion of the mind,' which are rectified by cleansing the body and purifying the blood. In connecting joy and sadness with the imagination, R. Nachman states that 'sadness is very harmful and gives power to the grossly corporeal evil inclination.'

R. Nachman, like Maimonides, sees in dreams the result of the activity of the imaginative faculty and 'the traces of prophecy' that have passed through the imaginative faculty.[48] R. Nachman's further development of this issue – that joy is a condition for attaining correct and true dreams – does not explicitly appear in Maimonides and is therefore derived from the connections between *joy* and the imaginative faculty, as well as between the imaginative faculty and the *dream*.

II. Faith and Imagination

According to R. Nachman, faith is a function of the imagination: 'the essence of faith is dependent upon the imaginative faculty;'[49] therefore rectifying the imaginative faculty 'causes holy faith to be rectified and purified.'[50] The proper functioning of the imaginative faculty itself is connected to and dependent upon the spirit of prophecy: 'the essence of the rectification of the imagination comes through the spirit of prophecy.'[51] From this we learn that faith depends upon a prophetic spirit, a point that R. Nachman makes explicitly when he says: 'the essence of the rectification of holy faith comes through the spirit of prophecy'[52] – a very significant determination in understanding the character of Bratslavian faith.

According to R. Nachman, rectified faith has a prophetic quality; it is not merely a personal attitude, but prophecy is dependent on a certain level of faith for revelation, 'the quality of the spirit of prophecy.' And since faith has a prophetic dimension, it too acts and passes through the imagination, the instrument for prophecy. Thus, the 'well-being' and purification of faith depend upon the 'well-being' of the imaginative faculty.

Proper faith is neither philosophical knowledge nor belief based upon knowledge of the tradition. Rather, it is a state in which a person 'sees' what he believes in. In the language of R. Nachman, 'to the believer, matters are so clear that it is as if he sees what he believes in with his eyes – such is the greatness of his complete faith.'[53] This faith, which has a prophetic aspect, can be described as something just short of visionary. Faith is clearly, therefore, more than the result of choice and decision;[54] it incorporates a strong, direct awareness of the divine, as though one is seeing with one's eyes, and is related to the mystical structure and hierarchy found in prophecy.

According to this approach, joy strengthens the imaginative faculty and thus strengthens *faith* and *prophecy*, both of which depend upon the 'wholeness' of the imaginative faculty. The argument for a connection between faith and the imaginative faculty and faith and prophecy may be described as the central juncture where R. Nachman's path – regarding both imagination and faith[55] – diverges from that of Maimonides.

1. Joy and Faith

R. Nachman, like Maimonides, sees joy as an instrument of central importance for strengthening the imaginative faculty and therefore an essential element in prophecy. For Maimonides, the importance of the imaginative faculty is limited to its role in prophecy. It plays no role in relation to the commandment to *know* God, the obligation of every individual,[56] but is solely relevant to an elite group that sees itself as destined to attain prophecy.[57]

In contrast, for R. Nachman, faith is also dependent upon 'a spirit of prophecy.' Therefore, increasing the activity and influence of the imaginative faculty will also apply to faith. Since faith is obligatory, the imaginative faculty plays a central and vital role in the religious life of every believer. This enlargement of the role of the imagination goes hand in hand with the significance of joy in facilitating religious worship as a determining factor.

Another important point of contention concerning the role of the imagination in religious worship involves the question whether it is possible to develop and perfect the imagination or whether it is an inherited trait that cannot be affected by a person's deeds and efforts.

Maimonides states firmly that unlike the intellect and character, which are amenable to development, the imagination is a fixed trait with which one is born,[58] and therefore cannot be improved.[59] A person is then obligated to improve his mind and character but, since he has no capacity, he is not obliged to attempt to improve and rectify his imagination. R. Nachman disagrees with this view, claiming that the imaginative faculty can be improved and rectified, and he provides his disciples with a range of techniques in order to accomplish this. Amongst his suggestions are creating original Torah thoughts[60] and coming close to true *zaddikim*.[61]

R. Nachman's understanding of faith as dependent upon a certain level of prophecy and upon the imaginative faculty (whose integrity depends upon a person's deeds) explains an important additional difference between his approach and that of Maimonides – a difference with halachic implications with regard to joy and the imaginative faculty.

While Maimonides acknowledges that the importance of joy goes beyond the vital role it plays in maintaining the 'well-being' of the imaginative faculty in prophecy,[62] his concerns about the negative influences of the *imaginative faculty* and *joy* lead him to place limits upon the experience of joy and imagination and consequently to drastically restrict the group of people for whom it is appropriate. According to Maimonides, worship intended to arouse great joy and fervor is limited solely to great men and exceptional individuals of rare quality who seek to attain prophecy. The common folk, who have nothing to do with prophecy, must keep a prudent distance from anything that arouses joy and the imaginative faculty. His position is expressed in a compendium of rulings and guidelines that place a boundary between the worship appropriate for the common man and that meant for the elite few who seek prophecy.

1. Maimonides states that the activities of the 'Joy of the Water Drawing' ceremony were limited solely to 'the greatest scholars of Israel, the heads of the yeshivas, the Sanhedrin, the pious, the elders and the

men of renown.'[63] Apparently, Maimonides saw that for this religious elite that seeks prophecy and a divine spirit of holiness, joy was a necessary condition, whereas others, who have nothing to do with this elite group and its aims, are warned not to take an active part in the joy.[64]

2. This viewpoint is connected to Maimonides' approach to melody, also a means of arousing joy and attaining prophecy. 'The prophetic schools made use of lyre, drum, flute and *kinor* when they sought prophecy.'[65] But for the common people, melody and song is restricted in a number of ways.[66]

3. Maimonides describes 'self-isolation' as an appropriate and praise-worthy means of attaining prophecy and great insights, when it is integrated with joy: 'the prophets did not prophesy whenever they wished to, but focused their minds and sat joyfully and with a happy heart, and entered a state of self-isolation;'[67] and also 'a person must focus his intellectual thought constantly upon his goal – and this is achieved in the main through "self-isolation" and separation. Thus, a pious person must separate and isolate himself a great deal, and only engage in (communal) intercourse with others when absolutely necessary.'[68]

But the behavior of the common folk must be absolutely different. Maimonides urges these not to isolate themselves but to join with the righteous and to remain in their company at all times. 'Therefore, a person must cleave to the righteous and sit with the wise always, in order to learn from their deeds.'[69]

There are other examples of this approach,[70] but the important point is that in each of the examples cited above, R. Nachman unequivocally disagrees with Maimonides. He sees joy, melody and self-isolation as central and important technique of worship to be employed by every individual. Indeed, because of the strong bonds that link joy, melody and self-isolation to prophecy, these are needed to help a person rectify his faith, which is dependent upon the spirit of prophecy.[71]

Without joy, a person cannot possess faith. Faith is an operation dependent on the faculty of the imagination, and the full expression of that faculty depends upon faith. And since faith is the foundation of the worship of God, every individual is obliged to maintain himself in a constant state of joy.[72]

R. Nachman, it should be emphasized, is not making the common claim that faith and trust in God make a person joyful. Rather, he is claiming the opposite: that joy leads to faith; that without joy there can be no faith. Sadness and depression lead a person to heresy and idolatry, for they do not allow the imaginative faculty to function. Since 'the essence of faith depends upon the imaginative faculty,'[73] faith too is lost. Moreover, sadness strengthens the negative aspects of the imagination, which is a physical faculty, and thus leads to idolatry.

An interesting example of this is found in R. Nachman's teachings concerning people who suffer thoughts of idolatry during prayer. He states that there is an evil inclination 'that is lowly and corporeal, and the evil inclination of most people is the blood itself. ... The essence of the confusions that they experience is as a result of the turbidity and confusion of the blood.' He continues:

> You can see that there are some people who suffer from thoughts of idolatry. Sometimes when such a person stands up to pray, an idolatrous image appears before him. And even though he himself knows that it is an illusion, he finds it hard to overcome. He sees the image standing before him, and he finds it exceedingly difficult to drive it out of his imagination and thought [...][74] There is no doubt that when a person is overcome by those illusions, he finds it exceedingly difficult to free himself of them and remove them from his thoughts. The more he tries, the more he rocks back and forth and throws his head around, the stronger those images become [...] Therefore, the principal solution for a person who has been caught in this and has such thoughts (whether thoughts of lust or thoughts of idolatry), the only solution, is to sanctify and purify his body so as to cleanse and purify his blood. As long as his body has not been sanctified and purified, there is no solution. [...] In addition, sadness is very harmful, and strengthens the thick, corporeal evil inclination.[75]

It is not clear from this passage whether R. Nachman relates depression and joy to the turbidity of the blood. One could say that he is making two unrelated statements about the imagination. The first is that cleansing and purifying the blood rectify the imagination, and secondly, that sadness strengthens the physical evil inclination of the imagination. In addition, it is unclear whether joy influences the person on a physiological level or otherwise.

However, R. Nachman, in his teaching *Al Yedei Zeiah Tovah*, clarifies his assertion[76] that there is, indeed, a link between the turbidity of the blood and sadness, as well as between the purity of the blood and joy.[77] And since the turbidity of the blood affects the evil imagination, clearly joy affects imagination by passing through the physical medium of the blood.[78] (This explanation is built upon the medical model of the four humors.[79])

Thus we come to understand that R. Nachman makes use of Maimonides' belief in physiological interdependence between the states of joy and sadness, on the one hand, and imagination and prophecy on the other. But since R. Nachman also sees faith as dependent on the imagination and prophecy, he posits a connection between joy and faith and between sadness and heretical, idolatrous thoughts.

2. 'All Sins Come about via the Imagination'

R. Nachman believes that 'a person does not sin unless a spirit of foolishness has entered into him. This is the case when divine inspiration passes through the imaginative faculty and is not subjugated to the critical attention of one's 'consciousness' (*da'at*), and the 'spirit of foolishness' is allowed to bring a person to madness. In light of this, we can understand R. Nachman's argument that every sin is a result of the activity within the imaginative faculty:

> When a man goes after the imagination in his heart – that is after one's desires, heaven forbid, which come from the imaginative faculty – it is literally an animalistic act, for animals also possess an imaginative faculty. And so when a person sins, heaven forbid, all the sins result from the imaginative faculty, from which all desires come …
> [R. Natan adds], and after he [R. Nachman] said that, we should give a name and call all desires of the 'evil inclination' by the name of 'the imaginative faculty,' and [he] says we need to call it and define it under another name, that the '*baal-davar*', the evil inclination needs to be called by another name, […], not to call it the evil inclination any more, but only by the name of the *imaginative faculty*, and he said this, as if it were a joke, but I understood that his intention was sure, but I was unable to understand what he meant.

R. Nachman's proposal to refer to the evil inclination as the imaginative faculty follows in the footsteps of the Maimonides, who states, 'The imagination is actually the evil inclination, for every imperfection in thought or in character comes from the imagination or is connected to its functions.'[80]

The idea that sins result from the imagination leads to another connection between sin and madness. Since sins come from the imaginative faculty, and since unmonitored activity of the imaginative faculty is madness, then every sin is an act of madness. Indeed, R. Natan clearly states, 'madness comes about via an error of the imagination, which is not conducting itself properly in accordance with the intellect.'[81]

Thus, we see that the imaginative faculty cannot be unequivocally defined as good or evil, but that it is involved in a variety of realms: ranging from the evil inclination and madness to faith and prophecy.

III. Casting Away the Intellect

In a number of his central teachings on the relationship between the intellectual activity and the imaginative faculty, R. Nachman makes reference to
the figure of Moses, represented as the zenith of the religious ideal, a man who
has attained the highest awareness accessible to a human being.[82] Seemingly
without regard to this in other teachings, R. Nachman teaches that a person
is obligated to seek after and obtain the elevated insights that Moses attained
in his lifetime.[83]

A careful reading of these texts reveals that R. Nachman is consistent both
in regard to the level and type of attainment represented by the figure of
Moses, and, more importantly, the hierarchy that he assigns to the various
means of attaining such insights. It is thus possible to describe and delineate
the hierarchy of various states of consciousness that a person is capable of
reaching.

1. Casting Away the Intellect and Removing the Rational Mind in the Teaching, Tiku Emunah[84]

Tiku Emunah is a long and complex teaching that addresses a number of inter-
related topics, one of the central ones being the relationship between *spiritual
insight* and *intellect*. Various attempts are made to categorize and define the
boundaries of religious worship with regards to the intellect (*mochin*) and
rational mind (*da'at*) and the function and role of the imaginative faculty.

R. Nachman begins his teaching with the words: 'The essential thing is
faith.' After discussing various situations in which a person's faith grows weak,
the connection between faith and health, and the interdependence of the
purification and elevation of faith in attracting converts, R. Nachman, in
Section Seven, introduces a discussion on spiritual insight and intellect. The
teaching is clearly carefully organized, although the discussion on spiritual
insight and intellect is scattered throughout and not centralized.

This teaching displays a marked reserve regarding the service of God with
one's rational mind, and includes a detailed description of serving God
without the participation of the rational mind. At certain stages in the shunting
aside of the rational mind, a person finds himself in a state of consciousness
that is not far removed from madness. In this teaching, Moses is identified with
the service of God as aided by the rational mind.

Stage One

Moses is the rational mind (*da'at*),[85] the mind (*mochin*), tefillin, […]
And this corresponds to the letter shin that is impressed onto the
head, tefillin, as the first letter of the divine name Sha-dai. It is a
contraction – i.e., every individual must contract his mind and

intellect, so as not to allow his mind to go beyond its limitations, so that his mind will not wander where it is not permitted, according to its level. Thus, our sages state, 'That which is hidden from you do not seek, and that which is concealed from you do not investigate.'[86] This corresponds to the divine name of Sha-dai, constriction. The name Sha-dai is a contraction of 'there is enough in his divinity for every creature' (as stated by Rashi in his commentary on Lech Lechah). That is to say, each creature is his own 'enough' – his own limitation in regard to divinity, beyond which he is forbidden to go with his intellect. Every individual has a limitation on and a constriction of his intellect, according to his level, so that even in matters of holiness he may not go beyond his limitation – 'that which is hidden form you do not seek,' etc. Thus the verse states, 'Lest they break through to God to see,'[87] etc. And thus God told Moses, 'I will place you in the crevice of the rock'[88] when Moses merited to see and attain the insights which he attained. In other words, God promised to protect him, to hide him in the crevice of the rock. That is the aspect of constriction, in which the mind does not emerge to wander outside its limitation.[89]

In this initial stage of the discussion on the levels of insight a person can attain with the help of his rational mind, R. Nachman states that a correspondence exists between a person's spiritual level and the level of insight he is able to attain. Every individual must be aware of his level and know his limitations, beyond which he may not go.

The insights described in this passage are of a particularly intellectual nature, and they are attained in consequence of the activity of the intellect and the rational mind. At this stage, there is no hesitation in regard to the importance, helpfulness and unique quality of rational thinking as a method of attaining insights, with the stipulation that this insight must correspond to a person's spiritual level. The idea that one must limit the field of his thought is supported by the example of Moses. Although God spoke to Moses directly, he too is described as requiring a boundary for his spiritual insights to keep his intellect from wandering.

R. Nachman's presentation of the danger of leaping spiritual levels and his prohibition against learning matters when one lacks the requisite maturity and preparation is part of a long tradition, as represented by the warning, 'In that which is too wonderful for you do not inquire.'[90]

Stage Two

The following section of this teaching (Section Eight) discusses the importance of purifying one's mind and the capability of a person who has purified himself to elevate fallen souls. In Section Nine, R. Nachman goes on to argue that it is possible to gain spiritual insights and even a certain level of revelation when the rational mind is absent.

> When the mind is pure (as a result of which 'pure statements' are made), then even when, during sleep, the mind is not present, and all that remains is the impression of the mind – which corresponds to speech, and then this impression itself is pure, in the aspect of a dream that comes via an angel. And that corresponds to the stage following Moses' passing away, when an angel of the army of Hashem came and said, 'Behold, I have come.' (Yehoshua 5:14). Moses' passing away corresponds to the absence of the rational mind, sleep, when the rational mind is absent, and only the impression of it remains. Then, 'I am the prince officer of the army of Hashem' – in other words, an angel. 'Now I have come' – at that point the impression remains in the form of an angel, a dream that comes via an angel.

R. Nachman here describes the insights that come to a person via an angel when his rational mind is absent. This is not to say that he is going beyond the limits of his intellectual ability, but rather that these insights do not even pass through the mind and the rational intellect. Rather, the path to insight without the 'rational intellect' travels a qualitatively different track, such that the meaning of the term 'insight' has less to do with concepts such as learning and wisdom and more with the concepts of revelation and prophecy.

Indeed, not only are such insights independent of the intellectual process, but they occur precisely when the rational mind is absent. Still, at the same time this passage presents an inter-relationship between the rectification and purification of the mind and the ability to receive dreams via an angel. Therefore, a relationship exists between the 'mind' and insight that comes via an 'angel.' That relationship, however, is a mere 'impression' left by the influence of the pure mind present before, but now absent. Only when a person's rational mind is absent can a person experience a prophetic dream that comes via an angel – 'now I have come.' The rational mind itself takes no active part in receiving the dreams; it only exerts an influence that comes from the impression it has left behind.

R. Nachman goes on to discuss the role of the imaginative faculty in attaining insights.[91] The imaginative faculty operates as an alternative to the mind, and through it a person receives the dream. The imaginative faculty carries out its work not during the time of sleep, nor when the rational mind is absent, but while the mind is still active. If a person has purified his mind, then even while it is absent its impression remains and influences the purity of the imaginative faculty. In such a situation, a person rises to the level of 'In our image, like our form,' receiving insights like the angels in whose image he was created. But if a person has polluted his mind before going to sleep, and his imaginative faculty is tainted by his animal nature, even at the moment when his mind is absent, his imaginative activity 'is compared to a beast's imagination.'

In addition, the idea that in order to attain an inspired state a person must have already worked on correcting and purifying his mind does not mean that R. Nachman is urging the development of the mind via intellectual effort. Rather, he is speaking of the need to develop other qualities of the mind – such as spiritual cleanliness and purity – that belong to the realm of rectifying character and refining desire, and not to the realm of developing intellectual ability.[92]

In this section, a qualified distinction is made in regard to the role of the intellect in attaining spiritual insight. Here, R. Nachman does not discuss who is fit to attain such inspiration or its parameters. Rather, he proposes an alternative path, which does not make use of the intellect, but rather the imaginative faculty – a path that is particularly available during sleep, when the mind is absent.

R. Nachman describes this inspiration as a result of an external source – i.e., an angel, 'the officer of the army of Hashem' – that may or may not come. It becomes clear that the angel itself is the faculty of the imagination, a revelation or spiritual inspiration in the name of Hashem. So, whereas on the one hand, he describes revelation via dreams as an occurrence of spiritual inspiration and prophecy coming from without, on the other hand, he describes it as an incidence of awareness that a person attains through the aid of his own internal abilities, the imaginative faculty. This tension is resolved when we recall that in R. Nachman's view, the imagination is the faculty through which prophecy passes.

An alternative path to spiritual insight, the dream, is a state of consciousness that frequently visits every individual. And the dream exemplifies well a state of consciousness outside the experience of the rational mind, with which even the most ordinary individual – he need not be a mystic or a madman – is familiar. The dream, therefore, acts as a bridge between a routine or normative state of consciousness (in which the rational mind acts as a dominant and central influence) and the exceptional states of consciousness that R. Nachman will describe in the course of this teaching.[93]

Although the absence of the rational mind during sleep is independent of a person's will, in order to assure its greatest efficacy a person must prepare himself for it by purifying and rectifying his mind. Such preparation will make it possible for his independently acting imaginative faculty to express the character of a person as being 'in our image, like our form' – angelic and not animalistic.

At this stage, R. Nachman does not propose that a person voluntarily cast aside his intellect and purposefully create a state in which the imaginative faculty remains the sole factor in the arena of consciousness. Rather, he advises people to properly prepare themselves for states in which, independent of their volition, their rational mind is absent.

Stage Three

In Sections Ten to Fourteen, R. Nachman deals with a variety of topics not germane to our study.

In Section Fifteen, R. Nachman returns to the topic of sleep, a state in which the intellect and rational mind are absent, describing it in positive terms: 'after the mind is rectified, then sleep, which is the absence of the rational mind, is good and exceedingly sweet.'

Here R. Nachman does not stop at discussing the absence of the rational mind that happens independent of a person's will, but in a most surprising way claims that a person must of his own volition 'cast aside his intellect' and create a state in which his rational mind is absent.

> Indeed, what is necessary is precisely to 'cast away the mind,' because it is necessary to cast aside all rational processes and serve God simply. This is because a person's deeds should outweigh his wisdom[94] – and mental understanding is not essential, but rather the deed.[95] And so a person must cast aside his thoughts and serve God simply, without any ideas. And this is not only the case in regard to the foolish ideas entertained by the common folk, but even to ideas that are truly intelligent, even those of a person who has a truly great mind. When a person comes to some type of service of God, he must cast aside all ideas and serve God with utter simplicity.

R. Nachman makes it perfectly clear that he is speaking of casting aside truly wise ideas regarding the service of God, not only vanities of this world and foolish ideas. From this we come to understand that when a person comes to serve God or perform a mitzvah, he must cast aside his rational thought processes and suspend his intellect.[96] The abandonment of one's rational mind becomes then a kind of spiritual exercise and the suspension of one's rational mind becomes a desired state of religious consciousness.

But R. Nachman does not stop at calling for an internal transformation. Instead, he directs a person to express his absence of rational mind with external acts of madness, such as rolling in 'mud and refuse,' which will cause others to regard him as mad.

> And a person must even behave himself and do things in a manner that appears mad for the sake of serving God, which is the aspect of, 'In her love you will be intoxicated constantly.'[97] For the love of God, a person must do things that appear mad in order to perform God's commandments and do his will. A person must roll in all sorts of refuse and mud in order to serve Him and perform His command-ments. And this is true not only in regard to a literal commandment, but to anything where God's will is involved – that is called a mitzvah. There are 613 commandments, and those 613 commandments have many branches. And anything that fulfills the will of God, when one pleases one's Father in heaven, is a mitzvah, a commandment. And a person must roll in all sorts of refuse and mud to do God's will and please Him.

R. Nachman's assertion does not purport to encourage greater dedication and devotion in the service of God. Nor is he merely speaking about a case in which it is not possible to perform a mitzvah without being derided and considered mad. Such behavior has nothing to do with 'casting away the intellect.' On the contrary, in such a case, a person must overcome his feelings and reach a logical decision as to his scale of values: is God's honor or his own of greater importance to him? But R. Nachman is not speaking of casting aside one's honor, but of casting aside one's intellect. Acts of madness are not occasional obstacles to be overcome; rather they are acts a person performs as a kind of prologue and preparation in order to serve God: 'when a person comes to some type of service of God, he must cast aside all ideas ...'

Performing acts of madness does not only involve a readiness to be viewed as mad by others. It means that one is truly ready to be mad.[98] R. Nachman's directive to his disciples is based upon the principle that 'hearts are drawn after deeds,' and its purpose is to create a 'mad' consciousness, free of the rational intellect and mind. This is not some symbolic act, but the actual casting aside of one's mind and the abandonment of one's rational intellect.[99] R. Nachman directs a person to make use of external, public acts in order to create a desired internal state.[100]

Acts of madness and of casting aside the intellect are part of a complex of practices meant to prepare a person for and lead him to a state of consciousness from which the rational mind is excluded and in which the imaginative faculty plays the central role. This state of consciousness opens a person to various mystical states of inspiration and revelation with the aid of the imaginative faculty.

This understanding of deeds of madness as a practice that helps a person attain an alternative state of consciousness and allows a person to have insights unavailable in his normative state of consciousness is supported by the continuation of the teaching:

> And then, when his love for God is so strong that he abandons all of his wisdom, and he casts himself into refuse and mud for the sake of serving God, in order to please Him, he affects his intellect positively. At that point he attains insights that transcend his intellect – insights that not even Moses gained in his lifetime: an understanding of why 'the righteous suffer and the wicked enjoy well-being' (see *Berachot* 7), which is a perversion of justice, and something that appears to pervert fairness, heaven forbid, which Moses himself did not understand in his lifetime – i.e., when the intellect is completely functioning, when it is not absent, which corresponds to Moses in his lifetime. On the one hand, the absence of the mind, the aspect of sleep corresponds to Moses' passing away, whereas, on the other hand, the presence of the mind, when the mind is present and not absent, corresponds to Moses in his lifetime. In this aspect it is not possible to understand why the righteous suffer and the wicked enjoy well-being. But when a person's love of God is so strong that he throws himself down and rolls in the refuse and mud in order to serve God, and acts literally like a slave because of his love for God, then he can attain an insight into that state which is known as 'Moses in his lifetime' (i.e., when the mind is present), in which he cannot understand why 'the righteous suffer and the wicked enjoy well-being.'

R. Nachman links the 'casting away of the intellect' to the ability to attain insights that transcend the level of the rational mind, which is the level of Moses in his lifetime. Astonishingly, R. Nachman describes the level that Moses attained in his lifetime as a low level in the service of God,[101] a stage at which a person serves God in the framework of normative consciousness characterized by the rational mind and intellect. This consciousness does not allow a person to reach certain insights attainable only with a consciousness emptied of its rational mind and intellect. Moses, 'who is the rational mind,' could not attain that state in his lifetime, and so was prevented as long as he remained alive from reaching the higher level of understanding, which contains the answer to the problem of why the righteous suffer and the wicked enjoy well-being.

R. Nachman states very clearly that even when a person engages in proper intellectual service, he cannot reach that level of insight. The very fact that his intellect is present prevents the spiritual apprehension of the insight. This has nothing to do with any particular flaw in one's intellect that can be rectified, but is an intrinsic limitation of the consciousness of the rational mind.

In order to explain what it means to cast aside one's intellect, R. Nachman contrasts the work of a slave with the service of a son when he claims that the highest stage of worship is achieved when a son voluntarily acts like a slave.

> There are some people in the aspect of son, who search through the hidden treasures of their father (see Zohar, B'har 111b), while others are in the aspect of a slave, who has but one role: that is to do his task, and who may not ask for any reason or explanation. He has one obligation: to do his work that he has been assigned. But there are also people who are the aspect of a son who so loves his father that out of that love he does the work of a slave, of what a simple slave must perform. He leaps from the great rampart, into the very midst of battle; he rolls in all sorts of mud and refuse, if only to please his father, carrying out actions that not even a simple slave would do. And then, when his father sees how strong his love is, so much so that out of his love he acts with total servitude, then he reveals to him even those things that he would not give to a [regular] son. Even the [regular] son, who is able to go through the hidden treasuries of the king, for him too, there are places where he is not allowed – insights that are withheld from him. But when the son sets aside his wisdom, and casts himself into servitude, his father has compassion on him and reveals to him that which is not given over to a [regular] son: why 'the righteous suffer and the wicked enjoy well-being' – something that not even Moses was able to understand in his lifetime.[102]

The son searches for insights in the hidden treasury of the king, using his reason and inquiry. But even though he is permitted to enter areas forbidden to normal people, he is likely to find that some insights are withheld from him. Only when he casts away the use of his reason and inquiry is he given access to those insights that are generally outside of his access.

This is not to say that the slave is superior to the son. Rather, the son who does the work of a slave is superior to a normal son. The slave is forbidden to ask questions and asks none; reason and inquiry are beyond his purview and the king's hidden treasuries are of no interest to him. His work and consciousness do not lead him to insight. His position is static and self-contained; it is not a preparatory stage to attain higher states of consciousness. The king's son, on the other hand, uses his reason and inquiry to attain more than the slave can. He is authorized to enter the king's hidden treasuries, where he attains what the slave does not.

But there is a third level: that of the son who serves as a slave. This son is interested in the king's hidden treasuries and walks through their midst, desiring and focusing on them. Nevertheless, he is not deluded into using his reason and inquiry as the peak of his service. Instead, he is prepared to serve the king by rejecting the path of reason and inquiry, by casting aside his wisdom and intellect, and by serving out of a state where his rational mind is not present. But this state of an emptied consciousness is only an intermediary stage, for he ultimately attains insights beyond the ken of a regular son.

Reaching insights beyond the grasp of the regular son and the slave is made possible only because of his complete dedication, as he casts aside his rational mind and performs acts of madness.[103]

We see therefore that the level of 'Moses in his lifetime' represents the rational mind and the intellect, which, no matter how high they may rise, cannot understand the suffering of the righteous. The level of 'the passing away of Moses,' on the other hand, which is higher than that of 'Moses in his lifetime,' expresses the absence of rational thought. This level must be preceded by the rational mind; in the language of R. Nachman's parable, it is the level achieved only by the son who first investigates the king's treasuries with his reason and inquiry, and who now casts aside his rational mind. This is something that the slave, who has never engaged in reason and inquiry, cannot attain. A person who has attained the state of consciousness of 'the passing away of Moses' is capable of arriving at an understanding of why the righteous suffer.[104]

R. Nachman's parable of the son and the slave contrasts the active nature of the son's search, aided by his rational mind, in the king's hidden treasure with, on the other hand, the passive nature of the slave-like behavior whereby he receives insights when his rational mind is absent. A person in this latter condition does not think, search or find; rather, insights are revealed to him from above.[105] R. Nachman's parable throws into sharp relief the nature of this kind of insight: it is a gift of loving-kindness that arrives only after a person casts aside the insights that he has reached with his intellectual faculties. These insights are not granted in response to his level of spiritual attainment or as a reward for his activities, but as an act of compassion and loving-kindness. The inspired nature of an insight when the rational intellect is absent brings it close in a phenomenological sense to prophecy and *unio mystica.*[106]

Casting aside one's intellect comprises an additional floor, as it were, in R. Nachman's structure of imagination-based worship. The foundation of this building is faith, which is itself a function of the imaginative faculty, and which possesses an element of prophecy. A level above is the revelation of the angel of imagination, as it appears in a dream, when a person is asleep and the functions of his rational mind are suspended. The top floor of the building is the state that transcends the level of 'Moses in his lifetime,' and requires a person to voluntarily cast aside his intellect.

This hierarchy is clearly presented in the structure of *Tiku Emunah.* The teaching opens with the statement, 'The essential thing is faith,' and describes the importance of faith and the methods of strengthening it. It then discusses the limitations of the intellect and the ways to attain 'correct dreams,' and finally speaks about the exalted level attained by 'casting aside one's intellect.' He also describes the path, explaining that one can reach this goal by engaging in acts of madness carried out as an expression of one's love of God and as part of the process of setting aside one's mind.

Worship via the imagination at differing levels of the state of 'the absence of the rational mind' prepares a simple person to come to faith and an elevated person to come to prophecy. To attain these goals, a person needs a purified mind and character, which make possible the unhindered activity of the imaginative faculty; this in turn can lead him to faith, correct dreams and prophecy.

2. Areas of Consciousness Void of the Rational Mind (Mochin)

Other teachings of R. Nachman also describe to various degrees the absence of the intellect and the rational mind as the operative condition allowing the imaginative faculty and faith to function.

In *Vayasev Elokim,* R. Nachman describes faith as both hidden and revealed:

> It is hidden – for if you ask a believer to explain his faith, he will not be able to provide you with an explanation, since faith is something that applies only when one does not have an explanation. Yet at the same time, it is revealed – which is to say that the matter is clear to the believer, as though he sees what he believes in with his eyes, because of the greatness of his complete faith.[107]

Faith is hidden from intellect, in that a person cannot provide an explanation for his belief. The certainty and strength within faith are not dependent on the rational mind and reason but on an experience similar to a vision – the person 'sees' what he believes in. As mentioned earlier, this visionary aspect of faith is one of the components that link faith to the creative faculty and to prophecy.[108] Faith, like prophecy, brings a person clear insights and knowledge, with the help of his imaginative faculty, like an image before his eyes.

In *Tiku Tochacha*,[109] R. Nachman describes in greater breadth how the imaginative faculty, faith, prophecy and the absence of the rational mind are linked:

> When prophecy 'spreads out', then the imaginative faculty is purified and rectified. As the verse states, 'By the hand of the prophets shall I be imagined.'[110] Because essentially, the imaginative faculty is rectified and purified when it is in the hand of the prophets. And when the imaginative faculty is rectified, then the true faith of holiness is rectified, and false faiths are nullified. This is because the essence of faith depends upon the imaginative faculty. In regard to matters that the intellect understands, faith is irrelevant. The essence of faith exists only where one's intellect is at a loss and one does not understand something intellectually. That is where faith is needed. When a person does not understand something with his intellect, then all that remains is the imaginative faculty. And there one needs faith. And so the essence of faith is on the level of the imagination. Therefore, when prophecy spreads out, as a result of which the imagination is purified and rectified, the true faith of holiness is rectified.[111]

This definition of the essence of faith as confined to realms beyond the competence of the intellect – 'what the intellect understands is not relevant to faith' – sharpens the tension between the intellect and faith and the imaginative faculty. This view of faith and prophecy as a mental expanse void of intellect[112] teaches that even a person in a normative state of consciousness possesses areas of consciousness in which his intellect and rational mind are quiescent. It is in those areas of consciousness where the imaginative faculty operates on its own that a person is in great need of faith; this is also the place of prophecy.

In describing the paradoxical and existential faith of R. Nachman, Joseph Weiss claims that it stands in stark opposition to the mystical perspective (of unifying with Hashem through the interdependence of faith and prophecy),[113] and in support of this thesis quotes the present teaching, while passing over the first and last sections, which discuss the connection between prophecy and faith.[114] Weiss begins the quote with the words: 'the essence of faith is,' and ends with the words: 'and there faith is necessary.' The omissions in between make it possible for him to present Bratslavian faith as detached from and even radically opposed to mysticism.[115] Reading the passage in its original context, however, makes it clear that, quite to the contrary, R. Nachman emphasizes the connection between the 'mystical prophetic experience' and the rectification of faith. R. Nachman claims that prophecy and faith, which are connected to the imaginative faculty and function within its parameters, have no relationship with the activities of the intellect and the rational mind. Rather, they exist 'where one's intellect is at a loss' – i.e., the realm of the imaginative faculty.

R. Nachman explains the dependence of faith on prophecy, in both a positive fashion – the rectification of holy faith is through the spirit of prophecy – and in a negative context – 'lacking prophecy, the imagination grows unclear and is liable to confuse a person with false beliefs.'[116] It seems to me that it would be difficult to express more clearly the mystic-prophetic nature of faith and its clear dependence on mystical-prophetic experiences of developmental stages and qualification. Bratslavian faith is no mere verbal profession, nor is it an internal transformation that occurs in a place empty of God and filled with paradox;[117] rather, it is an experience that contains mystical inspiration,[118] in R. Nachman's words, the spirit of prophecy.[119]

Notes

1 See Zeitlin, *R. Nachman M'Bratslav*, 22–24; Green, *Tormented Master*, 334–337; Margolin, *Haemunah V'Hakefirah*, 77–134.
2 See Ackerman, *The Philosophical Sermons of R. Zerachia Halevi*, 103–120. Harvey, 'The Teaching of Synthetic Prophecy,' 141–155. See Wolfson, *Through a Speculum that Shines*.
3 See R. Yosef Ashkenazi's *Peirush Kabbali*, 219–224. See Warbloswsky, *R. Yosef Karo*, 79.
4 See Ackerman, *The Philosophical Sermons of R. Zerachia Halevi*, 103–120. Harvey, 'Torat Hanevuah Hasintetit,'141–155. See Wolfson, *Through a Speculum that Shines*.
5 See Maimonides, *Guide of the Perplexed* – in particular, Part II, Chapters 36–38. See also Kreisel, 'Chacham V'navi,' 149–169. See also Ackerman, *The Philosophical Sermons of R. Zerachia Halevi*, 108–112.
6 See Warblowsky, *R. Yosef Karo*, 78–80; Idel, *Hebetim Chadashim*, 119–127; Idem, *Hachavayah Hamistit*, 32–36.
7 *Sefer Habrit*. See the author's introduction, 4. See also *Shaarei Kedushah*, Part 3, Gate 5, 89–92.
8 Ibid., 289–299, 486, 578–586.
9 See Feikazh, *Hasidut Bratslav*, 'The Influence of *Sefer Habrit* on the words of R. Nachman,' 249–252.
10 *Sefer Habrit*, 594; *Likutei Moharan*, 141:193.
11 *Likutei Moharan*,141: 3.
12 Idel, '*HaPerush HaMagi shel Hamusika*,' idem, *Hebetim Chadashim*, 68–69; idem, *Hachavaya*

Hamistit, 43–55.

13 *Psalms* 47:8.

14 *Likutei Moharan* 141:54.

15 *Kings* II 3:15; *Likutei Moharan* 141:54:6.

16 *Samuel* I 16:14.

17 *Psalms* 143:10.

18 *Samuel* I 19:24.

19 *Samuel* I 16:24.

20 Oppenheimer, *Hanevuah Hakeduma*, 5, 26–27, 146–147; idem., 'Akdamot L'she'elat Haekstaza,' 45–62; Levinstein, 'Ha'arot,' 79–83.

21 PT, *Berachot* 5:2

22 *Proverbs* 29:11.

23 *Likutei Moharan* 141:3.

24 See note 49, further on.

25 *Hakuzari*, Essay 4, Section 3, 161. See also Harvey, '*Torat Hanevuah*,' 144; Wolfson, *Through a Speculum that Shines*, 163–181.

26 *Likutei Moharan* 141:54.

27 *Likutei Moharan* II 5:13.

28 *Berachot* 55b.

29 A homiletical rendering of *Habakkuk* 2:17.

30 A homiletical rendering of *Psalms* 49:13.

31 *Likutei Moharan* II 5:9.

32 See Rashbam on *Bava Batra* 74b.

33 *Likutei Moharan* II 5:16.

34 *Sefer Habrit*, 289.

35 See *Shabbat* 11a.

36 *Psalms* 90:15.

37 *Ecclesiastes* 9:7.

38 *Likutei Moharan* II 5:10.

39 *Likutei Moharan* I 54:6.

40 See *Pesachim* 117a; *Yalkut Shimoni, Kings* II, Allusion 226, 762.

41 *Tormented Master*, 334–337 and note 7; *Likutei Moharan* I 54:6. In *Achvi Lan Mana, Likutei Moharan* I 25.

42 *Likutei Moharan* II 24.

43 See *Keter Shem Tov*, sections 15, 37, 87, 100, 111, 129, 229, 272, 302, 384, 412; *Tzava'at Haribash*, sections 9, 15, 43–45, 61, 67,75, 107–108, 110, 132, 137. See *Tormented Master*, 65–67, 138–139. See Shochet, '*Al HaSimchah*'; Yaakovson, *Torat Hahasidut*, 76–80; Tishbi and Dan, '*Chasidut*,' 809–811.

44 See Shochet, ' '*Al HaSimchah*' 40–42;

45 See the *Guide of the Perplexed*, part 2, Chapter 36; and also Blidstein, '*Hasimchah B'Rambam*,' 145–163; Fishbane, 'Joy and Jewish Spirituality,'151–172, and particularly 157–159. See Shochet, ' '*Al HaSimchah*,' 30–43

46 *Hanhagath Habriut, Ketavim Refuiyim*, Volume 1, Gate 3, paragraphs 12–19, 58–63; *Guide of the Perplexed*, Part 2, Chapter 36; Blidstein, '*Hasimchah B'Rambam*,'149–1151 and 161–195.

47 *Likutei Moharan* I 72.

48 *Guide of the Perplexed*, Part 2, Chapter 36.

49 *Likutei Moharan* II 8:7.

50 Ibid., 8:8.

51 Ibid. This is bi-directional, since prophecy is dependent upon the healthy functioning of the imagination.

52 *Likutei Moharan* II 8:7. At present, see Zeitlin, *R. Nachman M'Bratslav*, 308–309; Margolin, *Ha'emunah V'hakefirah*, 88–122, particularly 100.

53 *Likutei Moharan* I 62.

54 Green, *Tormented Master*, particularly 291–301, 313–314.

55 Rosenberg, '*Musag Ha'emunah*,' 389.

56 See *Mishnah Torah, Hilchot Yesodei Hatorah*, Chapter 1, paragraphs 1–6. see *Guide of the Perplexed*, Part 1, Chapter 50; Rosenberg, '*Musag Ha'emunah*,' 351–389; Heller Vilinski, '*Hitgalut Emunah Ut'vunah*,' 25–27; ibid., 41.

57 Maimonides, *Guide of the Perplexed*, Part 1, Chapter 73, 142–144; ibid., Part 2, 36, 241.

58 *Guide of the Perplexed*, Part 2, 36, 246 and 248.

59 Ibid., 246–247.

60 *Likutei Moharan* II 105; *Chayei Moharan, Avodat Hashem*, 78 (521), 330.

61 *Likutei Moharan* II 8:8.

62 Blidstein, '*Hasimchah B'Rambam*'

63 Maimonides, *Mishnah Torah, Hilchot Lulav* 8:14.

64 Ibid. And see Blidstein, '*Hasimchah B'Rambam*,' 158–150.

65 *Mishnah Torah, Hilchot Yesodei Hatorah*, 7:8.

66 *Teshuvot Harambam*, Part 2, *Teshuvah* 224, 398–400; See Levinger, '*Al Taam Han'zirut*,' 299–305.

67 *Mishnah Torah, Hilchot Yesodei Hatorah*, 7:8.

68 *Guide of the Perplexed*, Part 3, Chapter 51.

69 *Mishnah Torah, Hilchot Deiot* 6:2. See Levinger, '*Al Taam Han'zirut*,' 299–305; Idel, '*Hitbodedut K'rikuz B'philosophiah*,' 44–45 and note 22.

70 For example, Maimonides' attitude toward the Nazirite vow. See Levinger, '*Al Taam Han'zirut*,' 299–305.

71 Shochet, *Al Hasimchah*, 40–41.

72 *Likutei Moharan* II 24.

73 Ibid., 8:7.

74 *Shivchei Habesht*, 305–306. See Weiss, '*Reishit Tz'michatah*,' 57 and note 33.

75 *Likutei Moharan* I, 72.

76 *Likutei Moharan* II 6.

77 *Likutei Moharan* II 6.

78 Kama 23, 2 and 6.

79 Poko, *Toldot Hashigaon*, 72.

80 *Guide of the Perplexed*, Part 2, Chapter 12. See Klein-Bratslavi, *Hapeirush shel Harambam*, 209–226. Margolin, *Ha'emunah V'hakefirah*,108.

81 *Likutei Halachot, Choshen Mishpat, Hilchot Shluchin, halachah* 5, section 2.

82 *Likutei Moharan* I 64; ibid. 4:9.

83 *Likutei Moharan* II 5.

84 *Likutei Moharan* II 5.

85 *Etz Chaim*, Gate 38, Chapter 6, 215; *Tzafnat Paaneach*, 127, 135.

86 *Chagigah* 13a.

87 *Exodus* 19:11.

88 Ibid. 33:22.

89 *Likutei Moharan* II 5:7.

90 See, for instance, Idel, *'Latoldoth Ha'isur lilmod kabbalah lifnei gil arbaim'*

91 *Shaar Hakavanah* Part One, *'Derushei Haleilah,' Derush* four, 348. And see also *Sefer Habrit*, 288. A homiletical rendering of *Habakkuk* 2:17.

92 *Likutei Moharan* II 5.

93 Elior, Rachel *'Miziut B'mivchan Habidyon.'*

94 *Pirkei Avot*, 3:9.

95 Ibid., 1:17.

96 *Sanhedrin* 106b. *Likutei Moharan* II 44.

97 *Proverbs* 5:19.

98 *Sichot Haran* 67, 45.

99 Weiss, *Studies in Eastern European Jewish Mysticism*, 143–145; Liebes, *'Hatikkun Hak'lali,'* 201–219.

100 See *Likutei Moharan* II 23.

101 Liebes, *'Hatikun Hak'lali,'* 212–214.

102 See Liebes, *'Hatikun Hak'lali,* particularly 206–207.

103 Green, *Tormented Master*, 299; Nigal, *Hasiporet Hachasidit*, 245–258; see also Ysif, *Sipur Ha'am Ha'ivri*, 415–418.

104 *'Hatikun Hak'lali,'* 213–214.

105 Weiss, *'Hakushya B'torat R. Nachman,'* 44–145.

106 Regarding *unio mystica* and prophecy in Hasidism, see Shatz-Oppenheimer, *'Ha'imanantziah Haelo-hit Ush'eilat Hahitnab'ut,' Hachasidut B'Misktikah*, 110–121.

107 *Likutei Moharan* I 62.

108 See Wolfson's *Through a Speculum that Shines*

109 *Likutei Moharan* II 8:7. This teaching was delivered on Rosh Hashanah 571 (1810).

110 *Hosea* 12:11.

111 *Likutei Moharan* I 7.

112 *Likutei Moharan* I 64.

113 Weiss, *'Hasidut shel Mistikah V'chasidut shel Emunah,' Mechkarim*, 87–95.

114 Weiss, *Studies in Eastern European Jewish Mysticism*, 141.

115 Ibid., in the section called *Mahut Ha'emunah Haparadokslit,'* 133–149; See also Weiss, *'Hasidut shel mistikah av'hasidut shel emunah,'* 87–95.

116 *Likutei Moharan* I 8.

117 See Weiss, *'Hakushia B'torat R. Nachman,'* 109–149.

118 See Green, *Tormented Master*, particularly, 281–313; Feiazh, *'Tzaddik,'* 149–165; Green, *'L'bikorato,'* 509–509; Dan and Tishbi, *'Chasidut,'* 771, 804; Gris, *Sifrut Hahanhagut*, 232, note 5; Rapoport-Albert, *'Katnut,'* 7–33; Margolin, *Ha'emunah V'hakefirah*, 133–134, 152–185; Mark, *Sipurei R. Nachman*, in particular 9–29.

119 When these words were written, Fechter's important essay, *'L'sugyat Ha'emunah v'hak'firah b'mishnat R. Nachman miBratslav,'* had not yet been published.

TWO

On the Character of Mystical Experiences

This chapter is devoted to the further explication of the role of the intellect and its *absence* within a variety of mystical experiences, as described in the writings of R. Nachman. Section I explores the role of the nullification of the rational mind as a preparation for mystical experiences, and the character of 'consciousness' during and after mystical experiences. This section also continues to explore the figure of Moses as a prototype for prophecy and mystical experiences. Section II discusses the 'mysticism of faith,' which R. Nachman presents as an appropriate model of spiritual attachment and worship of God. Section III describes the organizational categories that R. Nachman suggests for various mystical paths and experiences and the hierarchical order in which he places them. Finally, in Section IV, I will consider the place of the rational mind in Bratslavian mysticism and analyze the teachings in which R. Nachman proposes the rational mind as a path to mystical unification.

I. The Nullification and Return of the Rational Mind in the Mystical Experience

In the previous chapter, we examined R. Nachman's directive for 'casting away the intellect' and performing 'acts of madness' prior to performing deeds in the service of God. 'Casting away the intellect' prepares and develops the necessary 'consciousness' for the functioning of the imaginative faculty, allowing a person to obtain insights not available to the rational mind, including mystical insights characteristic of revelation.

1. Moses in his Life and in his Death

The teaching *Anochi*[1] contains a salient description of the mystical experience including: the path leading to absorption within the Infinite One, the mystical experience during that absorption and the post-mystical state of consciousness.[2] I will begin by addressing R. Nachman's presentation of the various levels of mystical experience to which Moses corresponds, a presentation that resolves contradictions that we find in varying descriptions of the 'level of attainment' of Moses in other teachings of R. Nachman.[3]

Death as a Pre-Condition for Absorption into the Infinite – 'Moses in His Death'

> Whenever a person comes to a Torah scholar and tells him all that
> is in his heart[4] and the Torah scholar corresponds to Moses, who
> corresponds to 'Nothingness,' as the verse states: 'And wisdom –
> from Nothingness shall you find it,'[5] he is in this way absorbed into
> the Infinite [...], and that is the aspect of stripping away corporeality.
> This is because when a person wants to be absorbed into the will of
> the Infinite One, he must nullify his being. And thus the *Zohar*
> writes[6] that Moses passed away on the Sabbath during the time of
> *minchah*, the time of the revelation of the '*will of wills*,' which is the
> aspect of the will of the Infinite One, from which all wills receive
> their life-force. And Moses died then because Moses nullified all of
> his being. As the verse states: 'And we are what?'[7] That is the
> meaning of 'And God buried Moses in Gai'[8] that is the aspect of
> Nothingness, as we see from the verse, 'Every low valley – *geh* – will
> be exalted.'[9] 'He buried him in Gai in the land of Moab'[10] – that is
> the aspect of kingship, as we see from the fact that King David came
> from Moab. And this happened to Moses because Moses passed
> upward into the Infinite One, into the *will of wills* [...] which corre-
> sponds to the will of the Infinite One.[11]

R. Nachman predicates the ability to attain *unio mystica*, mystical absorption
into the will of the Infinite One, upon the nullification of being. The astonishingly radical nature of this prerequisite becomes clear upon realizing
that R. Nachman maintains that this requires, in effect, literal death.

    R. Nachman describes the death of Moses as a process in which Moses
was absorbed into God – an absorption that demands the nullification of
one's being and the loss of one's life. Our sages describe Moses as having died
'with a kiss.' Many kabbalistic sources, like R. Nachman, explain this to mean
that Moses died in the midst of a mystical experience and absorption into the
Infinite One.[12]

In His Lifetime as Well
At this point, one could conclude from R. Nachman's words – 'no man can
see me and live' – that it is impossible for anyone, even someone as great as
Moses, to be absorbed into the Infinite One and remain alive.[13] Further
along, however, R. Nachman moderates this position and states that it is
possible to arrive at this sort of attainment, even in one's lifetime:

> This is the meaning of the phrase, 'No man knows' – not even
> Moses knows, as our sages, may their memory be blessed, state.[14] And

so his nullification to the Infinite One occurred upon his death. But certainly in his lifetime, as well, he experienced the stripping away of the corporeal and he cleaved to the light of the Infinite One. However, that stripping away was temporary, corresponding to the aspect of 'the *chayot* raced and returned.'[15] This is because the Holy One, blessed be He, desires our worship on earth. As the poet states, 'You have desired praise from clumps of earth, from those carved out of clay.'[16] Thus it is necessary not to remain in the state of self-nullification until that time when the Holy One, blessed be He, will Himself come and take one's soul.[17]

Even in his lifetime, Moses was able to strip away the physical and cleave to the light of the Infinite One. But that attainment was temporary, limited to the level of 'racing and returning.'[18] R. Nachman develops an important distinction between *stripping away the physical* and the *nullification of being*. *Nullification of being* is an irrevocable experience that leads to death: 'since Moses nullified all of his being ... Moses passed into the Infinite One.' More than a mere state of consciousness, it is a condition with significant physiological consequences that lead ultimately to the total nullification of being i.e., death. In contrast, *stripping away the physical* refers to a more moderate state of consciousness, in which a person casts aside his physical awareness and is prepared with utter self-sacrifice to renounce his physicality. He does not, however, actually nullify his entire being. He enters a process of 'racing and returning,' which affects his life force: at the moment that he strips away the corporeal, he momentarily ceases to live and clings to the Infinite One. But this is a temporary state, and he does not entirely pass away into the Infinite One.

During this process of 'racing and returning,' one walks the razor's edge between life and death. This state can result in death; thus experiencing it is conditioned on the readiness to give up one's life.[19] The degree to which a person cleaves to and is absorbed into God is directly related to the degree to which he strips away or nullifies his physicality. Therefore, R. Nachman first deals with a cleaving to God that requires a person's death, and then moves on to discuss more moderate possibilities of such cleaving, in which a person nullifies his faculties but not his entire being. This latter condition can also occur during a state of fervent prayer:

> We see that sometimes a person prays fervently, reciting a few words with great feeling. This is due to God's compassion on him. At that moment, the light of the Infinite One opens for him and shines upon him. When a person sees this gleam – even though he may not see it consciously, his soul (*mazal*) does see[20] – immediately his soul

is on fire with great cleaving to cleave to the light of the Infinite One. And in accordance with the measure of the revelation of the Infinite One, in accordance with the number of words that have opened and gleamed, he recites all of those words with great cleaving, with total dedication, and with the nullification of his faculties.[21]

The revelation of the Infinite One described here is a measured one: 'in accordance with the measure of the revelation of the Infinite One.' This testifies to the relative and incomplete nature of this revelation. Like the stripping away of the physical, which is incomplete and temporary, so too, cleaving and revelation are available to a limited degree. Although a person may yearn for a more complete revelation, he must keep his mystical experience temporary and incomplete so as to remain alive.[22]

We see therefore that the highest level of cleaving to God is the level of 'Moses in his death,' the level of being absorbed entirely into the Infinite One, which involves the nullification and abandonment of one's rational mind. There are various levels of 'Moses in his death.' The highest, 'racing forth' without returning, which involves the nullification of a person's entire being as he passes away and is absorbed into the Infinite One, may be attained only with his death.

The lower level of 'Moses in his death' involves stripping away the corporeal and clinging to the light of the Infinite One, but maintaining one's existence, 'racing forth and returning.' On this level too, a person's self-nullification means that he leaves behind his rational mind, and returns to it only at the conclusion of cleaving to the Infinite One. Moses attained the level of 'Moses in his death' even while he was alive. This parallels the aspect of Moses as described in the teaching *Bo el Paroh*,[23] in which the Zaddik – 'in the aspect of Moses' – renounces speech and intellect (*seichel*) in favor of silence and faith.

This is completely different from the level and attainment reached by 'Moses in his lifetime,' the level of the rational mind (*da'at*), of insights accessible to the intellect (*seichel*) and rational mind.[24] Casting away that rational mind, on the other hand, raises a person to the state of 'Moses in his death.' This distinction between the levels of 'Moses in his lifetime' and 'Moses in his death,' implied in the teaching *Tiku Emunah*, is developed and explained in *Anochi*.

The depiction of the rational mind (*da'at*) and its absence, as two distinct levels of Moses himself,[25] responds to another perplexing difficulty arising from the assertion that 'casting away the intellect' represents the highest level of serving God.[26] This is clearly at odds with what we are able to appreciate of the Kabalistic-Hasidic tradition where 'Moses – he is the rational mind (*da'at*).'[27] A famous statement asserts that 'No one arose in Israel like Moses, a prophet who gazed at God's image,'[28] and in the kabalistic literature Moses symbolizes the peak of human consciousness and mystical achievement. These assertions lead to the manifest conclusion that the rational mind (*da'at*) is the central and paramount instrument with which to serve God and through which to attain mystical realizations.

R. Nachman's position that removing one's rational mind (*da'at*) and casting away one's intellect (*seichel*) represents the apex of religious worship[29] seems, therefore, to be the very antithesis of the core Jewish conception that Moses and his teachings surpassed those of all prophets and mystics and their attainments.[30] The meaning of this contradiction is not limited to the question of the figure and stature of Moses, both a thought-provoking question and one of significant halachic importance.[31] But it also shows R. Nachman's intention with regard to abandoning the rational mind in worshipping God to be a revolutionary one.

The claim that identifies Moses with the rational mind holds true in regard to 'Moses in his lifetime.' Moses, however, possesses an additional and higher level, attained by casting away the rational mind and removing the intellect, a level achieved by Moses in his lifetime only temporarily and briefly, while his normative state was on the level of the rational mind (*da'at*).

2. Cleaving to God and Not-Knowing
In the passage describing the level of Moses at his passing and the depiction of his spiritual attainment during his lifetime, the consideration of the process of nullification undergoes a change from the 'nullification of being' to the 'nullification of awareness and the rational mind.'

The cleaving to God that a person attains in his lifetime is characterized as a state in which he exists, but in which his 'rational mind (*da'at*) is nullified.' Just like 'faith,' 'correct dreams,' 'insights,' and 'prophecy,' cleaving to the Infinite One involves nullifying one's rational mind. This state of cleaving to God is different from both the cleaving to the divine intellect that Maimonides describes[32] and the rational nature of cleaving to God as described by many Kabbalists.[33] We see here a direct connection between the path and the goal, between the means of attaining mystical experience and the nature of that experience.

During the 'racing' phase of the mystical experience, when a person is nullified to the Infinite One, his rational mind and self-awareness are nullified. Note that the nullification of self-awareness, of 'not knowing oneself,' does not necessitate nullification of the rational mind. The rational mind can be an active, observing and dominant faculty during the mystical experience, except that the object of its awareness does not include the person himself. Rather, the focus is solely on the divine, leaving room for nothing else. In consequence, the person does not know himself; he does, however, know God. Therefore, nullification of self-awareness cannot call into question the character of the mystical experience as a conscious activity.

Further along in this teaching, R. Nachman discusses the post-mystical state of consciousness, the stage when a person ends his absorption in God and returns to his independent state of consciousness and rational mind:

> And when he returns to his rational mind, he then knows the Oneness and Goodness of the Infinite One. And then there is no difference between Hashem and Elokim, between the divine trait of judgment and the divine trait of compassion, because in the Infinite One there is no change of will, heaven forbid, for changes are nothing other than changes in appearances. But when a person clings to the Infinite One, where there is no change of will, because there God's will is simple, and afterwards the residue of that oneness remains with him, and he is in the aspect of 'and return,' then the remaining impression shows the rational mind that it should know that everything is good and everything is one.

At the stage of 'return' from the mystical experience, a person comes back to his rational mind and self-awareness. His rational mind again becomes the active and dominant faculty in his consciousness, and his previous experience, while cleaving to God, is translated into the language of his rational mind. Only now is his rational mind able to digest what happened; through the residual impression the person arrives at an understanding and rational knowledge that he was unable to attain before and during the experience. Only now, after the 'racing' phase of cleaving to God has ended, does the mystic 'know the Oneness and Goodness of the Infinite One.'

3. The Process of Returning from the Mystical State and the Post-Mystical Consciousness

Moshe Idel argues that, unlike customary descriptions in the world of mysticism of the return from the mystical state as a traumatic experience of abandonment and loss, according to Hasidism the 'post-mystical state' is described as non-traumatic, and is understood as 'a descent for the purpose of ascent.' It is seen as a part of the natural and desirable dynamic of the mystic's life. However, Idel describes R. Nachman's approach, as an exception to that Hasidic model, stating that for R. Nachman the return from mystical union with God is accompanied by the harsh trauma of abandonment and descent into a state in which a chasm separates man from God.[34] Similarly, Ada Rapoport-Albert claims that the states of 'smallness' and 'I do not know' that R. Nachman depicts are to be understood as states of 'falleness,' 'one of the significant descriptors of the mystic experience in general.'[35]

However, according to what we previously determined, one may arrive at the opposite conclusion: that the memory of the mystical experience is not the source of a traumatic experience of abandonment, but an active and encouraging element in his present awareness.[36] The residue of that experience is transformed into a positive and active component in his post-mystical consciousness. His view of the world and experience of reality are transformed by his having cleaved to the Infinite One and now take on a more positive character.

In addition, R. Nachman does not describe the state of the 'return' as having been forced upon a person against his will, for man is neither abandoned nor cast aside by the *Shechinah*. Rather, he describes this 'return' as a choice to return to his normal human condition, since it is only on earth that he is able to fulfill his mission as a 'physical entity' and thus do the will of God Who desires the service of man as man.[37]

> But when the mystic is stripped of his corporeality, which is the aspect of 'the *chayot* racing forth and returning.' The Holy One, blessed be He, desires our service. As the poet states, 'You have desired praise from clumps of earth, from those carved out of clay.' And so a person may not remain in the state of 'racing,' until such time as the Holy One, blessed be He, will Himself come and take his soul.[38]

Cleaving to the Infinite One constitutes a temporary cessation of human existence. Remaining in that state for too long a period is likely to end in death, a deplorable end, negating man's mission to offer praise to God as a human being. Therefore, he may not remain in the state of 'racing,' but must quickly return to his normal state of consciousness – to life.[39]

> A person who has some knowledge of God knows that God's essential delight and pleasure come when we enhance and sanctify His name in this low world. That constitutes God's essential delights and pleasures. As the poet states, 'You have desired the praise of clumps of earth, from those carved out of clay,' etc. God has *seraphim, chayot, ophanim* and supernal worlds that serve Him – nevertheless, the essence of His delight and pleasure occurs when the service of this lowly world rises upward.[40]

According to R. Nachman, the principle that man's worship in this physical, lowly world gives God more pleasure and delight than all the service of the *seraphim* and *ophanim* may be unimportant to someone who has experienced, even to a minor extent, the knowledge of God. Therefore, it must be clear to a person that he bears the responsibility for guarding his existence as a human being and not allowing himself to be drawn into a mystical cleaving to God from which he cannot return.

In an instructive passage found in *Shivchei Moharan*, R. Nachman tells that the essence of his own efforts and mystical worship was not in entering the mystical state but rather in the effort to emerge from it:

> R. Nachman said that for him the 'racing forward' is not his service of God. Rather, his basic service and effort is the 'return.' In other words, in serving God there are the 'racing out and the return,' which exist for every individual, even the most worthless of men, for every person is at times awakened to serve God, particularly during prayer, when at times a person's heart is filled with great fervor and he recites a few words with tremendous feeling. That is the level of 'racing out.' And afterwards, that awakening and fervor cease, and all that is left him is the residue – that is the 'return.' The essential worship and effort of most people is to attain to 'racing outward,' so that their heart will race forward and be inspired to serve God, etc. For such a person, the 'returning' is easy, since that is his nature. But for R. Nachman, the opposite was true, since he had broken and nullified his body entirely. Thus, the racing outward was his nature, and his main effort was to return. In truth, it is necessary for a person to return as long as he must live – for if not, heaven forbid, he will pass away prematurely. It is therefore necessary that there be a racing outward and then a return.[41]

This fascinating description teaches that the mystical experience was more than a component in R. Nachman's speculative thought or an unrealized desire,[42] but rather an indivisible part of his existence.[43]

Alongside an extensive treatment in Hasidic texts of those instances in which cleaving to God comes to an end against the *zaddik's* will, we find as well the repeated call for the *zaddik* to volitionally leave the state of cleaving to God in order to perform the commandments and act amongst the people or bring goodness and blessing to the world.[44] When the mystic abandons the state of cleaving to God of his own volition, the difficulty of returning to everyday consciousness is mitigated. For R. Nachman, although the stage of leaving the mystical experience of cleaving to God is a difficult and tiring religious service, it is precisely for this reason that it is not viewed as traumatic but rather as the volitional act of a person who chooses to return to earth and serve God as a living human being.

4. Suffering and Joy

R. Nachman's teaching *Vayomer Boaz El Ruth*[45] contains a description of the
various stages of mystical absorption similar to those described in the previously discussed teaching *Anochi.*[46] But unlike *Anochi*, in this teaching we also
find discussion of the difficulties that can transpire in the process of returning
from the mystical experience. These do not involve feelings of abandonment
or rejection from God's countenance, but separation from the positive
experiences that accompany absorption into the Oneness. Despite these
difficulties, R. Nachman describes the post-mystical stage as a positive
experience characterized by joy and renewal, not as something difficult and
traumatic.

Let us take a brief look at the stages of the mystical experience as
described in this teaching:

> In truth, during the time of self-nullification, when a person is
> nullified to the Ultimate, Who is all Good, all One, then sufferings
> are truly nullified. But it is impossible to experience this nullifi-
> cation permanently and constantly, for if one did, one would no
> longer be human. And so that self-nullification must occur in the
> manner of racing out and returning.[47]

Here, as in *Anochi*, the desire and obligation to remain 'human' lead to a
mystical experience based on the dynamic of 'racing out and returning.' But
at this point, R. Nachman adds a description of the pain and sufferings
apparently involved in the process of 'returning.'[48]

Nullifying oneself to the oneness of God eliminates even the sufferings
that exist in ordinary human consciousness – the awareness of being separate
from God – and transforms a person into a part of the divine oneness that
has no evil and no suffering. Returning from the experience of that stage
intensifies one's sufferings.

This description of the intensification of sufferings, however, does not
take into account the entirety of the transformation that has taken place in
the spirit of the mystic who now returns to human consciousness. Other
factors have changed in consequence of his nullification to the Infinite One,
Who is all Good, all One, and these serve to mitigate his sufferings and even
to lead him to joy:

> But afterwards, the sufferings are lessened and one is consoled,
> because of the new Torah insights that one attains because of the
> sufferings. This insight comes about as follows. As a result of his
> sufferings, a person comes to self-nullification. And afterwards, even
> though he returns from that self-nullification, the residue that

remains of that self-nullification brings about new Torah insights, for as a result of having been nullified to the Ultimate and having realized that all the sufferings are very great favors, he is filled with joy. And joy is a vessel for original Torah insights.[49]

As in *Anochi*, here too the residue that remains following the experience of unity maintains the positive character of the mystical experience even after its conclusion. This redeems the post-mystical situation from the intensification of sufferings that might have occurred and eases the pain. At the end of the process the person is filled with joy and is ready for new Torah insights.

Alongside a description of the inner logic and process that a person goes through as he returns from self-nullification, which are liable to lead to trauma and intensified suffering, R. Nachman describes a process of his inner being and consciousness that eliminates that danger and instead alleviates his sufferings and brings him to joy. R. Nachman's words accord with the conclusion of the teaching, *Vayomer Boaz*:

> And this is the aspect of our sages' statement that 'in the future, the Holy One, blessed be he, will make a circle for the righteous, and each one will show with his finger,' etc.[50] 'The circle' corresponds to the aspect of joy, which is the vessel with which to receive the Torah. [...] And all of this comes about through self-nullification. This is because the Torah comes about through the radiance of the residue that remains from the state of self-nullification, as that radiance travels through the vessels [...] And that corresponds to the aspect of 'will show with his finger.' 'Showing' is the aspect of the vision and radiance of the residue, from which the Torah comes. And that is the aspect of 'showing with the finger,' the aspect of the Torah, which is the aspect of 'the finger of God.'[51]

A person who casts away his 'rational mind' and his 'ordinary states of mind, which are vessels,' for the sake of attaining oneness with the Infinite One, a oneness that cannot be contained within the vessels of the ordinary mind and rational mind, now returns at the end of that unification to his regular consciousness. The impression and joy that remain within the person transform these vessels so that the Torah now comes through them. It is precisely now, in the post-mystical state, that the joyful man can receive Torah and via his intellect attain new Torah insights touched with the residue of the infinite.

This clarification of R. Nachman's attitude to the emergence from the mystical experience to the post-mystical state of consciousness underscores Idel's observation regarding the exceptional nature of Hasidic mysticism in its view of the emergence from mystical unification.[52] Clearly, even for R. Nachman of Bratslav, who has been portrayed as one of the great pessimists of Hasidism, as a 'tormented master,' the mystical experience and post-mystical state can help a person accept his regular life with its sufferings, rather than destroy the flavor of his life and vitiate its joy.

This provides us with an additional perspective on the unique place that cleaving to God holds in Hasidic life. This mystical cleaving is integrated relatively easily into regular life; it does not, following the mystical experience, disconnect him from life, from appreciating its importance or from maintaining both the ability and desire to act within its parameters. The Hasidic mystic chooses to return to life, to the community, to Torah and God's commandments, as a religious ideal that expresses the 'service of Hashem.' In Hasidic mysticism – and, it seems to me, in Jewish mysticism as a whole – we do not find the dark and harsh descriptions of the post-mystical state that abound in Christian mysticism.[53] The lack of such descriptions may indicate Jewish mysticism's high evaluation of this-worldly life.

Repeatedly, R. Nachman and Hasidic texts in general teach that the mystical experience must be viewed within the context of 'racing and returning.' This world-view sees the mystical experience as part of a broader framework. Mysticism plays a major role in that framework – a role that cannot be realized if a person 'races out' but neglects to 'return,' for that would be considered abandoning the framework within which the mystic must function.

5. Knowledge – Love

The differentiation between a mysticism of love and a mysticism of knowledge is important and fruitful.[54] But when we analyze R. Nachman's view of the nature of mystical experience, it becomes clear that this distinction loses its cogency and fails to offer a definition or description of his view of the mystical experience.

We have seen that, in R. Nachman's view, the mystic at the end of his experience attains a knowledge and understanding that he could not have attained outside of the mystical experience. This fits neatly under the heading of the mysticism of knowledge. On the other hand, the path of cleaving to God and the pinnacle of that cleaving depend specifically upon the mystic's nullification of his rational mind. Thus, as a whole this explanation cannot easily be categorized as congruent with a mysticism of knowledge.

Regarding the post-mystical knowledge of God's oneness, studying the nature of R. Nachman's view of that state shows that this view also cannot easily be categorized as conforming to the criteria of the mysticism of knowledge.

According to R. Nachman, God's oneness may be attained only through experience. Only someone who has experienced the unity between himself and the Infinite One possesses knowledge thereof, with the influence of the residue that remains of that unity. This new insight is not theoretical knowledge. He already possessed knowledge of the principle of God's oneness before his mystical experience – a theoretical knowledge obtained without recourse to self-nullification to the Infinite One. The novelty of his realization lies not in the formulation of his thought or even in the proofs that sustain it, but in a tangible experience of God's oneness, the sole key to understanding. For R. Nachman post-mystical knowledge, attained as a result of having cleaved to God, is not based on knowledge of a discursive nature, but is related to intuitive, non-rational understandings. The ability to understand the unity of the divine traits of loving-kindness and judgment and to understand man and God as a unity, characterize intuitive understanding, for these paradoxical combinations cannot be grasped by discursive thought. Rational approaches that see discursive comprehension as the measuring rod for all understanding and knowledge will completely reject the unification of such opposites.[55] That being the case, even after a person returns to his ordinary mind, to the post-mystical state of knowledge, his knowledge is not of a rational cast – neither in its character nor in the way that it was acquired.

R. Nachman says of this attainment that a person '*knows* the unity of the Infinite One and His goodness.' 'Then,' states R. Nachman, 'the residue shows him how to *know;* he then *knows* that everything is good and everything is one.'

One might still wish to describe R. Nachman's mysticism as that of knowledge, since intuitive knowledge too is a type of knowledge. However, it appears to me that it would be more correct to describe the knowledge of which R. Nachman speaks as being closer to erotic knowledge and to the mysticism of love, which is based upon an experience of oneness and commingling, rather than to associate it with the mysticism of knowledge, which is centered on learning.

6. Good, Evil and Mysticism

R. Nachman associates the experience of mystical absorption into God's oneness with the ability to understand the existence of evil in the world.

The question of evil may be broken down into various categories: falsehood and truth, the existence of moral evil, and reward and punishment – why the righteous suffer and the wicked enjoy well-being. This last category impinges upon the question of the meaning of suffering.[56]

At the beginning of this chapter we saw that in the post-mystical stage, when a person returns from having been nullified to the Infinite One: 'then he knows the oneness of the Infinite One and His goodness … Via a person's cleaving to the Infinite One, where there is no change of will – for there the will is simple, afterwards a residue of that oneness remains with him. Then he is made into the aspect of "and return." Then the residue makes itself known to his *da'at* and he knows that everything is good and everything is one.'[57]

In the divine oneness, no evil exists; rather, all is immersed in a complete oneness that is entirely good. When a person returns from a state of absorption into that oneness, he still retains within the residue of that former state, a fragment of that oneness that has within it neither good nor evil. The residue of that experience within oneness leads him to the awareness that in truth there is no evil in the world, and so he no longer recites the blessing, 'the true Judge,' which a person recites when a tragic event occurs, but feels instead that he should recite the blessing of thanks to 'He who is good and does good' for everything.

R. Nachman offers additional theoretical expansion on this topic in his teaching, *Amar R. Akiva*, which explains the interdependence between the creation of evil and the emergence from the divine oneness.

> And falsehood, which is evil, which is spiritual pollution, comes into being because of the distance from the One. This is because evil is oppositional – for instance, whatever goes against a person's will is experienced as bad. But within the One, there can be no opposition; rather, everything is good. As our sages comment on the verse, 'On that day, Hashem will be One,'[58] etc., everything will exist within the reality of 'He who is good and does good'[59] – for within One, we cannot speak of evil. And so in those future times, the verse, 'A lip of truth will be established forever,'[60] will be realized, for then everything will be one, [...] everything will be good.

In the state of oneness there is no evil, war, falsehood, suffering and tears. In this teaching, the state of oneness is described as preceding the creation of the world and as a state that will return in messianic days, on the day that 'Hashem will be one and his name will be one.' R. Nachman does not discuss the possibility of reaching that state of oneness at the present stage of being, before 'that day' has come. But he explains more completely why a person absorbed into oneness experiences a world without evil and suffering.

In his teaching, *Vayomer Boaz*,[61] R. Nachman discusses the question of evil in the sense of suffering and describes the mystical experience as having the power to nullify that evil. This corresponds to R. Nachman's words in *Anochi*:

> And know that this aspect – i.e., the aspect of oneness – is the aspect of the ultimate goal. As the verse states, 'On that day, Hashem will be One and His name will be One.'[62] 'On that day' is the ultimate goal, which is 'all good,' because the One is all good. As our sages

of blessed memory state on this verse, 'On that day Hashem will be one,' etc., But now is He not one? Rather, now we recite the blessing 'the true Judge' over evil and 'He Who is good and does good' over good. But in the future days, people will recite the blessing, 'He Who is good and does good' over everything.' So we see that the level of oneness is the ultimate attainment. And that is all good, for the ultimate is all good. This is because even in regard to all of the troubles, sufferings and evils that a person experiences, heaven forbid, if he looks at the ultimate, they are certainly not evils at all but rather great favors. This is because all sufferings are certainly purposefully directed by God for a person's good – whether to remind him to repent or to erase his sins. That being so, sufferings are great favors, for God's intent is certainly only for the good. So we see that in all the evils and sufferings that a person experiences, heaven forbid, if he looks at the ultimate purpose – i.e., at God's intent – he will experience no sufferings at all. [...] And afterwards, even though [this person] has returned from [his] self-nullification, from the residue that remains of that self-nullification, the Torah is renewed. This is because via his self-nullification to the ultimate, in the course of which a person has realized that all sufferings are very great favors, he is filled with joy. And the joy is a vessel for new Torah insights ... Via the renewal of Torah that this person attains due to the residue of his self-nullification, his sufferings are after-wards ameliorated.[63]

During the mystical experience, when a person is nullified to the ultimate, his sufferings disappear entirely. Post-mystical knowledge of the experience of being commingled into the oneness of God cannot be communicated to another or expressed in logical words. But the strong residue that remains of those moments of experiencing oneness and the eradication of sufferings suffices to ameliorate and moderate the sufferings.

According to this, R. Nachman's words in *Tiku Emunah*,[64] which discuss why the insight into the suffering of the righteous and the well-being of the wicked – which a person can understand only after he casts away his intellect and dedicates himself to God wholeheartedly – should be understood as an insight that comes as a result of the mystical experience of *absorption into the oneness of God*, not as an intellectual insight that comes down from above due to God's magnanimity. This is the conclusion also reached from an analysis of *Tiku Emunah*.[65]

And then when a person's love for God is so strong that he removes all of his astuteness (*chochmah*) and casts himself into refuse and mud

in order to serve Him, in order to please Him somewhat, that is good
for the ordinary mind. This is because, he can then understand, even
that which is higher than the ordinary states of mind, something that
even Moses in his lifetime did not attain: [i.e.,] 'why the righteous
suffer and the wicked experience well-being,'[66] which is a 'perversion
of justice,' for it appears to be unjust, heaven forbid, something that
even Moses in his lifetime did not understand. That is to say, the
person attains this insight even when his ordinary mind is whole and
not absent – which corresponds to Moses in his lifetime (as opposed
to the removal of the ordinary mind, which corresponds to sleep,
which is the passing away of Moses). The presence of the ordinary
mind – when the ordinary mind (*mochin*) is present and not absent
– corresponds to Moses in his lifetime. At that point, it is not possible
to attain that insight – i.e., to understand why the righteous suffer,
etc. [...] But when the son removes all of his astuteness (*chochmah*)
and casts himself into servitude, then his father has compassion
upon him and reveals to him that which is not revealed even to the
[regular] son – i.e., he reveals to him why the righteous suffer and
the wicked enjoy well-being – something that Moses in his lifetime
did not attain.[67]

Joseph Weiss defines the revelation granted the son who acts as a slave as an
'intellectual boon' that leads him to understand why the righteous suffer and
the wicked enjoy well-being.[68] This definition accords the revelation a
complexion of intellectual insight that is not attained via a person's intellectual activity – 'the answer descends with the dew of loving-kindness, not
from the strength of the thought.'[69] But although the path is not intellectual
and even involves 'casting away the intellect' and entering a state that is
similar to 'a type of madness,'[70] Joseph Weiss nevertheless describes the
outcome as a species of intellectual insight – 'an intellectual boon.' It seems
that Weiss's refusal to recognize the existence of mysticism in the world of
R. Nachman prevented him from understanding the particular nature of this
mystical loving-kindness and of the dynamic that impels it, and so he saw this
mystical experience as an intellectual boon.

According to the passage quoted above, R. Nachman's unmistakable
position is that the mystical experience of oneness is the sole path to gaining
any answer about the existence of evil and suffering in the world. Intellectual
endeavor is unable to provide any answers.[71] Rather, only mystical absorption
into the oneness of God, followed by the residue that remains afterwards,
makes a sort of insight into these questions possible.[72]

7. Intermediate Summary

R. Nachman's presentation of the mystical experience must be viewed, from a phenomenological perspective, as part of the genus of Hasidic mysticism, which is principally motivated by and marked by love rather than knowledge or the desire for knowledge.

We have seen that Bratslavian mysticism is unique in that it makes mystical attainment conditional upon service that demands casting away the intellect (*seichel*) and nullifying the ordinary mind (*mochin*) – a service that involves engaging in acts of madness and a strong emphasis upon the removal of the rational mind (*da'at*), both as preparation for the mystical experience and as a state that characterizes the very essence of the mystical process of clinging to the light of the Infinite One.

II. Mysticism of Faith

In the teaching *Ikar Hatachlit*,[73] R. Nachman contrasts the philosophers' ideal with the mystical ideal of cleaving to God as a result of faith and prayer. R. Nachman opens with a description of the philosophers' position and then portrays his own viewpoint.[74]

1. Rejecting the Aristotelian Model

Before analyzing the model that R. Nachman proposes, I wish to discuss that which he rejects. The perspective of the philosophers described in R. Nachman's teaching presents an Aristotelian model that rests upon the unity of the observer, observed and observing intellect. It is important to note that R. Nachman refrains from claiming in the name of the philosophers that man's purpose is to cling to God via intellectual unification, although variations of this viewpoint existed in Jewish philosophy, as well as in kabbalah and in Hasidism. Various kabbalists and Hasidic thinkers made use of the Aristotelian model of the unity of intellect, intellectual observer and the intellectually observed object in order to conceptualize and describe the mystical experience with God[75] or at least to describe mystical attachment to God as the *sefirah* of wisdom and the like.[76]

R. Nachman chooses not to deal with this approach, whether in its defense or otherwise, but declares his opposition to the view that the purpose of man is to involve himself in knowledge of intellectual insights. R. Nachman instead presents his own alternative model: that the ultimate goal, attained via faith and prayer, is unification with God.

R. Nachman thus does not explicitly discuss the possibility of cleaving to God via intellectual unification. This seemingly allows for two possibilities: either R. Nachman denies the legitimacy of that path, or he gives it his tacit approval.

The first view assumes that R. Nachman entirely rejects the Aristotelian model of intellectual unification, including its use as a means of cleaving to God. But if that is the case, why does he not say so explicitly? A possible answer is that R. Nachman did not know of any thinker of his generation who held that view, and so found no reason to dispute viewpoints that no one held.[77]

It is also possible that R. Nachman did not deal with this view because his conflict with the 'philosophers' is essentially a conflict with Maimonides, in particular with his *Guide of the Perplexed*; and since the model of intellectual unification with God is not found in Maimonides,[78] R. Nachman saw no need to confute it.[79] But a look at the continuation of *Ikar Hatachlit* makes that conjecture extremely unlikely, for R. Nachman goes on to denounce philosophers who deny the value of performing God's commandments, a position difficult to believe that R. Nachman would attribute to Maimonides.[80]

It appears that we must proceed in a different direction and state that R. Nachman does accept the model of cleaving to God via intellectual unification, and even agrees that this is a legitimate means of actualizing one's purpose in the world. But R. Nachman objects to two components in this view propounded by the philosophers. The first is their attribution of intrinsic value to knowing objects of intellectual inquiry aside from God. The second is their view that intellectual apprehension of God is the sole path to attaining the goal of humanity.

This understanding of R. Nachman's view is buttressed by his other teachings, in which he discusses the possibility of clinging to God by means of the rational mind. The central example of such a teaching is *Atika Tamir V'satim*,[81] with which we will deal at length further on. This teaching describes clinging to God via the rational mind – a state that is presented as the human ultimate, and which is profoundly similar to the model of intellectual unification.[82] Indeed, although R. Nachman does not mention the formula, 'intellect, observer and observed object,' there is no doubt that his model rests upon the idea of unification between the intellect and the observed object, and he presents the intellect as a tool for cleaving to God. I will deal at length with this model, which interweaves the formulaic language and structure of philosophical constructs with that of kabbalistic tradition, in Part IV of this chapter when addressing the topic of the mysticism of knowledge.

The claim that R. Nachman accepted the intent of intellectual unification with God and related to it as a possible goal raises a number of difficulties. The first has to do with the democratic argument. R. Nachman stated that the philosophers' ideal of knowledge cannot be the goal of humanity, because such a goal must be attainable by every individual. This claim should be equally relevant, if not more so, when the object of knowledge to be gained by intellectual unification is God. It is, however, possible that

R. Nachman sees the democratic argument as applicable only if there is just one means available to this universal goal; but if another path exists, the path of faith and prayer, accessible to everyone, there is no reason to dismiss intellectual unification, even if that approach is restricted to an elite few.

The second difficulty arises from R. Nachman's statement that 'in truth, for us the essence of attaining the goal is only by means of faith and practical mitzvot: to serve Hashem in accordance with the Torah in a wholehearted and simple fashion.' Apparently, in these words, R. Nachman denies that any other path to the goal exists; the one he describes is the 'only' path. However, the continuation of his words and the text that he cites in proof show that this is not the proper understanding of his words: 'As the verse states, "The beginning of wisdom is the fear of Hashem"[83] – the essence of the beginning and first step of wisdom is only the fear of Hashem; fear must precede wisdom.'

It thus appears that R. Nachman's concern is about precedence: what kind of wisdom is first and most important? Once we recognize that the fear of Hashem is the goal and foundation of all, then there is room for religious worship, which can even result in cleaving to God upon the path of wisdom. This distinction between path and goal is important, for it clarifies that even when R. Nachman accepts intellectual unification as a path to clinging to God, he does not see the ultimate goal contained in the unification of intellect, observer and observed object.

R. Nachman also rejects the idea that delight in attaining intellectual insights, whether in this world or the next, is man's highest purpose. Man has but one goal – cleaving to God – and delight in intellectual insights is not the way to achieve it.

A number of paths lie open before a person for attaining his purpose and cleaving to God. The one path open to all is prayer and practical mitzvot. The second path is worship that uses the intellectual faculties until the worshipper attains an intellectual unification with God. Intellectual insight is not the ultimate goal, but an instrument and means of attaining the goal of cleaving to God. This is the essential distinction between using the intellect to serve and cleave to God and the philosophers' ideal of intellectual unification as the ultimate goal in itself.

2. The Alternative Model – Unification via Prayer

Analyzing the alternative model to intellectual unification that R. Nachman presents in this teaching reveals that his rejection of the Aristotelian model is not as absolute as it initially appeared.

Against the philosophers' ideal of intellectual unification R. Nachman presents faith and cleaving to God with the help of prayer as man's goal. In certain states of being, man experiences identification between prayer and

God: 'prayer and Hashem are one, as it were.' Thus, when a person prays and his prayer is God, he cleaves to God.[84]

In the teaching *Ikar Hatachlit* the postulate of unification between man and his prayer is implicit, whereas in other places the unification of man and prayer is explicit.[85] The unification between the man praying and his prayer is also found in the teachings of other Hasidic thinkers, and stands at the foundation of the idea of cleaving to God with the help of prayer.[86] Here R. Nachman emphasizes the other pole of cleaving to God: the unification between prayer and God.[87] R. Nachman speaks of this idea in other places too, teaching for instance that 'the fervor that a person experiences in his prayer corresponds to Hashem himself, as it were, corresponding to 'He is your praise, and he is your God'[88] – that is to say he is himself the praise and the prayer.'[89]

The model of clinging to God that R. Nachman constructs here relies upon the unification of the person praying, his prayer and God. This model adapts the external structure of the Aristotelian tri-fold model, but apparently changes its meaning entirely. Corresponding to the unification of the observer, observed and intellect, R. Nachman presents the unification of another triad: the person who prays, his prayer and the object of his prayer – God. The structure of the formulation is identical but the knowledge is replaced by prayer. R. Nachman preserves the shell of the Aristotelian model but casts away its content.

This description though is not altogether accurate, for in a certain sense one can see in the model R. Nachman proposes a sort of variation on the Aristotelian model even in terms of content. If we see prayer as thought whose subject is God, then unification in prayer comes about through the unification of the thinker, the thought and the object of the thought. The similarity then between the Aristotelian model and R. Nachman's is not only structural but substantive too.

These models differ in two basic ways. The first is the object of the thought that leads to an intellectual unity. Is it the knowledge of the content of every object, or the knowledge of God? In R. Nachman's view, only thought about God gives meaning to man's life. The second distinction deals with the nature of the mental activity leading to unification. In the Aristotelian model, the intellect functions in a cognitive-rational sense ('to understand'). R. Nachman, on the other hand, recommends activity of thought closer to concepts such as focusing and concentration ('to think upon'). This second possibility proffered by R. Nachman is similar to the model of cleaving to God that is known as 'the cleaving in thought.'[90]

Thus, even as R. Nachman vigorously and emphatically rejects the Aristotelian model, he offers an alternative model that adapts the rejected model's structure, as it copies and transforms its content.

This topic turns our attention to an interesting point that touches upon the concepts and constructs with which R. Nachman describes the mystical experience. Without a doubt, both in this teaching and in *Anochi* (discussed above), R. Nachman offers a model of clinging to God that is similar to the mysticism of love and that rejects knowledge (even mystical knowledge) as the purpose of man. However, in none of the examples seen so far does he use models of cleaving to God based on erotic images of unification, as might have been expected in a mysticism of love, and as we indeed find in the Baal Shem Tov's descriptions of clinging to God during prayer:

> Prayer is commingling with the Shechinah. And just as at the beginning of the act of intimacy there is movement, so must a person move when he begins prayer. And afterwards he can stand without movement and cleave to the Shechinah with a great cleaving. And with the power gained from having moved, he can come to great enthusiasm, thinking, 'Why am I moving? It is no doubt because the Shechinah is standing before me.' And with that he will come to great fervor.[91] From the Baal Shem Tov: 'From my flesh shall I see' – just as in the physical act of intimacy a man can be fertile only when he employs his organ with desire and joy, so too in regard to spiritual intimacy, which is speech in Torah and prayer – when it is performed with an aroused organ, with joy and pleasure, then it is fruitful.[92]

These explicitly erotic images leave no doubt as to the connection between cleaving to God and the mysticism of love or of eroticism. A comparison of these images to the way in which R. Nachman describes cleaving to God points to the problem of labeling Bratslavian mysticism as a mysticism of love. There is a great gap between R. Nachman's descriptions and images of mystical unification and the rather shocking erotic images that characterize the mysticism of love in the Hasidic world. R. Nachman prefers to use models of cleaving to God based upon thought and knowledge, rather than his great-grandfather's shocking images.

It is then no less difficult to categorize R. Nachman's mystical experience as a 'mysticism of love' than it is to categorize it as 'mysticism of knowledge.' We will see that if we wish to assign a name to R. Nachman's mysticism, the title closest to R. Nachman's speech and spirit of language is 'mysticism of faith.'

3. Mysticism of Faith

The teaching *Ikar Hatachlit* has the quality of a manifesto, proclaiming man's purpose and the proper path upon which to walk. This is one of

R. Nachman's important proclamations that 'in truth, for us the essence of the attainment of the goal is only via faith.' Here, he presents an alternative to rationalistic religious approaches; this thus serves as a part of his proclamation of war against philosophers and the path of their 'sciences' (*chochmot*).

This is, therefore, also an excellent source for understanding R. Nachman's concept of faith. As we have seen, for R. Nachman faith is the goal of man, since it leads to unification with and mystical absorption into God. Faith and prayer are identified as one and the same: 'and faith – that is prayer.' The believer who prays reaches his goal of unification with God through the path of faith and prayer, for 'prayer and Hashem are one, as it were, and that is the essence of the goal in truth.'

For R. Nachman, faith, like prayer, is a specific level of cleaving to God.[93] Faith is not knowledge or proof of the existence of God, but a sense of His presence. Like prayer, it is existence in the presence of God – something not connected to the rational mind or to intellectual conclusions, but that depends upon an internal state in which a person feels that he is in contact with God or standing in His presence.

It goes without saying that R. Nachman is not claiming that the moment a person has faith or engages in prayer he enters into a trance, an ecstatic state or nullification of the ego. Rather, his internal state of faith is by its nature an expression of a sense of cleaving to God, of connection, of standing in the presence of the divine. This clinging to God exists even if it does not necessarily result in drastic changes of consciousness or an exceptional internal awakening.

Bratslavian faith, therefore, does not stand at the opposite pole of mysticism,[94] but is an integral part of the mystical framework of values, and explicitly connected to mystical goals of cleaving to and being absorbed into God.

III. Hierarchy in Mystical Paths (Via Mystica) and in Mystical Unification (Unio Mystica)

The teaching *Ohr Haganuz*,[95] which I will discuss in the following sections, and the teaching *Chotem B'toch Chotem*,[96] which I will discuss thereafter, present an organized structure of various models of religious worship and mystical experiences that are discussed in a number of R. Nachman's teachings. *Ohr Haganuz* and *Chotem B'toch Chotem* not only discuss models of service and religious insight, but explain the general structure within which these various models fit. As we will see, the hierarchy of models created in these two works is consistent across the span of R. Nachman's teachings.

1. Ohr Haganuz: Torah and Prayer – Revealed and Hidden

> When a person comes to the level of knowledge (*da'at*), he merits
> the attainment of Torah [...] But there are two aspects of Torah: the
> revealed aspect and the hidden aspect. Regarding the hidden aspect,
> that is gained only in the future days. But in this world, a person
> attains the aspect of the hidden via prayer with total dedication. And
> one attains prayer via the revealed Torah. This is because the
> revealed Torah corresponds to Sinai. As our sages state, 'Sinai [plain
> meaning of the text] and up-rooter of mountains [elevated under-
> standing of the Torah] – which of them is preferable?' And they
> answered that 'Sinai is preferable, for everyone needs masters of
> wheat [basic knowledge].'[97] Everyone needs the revealed Torah, but
> few are those who need the hidden Torah. And the aspect of Sinai
> is the aspect of humility. As our sages state, 'The Holy One, blessed
> be He, set aside all the mountains and only gave the Torah on Mt.
> Sinai' because of its low stature.[98] And our sages have stated[99] that
> the prayer of a humble person is not rejected, quoting the verse, 'A
> broken heart,' etc. [100] And via prayer with total self-dedication, when
> a person nullifies all of his physicality and there is no limitation, then
> he can attain the Torah of the future, which is not limited and is not
> grasped within limits.[101]

R. Nachman here presents two examples of insight – revealed and hidden –
and two examples of the means to attain those insights – rational mind
(*da'at*) and prayer.

The Torah has a layer of revealed and a layer of hidden teachings. The
rational mind can grasp the revealed aspect of the Torah, but cannot, in this
world, attain its hidden aspect. Only in the future will a person be able, with
the help of his rational mind (*da'at*), to attain that hidden aspect. But now
the path to that hidden aspect of the Torah is the path of prayer.

Prayer, a tool with which to attain hidden matters, requires total self-
dedication and is related to nullification of the physical. R. Nachman presents
total self-dedication as a person's trail-blazing progress from a state with
boundaries and physicality to a state without boundaries.[102] This state of
internal and conscious being makes possible the attainment of the hidden
Torah, which is also not finite. Prayer out of total self-dedication is attained
by learning the revealed aspect of the Torah.

In the teaching *Ki Ta'avor* as well, R. Nachman refers to two types of
attainment: 'for behold, the Torah is concealed and revealed, and the Holy
One, blessed be He, is also concealed and revealed. That is to say, that which
is revealed to us is the garment and the exterior, and that which is hidden

from us is the inner being. And behold, every person must encourage himself to attain the inner being, that which is hidden from him. But how can he come to that which is hidden from him? The answer is: with prayer for its own sake.'[103]

Both *Ohr Haganuz* and *Ki Ta'avor* present a clear hierarchy of two levels of attainment – revealed and hidden – and they both assert that the hidden secrets of the Torah and the inner nature of the Torah (the secrets of God and His innerness) are revealed with prayer and not via the path of knowledge (*da'at*) and Torah learning.

1.1 The Mysticism of the World to Come

R. Nachman draws an important additional distinction between the mysticism of this world and the mysticism of future days. He makes it clear that the mind will only be able to understand the secrets of the Torah (which are the secrets of God) in the future. At present, the hidden cannot be understood or conceptualized. A person can attain it only via faith, prayer with total self-dedication, and casting aside the intellect.

The mind as an intermediary, linking man and his God, cannot be realized in this world. It is a messianic and distant dream that will come into being only when the rules of reality will change, and the basic conditions of human existence will be transformed beyond recognition. Until then, contact with that future world exists only in the way of faith that purposely renounces the rational mind and chooses an alternative consciousness in order to arrive at contact with the Infinite One.

In the teaching *Bo el Paroh*,[104] R. Nachman deals with the topic of 'constriction (of God)' and 'the vacated space,' and with the intrinsic inability to reconcile contradictions and answer certain heretical claims with intellect (*seichel*) and the rational mind (*da'at*).[105] That reality remains in force only until the 'future times.' But when those future times arrive, it will even be possible for the rational mind to attend to the difficulties that come from the vacated space.[106]

An additional central teaching in which R. Nachman distinguishes between the 'future days' and the present reality is *Atika Tamir V'satim*,[107] which we will discuss at length in Part IV of the present chapter, dealing with the mysticism of knowledge.

1.2 Delight

Etkes claims that the goal of Hasidic mysticism is delight,[108] describing it as something of the highest order and contrasting the mysticism of delight with the mysticism of knowledge or rectification.[109]

Moshe Idel discusses the use of the term 'delight' by Hasidic thinkers[110] as an example of how kabbalistic terms shift meaning as they are used in

Hasidism. 'Delight' was originally used to describe the occurrences in the world of the *sefirot*, but was transformed into a description of the relationship between man and God. 'Delight,' therefore, is the psychological meaning that Hasidism (like the prophetic kabbalah before it) confers on descriptions of the erotic connection amongst the various elements in the world of divinity. These descriptions, which appear mainly in the kabbalistic literature that deals with the world of *sefirot*, are explained as expressing the internal state of a person when he is involved in serving God by cleaving to Him. 'And so it is in the trait corresponding to "the *zaddik* is the foundation of the world," that a person's spirit is connected to Hashem, the Life of life, and clings to Him with clinging and yearning, with a wondrous pleasure yearning and delight.'[111]

We also find in R. Nachman that cleaving to God leads to delight, a 'delight' with clear erotic connotations. However, there is a crucial difference. The goal of that cleaving to God is not the delight that a person immersed in cleaving to God experiences; rather, the goal is to give that delight to God.[112] The difference lies in two areas:

1. Delight again becomes or continues to be a concept dealing with occurrences in the world of divinity, not a psychological-internal concept of the condition of a person's world.[113]
2. The yearning of the mystic to cleave to and unite with God does not come from his yearnings for supernal delight attained during unity with God; his purpose is to give delight to God.

As we saw above, in the teaching *Ohr Haganuz*,[114] R. Nachman speaks of prayer out of total self-dedication, a self-dedication that he defines as follows: 'a person prays without any thought of his own interests, and he does not think of himself at all, and all of his essence and physicality are nullified, and he is nullified as though he does not exist in the world. As the verse states, "For your sake are we killed all the day"[115].'[116]

Via self-dedication a person attains the secrets of the Torah. And R. Nachman continues:

A person attains this through prayer, for 'the Holy One, blessed be He, desires the prayers of Israel.'[117] And when the nation of Israel prays before Him and fulfills His desire, then, as it were, He is made into the aspect of woman, in that He receives delight from us. As the verse states, 'a sacrifice by fire, [*isheh*, but this word can be vowelized as *ishah*, woman], a pleasing fragrance for Hashem.' [118] As a result of the pleasing fragrance that God receives, He is made into the aspect of a female. 'And a female circles a man'[119] – for the Holy

> One, blessed be He, is made into the aspect of a revealed garment
> – i.e., whereas He was initially in the aspect of being concealed, now
> He is revealed via prayer. 'And the Holy One, blessed be He, and the
> Torah are all one.' And then via prayer the Torah is revealed – i.e.,
> the secrets of the Torah.[120]

R. Nachman here presents a most interesting variation on the understanding of delight as the purpose of prayer and cleaving to God. God is
compared to a woman,[121] who wishes to fulfill her desire; by means of
prayer, the nation of Israel fulfills her desire and brings her delight. It is not
that man receives delight out of his contact with God; rather, God gains
delight from the prayer of man.[122]

These words continue R. Nahman's previous statements regarding
the total self-dedication required for prayer and cleaving to God. Such self-
dedication makes it impossible to see 'the delight of serving Hashem' as the
purpose of prayer and cleaving to God. It is not possible that a person who
is serving God 'without any self-regard' will believe the goal of that service
to be the delight that it brings him. Fully turning to God necessitates the
renunciation of any personal ambition, including the hope for the supernal
and spiritual delight that a person can attain when he prays and cleaves to
God.[123]

In other sources too, when R. Nachman makes use of erotic imagery
in referring to prayer, the delight that he refers to is God's and not the
worshipper's. This is the case when R. Nachman compares God to a woman
and Israel to a male during prayer,[124] and also when the person praying (or
the people of Israel) is female and God is the male. When R. Nachman
mentions delight, he attributes it to God as He pours forth loving-kindness:
'And that is the meaning of the verse, "He recalled his loving-kindness." The
term "He recalled" carries the meaning of pouring forth – i.e., when He
wishes to give loving-kindness to Israel … This is because words are formed
of the sparks, and in this way Hashem pours forth much good to Israel.
Thus the verse speaks of "The salvation of our God," for that is His
delight.'[125]

But even when the images of the connection between a person praying
and God are not erotic, we find the same demand for total self-dedication
during prayer,[126] joined by the assertion that 'Hashem has great delight
from this.'[127] We may conclude from these sources that Bratslavian
mysticism differs from the mysticism of delight not only in that it denies that
the individual's delight is the purpose of cleaving to God, but also in that
it demands total self-dedication – a demand that includes the renunciation
of any self-interest and gain from clinging to God.

1.3. Secrets of the Torah

Although he expresses himself in a refined and allusive manner, R. Nachman confers a radical erotic meaning to the term 'secrets of the Torah.' Prayer, in which the person praying unites in intimacy with the divine, leads to a state in which 'a female surrounds a male.' What occurs in prayer to make that which was previously hidden revealed, and how, then, does 'a female surround a male?' It is possible that R. Nachman is hinting that prayer, which is the time of congress that causes delight, reveals those parts of divinity that in general are hidden. Since divinity and the Torah are all one, during the time of prayer – the time of contact that gives delight to the divine – the secrets of divinity, which are the secrets of the Torah (that cannot be revealed in any other way), are revealed.[128]

As we saw earlier, the teaching *Ki Taavor Bamayim*[129] also discusses prayer for its own sake as the proper path to attaining the secrets of the Torah, the secrets of God. R. Nachman's words there support our present contention:

> And it is known that whoever receives delight from another is called female – i.e., in relation to that other. And so when Hashem receives delight from the prayer of Israel, he so to speak becomes female in relation to Israel. And thus the verse states, 'a sacrifice of fire [*isheh*, but this word can be vowelized as *ishah*, woman], a pleasing fragrance for Hashem.'[130] This is because via the pleasing fragrance that Hashem receives from the payers of Israel, he becomes the secret of woman. 'A female surrounds a male.'[131] That being the case, the inner being becomes the exterior being. And that is the meaning of the verse, 'When you pass through water. …' 'Pass through' comes from the language of revelation, as in the verse, 'And Hashem will pass through to strike the Egyptians,' [132] which Onkelos's Aramaic translation renders as, 'and Hashem will be revealed,' etc. 'And there is no water but Torah.'[133] And the meaning is that when you want the hidden aspects of the Torah to be revealed to you, 'with you am I' – i.e., see to it that you make the vessel that is called 'I.'

R. Nachman's explanation of the connection between the secrets of the Torah and prayer is concealed within the erotic perspective. The secrets of Torah correspond to the inner organs of the female divinity/Torah, which are generally hidden. The female encircling the male refers to the moment of intimacy when the woman in that sense surrounds the male. This is the revelation of the secrets of divinity, the 'secrets of the Torah,'[134] and the revelation of 'the inner being of the Torah,'[135] the inner being of divinity, which can be revealed only during the intimate union between man and God.

It stands to reason that the expressions 'hidden' and 'hidden parts' are associated with the anatomical term, 'house of the hidden parts'[136] (a reference to a woman's hidden organs) and to the word 'hidden'[137] in the biblical context, with its clear erotic connotations.[138]

R. Nachman's imagery of prayer as an activity in which a person makes divinity a vessel – 'and that vessel is made by every individual of Israel, when he prays in a manner that connects his thought to his speech'[139] – is strengthened when we read it in the context of the Talmudic statement that 'a woman is unformed'[140] and does not make a covenant with anyone but the man who makes her a complete vessel. As the verse states, 'The one who takes you, Your Maker, Hashem of Hosts is His name.'[141] In other words, the act of intimacy transforms the woman into a vessel.

In this Talmudic statement, the imagery of making a vessel expresses the connection between Israel and God as intimate union. In the Tanachic-Talmudic imagery, God is the male who makes a vessel of the Jewish nation. In R. Nachman's description, on the other hand, Israel is the male and makes divinity, corresponding to the female, a vessel during prayer.[142]

R. Nachman presents the delight of divinity and the fulfillment of its desire as the ultimate goal of cleaving to God. But in addition to that delight there is also an ancillary purpose with a more clearly theurgist role: this congress completes and rectifies a specific aspect of divinity and thus makes it into a 'vessel' – 'the One who takes you, your Maker.'

Although R. Nachman presents clinging to God as an activity not based in self-interest, one cannot deny that the person's desire for the revelation of the hidden pieces of divinity/Torah and its inner being is in fact actualized: 'when you desire that the hidden of the Torah be revealed to you, "with you am I" – i.e., see to it that you make the vessel that is called "I".'

This image of 'a female surrounding a male' as an expression of unity achieved during prayer can contribute to understanding the nature of mystical union that R. Nachman describes. This image emphasizes the dimension of the male being absorbed and swallowed into the female during intimate union. In this context, the image of divinity as a female swallowing up and the man's prayer as a male swallowed up is quite fitting, for the man is nullified in God and not God within man.[143]

The imagery of mystical union as being swallowed, as well as the image of mystical union as intimate union, is found both in general and in Jewish mysticism. It appears, however, that R. Nachman presents an interesting variation that combines the two images into one. The image of unification as being swallowed up or as the nullification of a drop of water into the sea generally describes a state in which a person's soul is no longer an entity identifiable as separate from the divine. Having been entirely nullified into the sea or into the one swallowing, it has no more independent existence.[144] On the other hand, the image of unification as erotic union generally describes the state of unification as a cleaving between two separate beings that are distinguishable from each other, both during the unification and afterwards.[145]

The image of intimate union as being swallowed up describes a specific kind of mystical union. On the one hand, the unification is a state of being absorbed and swallowed up into the innerness of God on the level of 'when he merits to be absorbed into the Infinite One.'[146] On the other hand, the person remains a distinguishable and independent being even during the time of the mystical experience. He comes in contact with the divine and is even swallowed into it, but is not entirely nullified.[147]

We see in this an allusion to the experience of a person in prayer[148] – at the very time that he feels absorbed into God and swallowed into Him, he still remains present in his experience as a distinct, existent being.

1.4. The Torah as the Body of God

There is a long tradition that regards the secrets of the Torah as the layer in which the secrets dealing with the 'body' of God are revealed; this perspective appears in the *heichalot* literature and afterwards in various permutations in kabbalah. R. Nachman's comparison of the secrets of Torah to secrets of the body of divinity may be understood as an additional stage in this tradition of describing God – a stage with a significant shift in meaning.[149]

The *Zohar* (in *Saba Demishpatim*[150]) describes the revelation of the secrets of the Torah as the revelation of the secrets of a young woman's body. The Torah is compared to a young woman who progressively unveils herself before her beloved, until she stands naked before him, and he knows all of her secrets.[151] In the *Zohar*, the secrets of the young woman are the secrets of the Torah, but God is not identified with the Torah. Therefore, in the *Zohar's* parable, the erotic imagery pertains to the relationship between man and the Torah, not between man and God.

In contrast, R. Nachman identifies God with the Torah in this context; thus, the secrets of the Torah are themselves the hidden limbs of God. In his essay on the feminine image of the Torah, Elliott Wolfson states that in the Baal Shem Tov's Hasidism, the woman serves as a central image of the Torah: the connection between the student and the Torah is like a dance, an erotic touch and even actual intimacy. Nevertheless, Wolfson's examples of feminine imagery relate to the Torah, not to God.

R. Nachman also makes use of the erotic imagery in his allusion that the secrets of divinity are not only the hidden places, but the inner limbs of the feminine that are revealed to the male when 'the female surrounds the male.'

A distinction of crucial importance between the *Zohar's* parable and R. Nachman's words lies in the manner in which the secrets of the Torah are revealed. In the *Zohar*, the secrets of the Torah are revealed through Torah

learning. For R. Nachman, in contrast, the path to the secrets of the Torah
is prayer. Thus, in identifying the Torah with God, R. Nachman sets out in
an entirely new direction – yet one that is also very ancient.[152]

1.5 A Note Regarding Gender and Mysticism

In his book, *Derech Ha'aspaklaria*,[153] Wolfson argues that Jewish mysticism is
characterized by 'absolute phallocentrism.' (In short, God is always related
to in mystical-vision as possessing male characteristics.) Even when God or
the Torah is described as female, the context makes clear that this female is
only a part of the male, and serves him in a double role: to reveal the male
on the one hand, and to cover and conceal it on the other. There is no doubt,
in his view, that the female dimension of divinity is hidden and swallowed up
within the male dimension, within the 'divine phallus,' which is, ultimately,
the all. The male kabbalist saw from his flesh only a male deity. Wolfson
expands on this theme in additional essays not only with regard to the
mystical vision and image but concerning the question of gender in Jewish
mysticism in general.[154]

Our study shows that these descriptions do not apply to the mystical
thought of R. Nachman. For R. Nachman, the highest mystical union that a
person can achieve is via prayer, in the course of which the human being
discovers the secrets of the Torah, which are the secrets of divinity. That unification is described as an erotic union, in which the mystic is compared to the
male and divinity corresponds to the female. The revelation that elevates the
soul of the mystic is not a revelation of the male phallus, but the 'house of
hidden parts' of the female. There is no hint that the female is transformed
into a component within the male or swallowed up into the male.

This vision is completely different than that described by Wolfson, both
regarding the one who swallows and the swallowed and the question of what
is revealed in the mystical experience. The question of gender is clearly
decided in these teachings of R. Nachman: divinity is experienced as female,
and the absorption into divinity is the desire of the mystic to unveil the
secrets of divinity and its inner being.

It is important to recall that this refers not to unification with God via the
Torah, which is the female, but an alternative to unification with divinity
directly by means of prayer.

1.6. 'The Holy One, Blessed be He, And the Torah Are All One'[155]

There is something unique in R. Nachman's mystical identification of Torah
and God, an identification that explains how via prayer and cleaving to God
the secrets of the Torah are revealed. By clinging to God one clings to the
Torah; the revelation of the secrets of God is the revelation of the secrets of
the Torah.

The sentence upon which R. Nachman relies in his claim for a unification of God and Torah, 'The Holy One, blessed be He, and the Torah are all one,' is apparently a partial reading of the original phrase, which includes Israel as part of the oneness. This expression, cited many times in Hasidic texts in the name of the *Zohar*, appears for the first time in the writing of R. Chaim Moshe Luzzatto.[156] However, as we have noted above, the roots of the idea of the unification of God and the Torah are much older, and are to be found in the earliest kabbalistic texts.[157]

The idea of mystical unity between the Torah and God served as a central component in shaping the path of cleaving to God,[158] but for the most part in a way different than, and even contrary to, R. Nachman's approach. It was generally explained that the unification of God and the Torah meant that a person who desired to cleave to God had to cling to the Torah,[159] since God and His Torah are one.

The difference in views is clarified when we compare R. Nachman's position to that of R. Shneur Zalman of Ladi, founder of Chabad Hasidism, who was a contemporary and interlocutor of R. Nachman.[160]

> As the *Zohar* states, the Torah and the Holy One, blessed be He, are all one. This means that the Torah is the wisdom and will of the Holy One, blessed be He, and the Holy One, blessed be He, Himself is all one, for He is the knower and He is the knowledge, etc., as stated earlier in the name of Maimonides […] However, as for the Holy One, blessed be He Himself, no thought can grasp Him at all, except when that thought is grasped and clothed within the Torah and its commandments. Then the thought is grasped and clothed in the Holy One, blessed be He, literally, for the Torah and the Holy One, blessed be He, are all one.[161] For an additional, exceedingly clear elucidation regarding the phrase 'grasps' stated by Elijah – i.e., 'no thought grasps You,' etc. – behold, in regard to any mind – when a person understands and realizes some concept with his intellect, the intellect grasps the concept and the person encompasses it in his intellect, so that the concept is grasped and surrounded and clothed within the intellect that has grasped and understood it. And also the intellect is clothed within the concept when the person understands it and grasps it with his intellect […] And also this person's intellect is clothed in those concepts. And this is a wondrous union that has nothing like it and no equal to be found in physicality that factors should be as one and unified, literally, from every side and aspect.[162]

R. Shneur Zalman here employs the Aristotelian model of intellectual union in order to explain the mystical idea of the unity of God and Torah. On the one hand, he presents the unity of God and Torah and, on the other, the unity of man and Torah. Since man and God know the Torah and are unified with it, they unite with each other. Thus a person who wishes to cleave to God must learn Torah; the more he delves into its laws and details, the more fully will he cleave to God.[163]

The learning that R. Shneur Zalman proffers as a way of cleaving to God is halachic in nature. He does not speak of the 'Work of the Chariot' nor of the secrets of the Torah, but of learning the 'revealed' Torah – the arguments of Abaye and Rava – with the claim that when a person learns and encompasses a halachic topic clearly with his thought, he cleaves to God via an intellectual-mystical unification that occurs at the time of the learning.[164]

The mystical unity of Torah, God and the student leads R. Shneur Zalman to a conclusion that is extremely important in both conceptual and practical terms. In Chapter 23 of his work he writes, 'With all the above, the statement in the *Zohar* that the Torah and the Holy One, blessed be He, are all one may be understood exceedingly well.' Again he explains the unity: 'He is the knower and He is the knowledge, etc. Thus, it is stated that "the Torah and the Holy One are all one".' And R. Shneur Zalman concludes: 'with this we may understand why involvement in Torah study is superior to all the other commandments, greater even than prayer, which is the unification of the supernal worlds.'

This presents a clear hierarchy based on intellectual unification with God. Learning Torah is the highest religious value, higher even than prayer. Prayer is seen here as 'the unification of worlds' in a hidden manner, whereas learning Torah is unification with God, 'since the supernal will is revealed literally in the spirit and garments of the person learning the Torah, that supernal will being the Torah itself.'[165]

R. Shneur Zalman of Ladi's approach is but one of a range of approaches sharing the idea of the unity of God and Torah proposed in Hasidism for cleaving to God via learning Torah. Some state that unification with God occurs when one learns the inner aspect of the Torah and its secrets, not its simple halachot;[166] others claim that a person cleaves to God by speaking the words of Torah aloud and forcefully, and the more energy he puts into his pronunciation the more he cleaves to God.[167] Uniting these viewpoints is the common denominator that since there exists a unity of Torah and God, one clings to God by learning Torah – the Torah is the intermediary between God and man.

This generally-accepted viewpoint throws into sharp relief the unique and contrary approach of R. Nachman of Bratslav. In R. Nachman's view, a person cannot learn the secrets of the Torah. Instead, he clings to God via prayer; and since God and the Torah are one, he also clings to the Torah, and then its secrets are revealed to him. Disagreeing completely with R. Shneur

Zalman, R. Nachman argues that the mystical unity of God and Torah helps explain the primary importance of prayer, since it is impossible to attain any secrets of God and the Torah by means of learning and the rational mind.

This is an excellent example of a case in which various authorities share basic mystical approaches and even the specific versions of those approaches, yet create different and opposing viewpoints that lead to divergent concepts, mystical praxes and the religious atmosphere that they shape.

1.7 Learning Torah in its Aspect of Being Revealed, Learning Torah in its Aspect of Being Concealed

In Hasidism, the central purpose of learning the secrets of the Torah was to attain a certain level of cleaving to God and revelation of the divine. Also, learning the classic kabbalistic texts, such as the kabbalah of the Ari and the *Zohar*, purported to impart to the practitioner a mystical experience. The central challenge in learning the hidden Torah and kabbalah, then, is not interpretive but experiential. The practitioner's goal is to transform his learning into an occasion of revelation. Scholarly expertise, the command of kabbalistic concepts and exegetical expertise were thus presented as secondary to the principal goal of cleaving to God and attaining divine revelation, without which the learning 'lacks soul.'[168]

In his explanation of the concept, 'secrets of the Torah,' R. Nachman echoes this goal. The secrets of the Torah are not knowledge that passes from teacher to student, whether in writing or orally, nor are they a secret exegesis of esoteric texts. The essence of learning 'secrets' is the mystic's contact with the hidden, a contact that consists of a personal experience of clinging to God.

The novel exposition regarding concepts such as 'secret' and 'secrets of the Torah,' which applies these terms to the experience of cleaving to God, is not unique to R. Nachman, however, but is employed by other Hasidic thinkers too.

For instance, R. Menachem Mendel of Premishlan writes:

'Hidden' is a term referring to something that a person cannot explain to someone else. For instance, the taste of food cannot be explained to someone who never tasted it. It is impossible to explain this to him in words – and that is called something that is hidden. The same applies to the love and fear of the Creator. It is impossible to explain the love in one's heart to another person – and that is called 'hidden.' But as for the fact that people call the wisdom of kabbalah hidden – how is it hidden? If a person wants to learn it, the book lies before him. And if he does not understand, he is an ignoramus, and for such a person the Gemara and *Tosafot* are also called hidden. But the concept of hidden matters in the entire *Zohar* and the writings of the Ari is all based on cleaving to the Creator.[169]

Similarly, R. Kalonymus Kalman Epstein writes in his *Meor V'shemesh*:

> And we too will expound on the verse in accordance with our words on the verse, 'The secret of Hashem is for those who fear Him.' The essential meaning of 'secret' is something that cannot be revealed. This does not mean learning kabbalah, which is something that a person is permitted to teach someone else. Rather, a true secret is the understanding of the existence of God. As the holy *Zohar* explains on the verse, 'Her husband is known in the gates,' each individual learns on his level, which is a matter hidden in the heart of every individual in accordance with his station and in accordance with the radiance of the light of Hashem in his heart. And it is impossible for one person to explain his insight to someone else, for even if he explains it to him, the other person won't understand it at all, for everyone understands in accordance with their own personal inquiry of Hashem. That is the meaning of 'The secret of Hashem is for those who fear Him': the existence of our Creator is a hidden secret for those who fear Him, those who attain great insight into His existence.[170]

Despite the similarity between R. Nachman's words and these two passages, it appears that R. Nachman goes a step further insofar as he defines the concept of 'secrets of the Torah' as insights attained in prayer. He does not speak of attributing another characteristic to learning the hidden Torah nor does he say that learning Torah must be accompanied by cleaving to God. Rather, he completely divorces the concept of the 'secrets of Torah' from the field of learning Torah, and transfers it instead to prayer. This step is important, for the high evaluation of involving oneself in the secrets of Torah is now attributed to prayer. The secrets of Torah are revealed not during learning, but during prayer with total self-dedication. A person who wishes to learn the secrets of the Torah should not turn to canonical kabbalistic texts but instead prepare his heart for prayer.[171]

In the teaching under discussion R. Nachman does not associate learning with cleaving to God.[172] Rather, he argues clearly that in the present era, until the coming of the messiah, it is not possible to come to secrets of the Torah via learning, but only through prayer.

In the tension between experiential mysticism and speculative learning and the intellectual mastery of mystical texts, the overriding tendency in Hasidism was to combine the two: to learn the canonical writings with an emphasis on the experiential character of the learning.[173] R. Nachman, however, clearly holds that experiential mysticism is the sole path to the secrets of the Torah.

However, R. Nachman states that prayer itself relies upon learning Torah and upon the rational mind, with an important and surprising caveat regarding the kind of text suggested as preparation for prayer: 'and one merits prayer via the *revealed* Torah.'[174] These words are astonishing, since one would think that learning 'the secrets of Torah' would bring a person to prayer, cleaving to God and mystical experience, whereas the revealed Torah – which deals with 'an ox that gored a cow' – is far from the world of prayer. R. Nachman's designation of the revealed Torah as a factor that makes prayer possible underscores his unique position and his general attitude toward the concept of clinging to God.[175] He not only proclaims the goal of cleaving to God and characterizes it as the ultimate goal of learning the secrets of the Torah, but also states that the rational mind does not serve to attain this goal. In order to attain and reveal the secrets of the Torah, a person must renounce his rational mind, cast away his intellect and pray with total self-dedication of soul and mind. Therefore, in contrast to other Hasidic thinkers, for R. Nachman the service of the rational mind (*da'at*) is directed in particular to the revealed Torah, to scholarly debate and clarifying halakhah and not to an attempt at arriving at the secrets of the Torah, the secrets of God.[176]

2. The Teaching Chotem B'toch Chotem[177]

R. Nachman's teaching *Chotem B'toch Chotem* also describes a structure in which the various types of mystical attainment are organized. Although this teaching is independent in structure and expression, its ideas are consistent with those of *Ohr Haganuz*, discussed above. This teaching is rich and complex and I will confine myself to a few observations dealing with the various models of cleaving to and absorption into God described therein.[178]

The second part of *Chotem*[179] is based on the presentation of two contrasting models of the worship of God: the worship of God on the level of 'let us do' as opposed to the worship of God on the level of 'let us hear.' Each model is characterized by a cluster of concepts, and each concept in one group finds its opposite half in the other: revealed versus hidden, son versus father, lower Eden and wisdom versus upper Eden and wisdom, a half statement in contrast to a complete statement, Torah in contrast to prayer, and 'his Torah' in contrast to 'the Torah of Hashem.'

These opposite poles do not deny each other's legitimacy, rather existing in parallel. Regarding the nature of these models, R. Nachman writes:

> For 'we will do and we will listen' is the aspect of hidden and revealed matters. 'We will do' is the aspect of revealed matters – i.e., the

commandments that every individual can perform on his level. 'And we will listen' is the aspect of hidden matters, that which is higher than and hidden from a person, with which he cannot serve God [...] And that corresponds to the aspects of Torah and prayer, respectively. 'We will do' – that is the aspect of Torah – i.e., revealed matters, which a person knows how to perform. 'And we will listen' – those correspond to the aspect of hidden matters, the aspect of words of the Torah, the words of the Torah that surround each commandment, which are the aspect of the hidden [...] where a person does not know how to use this to serve Hashem, be He blessed. This latter is the aspect of prayer, which is cleaving to God, for 'hearing is dependent upon the heart.'[180] As the verse states, 'And you give your servant an ear that hears.' [181] 'And service of the heart – that is prayer'[182] – that is to say, self-nullification and clinging to the Infinite One, for the Infinite One is the aspect of that which cannot be grasped. And since a person has no grasp of that (i.e., the words of the Torah surrounding each commandment, as above, since that is the aspect of the hidden), that is the aspect of prayer, of cleaving to God, which is none other than nullification to the Infinite One.[183]

'We will do' represents the service of Hashem that can be understood. This service is the aspect of Torah with which one involves oneself by learning. On the other hand, 'we will listen' is the hidden: those layers that a person cannot understand and learn. One can reach them only by passing through the service of the heart, which is prayer. This prayer involves clinging to and nullification into the Infinite One. Contact with the Infinite One is contact with the layer that a person cannot comprehend, because it is infinite. Therefore this layer is hidden and cannot be grasped by the rational mind but solely via prayer, self-nullification and clinging to the Infinite One.

The hidden or revealed nature of insights is not fixed, but depends upon a person's level and deeds:

And there exists on every level, as well as in every world, the aspects of 'we will do and we will listen,' for every individual on his level possesses the aspect of 'Let us do,' the aspect of Torah – i.e., those matters that are revealed to him – and the aspect of 'Let us hear,' which is the aspect of hidden matters, the aspect of prayers, as above. This is because when a person rises to a higher level than the first level he was on, then that which was his 'we will hear' is now considered the aspect of 'we will do,' and he attains another aspect of 'we will hear.' And so it goes from level to level. And so every individual, in accordance with his level, possesses the aspect of 'we will do and we will hear.' And also in every world, there is the aspect of 'we will do and we will hear.' This is because that which, in relation to this world, is the aspect of 'we will hear,' is in the higher world of spheres (*galgalim*) the aspect of 'we will do,' and those spheres possess an aspect of 'we will hear' that is higher than their level of 'we will do.' And so it goes from world to world. And that is the aspect of 'the Torah of Hashem and his Torah.'[184] At first it is the Torah of Hashem, which is the aspect of the hidden, 'the hidden things are for Hashem our God.' And afterwards, when a person rises to a level higher than that, it becomes his own Torah. This is because the 'we will hear' becomes the 'we will do,' which is the aspect of 'and the revealed matters are for us and for our children.' And that is: 'The hidden matters are for Hashem our God'[185] – that is the aspect of 'We will hear.' 'And the revealed matters are for us and for our children' – that is the aspect of 'We will do.' 'Forever to do all the words of this Torah' – that a person will go from level to level, that he will come to a world in which the 'we will hear' becomes 'we will do.'[186]

Although the nature of insights is different from person to person and from level to level, the existence of the basic form of revealed and hidden layers is not merely an incidental or human phenomenon, but a foundational structure that exists in all worlds, from the very lowest up to the beginning of the world of Emanation:

And every person must proceed from level to level and from world to world, until he merits each time to attain a higher aspect of 'we will do and we will hear,' so that every time for him the aspect of 'we will hear,' the aspect of the hidden, the aspect of prayer, the aspect of words of the Torah that surround the commandment, the aspect of the Torah of Hashem, will become the aspect of 'we will do,' the aspect of revealed, the aspect of Torah, the aspect of 'his Torah.' And he will have a higher aspect of 'we will hear,' etc. And so it is every time he goes from level to level and from stage to stage, until he comes to the primal beginning point of creation, which is the beginning of Emanation. And there an aspect of 'we will do and we will hear' also exists. And the aspect of 'we will hear' that exists there is truly 'the Torah of Hashem.' This is because in each world and on each level, the 'Torah of Hashem' is only so in a relative sense, because only because it is hidden from a person is it called 'the Torah of Hashem,' and when he comes to that level, it becomes 'his Torah.' But the aspect of the 'we will hear' at the beginning of Emanation is truly 'the Torah of Hashem,' for there is nothing higher than that, nothing higher than that which is literally the Torah of Hashem. And afterwards, when this person is absorbed into the Infinite One, then his 'we will do' is literally the aspect of 'the Torah of Hashem,' and his 'we will hear' is the aspect of the prayer of Hashem. This is because there is a 'Torah of Hashem.' As our sages teach, 'I performed it first.'[187] And as it is stated, 'The Holy One, blessed be He, clothes the naked and visits the sick,' etc.[188] And so do our sages state, 'From where do we know that he Holy One, blessed be He, puts on tefillin?' etc.[189] And there is 'prayer of Hashem.' As our sages state, 'From where do we know that the Holy One, blessed be He, prays? As the verse states, "And give him joy in my house of prayer".'[190] So we see that there is a 'Torah of Hashem' and there is a 'prayer of Hashem.' And when a person merits to be absorbed into the Infinite One, then his Torah is literally the Torah of Hashem, and his prayer is literally the prayer of Hashem.

This division into two models is not an intermediate stage until the messiah's arrival, but a foundational structure that is found *ab initio* 'on every single level and also in every single world' – for the angels, in each individual, and on each level on which a person exists.

R. Nachman presents a complex map with many stages of terms and situations, in each of which the distinction between 'we will do' and 'we will hear' is relevant. In order to simplify the path, we will schematically outline the three central stages, in each of which the level of 'we will hear' is higher than the level of 'we will do.'

Stage One: Crossing through all the Worlds to the Point of Creation
    We will do = Torah = His Torah
    We will hear = prayer (cleaving to the Infinite One) = the Torah of Hashem (in a relative sense)

Stage Two: The Beginning of the Point of Creation, the Beginning of Emanation
    We will hear = The Torah of Hashem *in truth* (the Torah of Hashem *literally*).

Stage Three: After one is Absorbed into the Infinite One
    'We will do' = Torah of Hashem *literally*
    'We will hear' = the prayer of Hashem *literally*.

2.1 Distinguishing Between States of Mystical Unity

We thus see that the two models also exist in the framework of absorption into the Infinite One: 'and after a person is absorbed into the Infinite One, then the "let us do" is the aspect of the Torah of Hashem literally, and the "let us listen" is the aspect of the prayer of Hashem.'[191] From this we may infer that according to R. Nachman the state of mystical unification is not one simple state. Not all of the paths that lead to absorption into the Infinite One arrive at the same level.

Not only are there various ways of making contact with the holy and with the world of divinity, but even within the unio-mystical states of self-nullification and absorption into the Infinite One there are distinctions, and a difference still remains between the two ways of unification with God: 'we will do' and 'we will hear,' Torah and prayer. The difference between these two models remains extant not only during the course of the Hasid's spiritual journey, but even at the climax of that journey: even as he is absorbed into the Infinite One, there is no simple oneness but rather diversity and multiplicity.

2.2 The Spectrum of Types of Mystical Unification

R. Nachman refers to the two models of 'we will do' and 'we will hear' as 'two ornaments' – i.e., the crowns that the angels placed upon the head of every Jew at Mt. Sinai, referred to in the verse, 'Eternal joy upon their head.'[192]

However, R. Nachman's view of the relative value of these two models is complex and ambivalent. A person is obligated to transfer his service of God from the aspect of 'we will hear' to that of 'we will do,' indicating the superiority of the latter. On the other hand, though, R. Nachman describes the service of 'we will hear' as attaining from its very inception a state of cleaving to the Infinite One, something that does not exist in the service of 'we will do.' Similarly, the 'prayer of Hashem' exists at the highest levels, higher even than that of the 'Torah of Hashem.' 'Prayer of Hashem' is not referred to in a relative, temporary sense; it is a final state with no superior.

There can be no doubt that R. Nachman places prayer at the top of the hierarchy and Torah one step below it.

2.3 Rational Mind and its Absence in the Mystical Path and in Mystical Unification

The complex framework that R. Nachman presents in *Chotem* fits in well with his notions regarding the place of the rational mind, as well as its absence, in relation to the mystical path and to mystical unification. Although there are insights that are the aspect of 'Torah,' which one can attain with reason and inquiry, the highest insights are those corresponding to prayer, connected to those realms that cannot be grasped and understood.

At both the beginning and end of a person's mystical journey, prayer is the highest and most effective means of attaining the 'secrets of the Torah' and the hidden layer of the Torah and divinity.

In *Chotem*, the path of Torah, which possesses the character of scholarship as in-depth research aimed at gaining understanding and knowledge, is presented as a path that can lead to mystical union, at the pinnacle of which a person merits to be absorbed into the Infinite One and an identity is forged between 'his Torah' and the 'Torah of Hashem.' But even this pinnacle is described as no more than an aspect of the revealed Torah, unlike the aspect of the hidden Torah, which cannot be known rationally, but which exists on the level of 'the prayer of Hashem,' higher than the level of 'the Torah of Hashem.'

In this teaching, which presents rational thought as a way of serving Hashem and whose pinnacle is mystical cleaving to God, R. Nachman states that at the peak of the ladder of religious worship, and at the peak of the ladder of spiritual insights and religious goals, exists a manner of worship that has no 'reason and inquiry.' Only mystical experience, characterized by cleaving to God out of faith and disconnection from the rational mind, can bring a person to the highest absorption into the unification of God through prayer, when a person's prayer is the prayer of Hashem, 'in truth' and 'actuality.'

R. Nachman could well have concluded this teaching with the language with which he closes the teaching *Ikar Hatachlit*: 'That is our essential goal: that prayer should be absorbed into God's oneness, in the aspect of "He is your praise and He is your God,"[193] for prayer and Hashem, be He blessed, are one, as it were, and that is truly the essence of the goal.'[194]

IV. If I Knew Him I Would Be Him: Knowledge (Da'at) *as a means of Attaining Mystical Unification*

The descriptions of mystical experiences discussed to this point are characterized by an absence of the ordinary mind and by 'casting away the intellect.'

But this apparently directly contrasts other teachings of R. Nachman, in which we learn that rational thought is the core of the mystical experience and functions as the path to unification with God.[195] In those other teachings, Bratslavian mysticism bears a similarity to what may be termed the 'mysticism of knowledge.'[196] *Atika Tamir V'satim*[197] is one of the principal teachings in which R. Nachman develops this theme of the path of knowledge in mysticism.

Atika Tamir V'satim claims that clinging to and unifying with God via knowing and knowledge is part of a more general view of the place of knowledge. In brief, the lack of knowledge is the root of all the world's maladies, whereas an abundance of knowledge constitutes the rectification of the world. Everything that a person may lack, whether personally (such as income, health and children) or more generally (such as exile), results from a lack of knowledge (*da'at*).[198] It is thus understood that the elimination of these imperfections and 'the essence of redemption come about by means of the rational mind.'[199] Further on, the role of rational mind as a tool for cleaving to God and as a means of attaining the mystical experience will be examined.

1. *'If I Would Know Him, I Would Be Him'*

R. Nachman describes knowledge as an intermediary by means of which a person can arrive at a state of absorption into the one – i.e., absorption into God.

> And via knowledge (*da'at*), people are absorbed into His oneness and live an eternal life, as he does. This is because via knowledge, they are absorbed into Him. As the wise man stated, 'If I knew Him, I would be Him.'[200] And the essence of absorption, of a person being absorbed into the one, comes about through the knowledge of Him, be He blessed. As the wise man stated, 'If I knew Him, I would be Him.' This is because the essence of a person is his intellect (*seichel*). And thus, wherever the intellect thinks, that is where the entirety of a person is. And when he knows and attains the knowledge of Hashem, be He blessed, he is there literally. And the more he knows, the more is he absorbed into the root – i.e., into God, be He blessed.[201]

The wise man's phrase, 'If I knew Him, I would be Him,' has a long history in Jewish thought, and its usual meaning is that a person cannot know God.[202]

In *Derashot HaRan* by R. Nisim ben R. Reuven Gerondi of the fourteenth century, for example, we find:

> 'And he said, "Show me now your glory".' Moses did not mean by this to attain the truth of the essence of Hashem, be He blessed, as it is – heaven forbid that Moses should request that. There had

already come unassailable proofs that God's essence may be revealed only to His own essence, and that anything else is impossible. Thus once, when one of the sages was asked what the Creator is, he answered, 'If I knew Him, I would be Him.'[203]

R. Yosef Albo in *Sefer Ha'ikarim* similarly states:

> And so it is impossible for any being to attain God's essence, except for God Himself. As the sage responded when he was asked if he knew the nature of God, 'If I knew Him, I would be Him' – i.e., there is no living being that can understand His essence except for God Himself, be He blessed.[204]

This statement of the sage has also been explained in this spirit outside the realm of philosophy. Thus, for instance, the Maharal of Prague writes, 'It has been said that we cannot know God's nature. Thus, it has been said, "If I knew Him, I would be Him".' [205]

We also find in the Hasidism of the Baal Shem Tov these words of the sage describing the impossibility of understanding God. Thus, we read in the writings of R. Yaakov Yosef of Polnoye:

> In the light of this information, it is difficult to understand how [the biblical verses can command, 'Cleave to Him,' etc., or 'Know the God of your father.' Knowledge is comprehending. This argument of mine is to be found written in *Derashat HaRan*, which tells that one sage asked his comrade, 'Do you know of the Creator, be He blessed?' to which the latter replied, 'If I knew Him, I would be Him.' Understand this. It is impossible to know God, as that sage replied. And so it is difficult to understand how the Torah has commanded something that is impossible – to know Him and comprehend Him.[206]

As for R. Nachman, he quotes the sage's statement faithfully, but invests it with the entirely opposite meaning: man *can* know God, and at the moment that he knows Him, he will indeed be a part of Him and absorbed into Him. 'Via knowledge one is absorbed into Him, as the saying of the wise man: "If I were to know Him, I would be Him".' [207]

The fundamental religious presumption behind the wise man's statement in its kabbalistic context is that an unbridgeable chasm separates man from God. Since man cannot be God, and since 'if I knew Him, I would be Him,' by definition it is impossible for man to know God.

R. Nachman's basic presumption, however, is entirely different. According to him, the chasm between man and God can be bridged. Man can come in contact with God and, moreover, man can indeed be transformed into God (in a sense), by being absorbed into God, uniting with the unity of God and being transformed into a part of Him.[208]

In this sense, R. Nachman has inherited the Hasidic concept, whose spiritual and ideational world is built on the doctrine that every individual, not only the elite few, can cleave to God.[209] R. Nachman agrees with this position, widespread in Hasidism even among thinkers whose spiritual outlooks are otherwise very different from each other, that cleaving to God is not only contact but unification with Him and absorption into Him. [210]

2. *'In The Place Where the Intellect Thinks, that is Where the Entire Person Is'*

In explaining how knowledge helps gain absorption into God, R. Nachman uses the widespread Hasidic formula that describes the connection between thought and cleaving to God: 'whatever a person thinks of, there he is, in his entirety.'[211] R. Nachman cites this saying, but with a meaningful difference: 'the essence of a person is his intellect; and so whatever his intellect thinks about, there the entire person is in his entirety.'[212]

This saying, which appears in different versions in Hasidic teachings, is often quoted in the name of the Baal Shem Tov, R. Nachman's great-grandfather.[213] *Keter Shem Tov* states that 'whatever a person thinks of, there he clings,'[214] and R. Yaakov Yosef testifies, 'I heard explicitly from the mouth of my teacher that whatever a person thinks of, he is there entirely,' and 'in the name of my teacher, I heard at length – and I will write it in brief – that whatever a person thinks of, there he is entirely. This applies to matters of the spirit – if he thinks of something spiritual, his soul is there,' etc.[215]

In these statements, the terms 'think' or 'the thought of man' do not necessarily relate to cognitive activity and an intellectual effort to attain new understandings and insights. The term 'thought' rather describes the object of a person's consciousness. The term 'thought' in a Hasidic context is not cognitive but serves in a broader sense, including various modes of mental activity.[216]

The statement connecting thought and cleaving to God is frequently cited when discussing maintaining awareness of God, as in the verse, 'I have placed Hashem before me always.' Its role is to explain how constant focus on God leads a person to cleave to Him.[217]

By altering the expression 'a person thinks' to 'his intellect thinks,' R. Nachman confers a cognitive character to the thought process that leads to absorption, for 'intellect' more clearly denotes discursive thought and cognitive process than does the less concrete and more inclusive term 'thought.'

Also, the context in which this terminology is found ratifies its intellectual-rational connotation. Whereas this statement is generally cited in the context of the importance of constant cleaving to God and the need to focus one's thought solely on God,[218] R. Nachman describes a different path of self-advancement that has nothing to do with constant focus on God, but is rather dependent on the extent of one's intellectual grasp. R. Nachman sets forth a clear hierarchy of the stages of unity: 'when a person knows and understands the knowledge of Hashem, be He blessed, he is there with God literally. And the more he knows, the more is he incorporated into the root, i.e., into God, be He blessed.'[219] It is difficult to imagine a clearer expression of the link between knowledge and absorption into God. The intellectual function has been transformed into a means of absorption in God. Intellectual attainment is the measuring rod for the degree of absorption into God.

This model is intrinsically different than the standard Hasidic model, which deals with the connection between a person's focus in spirit and thought on God, on the one hand, and on cleaving to Him, on the other, without any reference to and connection with the degree of the Hasid's cognitive apprehension.[220] R. Nachman takes the Hasidic phraseology that speaks of cleaving to God as the focus of one's spirit and reshapes it to serve another mean: that of expressing the Aristotelian view regarding the union of observer, observed and intellect, relying upon the fundamental axiom, which has an unmistakable Aristotelian quality, that 'the essence of a person is his intellect.'

At the beginning of the section in which R. Nachman presents the Aristotelian model of intellectual unity as a path to clinging to God, he also offers another model of cleaving to God: returning to the root. This model resembles the neo-Platonic view of the return to the supernal root, and of states of cleaving to the root and the universal soul.[221]

> Eternal life is only for Hashem, be He blessed, for He lives forever. But whoever is absorbed into his root, i.e., into God, be He blessed, also lives forever. This is because, since he is absorbed into One and he is one with Hashem, be He blessed, he lives an eternal life as does Hashem, be He blessed. And so only Hashem, be He blessed, possesses perfection, and besides Him everyone is lacking – but whoever is absorbed into Him has perfection. And the essence of being absorbed into God, of a person being absorbed into One, comes via the knowledge of Him, be He blessed. As the wise man stated, 'If I knew Him, I would be Him.' This is because the essence of a person is his intellect, and so whatever his intellect thinks of, there he is in his entirety. And when this person knows and attains the knowledge of Hashem, be He blessed, he is there literally. And the more that he knows, the more is he incorporated into the root – i.e., into Him, be He blessed.[222]

That R. Nachman combines two separate models that employ different sets of terms and whose philosophical-theological roots contradict each other is not the surprising element of this teaching, for such combinations characterize the work of many kabbalists and Hasidic thinkers.[223] It is surprising that R. Nachman, the great fighter against philosophy, links these models in a way that makes the neo-Platonic model subservient to the Aristotelian model, insofar as he emphasizes the intellectual component in cleaving to God, and explains the return to the source as relying as well upon intellectual unification and the rational mind.

Before we explain how R. Nachman integrates the mysticism of knowledge (*da'at*) into the framework of general mystical thought, we can somewhat mitigate this problematic issue by offering a more circumscribed description of the role of the rational mind in experience.

Despite R. Nachman's description of the central role of the rational mind and the intellect in the process of uniting with God, a distinction should be made between his view and the mysticism that makes knowledge its cynosure. Some mystics describe the essence of their mystical experience as a revelation of secrets and as an experience leading to a certain knowledge not previously possessed.[224] R. Nachman apparently has an exactly opposite perspective. Knowledge is not the result of mystical unity – on the contrary, it is the path that leads to absorption into the divine. In his words, 'A person who merits true knowledge (as above), to know God, be He blessed, experiences no difference whatsoever between life and death, because he clings to and is incorporated into God, be He blessed, in both his life and in his death';[225] and, in an even more clear expression: 'Via knowledge, people are incorporated into God.'[226] The goal is unification; knowledge is the vehicle.[227]

As stated above regarding *Ikar Hatachlit*,[228] R. Nachman does not in principle deny intellectual unification as a means of reaching oneness and cleaving to God; rather, he protests against portraying knowledge and intellectual unification as the goal. The goal, rather, is unification with God, which can be attained by various means: cleaving to God in prayer is one and knowledge is another. All of this contrasts with the view of the 'philosophers' with whom R. Nachman takes issue in *Ikar Hatakhlit*. They claim that man's goal is knowledge; thus a person incompetent to learn and attain knowledge cannot reach true fulfillment. However, even defining the place and role of rational mind as just one of a number of methods that can bring a person to unite with God still fails to bridge the gap between R. Nachman's teachings that advocate 'casting away the intellect' and removing one's ordinary and rational mind, on the one hand, and R. Nachman's teaching *Atika*, on the other, which exalts the rational mind and the mystical path that makes use of knowledge.[229]

The key to understanding this contradiction in R. Nachman's words is to be found in a central and critical distinction briefly discussed in the first part of this chapter: speculative teachings and perceptions that describe mysticism in a future messianic age, and those teachings and perceptions in which R. Nachman describes present-day reality with its paths of present-day mysticism.

2.1 The Mysticism in the World to Come

R. Nachman states repeatedly throughout his teaching *Atika* that absorption into God via knowledge is not part of present-day reality. Rather, he is presenting a speculative description of the mysticism that will exist in future days. Only in that future era will an additional way of absorption into God be developed, a way that will be part of the new reality characterizing existence in the time when the prophecies regarding 'the earth being filled with the knowledge of Hashem like waters covering the sea' will be realized.

Man as man cannot receive supernal knowledge, which is an aspect of divine inspiration, and remain a man. Our sages' statement that 'there will arrive years that you will say I have no pleasure in them' – those are the days of the messiah, which have neither merit nor guilt'[230] here receives a mystical explanation: in the future era, when the earth will be filled with the knowledge of God, man will be absorbed into God and no longer belong to the category of man who possesses free will. Instead, he will move to existence as an angel, having neither merit nor guilt. The assigning of the mysticism of knowledge to the future era explains why the apothegm of the sage, 'If I knew Him, I would be Him,' uses the word 'if' and is not presented as something that can be presently realized.

3. Mystical Messianism

According to R. Nachman, the root of all the good destined for us in the messianic age stems from the actualization of mystical unifications and absorption into God.

The exile, the inability of the wolf to dwell with the lamb, anger, difficulties in making a living and problems of health, problems with one's children, 'and all other imperfections,' the chief of which is death – all of these will be resolved as a result of mystical union with the Creator, be He blessed, for 'whoever is absorbed into Him possesses perfection; and the essence of being incorporated into God, of being incorporated into One, comes about by means of knowledge.'

Since the descriptions of the future days do not point to the present-day reality in which a person acts, he cannot easily derive from this teaching appropriate deeds, customs and ways of living. Rather, R. Nachman describes a distant ideal: the world-to-come of the mystic, a world in which a person comes to be absorbed into God, following which there is no separation from Him, a union after which there is neither exile nor death. This image of the redemption and messianic mysticism has no connection to the present world.

And although, R. Nachman asserts that 'the essence of the redemption comes about through knowledge,' he does not conclude that a person must here and now attempt to unite with the Creator via knowledge and thus redeem himself and the world.

Instead, he constructs an entire framework of a way of life and behavior that will make it possible for a person to be absorbed into God even in this world – an absorption into God of racing out and then returning as he sees the deadly danger of being drawn into the mystical state. This awareness may not be allowed to frighten him away from taking a chance and entering into the mystic state; nevertheless he must see the loss of life as a danger and take care to guard his life. And as R. Nachman states in another context, 'A person must have two types of expertise – i.e., expertise in racing out, and expertise in returning. As the verse states, "Fortunate is the one who comes in and comes forth[231]".'[232]

But not even here, in the teaching *Atika*, does R. Nachman enter into discussion of speculative images that lack any relevant ramifications in a person's spiritual and religious world. Instead, R. Nachman discusses concepts that are relevant to this world and to every human being. The structure of 'surrounding' and 'inner' forces is to be found not only on a supernal plane, where a person is no longer a human being. Rather, 'every individual in himself has an inner and a surrounding being.'[233] It is true that there is an aspect of bringing the surrounding forces within, involving the person's absorption into the One and attaining eternal life, which will take place only in the future era. But there is also an aspect of bringing the surrounding forces into the inner being that exists also in this world, in a way that is not connected with absorption into God and does not grant eternal life, but which is a dynamic of learning and attaining insight that relates also to the realms that a person can achieve with his human intellect.

In the teaching *Bo el Paroh*, R. Nachman states that 'it is impossible to attain anything at all of the aspect of the vacated space until the future era,'[234] and so 'there is no answer to this heresy, since it comes from the vacated space [...] Only the people of Israel, via faith, pass over all the sciences (*chochmot*) and even over this heresy that comes from the vacated space, for they believe in Hashem, be He blessed, without any inquiry and cleverness (*chochmah*) but with a complete faith.' The *zaddik* as well, who deals with and investigates these diffi-culties, comes to terms with them not by resolving questions but solely via faith.[235] The 'future era' with its attainments via knowledge is not accessible even to 'a great zaddik, who is the aspect of Moses.'[236]

Man must be prepared to serve God with faith even in a reality where his rational mind and intellect lead him to conclude that the world and man are immersed within a space vacated of God. Until the arrival of 'that day,' a person's rational mind cannot assuage his wounds, his doubts and distance from God. And so the sole possible path is faith. Moreover, man is required to consciously renounce his rational mind, for only thus can he arrive at the states of unification with God on the path of faith and prayer.

Conclusion

Study of the sources discussed in this chapter shows that mysticism occupies a central place in the theoretical writings of R. Nachman of Bratslav. R. Nachman's formulations are not mere incidental comments or a few scattered and parenthetical remarks. Rather, they comprise a methodical, mystical perspective, which discusses distinctions between various types of mystical experiences and various mystical paths, attempting to disclose an order and inner logic in the relationship between the various types of mysticism. Anyone who studies these teachings realizes that R. Nachman was very conscious of the existence of various mystical methodologies and their ramifications. It is clear that R. Nachman saw himself as having to meet the challenge of clarifying the various paths of mysticism, of mapping them out, explicating their goals, and assigning a scale of values to the rich and many-faceted world of mysticism.

Notes

1 *Likutei Moharan* 4:9. Taught in Zlatipole in the years 5561–5562 (1801–1802).

2 See Weiss, '*Hasidut shel Mysitcka av'chasidut shel emunah*,' 87–95; also idem, the entire second part, '*haguto u't'udato h'aaztmit shel R. Nachman*,' 178–96; Green, *Tormented Master*, 27–328; Tishbi and Dan, *Chasidut*, 771, 804; Gris, *Sifrut Hahanhagot*, 232, note 5; Piekarz, '*Tzaddik*,' 160–161. Rapoport-Albert, '*Katnut*,' 7–33. Margolin, *Ha'emunah V'hakefirah*, particularly pages 133–134, 152–185.

3 See above, the notes in Chapter 1 at the beginning of Part III.

4 See Rapport-Albert, 'Confession in the Circle of Rabbi Nahman of Bratslav.'

5 Homiletical interpretation of *Job* 22:12.

6 *Zohar*, Part II, 88b.

7 *Exodus* 16:7.

8 *Deuteronomy* 34:6.

9 *Isaiah* 40:4.

10 *Deuteronomy* 34:6.

11 *Likutei Moharan* 4:9.

12 *Guide of the Perplexed* III, 51. Regarding the 'death of a kiss' in Kabbalah, see Idel, *Hebetim Chadashim*, 14, 62, 85–88, 90, 96; Idem, *Hachavayah Hamistit*, 130–134; Fishbane, *The*

Kiss of God, in particular, 36–37, 44; Idel, *R. Menachem Recanati Hamekubal*, 142–160.

13   *Otzar Hamidrashim*, Jerusalem 729, 84.

14   *Sotah* 14a.

15   *Ezekiel* 1:14.

16   From the Yom Kippur prayer book.

17   *Likutei Moharan* 4:9.

18   See Scholem, *'Deveikut,'* 341; Etkes, *Baal Hashem*, 141–144; Elior, *'Kabbalat Ha'ari,'* 392–397; Tishbi and Dan, *Chasidut*, 782, 802.

19   See Chapter 3, Part II.

20   *Megillah* 3a.

21   *Likutei Moharan* 4:9.

22   See Chapter 3, Part II.

23   *Likutei Moharan* 64.

24   See *Likutei Moharan* II 5:7. R. See *Likutei Moharan* I 6, 21, 56; and *Likutei Moharan* II 5, 7, 26, 72 and elsewhere.

25   See the previous note.

26   This is also the implication of the teaching *'Ki MerachamamYanhigam,' Likutei Moharan* II 7:8.

27   *Likutei Moharan* I 66.

28   *Zohar* (see, for instance, Part II, 221a and Vital, Chaim *Etz Chaim, Heichal Nukva, Shaar Leah V'rachel* [Gate 38], Chapter 6, 215).

29   From *Yigdal*, found in the morning services and based on Maimonides' Thirteen Principles of Faith.

30   See above, Chapter 2, Part III.

31   *Yevamot* 49b. And see Maimonides, *Peirush Hamishnayot, Sanhedrin 10*:1, Seventh Axiom; *Introduction to Pirkei Avot*, end of Chapter 7; *Mishnah Torah, Hilchot Yesodei Hatorah* 7:6; *Guide of the Perplexed*, Part 2, Chapter 35.

32   See Liebes, *Hatikun Hak'lali*, 212–214; Mundstein A., *'Al Hatikun Hak'lali,'* 199, note 5; Liebes, *'Magamot B'cheker Hachasidut,'* 226.

33   *Guide of the Perplexed*, part 3, chapter 51, 406.

34   R. Avraham Abulafia. See Idel, 'Avraham Abulafia v'haiichud hamisti,' *Perakim B'kabbalah N'vuit*, 5–38; idem., *Hebetim Chadashim*, 57–58; idem., *Hachasidut*, 405–406.

35   Idel, *Hachasidut*, 403–404.

36   Rapoport-Albert, *'Katnut,'* 18–19, and note 65.

37   See Idel, *Hachasidut*, 231–241, 403–406.

38   Etkes, *Baal Hashem*,142–144, 431, 435.

39   *Likutei Moharan* I 4:9.

40   Idel, *Hachasidut*, 233–238; *Keter Shem Tov*, 121, 16a; See Etkes, *Baal Hashem*, 141; see Idel, R. *Menachem Rakanti Hamekubal*,142–160; Fishbane, *The Kiss of God*, 36–37; 50.

41   *Likutei Moharan* II 7:4.

42   *Chayei Moharan, Gedulat Noraot Hasagato*, 12 (252), 207–208.

43   As is claimed by Shoham, *Yetzirah V'hitgalut*, 318.

44   See Idel, *Hachasidut*, 231–241.

45   *Noam Elimelech*, Part II, 530; see Idel, *Hachasidut*, particularly 202–231.

46   *Likutei Moharan* I 65.

47   *Likutei Moharan* I 4:9.

48   *Likutei Moharan* I 65:4.

49   Ibid.

50   Ibid.

51   *Taanit* 31.

52   *Exodus* 31:18.

53   Idel, *Hachasidut*, 403–404.

54   Underhill, 'The Dark Night of the Soul,' 380–412.

55   See Idel, *Hachasidut*, 40–60, 405

56   See Weiss, *Mechkarim*, particularly 120–124.

57   *Likutei Moharan* I 13.

58   *Likutei Moharan* I 9.

59   *Likutei Moharan* I 8.

60   *Zechariah* 14:9.

61   *Pesachim* 50.

62   *Proverbs* 12:19.

63   *Likutei Moharan* I, 51.

64   *Zechariah* 14:28.

65   *Likutei Moharan* 65:3–4.

66   *Likutei Moharan* II 5.

67   See above, Chapter 5, Part III.

68   See *Berachot* 7.

69   *Likutei Moharan* II 5:15; see Liebes, *Hatikun Hak'lali*, particularly 216–217.

70   Weiss, *Mechkarim*,143–145.

71   Ibid.,144.

72   Ibid.,143.

73   See also *Likutei Moharan* I 56:9.

74   See *Likutei Moharan* I 56:9; and *Likutei Moharan* I 21:11.

75   *Likutei Moharan* II 19.

76   Ibid.

77   See Idel, *Hebetim Chadashim*, 57–58, 64–67, 231–235, 255–258.

78   Idid., 64–65.

79   R. Shneur Zalman of Ladi, R., *Tanya*, chapter 4–5.

80   See *Mishnah Torah, Hilchot Yesodei Hatorah* 2:8–9.

81   See Weiss, *Mechkarim*, 112.

82   *Likutei Moharan* II 19; see Wolfson, *Pilon*, Volume One, 43–47.

83   *Likutei Moharan* I 21.

84   *Likutei Moharan* I 21:11.

85   *Psalms* 111:10.

86   Weiss, *Mechkarim*, 93 *Likutei Moharan* I 22:9.

87   *Likutei Moharan* I 75.

88   R. Simchah Bunim of Pesishchah, *Kol Simchah, Parshat Noah*, 11. R. Tzadok Hacohen of Lublin, *Kometz Haminchah*, Part 2, Section 32, 37.

89   See R. Efraim of Sudalkov, *Degel Machaneh Efraim, Parshat Terumah, Sheini*, 112.

90   *Deuteronomy* 10:2.

91   *Sichot Haran*, 52, 37. See also *Likutei Moharan* I 4:9.

92   Scholem, '*Deveikut,*' 340. See Elior, R., '*Rik U'besht,*' 689–696. See Idel, *Hebetim Chadashim*, 64–67, 255–258; Idem., *Hachasidut*, 405–406.

93   *Tzava'at Haribash* 68,11.

94   *Keter Shem Tov* 16,7.

95   R. Yaakov Yosef of Polnoe, *Ketonet Passim*, 323; *Tzafnat Pa'neach, Vayakhel*, 405.

96   As Weiss argues in '*Hasidut shel Mistika v'hasidut shel emunah,*' 87–95.

97   *Likutei Moharan* I 15. *Chayei Moharan, Makom Yeshivato Un'siyotov*, 11–12.

98   *Likutei Moharan* I 22.

99   *Berachot* 64a.

100 *Sotah* 5.

101 Ibid., 72.

102 *Psalms* 51:19.

103 *Likutei Moharan* I 15:4.

104 *Tiku Emunah*; *Likutei Moharan* II 5.

105 *Likutei Moharan* I 73.

106 *Likutei Moharan* I 64.

107 See Weiss, *Mechkarim*, 139–143, 121–127. Green, *Tormented Master*, 305–312.

108 *Likutei Moharan* I 64, end of section 1.

109 Ibid., I, 21, sections 4, 6–11. See also *Likutei Moharan* II 7:6.

110 Etkes, *Baal Shem*, 140.

111 See Idel, *Hachvayah Hamistit*,140–143, and note 51.

112 Idem., *Hebetim Chadashim*, 166.

113 *Sefer Hatanya, Igeret Hakodesh*, Chapter 15. See, for instance, *Tzafnat Pa'aneach*, 135; *Ketonet Passim, Vayikra*, 8; *Tzav*, 45; and *Nasso*, 213. And see Idel, *Hebetim Chadashim*, 367, note 366.

114 See Idel, *Hachasidut*, 246–247, 319–326.

115 *Chayei Hanefesh*, manuscript Munchen 408, 65b, published in Idel, *Hachavayah Hamistit*,140.

116 *Likutei Moharan* I 15.

117 *Psalms* 44:23.

118 *Likutei Moharan* I 15:5.

119 See *Chullin* 60b.

120 *Numbers* 28:24.

121 *Jeremiah* 31:22.

122 *Likutei Moharan* I 15:5.

123 See Idel, '*Dimuyim Umaasim,*' 31–39. Idem., *Hebetim Chadashim*, 222.; idem., *Hachasidut*, 243–251.

124 See Liebes, '*Hamashiach shel HaZohar,*' 177–194.

125 From the teaching *Ki Taavor*, *Likutei Moharan* I 73.

126 *Likutei Moharan* I 74.

127 *Likutei Moharan* I 94.

128 *Tzavaat Haribash* 35, 6a; also *Likutim Yekarim*, section 2, 1a; and section 31, 5b.

129 *Likutei Moharan* I, 80.

130 *Zohar*, see Liebes, '*Hamashiach shel HaZohar,*' 200–201.

131 *Likutei Moharan* I 73. *Chayei Moharan, Nesiato l'eretz Yisrael,* 15 (142), 135.

132 *Numbers* 28:24.

133 *Jeremiah* 31:22.

134 *Exodus* 12:23.

135 *Bava Kamma* 17.

136 *Pesachim* 119a; in *Chagigah* 13a

137 *Likutei Moharan* I 33:5.

138 *Mikvaot* 8:5; *Chullin* 129a.

139 *Numbers* 5:13.

140 *Yevamot* 11b.

141 *Likutei Moharan* I 74.

142 Rashi comments: 'Before she is taken sexually she is unformed – meaning, an unformed vessel.'

143 *Sanhedrin* 22b.

144 *Sanhedrin* 22b; *Reishit Hochmah* I, *Shaar Ha'ahavah,* Chapter 4, 251–252. For more on erotic images in prayer and cleaving in R. Eliyahu de Vidash, see, M. Fechter, '*Tefisat Had'veikut B'tz'fat,*' particularly 96–110.

145 See Chasin, *Shirah Umythos,* 36–37.

146 Idel, *Heibetim Chadashim,* 85–91.

147 Idem, '*Dimuyim Umaasim,*' 39; Wolfson, *Through a Speculum that Shines,* 362–363.

148 *Likutei Moharan* I 22:10.

149 See Idel, '*Universalization and Integration*'

150 See idem, *Hebetim Chadashim,* 45–47, 53–56.

151 Idem., 'Tefisat Hatorah,' Wolfson, 'Female Imaging of The Torah,' Circle in the Square, 22–26; see Idel, *Hebetim Chadashim,* 255–260.

152 *Zohar,* Part II, 98–99.

153 See Idel, *Hebetim Chadashim,* 239–242; and Liebes, '*Zohar V'eros,*' 94–98. R. Yosef Gitatilla, *Shaarei Orah,* 1, 195–196. See also Lachover, '*B'Shaar Hamigdal,*' 29–78.

154 See *Chayei Moharan, Inyan hamachloket she'alav,* 1 (392), 264.

155 Wolfson, *Through a Speculum that Shines,* 395–397.

156 See idem, *Circle in the Square;* see also idem, 'Female Imaging of the Torah,' 22–26.

157 *Likutei Moharan* 15:5.

158 Tishbi, '*Kudsha brich Hu v'oraita,*' 480–492; ibid., '*Hashlamot,*' 668–674; Idel, '*Shtei Ha'arot,*' 213; *Zohar Parshat Beshalach,* 60a; *Parshat Bereishit,* 24a; See Chalamish, *Netiv L'Tanya,* 44–45, note 12.

159 See Idel, *Hebetim Chadashim,* 255–260.

160 See Fechter, '*Tefisat Hadeveikut B'tzvat.*'

161 Weiss, '*Talmud Torah L'shitat Habaal Shem Tov',* 151–159; Shatz-Oppenheimer, '*a'ayat limud torah b'chasidut,*' *Hachasidut b'mistkah,* 157–167. See Idel, *Hachasidut,* 316–346.

162 *Chayei Moharan, Nesiyato L'eretz Yisrael,* 21 (150), 139. And see Green, *Tormented Master,* 101–102; *P'ulat Hazaddik,* 412–414.

163 *Tanya,* Chapter 4.

164 *Tanya,* Chapter 5.

165 Ibid.

166 See Idel, *Hebetim Chadashim,* 407, note. 225; Etkes, *Yachid b'doro,* 192–199.

167 *Tanya*, Chapter 23.

168 See Idel, *Hachasidut*, 334.

169 *Ohr Ha'emet*, 16a [31]; See Idel, *Hachasidut*, 331–336.

170 Ibid., 334.

171 R. Meshulam Feivish Heller, *Yosher Divrei Emet*, 122, section 22.

172 *Meor Vashemesh, Parshat Ki Tavo*, 232.

173 *Esh Kodesh, Parshat Ki Teitzei*, year 700, 59.

174 Idel, *Hachasidut*, 326.

175 Ibid., 321–322.

176 *Likutei Moharan* I 15:4.

177 *Yosher Divrei Emet*, section 24, 123b.

178 *Likutei Moharan* II 5:15.

179 *Likutei Moharan* I 22.

180 See Green, *Tormented Master*, 314–315.

181 From section 9 and onward.

182 *Tikkunei Zohar Tikun* 58.

183 *Kings* I 3:9.

184 *Taanit* 2a.

185 *Likutei Moharan* I 22:9.

186 See *Avodah Zarah* 19a.

187 *Deuteronomy* 29:28.

188 *Likutei Moharan* I 22:10.

189 *Talmud Yerushalmi Bikurim* 3:3.

190 *Sotah* 14a.

191 *Berachot* 6a.

192 Ibid. 7a.

193 See Idel, 'Universalization and Integration,' 45–46.

194 *Likutei Moharan* I 22:9.

195 *Deuteronomy* 10:21.

196 *Likutei Moharan* II 19.

197 Green, *Tormented Master*, 315–316.

198 See above, note 36.

199 *Likutei Moharan* I 21.

200 *Nedarim* 41; *Isaiah* 5; *Likutei Moharan* I 21:11.

201 *Kol Hachesronot*; *Likutei Moharan* I 172.

202 *Likutei Moharan* I 21:11.

203 Ibid.

204 Green, *Tormented Master*, 439, note 59.

205 *Derashot Haran, Haderush Har'vi'* I, 13, column 2–3.

206 *Sefer Ha'Ikarim, Ma'amar Sheini*, Chapter 30, 97b.

207 *Derech Chaim*, Chapter 5, 233.

208 *Ben Porat Yosef*, Introduction, 9 column 3 (page 18). See also 5 column 1 (page 9).

209 *Likutei Moharan* I 21:11.

210 Scholem, 'Deveikut,' 336–337; Idel, *Hebetim Chadashim*, 77–91. Regarding this, see ibid., 46; idem, 'Universalization and Integration.'

211 See Scholem, '*Deveikut,*' particularly 330–331.

212 Idel, *Hachasidut,* 403–406.

213 *Toldot Yaakov Yosef, Chayei Sarah,* 23a.

214 Ibid.

215 In R. Yosef Karo, *Maggid Meisharim,* 139–140; and Elior's essay '*Rik U'besht,*', 689–691. See Idel, *Hebetim Chadashim,* 64–67.

216 *Keter Shem Tov,* 16, 58, 71.

217 *Ketonet Passim,* 278. R. Efraim of Sodilkov, *Degel Machaneh Efraim, Parshat Bereishit,* 4, d.h. *vayomer.*

218 See Scholem, *Deveikut,* 340.

219 Idel, *Hebetim Chadashim,* 60.

220 See Elior, '*Rik U'besht,*' 692–698; Etkes, *Baal Hashem,* 141–144; Idel, 'Universalization and Integration,' 55–56; *Keter Shem Tov,* section 217, 28; *Shivchei Habesht,* 174, 92.

221 *Likutei Moharan* I 12:11.

222 *Yosher Divrei Emet,* 122a.

223 See Idel, *Hebetim Chadashim,* 56–60.

224 *Likutei Moharan* I 21:11.

225 See Idel, *Hebetim Chadashim,* 59.

226 *Sefer Hachezyonot,* the journal of R. Chaim Vital, R. Yosef Karo's *Maggid Meisharim;* James, *Hachavayah Hadatit,* 268–276.

227 *Likutei Moharan* I 21:11.

228 Ibid.

229 Dan, *Al Hakedushah,* 276–277; and see above, note 37.

230 Above, Part II.

231 Green, *Tormented Master,* 316.

232 *Shabbat* 151b.

233 *Zohar Vayakhel* 213b.

234 *Likutei Moharan* I 6:4.

235 *Likutei Moharan* I 21:9.

236 *Likutei Moharan* I 64:2.

237 *Likutei Moharan* I 5.

238 *Likutei Moharan* I 3.

239 See Scholem, *Major Trends in Jewish Mysticism,* 329–337. Idel, *Messianic Mystics,* 58–100, 212–247.

THREE Unification: Hints, Sparks and Melody –
On the Bratslavian Service of God

Introduction

The present chapter will focus on the religious practices of Bratslav Hasidim, beginning with a theoretical examination of basic religious practices and progressing to a treatment of the implications of these practices. I do not intend to focus on details of particular behaviors, but rather to discuss the existential and theological meaning of specific customs and modes of worship as designed by R. Nachman and which characterize Bratslav Hasidim.

Examining the way of life of Bratslav Hasidism and the meaning of certain customs can instruct us as to the place occupied by various components in the worldview of Bratslav Hasidism. In addition, a sound portrayal of the place occupied by the theoretical components of R. Nachman's teachings can provide us with the proper context and a deeper understanding of his thought. This kind of examination is particularly germane to Bratslav teachings, which are clearly intended to shape the Hasid's religious life and self-expression. Although Bratslav teachings make rich use of the breadth of Jewish culture throughout the generations, they should also be understood as emerging predominately from Hasidic religious life and its paths, and in addition, primarily, as a means of return to that life.

As this chapter will show, the contrast between the 'presence' and 'absence' of rational mind (*da'at*) is central to understanding the various methods of serving God that R. Nachman developed for his disciples.

The backbone of this chapter is the teaching *Vayihi Miketz,* which R. Nachman delivered on Shabbat Hanukah 5565 (1804) (*Likutei Moharan* I 54). This teaching contains a concentrated discussion of a number of the spiritual practices that characterize Bratslav Hasidim. The doctrine of 'hints,' the topic of melody and song, the doctrine of good points and *hitbodedut* are all discussed in this teaching as models of conduct that R. Nachman derived from two distinct ontological perspectives on the existence of holiness in the world.

Vayihi Miketz presents an important discussion on night and sleep as times particularly suitable for some of the spiritual activities proposed in this teaching. As we shall see in Section II of this chapter, sleep, night and dream are all indications of states of consciousness marked by the absence of the ordinary mind (*mochin*) and rational mind (*da'at*).

It is significant that this one teaching describes such a broad range of perspectives and modes of behavior that, were we to find them described in separate teachings delivered at various times, might lead us to engage in specious speculation regarding the development of R. Nachman's views. The existence in the same teaching of various models, that seemingly contradict one another, demonstrates how R. Nachman blends a variety of ontological and behavioral models into one lesson.

Strangely enough, the academic literature has not, to the best of my knowledge, produced even one analysis of a complete teaching of R. Nachman. R. Nachman's words have been split and parsed into individual units, sentences and even phrases, but a proper understanding requires an awareness of a teaching's complete context and structure.

Part I – The Unification of 'Hashem Elokim'

I. Founding Principles

Vayihi Miketz opens with a description of the importance of 'the unification of *"Hashem, Elokim"*.' According to this teaching, 'unification' is not brought about through a Hasid's prior knowledge of the structure of worlds or the inner dynamic of the divine as described in the kabbalistic literature, nor through the implementation of the mystical meditations (*kavanot*) of the Ari.[1] Rather, this unification is a mental and internal process on the part of the Hasid connected to acts of worship, such as extracting the spirit of joy from the spirit of sadness, judging others favorably and, in particular, finding the traces of holiness in this world.

R. Nachman defines 'unification' first and foremost as a constant awareness of the world-to-come. The specific is made tangible in the revelation of holiness in every thought, speech and action in this world. The assumption that holiness is to be found in every area of the world is the common denominator linking everything in this teaching together. Regarding the manner in which holiness exists in the world, *Vayihi Miketz* provides various descriptions from which we may derive that for a person to come in contact with holiness one singular path is insufficient; rather multiple paths must be taken.

In *Vayihi Miketz*, we can identify two central ontological models describing the presence of holiness in the world, and three ways of conducting oneself derived from these ontological models and their engagement with man's encounter with holiness and with the world.

II. The First Ontological Model: Levels of Holiness – the Emanation of Divinity

R. Nachman introduces section two of *Vayihi Miketz* by presenting a theoretical foundation for his subsequent description of how a person should conduct himself in regard to the holiness existing in everything.

> For the entirety of this world *clothes* the lower levels of holiness – i.e., the aspect of the feet of holiness, the aspect of 'and the earth is my footstool.'[2] Even though the supernal levels of holiness also have a revelation in this world, that revelation is not clothed in essence in this world, but is rather an illumination that shines in the aspect of feet. The aspect of feet, however, is revealed in essence in this world.

This introduction describes the presence of holiness in the world as part of a complete structure of devolution of holiness in the world, where no displacement between the world and God exists. This image of gradation from the supernal worlds to the physical world uses an anthropomorphic description of a body of holiness whose lowly parts, 'the feet of holiness,' are revealed on the earth. This is R. Nachman's general metaphysical model, which calls upon man to seek the footprints of God in the world, His footstool.

III. First Behavioral Model: Understanding Hints – Holiness in Speech

R. Nachman confers a specific character to the presence of holiness and divinity in the world by describing them as 'hints.'

> And every day contains thought, speech and deed. And the Holy One, blessed be He, constricts His divinity from the Infinite to the infinitesimal, to the central point of the physical world upon which He stands, and He brings every individual thought, speech and deed, in accordance with the day and in accordance with the person and in accordance with the place.[3] And He clothes within that thought, speech and deed that He brings a person hints with which to bring that person to His service.

R. Nachman here takes an additional and unexpected step, explaining that the presence of holiness in the world is a personal message sent to a specific person, at a specific time and place. The low level of holiness found in a person's thoughts and deeds is a hint containing a hidden summons to man to come close to God. According to this view, man's role is to decipher these hints.

> Therefore, a person must think deeply into this and expand his comprehension, and understand what the hints mean specifically, clothed within the thought, speech and deed of this day, which Hashem, be He blessed, sent him. This is pertinent to labor or business, and whatever Hashem, be He blessed, sends a person each day. A person must deepen and expand his thought upon this matter in order to understand the hints of Hashem, be He blessed.

The meaning of 'hints with which to bring that person to His service' is not clear from R. Nachman's words. Does he intend to say that these hints are minor instances of prophecy sent to a person to guide him along the proper path and from which he must learn what to do and how to do it, or is he speaking of a more undifferentiated heavenly proclamation, a more amorphous message that breaks through the world and calls upon man to come close to God?

The same question pertains to the guidance that R. Nachman offers at the end of the teaching: 'and understand these words well, in order to put them into action.'[4] This is no doubt a directive to internalize this teaching and transform it into a part of one's life, but the phrase provides insufficient information about the nature of the hints and the degree of their specificity.

1. Understanding 'the Hint' as a Rational Process

Generally speaking, Bratslav Hasidim, from R. Natan of Nemirov to the Hasidim of our day, have accepted the former interpretation of these 'hints.' A person is indeed required to draw specific conclusions on how to act from the hints sent to him from above.

Thus, R. Natan relates in *Yemei Moharant*:

> And as soon as I learned that R. Dovid ... had come here from the land of Israel – and it is generally my habit to look at the thought, speech and deed that Hashem, be He blessed, sends me every day, for they certainly contain some hints for what I must do to come close to Hashem, ... – I suddenly had the thought, 'What does this mean?' And I realized that a hint had been sent to me to remind me of the land of Israel, and I immediately began to think into the matter of yearning to come to the land of Israel.[5]

Yemei Moharant provides another example of interpreting hints as providing clear instruction:

My thoughts were very confused and unclear and I did not know what to decide in regard to the printing. I thought about going to Mohilov, where there was a printing press in which my father-in-law R. Tzvi and his partner R. Leib were involved. I wanted to go there immediately and do business with the printer there, so that when R. Naftali came we would go to print without delay. But I saw that I did not even have enough money to pay for the trip to Mohilov and to give him a small deposit. And so I was unable to make up my mind. At that point, Hashem, be He blessed, demonstrated His awesome wonders, so that as I was passing outside the holy community of Nemirov, I suddenly lifted my eyes and saw R. Leib of the holy community of Mohilov, who had a partnership in the printing press there. I was very moved, and I understood that this came from Hashem – that this devolved from Him, be He blessed, the fact that R. Leib had come here today and that matters should so develop that I should see him, for it was not in the normal course of events that I should meet him, for he had no dealings with me and it had never occurred to him that he would meet me, if not for the compassion of Hashem that brought this about with His wondrous providence. So I immediately took heart and went to him and entered into a financial agreement with him regarding the printing. And afterwards there were a few other episodes of such a nature.[6]

R. Natan made his decision about the printing on the basis of his understanding of a 'hint' hidden in his unexpected and surprising meeting with R. Leib.

This way of understanding hints is accepted and used today in Bratslav Hasidism. Thus, a student of one of the Bratslav yeshivas of our day tells:

There are many occurrences in which natural events receive assistance from without, as it were, a nudge in the desired direction. Those are hints of the involvement and partnership of a supernal power in all the paths of our lives. Yesterday, I wanted to sit and learn with a colleague outside the building, in the sun. But people were already sitting there. My colleague said to me in a rebuking tone, 'Come on, let's get up and go over there.' The moment we stood up, those students got up, and the place was free. Many times there are combinations of events that cannot be mere circumstance. For instance, when you want to buy something or go somewhere or do something that appears important to you, if you are aware, you can notice that many times obstacles that could have existed disappear and that everything goes well, whereas at other times the opposite is true – you feel that things are not coming together, that there are illnesses, arguments, inner alienation from Hashem. A person who is prepared constantly to notice what is happening to him sees that there is a connection between these 'hints,' these 'little miracles,' these 'signs,' and his path in serving Hashem. Hashem, as it were, expresses His will to you in this way, encouraging you or testing you and placing challenges in your way.[7]

This understanding of the hints about which R. Nachman speaks develops in a person a mind-set that at every moment he is hearing God's hints directed to him personally, guiding his deeds and encouraging or discouraging him on his way. God sends prophecy to man constantly, and if a person is attentive and prepared to invest constant effort 'to deepen his thought in that and to enhance his comprehension, and to understand the hints in detail, hidden in the thought, speech and deed of the day, which Hashem, be He blessed, has sent him,'[8] he is enriched with a species of small prophecies that guide him on his way.

Man lives in constant dialogue with God. Man acts and God responds with His hints. God hints and man draws conclusions from the hints and responds with his deeds. This is not a monologue of man turning to God, but a manifest dialogue of hints and deeds.[9]

Although such a reading of R. Nachman's teaching is defensible, it seems to me that understanding 'hints' solely in this manner might lead to a misunderstanding of R. Nachman's intent. R. Nachman's call for a literal mystical meeting of a personal nature in the here and now with God, with holiness in the world, is understood according to this interpretation as a call for a person to develop an interpretive mechanism for deciphering hidden codes instructing him how to act, rather than helping him attain a mystical encounter with holiness.

According to this approach, interpreting hints with the help of one's rational faculties is based on the presumption that our world is under the providence of God, Who acts in the world. If R. Leib happens to come within R. Natan's purview, it means that he was sent to inspire R. Natan to engage in some arrangement with him. If students got up the minute someone stepped outside, it was specifically for that person's sake that they stood up. Understanding these hints is not based on any mystical experience. The mystical strain is, at best, attenuated and ancillary.

According to the first interpretation, when a person understands the hint, when he removes the garment hiding the deeper meaning of reality, a guidebook is revealed to him that teaches him what to do. But the goal of R. Nachman's teaching is to uncover the holiness and divinity in the world.

2. Understanding 'the Hint' as a Mystical Experience

It seems to me that R. Nachman's approach to 'hints' refers to an experience of a completely different nature than described above, one closer to our second interpretation. This second way of interpreting the doctrine of hints is described by R. Natan and supported and authorized by other sources as well.

R. Natan writes in a letter to his son R. Yitzchak:

> The teaching *Azamra L'Elokai B'odi* [...] although the advice revealed in that teaching is good for all, sweet for the soul and healing the bone, and has already revived many souls who have followed its path, nevertheless, at times it is difficult for a person to revive himself even with this teaching unless Hashem, be He blessed, helps him understand the hints that He grants each individual in each place – the truth that this person is still beloved of the Holy One, blessed, etc. And also, the teaching about the son and the student informs all those who are downcast and of little [apparent] worth in the world that Hashem is still with them and near them, etc., for 'the entire world is filled with His glory.' The essence of this holy knowledge must be received in the aspect of hints, for 'no thought grasps Him at all,' not at all. Only 'her husband is known in the gates' – 'to each individual in accord with what he imagines in his heart.' That is the aspect of hints. So every individual must take care to understand these hints until he draws onto himself God's divinity, be He blessed, wherever he is, and understand that 'the entire world is filled with His glory,' in the aspect of, 'And every created being will understand that You have made it,' etc. And it is not possible to speak of this at length. But 'a wise man needs but a hint.'[10]

According to these words, the 'hint' is not intended to offer guidance on how to act, one way or another, but to reveal the divinity that exists in the world, of which it is said, 'No thought can grasp Him at all,' and which is thus attained solely through the 'reckoning of the heart' and via the hint. That which is hinted at is a realization that 'the entire world is filled with His glory;' this requires a man to 'draw down upon himself God's divinity, be He blessed' rather than advice about printing books or buying some object. According to this explanation, understanding hints is the apprehension of divinity that exists in the world, and particularly in the area of mystical attainments.

The clearly mystical character of the encounter with the hints that God sends a person in order to draw him close can also be learned from the following of R. Nachman's talks:

From all things, the glory of Hashem, be He blessed, cries out, for 'the entire earth is filled with His glory.' And even from the stories of the gentiles the glory of Hashem, be He blessed, cries out. As the verse states, 'Tell amidst the gentiles His glory'[11] – even in the stories of the gentiles, the glory of Hashem, be He blessed, cries out, for His glory, may He be blessed, cries out constantly, calling and hinting to a person to come close to Him, be He blessed. And God, be He blessed, will bring a person close to Him with compassion, with love, and with great affection. And the fact that a person at times grows fervent in the midst of his prayer and begins to pray with fervor and great desire, and his prayer is fluent and effortless in his mouth – that is the light of Hashem, be He blessed, Himself, as it were, clothed within him, calling him to His service, be He blessed, for the fervor with which a person grows fervent in his prayer – that is the aspect of Hashem, be He blessed, Himself, as it were, the aspect of 'He is your praise and He is your God'[12] – that He, be He blessed, is Himself the praise and the prayer.[13]

In this talk, as in the doctrine of hints in *Vayihi Miketz*, the appeal to understand the hints of Hashem and to hear the call to come close to Him assumes that God's presence is imminent in the world and that a person is able to experience that presence. But whereas in *Vayihi Miketz* the mystical nature of the doctrine of hints is not clear, in this talk it is more apparent.

In this teaching, R. Nachman describes a manifestly mystical experience of unity between a person and his prayer, and the unity of that prayer with God. A person's prayer constitutes contact with 'the light of Hashem, be He blessed, Himself,' and this light 'calls this person to God's service.' It is clear that hearing the divine outcry bursting forth from the tales of gentiles does not lead to any particular directive in practical terms. Rather, it is an expression of 'the whole world is filled with His glory,' as a result of which 'His glory, be He blessed, cries out constantly and calls and hints to a person to draw close to Him, be He blessed.' The hint and the call to come close to God are the essence of the contact with 'the light of Hashem, be He blessed, Himself.' And when a person experiences that 'the whole earth is filled with His glory,' it is not only a whispered hint, but an outcry summoning a person to step forward and come close to God.

This outcry is heard at all times – 'He cries out constantly.' And it breaks through 'from all things,' not only from a specific incident or place, since 'the entire world is filled with His glory.' Although this outcry echoes from one end of the world to the other, it is still defined as a hint and not a direct communication, and thus hearing this quiet outcry requires great attention and spiritual sensitivity. R. Nachman, who used to 'cry out with a

whisper to Hashem, be He blessed,'[14] and said that 'it is necessary to cry out
from the heart only, in correspondence with the verse, "Their heart cried
out to Hashem",'[15] which is the outcry of the heart itself 'without a voice,'[16]
directs his Hasidim to hear 'the glory of Hashem crying out.' This outcry too
though is expressed as a hint without a voice, which cannot be heard by
everyone.

The mystical nature of prayer and the experience here described
become evident when in the course of his talk R. Nachman contrasts this
prayer with prayers of a non-mystical cast, in which a person does not come
in contact with the divine but stands before God from a distance, praying
without a sense of contact with Him.

> And sometimes a person prays before Hashem, be He blessed, as
> it were, and even when Hashem absents Himself and distances
> Himself, heaven forbid, from this person, he still needs to pray and
> cast his prayers after Him, be He blessed. This corresponds to the
> verse, 'Cast your burden upon Hashem.'[17] This person needs to
> throw and cast prayers after God, be He blessed, when God absents
> Himself and distances Himself from this person. And that is the
> aspect of 'Fortunate is the man who knows how to shoot arrows,'
> etc., as stated in the *Tikkunei Zohar* (*Tikun* 21) – that a person must
> shoot prayers after God, be He blessed ...[18]

Shooting arrows creates communication between distant entities that would
otherwise have no contact. This is the way to maintain a dialogue when there
is no direct mystical connection. R. Nachman's description of this prayer, in
contrast to the prayer previously described, underscores the mystical
character of prayer in which 'He, be He blessed, is Himself the praise and
the prayer,' when a person hears the hints of God in his fervent prayer.

3. Holiness as Personal Relationship

Without a doubt, the description of God's holiness in the world as a 'hint'
makes our contact with that holiness resemble personal communication with
God; this does not exist in the Platonic elevation of thought, in the Hasidic
version of that practice,[19] or in the kabbalistic doctrine of the raising of
sparks. And that quality of personal communication exists even if we understand the 'hint' as a call for general mystical contact with holiness and not
as providing practical guidelines.

The definition of holiness as a heaven-sent hint and a call directed
toward man is seemingly at odds with the kabbalistic description of holiness
in the world as a necessary emanation from the Infinite One to the farthest
worlds. Holiness understood as emanation can at most lead to the need to

reveal the holiness within existence. But it is difficult to see how one could understand that holiness as a personal message sent to a specific person.

R. Nachman's call to see the hint that arises specifically from a particular day and a particular deed, which was sent to him by God, lends to the devolution of worlds a dimension of directed, goal-directed and willed action, not of an emanation that is 'programmed.' Thus, the contact with divinity attains a quality of personal connection.

This explains R. Nachman's need to integrate the concept of constriction – 'that the Holy One, blessed be He, constricts His divinity'[20] – into his general explanation of the devolution of levels of holiness. The description of holiness as emanating from God, and as comprising levels of devolution from Him, is at odds with the view of holiness in the world bearing a message of a personal nature. Nevertheless, if the presence of holiness results from God's decision to constrict Himself, then one may see a personal hint and message in the manner, time and place that holiness is revealed to a person.

Also, the anthropomorphic description of holiness as a complete entity, as a divine body for whom the earth is its footstool – 'the aspect of feet of holiness' – provides language and images that constitute a basis for an inter-personal relationship between man and holiness – something more difficult to develop in the framework of a description of holiness as an emanation.[21]

And so the images R. Nachman uses in order to describe the presence of divinity in the world are congruent with his goal of imparting a personal dimension to the divine presence in the world

In the continuation of *Vayihi Miketz*, R. Nachman discusses various levels of holiness: a low level of holiness is revealed 'in the matters of this world,' and a higher holiness exists in Torah and mitzvot. This gradation holds true even for 'a person who knows and understands this – i.e., who merits to understand the hints that Hashem, be He blessed, sends him in everything.'[22] R. Nachman directs the Hasid not to involve himself much with the holiness found in the matters of this world but instead to increase his Torah learning and performance of mitzvot. R. Nachman supports this requirement with two explanations: The first is that it is inherently dangerous to make contact with the *kelipot* (husks) that surround the low level of holiness and attempt to draw vitality from it. And the second is that the high level of holiness hidden in Torah and mitzvot is intrinsically superior to the holiness found in the world.

IV. A Second Model of Conducting Oneself: Unconscious Contact with Holiness – the Silence of Holiness

Although in Section 2 of *Vayihi Miketz* R. Nachman characterizes contact with low-level holiness as an activity in which a person is called 'to deepen his thought in this and to enhance his comprehension' in order to understand the 'hints' being sent to him, in Section 3 he argues that it is possible to attain those insights without intellectual work, and even if one is not conscious of any contact with holiness: 'and for the masses, who do not have the intellect to delve deeply into all this, to understand these hints mentioned above, all of this takes place by itself, through sleep and wearing tzitzit and tefillin and learning Torah and engaging in prayer and in business activities.'

There is something of a revolution here regarding our understanding of what occurs during contact with holiness: for if contact with holiness means understanding the hint hidden within, how can this occur by itself? The examples that R. Nachman cites, particularly sleep, accentuate this problem.

The claim that the 'common people' can be partners in remembering the world-to-come and achieving mystical unification would be easier to understand if the 'common people' would at least, although incapable of understanding the specific 'hints' that come through the events of this world, be aware of the 'hints' concealed in everything and of the fact that God communicates with man through everything. This awareness would change their relationship with the world, since it would enable a dialogue between man and God, even one that is mute. But the examples R. Nachman uses to illustrate his point make this explanation untenable. It is hard to claim that a person possesses a general, minimal awareness during sleep. Similarly, it is not reasonable to assume that the masses can maintain consciousness of this sort as they engage in their business affairs.

According to the model of serving God through 'hints,' the essence of mystical unification is to be found in understanding God's message and hints within the holiness in the world. Thus, this unification is essentially a mental event. Yet now, R. Nachman argues that this unification may be attained by means of an experience in which a person has no awareness at all. It is not exactly clear what R. Nachman means when he states that this happens 'of itself'; how memory (of the world-to-come) and mystical unification happen (of themselves) and their significance require further clarification.

R. Nachman does not clarify this difficulty immediately. First, he expounds in detail on the verse, '*Hashem Elokim*, You have been very great,' discussing how the masses make unifications even without investing their intellect and without understanding any divine hints, but simply by sleeping, wearing tzitzit, and so forth. Afterwards, in the latter half of this teaching, R. Nachman offers a fresh explanation of the presence of holiness in the world – and although he does not relate to this question directly, he does offer a new understanding of this particular difficulty.

V. *A Second Ontological Model: Shattering of the Vessels – Sparks and Letters*

As in the beginning of *Vayihi Miketz*, R. Nachman discusses the theological meaning of the existence of holiness in the world, after which he describes a person's role in relation to this holiness. 'For everything in the world has within it sparks of holiness that fell at the time of the shattering of the vessels – and that shattering is the aspect of letters that were broken and fell into all the things of this world.'

This description of holiness that exists within everything introduces a new ontological model of the existence of holiness in the world and of a person's relationship to it, a model based on the Lurianic teachings of 'the shattering of the vessels' and 'raising the sparks.'[23]

This is not a graduated devolution of holiness from an infinite pinnacle to the feet of physical existence, nor of God, Who with specific intent constricts Himself in order to come to 'the central point of focus of the physical world,' sending hints to a person through its entities.

Comparing the opening sentences of the two models clearly demonstrate that the picture R. Nachman paints at this point is significantly darker and less holy. Section Two of *Vayiki Miketz* states, 'This entire world is a garment for the lower levels of holiness' – i.e., all of existence consists of a devolution of holiness. Section Three, on the other hand, states that 'everything in the world contains sparks of holiness.'

These are two different explanations of the nature of reality, the first describing a reality that acts as a garment for holiness and the second describing a reality that is not holy in itself, but contains within it 'sparks of holiness.'

According to the second view, man does not meet with a complete state of holiness in the world, but rather with mere scattered shards of holiness. And these shards of holiness were not sent, but merely 'fell' into objects, in which no hints and coherent speech are directed to a person; they are, rather, no more than 'shattered letters.' Clearly, it would be difficult to conceptualize these shards of holiness as the Creator's personal speech with man – a speech in which reality is revealed to be God's call to man to come close to Him.

This second viewpoint, therefore, necessitates a radical change in defining the role of man in regard to holiness. And indeed, R. Nachman offers a portrayal completely different from that presented in Section 2 of the relationship between man and sparks of holiness:

> And every object has its hour,[24] and in this hour it must come to a
> specific person, who shares the same root with the sparks within that

object. And when that object comes to that person, and he receives life-force from that object – i.e., from the broken letters that are there – as a result, the shattered letters are incorporated into the person, into his life-force, and they are made into a complete structure, which spreads throughout the life-force of his entire body. And as a result the letters are made complete, and they attain completion. And that item must be allowed to remain with that person to use until the letters and sparks that have a relationship with his root are ended. And then it goes from his possession to someone else, for the time has come for the remaining letters to have an ascent – those letters that share a root with another man – and thus it goes into that other man's possession. And sometimes, the item returns to the man who had it first, because at first he did not have the necessary parts of *nefesh* and *ruach,* and so he was not able at that time to complete these letters. But now that these parts of his *nefesh, ruach,* and *neshamah* have come to him, through them he is able to complete those remaining letters. But in the meantime, it had to remain with someone else.

This example shows a partnership between the person and the spark that he encounters. Nevertheless, the hidden holiness within objects isn't sent to him in order to help him and teach him how to come close to God. Here, man is called instead to help reconstruct the shattered spark of holiness. The letter or spark remains with the person until he rectifies it and transforms it from a fragment into something whole. And then, when his role in reconstituting the spark is finished, the spark leaves him and moves on to someone else.

Although the human being is not the focus of this work, he can receive an illumination and vitality added to his spirit consequent to raising these sparks, and he can thus also bring about unifications:

And when he completes those letters, he is given an additional illumination in his *nefesh, ruach,* and *neshamah,* as a result of the illuminations of those letters that came to him and were completed by him. And as a result of this illumination, he shines on the root of his *nefesh, ruach,* and *neshamah* – which is in the *zaddik* and in *Knesset Yisrael,* which are the roots of all souls … And as a result of this shining, the *zaddik* and *Knesset Yisrael,* which are called 'give and take' (or 'business dealings')…, are united.

The illumination attained by the *nefesh, ruach* and *neshamah* is not presented as the goal of raising the shattered letters, but as an ancillary consequence.[25]

One of the ramifications of this explanation touches upon the point with which R. Nachman opened in Section 3: the unification of '*Hashem, Elokim*' performed by the common people.

R. Nachman does not consider the rectification of sparks and the performance of unifications to be dependent upon the knowledge of *kavanot*. He does not even require a person's conscious activity for the purpose of this rectification. The activity occurs 'of itself' and thus can be found even in a person whose intellect is not profound. The basic fact of a person's contact with the world raises the sparks that exist within it.

Therefore, even the common masses, who lack the intellect to delve deeply in order to understand God's hints, can be active partners in relating to holiness, even if they know nothing about the shattering of the vessels and the 'death of the kings' in the *kavanot* of the Ari. Even during sleep or while engaged in business, they automatically raise the sparks relevant to them.

R. Nachman here joins many Hasidic thinkers who see the raising of the sparks as an activity open to every individual,[26] in contrast to the implication of the Ari's kabbalah. The connection in the kabbalah of the Ari between *kavanot* and the raising of sparks indicates that the raising of sparks is a service intended solely for the kabbalistic elite, and involves prior kabbalistic knowledge. And not only prayers and mitzvot require *kavanot*. Even mundane activities such as eating and drinking, which are opportune occasions for the raising of sparks, involve '*kavanot* of eating' and the like.[27] Also, the raising of sparks during sleep[28] involves first engaging in *kavanot* of sleep[29] and *kavanot* of the prayer 'In Your hand do I deposit my spirit,'[30] which – like the other *kavanot* of the Ari – require intellectual effort and prior kabbalistic knowledge.[31]

The goal within Hasidism to eliminate the need for *kavanot* in raising the sparks may be seen as part of a broad-based opposition to using *kavanot* in prayer – an opposition that comes from a view different from that of the Ari regarding the proper provenance of cleaving to God and the correct manner of that cleaving.[32]

The Evil Eye and the Imaginative Faculty

Sections Four and Five of *Vayihi Miketz* return to the opening topic – remembering (the world-to-come) – and constitute a sort of introduction and background to the third model presented in Section 6. In these sections, R. Nachman warns against two dangers liable to injure a person's recollection of the world-to-come. The first is falling to the level of the 'evil eye,' which can bring about forgetfulness. The meaning of this danger grows clearer when we understand it as being the opposite of 'a good spirit,' the phrase R. Nachman uses to characterize the third model of conduct, which he discusses further on in *Vayihi Miketz*.

The second danger comes from the imaginative faculty. Thus, says R. Nachman, 'a person must guard his eye from the imaginative faculty.' When the rational mind is absent, the imaginative faculty grows stronger. At this stage, the absence of the rational mind and the strengthening of the imagination are described as causing a negative situation, which might allow a person's animal spirit to rule over him.[33] In this context, R. Nachman mentions the dream as an example of the state in which the rational mind is absent and the imaginative faculty gains ascendance. This greater strength of the imaginative faculty can damage a person's memory and cause him to fall into forgetfulness. The strengthening of the imaginative faculty, then, contradicts the goal of always remembering the world-to-come.

In the passage beginning with the words, 'and to subjugate the imaginative faculty' in Section 6, R. Nachman introduces a way to deal with these two dangers – the evil eye and the imaginative faculty – that is meant to lead a person to the recollection of the world-to-come. This is a third model for conducting oneself in order to relate to the holiness in the world.

VI. The Third Model of how to Conduct Oneself: Melody

Melody is an additional path to realizing the prerequisite to remember the world-to-come and to come in contact with 'the feet of holiness clothed in this world.'[34]

In Chapter 1, while discussing the ambivalent character of the imagination and its connection to prophecy, I described a number of viewpoints regarding the process of creating melody and the meaning of melody. Now, we will see how melody serves as a model of contact with the holiness that rests within the world, against the background of the two other models that R. Nachman formerly introduced in *Vayihi Miketz*.

1. The Ontological Foundation – Two Previous Models

Unlike his approach to the previous models of worship, R. Nachman does not provide the model of melody with its own ontological description of the existence of holiness within the world. This is because, as we will see further on, R. Nachman's 'doctrine of melody' relies on his two previous ontological models found in the opening of this teaching.

From a phenomenological standpoint, the two previous models of contact with holiness stand at polar opposites. Whereas one describes an intensive conscious activity that demands that a person 'intensify and increase his thought in this'[35] in order to understand the specific message directed to a person in every created thing, the second can occur automatically, entirely lacking personal awareness.

From this standpoint, the third model mediates between its two predecessors. It does not describe an activity that demands profundity of thought
or expansion of intellect, but rather the development of awareness that
does not occur spontaneously, but is the fruit of activity and a clear, internal
preparation. Melody is such an intermediate state. This idea is expressed also
in melody's reliance on the two previous ontological models of the existence
of holiness in the world.

Melody is created by gathering together scattered parts of a good spirit
and joy, which are components of the spirit of holiness and the spirit of
prophecy. And when these are gathered together into one complete melody,
that melody can bring a person to divine inspiration and prophecy.[36]

The separation of good from evil precedes the gathering of the components of the spirit.[37] The *a priori* assumption that makes it possible to summon
a person to gather together the components of the good spirit and prophecy
is that the elements of the spirit of prophecy and joy have been scattered
across the world. These particles are separated from each other and mixed
with other components: an evil spirit and sadness. Man's role is therefore to
separate the good from the bad and to combine the elements of the good
into one complete melody.

It is not difficult to identify the basic model that R. Nachman is developing as the doctrine of sparks. Parts of holiness fell, were separated from
each other and were scattered throughout the world, and are now in a state
of dispersal and admixture with evil. Man's role is to extract the good from
evil, holiness from the husk, and then to raise the sparks and in so doing build
anew the structure of holiness.[38]

The doctrine of sparks does not in itself necessarily assert that raising the
sparks can lead to prophecy or to a holy spirit. As R. Nachman described
earlier (in Section III), raising sparks can occur even without a person's
awareness, as an activity that occurs of itself. Raising sparks, is therefore, not
a way to attain a holy spirit, and should not be seen as a mystical practice
centered on man.

Although raising sparks may be associated with the illumination and
added vitality of a person's soul, in its essence it is a theurgic activity, whose
goal is the rectification of divinity and of the world of holiness. As for the
prophetic dimension of melody, R. Nachman must base that on something
else – i.e., on the doctrine of hints.

Indeed, in the exposition that concludes the section of *Vayihi Miketz*
dealing with melody, R. Nachman connects the doctrine of hints with melody.

And thus the verse states, 'Who rose to the heavens and descended,
who gathered the wind in His hands, who wrapped the water in a
garment, who set up all the ends of the earth?'[39] 'Who rose to

heaven and descended?' – that is the aspect of the musician, for the musician goes up and down with the tune … 'Who set up all the ends of the earth?' – for in this way he sets up the aspect of feet that are clothed in this world. 'The ends of' – that is the aspect of feet. As the verse states, 'And he made me pass through water, water up to the ankles.'[40] This is because via playing music with the hand, … the imagination is subdued, and then one attains memory, …which is the aspect of knowing how to understand all of the hints that are in everything in the world, which is the aspect of divine vitality, the aspect of the feet of holiness, which are clothed within all things in the world.[41]

As we saw earlier, the goal of revealing hints is to come into contact with the 'divine vitality' that exists within the world; it is not a theurgic activity. In the doctrine of hints, contact with the hints is intended neither to rectify the hints nor is it part of the general purpose of rectifying divinity or the holiness that fell into the world. It is not the spark that must be raised and helped, but it is the man who is in need of a hint to help him come close to his God.

Separating and extracting good from evil, gathering together the scattered parts and building them anew: these are the basic elements in the doctrine of sparks (which have no root in the doctrine of hints), and they serve as basic building blocks in the doctrine of melody.

Thus, in his doctrine of melody, R. Nachman makes use of both the doctrine of hints and the doctrine of sparks.

VII. *The Mystical Path:* Vayihi Miketz

In *Vayihi Miketz*, melody is essentially compared to a path to making contact with the holiness that resides within the world; it is not the path itself.

R. Nachman, as we saw, relies on the model of raising sparks – a model that applies to theurgic activity – and although he adapts its structure of extracting, gathering and joining, he shifts its goal. In his adaptation, it is not directed toward rectifying the supernal worlds but at arriving at a holy spirit and prophecy or, at the very least, at contact with the good spirit, the spirit of holiness, which resides within the world.

1. *The Essence of the Similarity*
Melody is apparently not a body of speech, but an accompaniment to the spoken word. It possesses no defined content and thus has nothing to do with the realm of the intellect (*seichel*) and the rational mind (*da'at*). Rather, melody and tune intensify and give force to spoken words. Melody shapes the

paths of words and grants them vitality and firmness. Words spoken without melody are like a body that lacks life, and are as a result sometimes even incomprehensible. To understand something to its depth necessitates understanding its melody. Relating only to the body of the words without understanding their spirit and the source of their vitality is an incomplete understanding. And so, when R. Nachman expresses the hope that he and his teaching will be understood, he states that this must also include the melody of his teaching and even its dance:

> R. Nachman said: The world has still not understood (tasted) me. If people would hear just one teaching that I deliver with its melody and dance, they would all be completely nullified. That is to say, the entire world in its entirety, even the animals and plants and everything in the world would all be nullified with an expiration of the spirit out of an exceedingly great impact of wondrous and extraordinary delight.[42]

Melody exists even without words. Its power and intrinsic strength and vitality do not necessitate any dependence on limited speech. R. Nachman describes melody as having the quality of granting life, and so a person who feels that he lacks life must employ its assistance:

> R. Nachman said: It is good for a person to accustom himself to revive himself with a melody, for melody is a very great and exalted matter, and has great power to arouse and draw the heart of a person to Hashem, be He blessed. And even if a person cannot sing, nevertheless at home by himself he can revive himself with a melody to the degree that he can sing it, for the quality of melody cannot be imagined.[43]

Melody grants a person vitality and power, even though it does not tell him anything specific. There is no transference of content here, but transference of vitality. Melody is the spirit that gives life to the words in the sense that it is a spark of holiness from which words draw their vitality.

As we will see further on, the ability to hear a tune and sing is the ability to come into contact with the spirituality hidden within things, with the holiness in them that grants them vitality and meaning.

R. Nachman calls on man to come into contact with the spark of holiness hidden within things through melody – not via a process of elevation that occurs by itself (as in the case of the sleep and eating of the common man), nor as an attempt to understand the specific hint sent to a person, but via hearing and revealing the good spirit and joy within the world. From amidst the mixture of sounds and spirits that the imaginative faculty transfers to him, a person must extract the good spirit and the joy, and from the collation of these sounds build the spirit of holiness and prophecy. The vitality of holiness within things is not mute; however, I do not maintain that it speaks with words or specific messages.

This way of service possesses a mystical-existential quality. It is not a practice that a person performs with the help of *kavanot* or by means of his deeds, but by increasing his awareness of the holiness within the world and his encounter with it. A person must feel the good spirit as a wind blowing through the world. He must hear the song of each blade of grass and the melody of everything in the world. He is summoned to a meeting with existence, not only on its prosaic plane but also by means of song and melody, so as to take note of the splinters of spirituality and holiness hidden in the world and to combine them together into a melody that is fully and clearly filled with holiness and prophecy. Melody and song are not only the representative demonstration, but are also the actual instrument for a person's encounter with reality, which is not merely silent and sealed but possesses vitality and holiness. Melody reveals a festal and spiritual landscape, which prose, with its dry verbal description, is unable to discover.

Song and music are those planes on which a person feels that he has come into contact with something spiritual and festive, even if it is not delimited and concretized into clear speech. It is precisely here that faith encounters song and melody; faith is the approach to that additional plane of existence, a plane of holiness, spirituality and divinity, which cannot be revealed in prose.

As R. Natan phrases it:

> But after the splitting of the Red Sea, at which point they attained complete faith as a result of drawing down the complete faith from the aspect of the Ancient of Ancients, from the aspect of the light of the messiah, from the aspect of the 'head of faith,' at that point they attained song, the aspect of 'Come, gaze from the head of Amanah,' which can be homiletically rendered, 'Sing from the head of faith'. 'Sing' – that is the aspect of 'and they believed in Hashem and in Moses His servant,' after which 'Moses sang,' for the essence of song comes when one attains full faith, from which all songs and melodies are derived.[44]

In this view, faith makes song possible. If a person does not believe that something more than 'this world' exists, the world does not arouse song within him. Faith arouses all songs and melodies,[45] and these teach a person more than the contents of the words he speaks. Melody is the inner stratum that reveals the hidden nature of that which stands before a person.

2. Melody and Prayer

Prayer, which R. Nachman sees as the clearest expression of the activity of faith,[46] must be aided by the sounds and melodies that it hears, as R. Nachman writes elsewhere:

> Know that when a person prays in the field, then all of the grasses enter into his prayer and help him, and give power to his prayer. And that is the aspect of prayer called *sichah* which means both 'speech' and 'herbage.' This corresponds to the verse, 'Herbage of the field.'[47] This is because all of the herbs of the field give power and assistance to his prayer. And that corresponds to the verse, 'And Isaac went out to speak in the field.'[48] This is because his prayer was made possible by the assistance and power of the field, insofar as all of the grasses of the field gave power and assistance to his prayer, for which reason prayer is called *siach*.[49] And therefore the passage of curses states, 'And the earth will not give its produce.'[50] This is because all the produce of the earth must give power and assistance to a person's prayer. And when there is a blemish and impediment to this, then the verse states that 'the earth will not give its produce.' This is because even when a person does not pray in the field, the produce of the earth still gives aid to his prayer – i.e., in regard to everything that is close to the person, such as his eating and drinking and the like. But when he is in the field, when he is closer to the grasses, then all of the grasses and all the produce of the land give strength to his prayer. And so the word *yibul* (produce) is the acronym for *vayetzei Yitzchak lasuach basadeh* – 'And Isaac went forth to speak in the field' – meaning that all of the produce of the earth prayed together with him.

And in another talk, delivered in the spring of 5565 (1805), R. Nachman directed his Hasidim to go out to the fields, particularly in the spring, and pray amidst the plants with the arousal to life that characterizes the spring.[51] The song of the grasses and plants causes a person to cling to the arousal and life-force within that song, and those grasses arouse yearning and longing for God. The sparks of holiness hidden in every herb and plant desire to rise and return to their source. They take along with them one who yearns for and desires God but also, by being incorporated into man and into his prayer, they themselves are elevated.[52]

The essence of R. Nachman's discussion on melody has until now focused on the mystical arena – i.e., on the ability of melody to serve as a tool and expression of a person's contact with the holiness and spirituality hidden within the world. But this teaching clearly also discusses other associations and qualities of melody : those relating to the realm of magic.

VIII. Chapter of Song: Melody as a Theurgic Magic Activity – an Alternative Basis to The Doctrine Of Melody

Turning our attention to the theurgic and magical perspectives of melody is important in both providing additional layers of understanding of R. Nachman's relationship with melody and uncovering an additional postulate of R. Nachman's doctrine of melody. From this postulate we learn that R. Nachman's doctrine of melody cannot be analyzed solely against the background of the Lurianic doctrine of sparks. Rather, R. Nachman's unique approach must be understood against the background of a broader array of sources.

Our discussion of the influence of melody on the grasses and the sparks hidden therein revealed a certain perspective on the theurgic and magical goals of melody. Relating to sparks as something that can lead to rectification and elevation imparts a theurgic dimension to the activity of raising sparks. This is because rectifying and elevating sparks of holiness in the world is connected to the rectification of divinity and as such should be classified as theurgic.

However, in *Likutei Moharan* II 63, R. Nachman states that via melody a person gives grasses the power to blossom. This definition of the act of melody cuts across the blurred line dividing theurgic and magical activity and grants the act more of a magical quality. Indeed in *Likutei Moharan* II 63, the magical characteristics of melody are at the heart of R. Nachman's discussion:

> Know that when our patriarch Jacob sent his sons, the ten tribes, to Joseph, he sent along with them the melody of the land of Israel. And that is the secret of, 'Take of the choice fruits (*zimrat*) of the land in your vessels,'[53] etc., the aspect of tune (*zemer*) and melody that he sent with them to Joseph. And as Rashi expounds, *zimrat* is related to the word for 'tune,' etc [...] And that corresponds to the verse, 'From the end of the earth have we heard songs'[54] – that tunes and melodies come forth from the end of the earth. This is because the melody is made by means of the grasses that grow in the earth [...] And as a result of the shepherd knowing the melody, in this way he gives strength to the grasses, and then the animals have food to eat. And that corresponds to the verse, 'The buds have appeared in the land, the time of singing has arrived.'[55] That is to say that the buds grow in the land by means of the tune and melody that relate to them ... So via the tune and melody that the shepherd knows, he gives strength to the grasses. [...] And there are many distinctions in melody. This is because there is a complete, self-contained melody, and there is a melody in movements, and one can divide melody into movements and sections.

And know that the king possesses the entire melody, entirely, completely. But the ministers have only a part of the melody, each according to his place. And so Daniel told Nebuchadnezzar, 'You are a tree, etc., and sustenance for all is in it.'[56] This is because through Nebuchadnezzar – who was king and who possessed the entire melody – all the sustenance was drawn down, for sustenance is drawn down by means of melody.[…] And so although our patriarch Jacob did not know that the minister was Joseph, for he knew nothing besides what his sons, the tribes, had told him of Joseph's behavior, he sent Joseph a melody appropriate for a minister such as he, in accordance with what he had heard from his sons of his ways and behavior. This is because Jacob wanted to affect him via the melody, so as to attain what he required. Thus, Jacob sent Joseph that very melody of the land of Israel. And this is as he told his sons, 'Take from the choice fruit (*zimrat*) of the land in your vessels.' That is to say, they should take the aspect of the melody […], which is the aspect of the *zimrat* of the land … in their vessels. 'And bring down to the man a gift: a little balm and a little honey, laudanum and lot, nuts and almonds.' These are the aspect of the various elements of the melody, for the melody is made of the produce of the land […]

It thus becomes clear that just as man hears the song of the grasses, so too are the grasses influenced by the song of man. The song that a man sings acts upon the grasses and grants them power; his melody also has the ability to draw blessing and sustenance for other people. This drawing down of blessing and sustenance comes about through divine effulgence upon the ministers. Every minister possesses a certain portion of the melody in keeping with the amount of sustenance that is drawn down through him. However, the king possesses the complete melody and is thus the supplier of sustenance for everyone.

Jacob, who knew the nature of melodies and their power, sent the melody appropriate for a certain minister in Egypt in order to influence him to fulfill his family's request and supply their sustenance. Jacob does not use melody as a way of turning to God, but clearly used melody as a magical tool to attain income and food.

1. Theurgic and Magical Perspectives on Melody

There are many ancient sources describing the theurgic and magical uses of melody.[57] Here I will focus on those that are clearly echoed in R. Nachman's words, and that can therefore shed light on his teachings.

The magical power of melody is described by R. Nachman as part of a general view of the world in which every heavenly minister and nation possesses a unique melody that helps them attain divine effulgence and sustenance. A person who knows the secrets of each melody has the ability to influence these heavenly ministers and the divine effulgence that flows through them.

A description of this type appears in the words of R. Yitzchak Abarbanel, in his commentary on the book of *Kings*, written in 1493, in the framework of a discussion of the songs composed by King Solomon.[58]

Solomon is presented as a magician possessing the knowledge of the secret of the heavenly ministers and of melodies that can help him bring down effulgence into the world. R. Yitzchak Abarbanel's portrait of Solomon is equivalent in great measure to the image of Jacob that R. Nachman limns in *Likutei Moharan* II 63. The background in both circumstances is a world that draws its vitality and the effulgence of blessing and sustenance via melody. Thus, a person who knows the secret of melody possesses a magical tool of great power, with which he can draw down effulgence to the world. Also, the image of the king or kingdom that knows all melodies or the complete melody, appears, although in different form, in the writings of both Abarbanel and R. Nachman. It should be noted that R. Yitzchak Abarbanel tempers his words and uses phrases such as 'perhaps' and 'it seems.'

Certain components of this view were described even earlier by R. Yehoshua Ibn Shuib, a Sephardic kabbalist and student of the Rashba, in his book, *Derashot al Hatorah*:

> We should learn from an exceedingly small creature, the ant. This is because Hashem placed wisdom and craftiness and stratagems in animals, and these traits are a special quality within animals, just as there are special qualities in stones and in grasses. And this is the meaning of the verse, 'From before Him, animals of the earth.' And our sages stated, 'We learn modesty from the cat, not to rob from the ant …' And there is no doubt that such a quality is a spark of the supernal soul. And as viewed by philosophers, it is a spark of the active intellect […] And it is not due to any knowledge or intellect within them, but is rather due to the fact that Hashem gave them this power and special quality so that people might grow wise from them. And our sages composed *The Chapter of Song*, in which the animals praise the Creator, or their heavenly ministers and their powers praise Hashem, for every creature and even the grasses have their own powers in heaven.[59]

The picture presented by R. Yehoshua Ibn Shuib is more incomplete than that of R. Abarbanel. Nonetheless, his exposition contains two important components that appear in the teachings of R. Nachman and not in the teachings of R. Yitzchak Abarbanel.

The first component is the connection between 'the appearance of this world' and the *Chapter of Song*. The *Chapter of Song* is an ancient text first mentioned in the tenth century. It contains songs and praises to God as spoken by animals and other creations; most of the praises are taken from *Psalms*, and the remainder from other books of the biblical canon.[60] *Likutei Moharan* II 63, where R. Nachman discusses the topic of heavenly ministers and melody, also has a connection with the *Chapter of Song*: 'and in accordance with the grasses and the place where the shepherd grazes, he possesses a melody, the aspect of the *Chapter of Song*. And from the song of the grasses is made a melody of the shepherd.'

Further on we will see that other sources point out a connection linking the *Chapter of Song* and the song of the heavenly ministers and the magical power of melody. These are apparently part of a tradition of theurgic and magical exposition on the *Chapter of Song* spanning many generations.[61]

The second component is the expression, 'a spark of the supernal soul.' I will point out that in *Vayihi Miketz* R. Nachman explicitly associates the sparks mentioned in connection to the doctrine of melody with the shattering of the vessels. Thus, a fully-developed approach must maintain that   for R. Nachman a doctrine of sparks is based upon the symbol of the shattering of the vessels.

It is possible, however, that R. Nachman has interwoven various sources and perspectives on the sparks into one approach. Thus, the connection that R. Nachman makes between sparks that came from the shattering of the vessels and the doctrine of melody may be influenced by other teachings that connect melody with sparks but that do not indicate a relationship between sparks and the shattering of the vessels.

2. R. Moshe Cordovero

One finds in the teachings of R. Moshe Cordovero the first mention of other components that appear in R. Nachman's doctrine of melody in addition to those already described. In *Ilmah Rabati* we see a few references to 'the secret of the *Chapter of Song*':

> Creatures large and small, beasts and animals of the forest and the elements and their compounds as found in inanimate matter and plant life and animal life that are not subject to reward and punishment – our sages alluded to them in their statement, 'Man for the sake of animal' [...] And that is to say that all of these entities have heavenly ministers in charge of them. And their heavenly ministers praise and sing to their Creator. And their song

and tune rise and draw down the light of the Infinite One and vivify these entities. And this is the meaning of the verse, 'Praise Hashem from the heavens,' and the entire psalm. And that is called the *Chapter of Song*. And that song gathers together as a single unit and rises. And it was regarding this that the sages gave a hint of the secret of the *Chapter of Song*, in that it says, 'The heavens – what do they say? The earth, what does it say? And the winds, what do they say? The dog, what does it say? The cat, what does it say?' and so forth. And this song that rises and is integrated together is gathered by the minister of the world called Metatron, since he is in charge of the song of the singers, to gather everything together and bring it within and draw forth the light of the existence of lower beings, and to give them some of their sustenance and effulgence. And when the song of the angels rises to the throne, and the praise of the throne rises to the *sefirah*, and the praise of the *sefirah* to the Infinite One, everything is gathered together and one praise and an all-inclusive song is made. And then light that vivifies all of them is drawn down.

And behold, the one who expresses his song is the most praiseworthy of all […] for he has the power of speech […] And he has the ability to add and make new cosmic intimate unions. And so if there is a person and he offers praises, all of the other beings are secondary to him and fall under his influence. And he is the one who goes and raises his song as the primary song and tune, and all are subdued under his hand […] But when there is no man […] the Shechinah returns to the heavenly minister of the world and then the world and all beings are given their sustenance, to the extent that is appropriate and suitable.[62]

This all-inclusive picture of heavenly ministers that sing and of man who, with his song and tune, can cause 'all of them to be subdued under his hand' is made by both R. Moshe Cordovero and R. Nachman.

Racing Out and Returning: Raising the Light and Bringing Down the Effulgence
In R. Moshe Cordovero's writings we find for the first time the description of melody and song as a dynamic with two stages: the first, 'raising the light' and the second, 'bringing down the divine effulgence.'

The existence of both phases teaches that R. Moshe Cordovero is describing a bi-directional process: 'to gather everything and to bring it within, and to draw up the light of the existence of the lower beings and to give them some of their sustenance and effulgence.' This is a structure of 'racing out and returning.' On the one hand, there is ascent, defined as a process that draws forth the 'light of the existence of beings,' and thus can apparently lead to the nullification of being. And on the other hand, the second stage – 'and to give them a little of their sustenance and effulgence' – thus, of course, strengthens their existence.

Or in another form: 'and their song and tune rises and draws down the light of the Infinite One and vivifies them' – that is ascent. And afterwards the drawing down of light gives life-force to created beings.

And we see similarly further along: 'and with the ascent of the song of the angels to the throne ... everything is gathered and one praise is made, an all-inclusive song and then there is drawn down light that vivifies them all.' The song rises upwards and then draws down light from the Infinite One to vivify all beings.

An equivalent structure exists in the teachings of R. Nachman. He describes a process that begins with created beings and rises with the aid of melody, 'for via the grasses that grow upon the earth, melody is formed.'[63] The matter is explained more clearly in *Likutei Moharan* II 11, as we saw above: 'when a person prays in the field, then all of the grasses come within his prayer and aid him and give him power in his prayer. And that is the aspect of prayer called *sichah*, the aspect of "speech of the field"[64] – meaning that all of the herbage of the field give strength to and aid his prayer ...'

The speech of the grasses imparts power to the prayer; a person must gather those powers and raise them upward. The prayer and melody though give strength to the grasses: 'and as a result of the shepherd knowing the melody, he gives strength to the grasses ... Thus, via the tune and melody that the shepherd knows, he gives strength to the grasses.'[65]

Gathering the Songs

We find in R. Moshe Cordovero's teachings the idea that it is necessary to gather the parts of the song and raise them as one song: 'and this song is gathered entirely together and rises,' 'and this song that rises and is incorporated together, is gathered by the minister of the world called Metatron, because he is in charge of the song of the singers, to gather everything and to bring it within.'

R. Nachman turns this motif from the realm of Metatron's activity also to the activity and role of man: 'and he must know musical playing, that he should know how to gather and draw together and find parts of the spirit, one at a time, in order to build the melody.'[66]

It is man who must gather the parts of the good spirit and create a melody of joy and it is he who must hear the song of the grasses and as a result sing his own prayer. For R. Nachman, the process of gathering includes also the process of extracting the good and rejecting the evil; this does not exist for R. Moshe Cordovero in the context of the doctrine of melody.

Regarding the Question of the Ontological Model
In discussing the following quotation from R. Moshe Cordovero, I wish to focus not on one motif or another, but on the framework of the discussion, that is on the context in which to understand the *Chapter of Song* and its place in the totality of R. Moshe Cordovero's thought:

> And the supernal effulgence is spiritual. And it is drawn from level to level until it comes to the coarseness of this level [of our world]. And just as the levels devolved from one state to another until they came to this state, so literally is the matter of their on-going existence. And thus it is written, 'And You vivify them all' – just as He vivifies them, so does He maintain them, and just as He maintains them, so does He vivify them. And so the light devolves from level to level, drawing deep waters from above to below, to this physical plane. As the verse states, 'I will answer the heavens and they will answer the earth.' And in regard to a lack of divine effulgence, the verse states, 'And I will place your heavens as bronze and your earth as copper.' And the verse states, 'And He will stop the heavens and there will be no rain and the earth will not give its produce.' And as a whole this level of reality contains the entire matter of the *Chapter of Song.* As our sages said, 'If you place His sovereignty in the land' – there is no blade of grass that does not have a heavenly minister striking it and telling it, 'Grow.' And that is referring to heavenly ministers of mountains, ministers of hills, ministers of grasses, ministers of herbs, ministers of plants of the earth, ministers of grain, ministers of trees – all of them authorized to draw down the divine effulgence and the power. And that grows coarser until that power is transformed into physicality. And if not for this life-force that is sent down, no creature of any sort could exist – neither above nor below. And this form is literally the seal of the supernal form […] And the light of the Infinite One, which is clothed in *atzilut* and from there is clothed in *beriah*, and from there is clothed in *yetzirah*, and from there is clothed in *asiah*, descends from level to level until it comes to [its] goal: providing sustenance and support for the lower created beings […] And if a thoughtful person delves into this matter, he will see how they all come from God and are absorbed into Him and live with His life-force that has been sent to them, and that the entire existence of beings is grounded in Him. And when we gain suste-

nance from those creatures inferior to Him, such as plant and animal life, we are not sustained by anything outside of Him [...] And He is He, and everything is one, and there is nothing separate from Him [...] And the thoughtful person should delve with his mind in the manner of 'racing out and returning,' and he will find that there is something hidden in these words of ours, which it is not fitting to reveal, not even by one individual orally to another. And if [a person] merits, he will intuit the secret of Hashem on his own, and the person who attains it should not speak it with his mouth, for this matter is 'not revealed even from the heart to the mouth.'[67]

The *Chapter of Song* is a part of an inclusive view of a devolution of worlds from the light of the Infinite One to the physical world. The *Chapter of Song* is an expression of the presence of the divine in the word.

We can understand from R. Moshe Cordovero's words, although this is not the only possible interpretation, that the song referred to is not only a song of created beings to the Creator, but also a song of divinity that exists within the world. It is the revelation and expression of the divine life-force found in everything. The devolution of worlds descends to the lowest of created beings, to every blade of grass, clothed within all levels until 'the goal: sustenance and support for the low created beings,' and is revealed in the song that rises from all beings on their respective levels.

R. Moshe Cordovero explicitly describes the presence of God in a manner suggesting pantheism when he defines the relationship between God and the world as a relationship of identification – 'and He is He and all is one, and there is nothing separate from Him.' As part of this viewpoint of the devolution of the worlds and the oneness of God and the world, R. Moshe Cordovero states, 'Within the whole of this level is the entire matter of the *Chapter of Song*.'

This passage also states that the light clothed in the world gives life to everything. But the context indicates that R. Moshe Cordovero does not deal with the magical aspect of that light and with the possibility of one using it to subdue all created beings under his hand. Rather, he focuses on the question of the identification of God and the world, with an ontological description of the presence of divinity in the world and of man's ability to experience that divine presence.

R. Moshe Cordovero concludes by stating that the insights he discusses cannot be attained through the regular path of knowledge but only via 'racing out and returning.' And even after a person attains them, he cannot conceptualize them verbally. This refers not to the problem of transmitting them to another, for even the person who attained these insights cannot verbally describe his experience to himself, 'for this matter is not revealed from the heart to the mouth.'[68]

Basing himself on these words, Yosef ben Shlomo writes:

> From an intuitive realization regarding 'racing out and returning' (which marks the type of awareness of all mystical, supernal truths), the kabbalist can come to a mystical, supernal experience in which he sees that the divine essence in itself spreads throughout the worlds [...] He sees as well from his own perspective the immanence of God in the world. It is possible to say that at this ecstatic moment the kabbalist comes to the boundary of all human understanding.[69]

R. Moshe Cordovero's words bring us back to the discussion in *Vayihi Miketz* where the topic of melody and song is mentioned as part of a discussion about the presence of holiness and divinity in the world. Similarly, we saw that R. Nachman links melody with the model of the devolution of holiness throughout the world – i.e., the ontological model of divine 'hints.'

R. Nachman too could thus have said: 'This level includes the entire matter of the *Chapter of Song*' – i.e., the topic of the *Chapter of Song* may be found to be embedded in the entire discussion regarding the presence of God in the world and in the possibility of understanding Him. Also, R. Moshe Cordovero's insistence that these insights cannot be expressed in words, not even to oneself, is clearly echoed in R. Nachman's words particularly in *Bo el Paroh* (*Likutei Moharan* I 64), to be discussed further on in Chapter 4.

For now, it bears repeating that the entire essence of the doctrine of melody is its relation to those insights that cannot be distilled into speech and designated by words. Thus we see in R. Nachman's approach a development and continuation of Cordoverian teachings not only regarding magical perspectives of melody, but also, and perhaps essentially, in R. Nachman's teachings emphasizing the mystical and ecstatic aspects of song and melody.

3. The Chapter of Song in The Kabbalah of the Ari

Most of the components of R. Moshe Cordovero's perspective found their way into the Ari's approach.[70] The *Chapter of Song* is linked to the ruling heavenly ministers and their ability to draw divine effulgence and vitality to created beings. The Ari also describes a person's ability to use the magical power of melody in order to send divine effulgence to created beings.

> The *Chapter of Song* and what it is about: Know that all created beings in the world are supervised by a heavenly minister. And that is the secret of, 'There is not even one grass blade here below that does

not have a constellation striking it from above and telling it "Grow".'
And behold, via that minister, divine effulgence is drawn to it. And
behold, that heavenly minister cannot bring down any divine effulgence before he first recites song. And via that song, he receives his
own sustenance and life-force, making it possible for him to transmit
divine effulgence below. So all of those songs are of the ministers and
the supernal constellations [...] And indeed, the *Chapter of Song*
states that whoever recites it daily attains a number of levels. And the
reason is that, as you know, man was made in the image of God. And
just as all the upper entities are dependent upon and grasp God's
divine structure, be He blessed, so also all lower creatures grasp the
structure of lower man, and through him they are all blessed. And
so a person who recites the *Chapter of Song* and is able to have in mind
all of the creatures alluded to in it and recites those songs causes
divine effulgence to rest upon all of those created beings.[71]

Malachi Beit-Aryeh states that the Ari makes two original contributions to
R. Moshe Cordovero's explanation of the *Chapter of Song*. The first 'original
contribution of the Ari is in explaining the value and the meaning of the
Chapter of Song as a liturgical text for the mystic.' The second is that the Ari
underscores the anthropomorphic perspective of the *Chapter of Song*.[72]

Beit-Aryeh's statement that the Ari viewed the *Chapter of Song* as 'a liturgical text for the mystic' is not clear, since the Ari's words contain no allusion
to the mystical function of the *Chapter of Song* but solely to its magical function
as a means of bringing divine effulgence into the world.

It seems that Beit-Aryeh uses the word 'mystic' to refer both to magician
and mystic: to a person whose goal is to directly influence the world via non-
physical means, and to a person whose goal is to experience contact and unity
with God or with the upper worlds.[73] If this is the case, then he is correct to
emphasize the magical nature of the *Chapter of Song* and explain the importance of reciting it, for that recital serves as a tool to bring divine effulgence
and life-force to created beings.[74]

However, if we consider the mystical aspect of the *Chapter of Song* – and
ask whether according to the Ari its text serves as a means to attain mystical
experiences or if the song of created beings serves as a means to attain
mystical arousal or is connected in any way with spiritual arousal or any
mystical insight – the answer is negative, at least from the sources of which I
am aware and from those cited by Beit-Aryeh.

A mystical understanding of the *Chapter of Song* is thus not the Ari's
original contribution. Indeed, in R. Moshe Cordovero's writings the *Chapter
of Song* is already understood to provide a clearly mystical experience, whereas
the Ari emphasizes its magical function. [75]

It becomes clear that the mystical function of the *Chapter of Song* as found in the teachings of R. Moshe Cordovero is not found in the kabbalah of the Ari. It thus appears that R. Nachman took the mystical explanation of the *Chapter of Song* and the view of melody as a *mystical* tool, as distinguished from a *magical* tool, from the kabbalah of R. Moshe Cordovero and not from the kabbalah of the Ari.[76] Further on in the chapter, when we discuss the Bratslavian service of *hitbodedut*, we will see an additional example of R. Moshe Cordovero's possible influence on R. Nachman.

4. *Hasidism:* Shivchei HaBesht
An interesting and significant story that conveys the Baal Shem Tov's attitude toward the song of created beings is to be found in *Shivchei Habaal Shem Tov.*

> A story: The rabbi and preacher, R. Aryeh Leib of Polnoyye, very much desired to learn the speech of animals and birds and the speech of palm trees, which he required in order to help him properly deliver rebuke. And since his intention was for the sake of heaven, he decided to travel to the Baal Shem Tov and ask him to teach him those sciences. And he was sure that the Baal Shem Tov would do so, since his intentions were for the sake of heaven. And when he came to the Baal Shem Tov [...] after he left the inn, the Baal Shem Tov told the preacher to sit with him in his wagon, and he sat with him. And the Baal Shem Tov told him, 'I know that your entire purpose in coming to me was only to learn the subject of the speech of birds and so forth. Come and I will teach you well. 'And first of all, you know that in the supernal chariot there is the face of an ox, the face of a man, the face of an eagle, and the face of a lion. And the choicest of them in the chariot is the face of a man, from which vitality is drawn to lower man. 'And from the face of the supernal oxen, after a devolution of levels via cause and effect, and after many constrictions, life-force is drawn to all animals below.' And that is the secret of the *Chapter of Song,* for the level of speech in the supernal chariot regarding every animal, correspondingly devolves lower and lower, into animals and birds. 'And so a person who is wise and understands of his own mind and looks at everything at its root above in the supernal chariot can know the source of all the details of the ways of speech of animals, wild beasts and birds. 'That is the general explanation of the matter.' And in regard to details of these matters, the Baal Shem Tov told the preacher awesome and wondrous secrets, until the preacher knew the matter clearly. And the Baal Shem Tov – since he had revealed to him the essence of the depth of the secret of this subject – parenthetically explained to him

passages from the Zohar and Tikunim. And the preacher listened to these with one ear, while with the other ear he heard how the birds were talking and how the domestic animals and wild animals were speaking. And the Baal Shem Tov explained all of those secrets to the preacher on this trip until they came close to the city. And when they approached the city, the Baal Shem Tov asked him, 'Have you have understood this matter well?' And the preacher told the Baal Shem Tov, 'Yes.' And the Baal Shem Tov passed his hand over the face of the preacher, and the preacher forgot all of the details of the secrets of this subject, and all that he remembered was the introduction. And the Baal Shem Tov laughed and said, 'And if it was necessary for you to know this matter, I myself would hurry to teach you that which was useful for you to serve the Creator. I taught you all of this in order to slake your thirst, but you have forgotten it because this is not part of your service, and "you shall be wholehearted," etc.' And this suffices for a person of under-standing.[77]

The Other Ear

Here for the first time, with R. Nachman's great-grandfather, we see that the *Chapter of Song* is heard outside, as people are traveling in a wagon. With one ear the preacher could hear the words of the Baal Shem Tov, 'and with the other ear he heard how the birds are speaking and how the domestic animals and wild animals are speaking.' The revelation of the secret of the *Chapter of Song* gave the Preacher of Polonya the ability to hear the speech of the wild animals and the birds, in addition to a theoretical understanding of the *Chapter of Song*. The song is the speech of the animals and palm trees themselves, not the song of their heavenly ministers. Indeed, the Baal Shem Tov's 'introduction' states that the chariot above and the face of the animals and birds and man above correspond to those below, and that those above bring down divine effulgence in a graduated fashion to those who receive them below. But the statement remains that 'whoever is wise and under-stands with their own mind and looks at everything at its root above in the supernal chariot can know the source of the details of the ways of speech of the domestic animals and wild animals and birds' here below.

Thus in contradistinction to R. Moshe Cordovero and the Ari's expla-nation of the *Chapter of Song*, which states that the heavenly ministers sing in the high heavens, the secret of the Baal Shem Tov's melody is that a person can hear the *Chapter of Song* arising from the speech of birds and animals here on earth. And indeed, the Preacher of Polonya attained this ability for a few blessed minutes in which he knew the secret of the *Chapter of Song*.[78]

The Maggid of Mezeritch was one who learned the speech of palm trees and the *Chapter of Song* from the Baal Shem Tov, and across whose face the Baal Shem Tov did not pass his hand. So testifies R. Shlomo of Lutzk, a student of the Maggid, in his introduction to *Maggid Devarav L'yaakov.* 'And once I heard from the Maggid's holy mouth that the Baal Shem Tov taught him the speech of birds and the speech of palm trees, etc.'[79] This testimony correlates with a story cited in the name of the author of the *Tanya*, R. Shneur Zalman of Ladi:

> After the rabbi, the Maggid of Mezeritch, passed away, his students began to speak among themselves and to consider the details of his deeds and actions. And the rabbi of Ladi stated, 'None of you knows what our rebbe did regularly every day at dawn. He went for a walk to the swamps and pools of water where the frogs croak.' And no one knew what the rabbi, the Maggid of Mezeritch, had intended by that. So the rabbi of Ladi said, 'I will tell you our rebbe's intent. He went to learn the song that the frogs sing to Hashem ..., as is explained in the *Chapter of Song*. He wanted to hear how they praise and laud Hashem, be He blessed.'[80]

This pleasant story clearly exemplifies the change introduced by Hasidism regarding the *Chapter of Song*. The widespread custom of kabbalists and others of reading daily the text of the *Chapter of Song*, which opens with a description of the frog's song and the praises to God, is transformed into a custom of taking a daily walk at dawn alongside swamps and pools of water in an attempt to hear the song of the frogs. They did not go out to hear the song of the heavenly minister of frogs, nor even *kavanot* and divine hints hidden in the verses of praise attributed to the frog in the *Chapter of Song*, but literally to hear the frogs croak in an attempt to ascertain from them how song and praise rise to God.[81]

The Chapter of Song *and the Elevation of Thoughts*

The Baal Shem Tov's position can been seen as mildly opposing the view of the *Chapter of Song* as a text, even a text with divine hints and *kavanot* in the style of the Ari. At the very least, it appears that the Baal Shem Tov presents an alternative to that view. For the Baal Shem Tov, the secret of the *Chapter of Song* is contemplative mystical activity, in many ways similar to his method of 'raising foreign thoughts.'[82] The basic idea is that a person sees only a reflection, a branch of the root that exists in the supernal world. And thus he must raise his thought from that concrete sight to 'its root above.'

Like R. Moshe Cordovero and R. Nachman's approaches, the Baal Shem Tov's too is presented as being opposite to that of the Ari. The divine effulgence descends from above to give life to the world. But despite the existence of a theological and ontological background from which one might be able to infer the ability of magical activity to draw down the divine effulgence, the Baal Shem Tov focuses on the mystical context of the *Chapter of Song*, not on drawing down divine effulgence. It appears that the service of God associated with the *Chapter of Song* forms a coherent part of the Baal Shem Tov's mystical teaching and is intimately connected to his doctrine of raising foreign thoughts – a doctrine that some have seen as the Baal Shem Tov's novel contribution to Judaism.[83]

R. Nachman's doctrine of melody takes the words of the Baal Shem Tov a step further. R. Nachman clearly and unmistakably calls on people to go out to the fields to hear its song. This Chapter of Song is completely disconnected from the text of the *Chapter of Song* that the kabbalists recited daily. The Bratslavian Chapter of Song summons a man to close his books, including the *Chapter of Song*, to go outdoors to the fields and hear the song of the grasses. This edict that a person connect his own song to the song of created beings is not related to the face of man on the supernal chariot, nor to praising God and intertwining one's praise with the song of the heavenly ministers. This is a summons to man to physically join the choir of song and melody, to stand amidst the grasses and trees, and from their song, and together with their song, pray and pour forth his own melody.[84]

5. R. Levi Yitzchak of Berditchev

R. Yitzchak Abarbanel describes King Solomon as a magician who knew how to affect the heavenly ministers by making use of song. R. Nachman describes the patriarch Jacob as a magician who uses melody in order to influence the Egyptian minister in charge of food.

R. Levi Yitzchak of Berditchev adds Mordecai to the list of magicians who knew the secret of song and used it to cause ministers and kings to view them kindly.[85] R. Levi Yitzchak of Berditchev maintains that Mordecai 'arranged' the Purim miracle with the help of song and forced the heavenly ministers to do his will, so that they compelled Achashverosh to change his mind and alter his relationship with the nation of Israel.[86]

R. Nachman's viewpoint is so similar to those of the Baal Shem Tov and R. Levi Yitzchak of Berditchev that they apparently overlap. Yet a comparison also reveals the uniqueness of the Bratslavian doctrine of melody. For R. Levi Yitzchak, and even more clearly for the Baal Shem Tov, the ability to act in the magical realm is not granted to every individual. R. Levi Yitzchak limits this ability to a *zaddik* who has special knowledge, since a regular person cannot hear the song of the heavenly ministers and is not expected to know 'how the seventy ministers draw effulgence from holiness and their influence and their songs and their service.' According to R. Levi Yitzchak, serving God with melodies does not belong in the religious service of a regular person; rather, 'only the *zaddik* recites that song.'

The Baal Shem Tov sees in the knowledge of melody 'awesome and wondrous secrets,' 'the secret of The *Chapter of Song*,' which he conceals even from the Preacher of Polnoye. The Baal Shem Tov states that if the preacher required that secret for his service of God, the Baal Shem Tov would teach it to him, indicating that the *Chapter of Song* is not intended as part of the divine service of every man. The Baal Shem Tov's words that only '*a person who is wise and understands of his own mind* and looks at everything at its root above in the *supernal chariot* can know the source of all the details of the ways of speech of animals, wild beasts and birds' teach that he saw engagement with the *Chapter of Song* as identical to engagement with the Work of the Chariot, limited by the strictures of the mishnah in *Hagigah*: 'We do not expound … on *the chariot* to an individual unless he is *wise and understands of his own mind.*'[87]

Unlike the Baal Shem Tov and R. Levi Yitzchak, who extend the esoteric approach that characterized the attitude toward the *Chapter of Song* in the kabalistic tradition,[88] R. Nachman views service with melody and with the song of the created beings as a path meant for every individual. It is true that R. Nachman describes Jacob as possessing special knowledge, and in several places he presents melody as part of the service of the *zaddik*, but alongside this he more broadly describes worship with melody as intended 'for every shepherd.' Every individual is called upon to go out and pray in the fields and take part in the song of the grasses.

Making the service of melody relevant for a wider populace is not restricted to using melody as a means of cleaving to God or as 'reviving oneself with a tune,'[89] but even includes melody's magical dimension. As we saw at the beginning of this discussion, R. Nachman recommends that a person sing the melodies of the nations that are subjugating him in order to cause them to cease their evil deeds. Enlisting every individual to thus magically make use of melody rests on the postulate that the melody to be known is not the heavenly melody sung by the heavenly ministers of the nations in the supernal heavens, but the literal melody sung by the gentiles themselves.[90] Thus, in order to sing the melody of the nations one need not be a wise person who understands of his own mind the Work of the Chariot.

The mention of this topic in *Sefer Hamidot*, a guidebook for proper behavior written by R. Nachman, proves that R. Nachman's directives are meant for the broad public and do not require *a priori* esoteric knowledge. Like all such guidebooks,[91] *Sefer Hamidot*, also known as *Sefer Ha'otiot*, does not purport to present kabbalistic or other theories, but to briefly and summarily suggest proper behavior based on the conclusions drawn from the in-depth study of the Torah.[92]

The statement in *Sefer Hamidot* that 'with the melodies that you sing, you awaken the Holy One, blessed be He, to look upon that nation whose melody you sing. Why? Because it is subdued within you'[93] is directed to every individual and does not require any prior kabbalistic knowledge nor any unusual ability in hearing the heavenly song. This is a simple directive to sing the melodies that the gentiles who are persecuting the Jews are accustomed to sing.

6. Between Sorcery and Melody: Prayer as an Alternative to Magic

It is instructive to note that elsewhere R. Nachman constructs an entire teaching that features 'all blades of grass,' prayer as 'the speech of the field' and the supervising heavenly ministers as the conduits transmitting strength to grasses and granting them healing power. That teaching, however, is apparently meant to neutralize the magical aspect of the heavenly ministers by presenting prayer as an alternative to magical activity and the 'word of Hashem' as an alternative to the heavenly ministers.[94]

R. Nachman sees the power of doctors and medicines as dependent upon an astrological and magic framework of the transference of powers from the supernal worlds and stars to the grasses, from which medicines are prepared. The healer is seen as a type of magician proficient in his powers and usages.[95] Healing does not rely upon a chemical and biological causative structure that is visible to the sight of human beings and susceptible to their understanding, but upon the special power of the grasses as coming from the stars, the constellations and the supernal ministers.[96]

The proposal that prayer and the master of prayer serve as an alternative to doctors and to curative, medicinal plants is not based on a denial of the medical worldview nor on skepticism regarding the ability of medicine to heal, but on adding a layer that ascends that naturalistic structure. 'The word of Hashem' stands above everything and gives life to the entire framework. Thus, as soon as the word of Hashem enters the framework there is no more differentiation between one blade of grass and another, or between one heavenly minister and another, for He Who told one grass to heal will tell another grass to heal.[97]

And when does the word of Hashem enter the framework as an active factor and not only as vivifying force? When a person makes use of prayer and the master of prayer. As R. Nachman states:

> And that is what Hizkiyahu said, 'And that which is good in your eyes I did,'[98] regarding which our sages say that he placed the prayer of redemption next to the prayer of *Shemoneh Esrei*, and he

hid away the book of cures. And this is all one, for by placing redemption next to prayer – i.e., by redeeming liberated prayer from exile – in that way he hid away the book of cures.[99] This is because when prayer is liberated, then all medical cures fail, for people are healed by the word of Hashem ... And then all of the doctors are ashamed of their medicinal cures, for then there is no power to any healing modality, for all of the grasses re-invest their power into prayer, which is the aspect of 'the word of Hashem,' which is their supernal root [...] This is because it is the obligation of all the grasses and every herb of the field that when a person stands to pray (at which point he corresponds to the word of Hashem, which is their supernal root), then they re-invest their power into that prayer, which is their supernal root. And when a person prays in regard to a disease, whatever it may be, then those grasses that have the power to heal that illness are obligated to re-invest their power into his prayer, which is their root, corresponding to the word of Hashem [...] And that corresponds to 'And Isaac went out to speak (*suach*) in the field'[100] – that his prayer joined together with the herbs (*siach*) of the field. This is because all of the herbs of the field returned their power and gave these powers into his prayer, which was their root.[101]

The master of prayer as an alternative to the doctor and prayer as an alternative to the book of cures are presented in a framework of that worldview whose foundations we examined in the context of melody. In a technical sense, this is not a view of an alternative reality but a completely different set of values regarding that same reality. A person should turn his concern for being healed to God and rely upon the word of Hashem, not upon heavenly ministers, grasses and doctors.[102]

In the continuation of this teaching,[103] R. Nachman discusses the secret of how Esther found favor in the eyes of all who saw her, a success we know was decisive in the Purim miracle. Here too, R. Nachman posits an alternative to the act of magic, an alternative that seems directed also to contradict the magical explanation that R. Levi Yitzchak of Berditchev gave to the Purim holiday. R. Levi Yitzchak explained that Mordechai knew the secret of melody and sang the melodies of the king, thus forcing the king to love him and do his will. R. Nachman employs a similar structure, but at its center stands not the magician Mordechai but the master of prayer, Esther:

And that is the aspect of gaining favor, corresponding to the verse, 'And Esther gained favor in the eyes of all who saw her' (*Esther* 2:15), regarding which our sages explain that 'each person saw her as a

member of his nation' (*Megillah* 13). This is because the master of
prayer is the aspect of the word of Hashem, which is the supernal
root, from which all the powers and all the host of heaven receive
their effulgence. And so, to all the host of heaven and all the
supernal ministers – to each one, he appears as though he belongs
to its nation – i.e., he finds favor in their eyes, and it appears to each
one that he is dealing with it alone, for they all receive effulgence
from him.[104]

Like R. Levi Yitzchak, R. Nachman too speaks of the ability to find favor in
the eyes of every nation and every king and supernal minister. But in contrast
to the words of R. Levi Yitzchak of Berditchev and in apparent contrast to his
own words in *Likutei Moharan* II 63, R. Nachman states here that the means
to attain this ability is not knowledge of the king's unique melody but prayer.
Further on, we will see that R. Nachman contrasts the *zaddik*, who is the
master of prayer, with the heavenly ministers and doctors and also with
zaddikim who use magic.

And that corresponds to, 'For you have found favor in my eyes and
I know you by name' (*Exodus* 33:17). This means that via the aspect
of gaining favor – which corresponds to 'and the host of heaven will
bow down to you,' i.e., that everyone receives and borrows from him
– he gains favor in their eyes. This corresponds to, 'It appeared to
each individual as though he belonged to his nation' … . As a result
of that, 'And I know you by name' – you will then be able to know
and recognize all of those famous men, masters of the name. This
is because a person who is famed and possesses a name due to his
arrogance falls before this person.[105]

In the framework of the host of heaven are also 'famous men, masters of the
name.' 'Famous men' is a term that R. Nachman regularly uses to refer to
Hasidic *zaddikim*, amongst whom are 'famous men of falsehood,' whom R.
Nachman did not hesitate to excoriate.[106] Here, R. Nachman refers to
famous men as 'masters of the name,' using the double meaning of the
phrase 'master of the name:' a famous person whose name has gone through
the world and a person involved in holy names and magic.[107] Here too we
notice that although R. Nachman disassociates himself from these 'famous
men, masters of the name,' he does not deny their abilities.[108] He does,
however, offer an alternative superior to them: the *zaddik*, the master of
prayer.

R. Nachman's trenchant attack on 'masters of the name' and doctors
raises the following question: what is the difference between the melody that

Jacob sent to influence the minister of Pharaoh and the way that doctors and masters of the name use their knowledge to affect the heavenly ministers and the grasses? And, what is the difference between singing the melody of a particular nation in order to turn its heart to you for good and the use of grasses for healing?[109]

It appears that R. Nachman's reservation is to be understood specifically against the background of his doctrine of melody. To be 'one who knows music' is not a simple technical matter but an inner process of extracting the good spirit from the evil spirit. As stated, R. Nachman does not deny the magical stratum of melody, but apparently opposes the use of any magic that is detached from the spiritual and inward dimension; such usage was the *modus operandi* of 'masters of names' and doctors. In R. Nachman's view, a person engaged in magical activity that possesses no trace of spirituality and holiness and that is not part of an inner process is engaged in witchcraft; even if his deed is effective, he should refrain from it. R. Nachman is not opposed to attempts to bring healing and relief via the power of grasses, but only in the context of prayer and connection with the word of Hashem.

R. Nachman requires that those who deal with the powers of the grasses must be able to hear the song of the grasses and integrate it into their prayer; they must also be able to gather and draw together voices of joy and of a spirit of holiness from the aggregate of spirits and voices, so as to construct from them a melody of joy. The ability to uncover this spiritual dimension, an ability R. Nachman calls 'knowing music,'[110] endows high value on the activity with grasses of which R. Nachman speaks, for it can lead to a spirit of holiness and prophecy. Contrarily, magical activity disconnected from the word of Hashem and from prayer is like the activity of the 'masters of the name' and doctors, against whom R. Nachman inveighs.

This point of view is expressed clearly in R. Nachman's attitude to prayer accompanied by the *kavanot* of the Ari:

> One of 'the men of our peace' told me that he was speaking with our rebbe, of blessed memory, about the service of Hashem, as was our rebbe's way. And our rebbe, of blessed memory, understood that he was involved somewhat in making use of the *kavanot* in his prayer. And our rebbe, of blessed memory, grew very stern with him and told him to no longer involve himself with that, and not to pray with *kavanot*. Rather, he should only have in mind the simple meaning of the words. (This is the case even though this man had learned the writings of the Ari, of blessed memory, in accordance with R. Nachman's directive – nevertheless, R. Nachman did not want him to pray with *kavanot* at all.) And our rebbe, of blessed memory, told him that if a person is not fit to pray with *kavanot* but does so anyway,

doing so is comparable to witchcraft. This is because in regard to witch-craft, the verse states 'Do not learn to do,'[111] regarding which our sages expounded, 'Do not learn to do – but you may learn to understand and to teach.'[112] The same is true regarding *kavanot* – not to mention the two in the same breath – one must learn them only to understand and to teach, but not to use them – i.e., not to have them in mind while in prayer, if one is not fit for that. And R. Nachman said that the essence of prayer is cleaving to Hashem, be He blessed, and it would be better to pray in the spoken language. This is because when a person prays in his spoken language, then his heart is close to and cleaves a great deal to his words of prayer, and he can bring himself to cleave exceedingly to Hashem, be He blessed. However, the Men of the Great Assembly arranged the order of prayer for us (since not every individual is able to arrange the order of prayer for himself, as has been stated). Therefore, we are obligated to pray in the Holy Tongue, as it has been arranged for us. But the main thing is only to have in mind the simple meaning of the words. And that is the essence of the prayer that we pray before Hashem, be He blessed, for every-thing. And in this way we come close to cleave to Him, be He blessed. And a person who speaks the Holy Tongue regularly, such as a resident of Jerusalem, has no need to think of the meaning of the words in his mind. But he must turn his ear to what he is saying. And this is the essence of his intent in prayer. And for the true *zaddikim* who are great in stature, all of the *kavanot* of the Ari, of blessed memory, etc., are the simple meaning of the words. This is because their understanding of the words includes all of the *kavanot*.[113]

The *kavanot* are an activity suitable solely for a person for whom they constitute his natural language, and which he can use to help him cling to God. If they are engaged in mechanically, as though they are a foreign tongue, then, even if the person believes in them, his prayer corresponds to witchcraft. The central distinction as to whether one is engaging in the equivalent of witchcraft or legitimate prayer depends whether the person praying with *kavanot* can cleave to God.

R. Nachman explains the analogy with witchcraft as being rooted in our sages' teaching: 'Do not learn to do, but you may learn to understand and teach;' *kavanot* too should be taught, but one should not pray with them. It appears, though, that this explanation is intended less to clarify the meaning of the analogy than it is intended to moderate the shocking equation between praying with the *kavanot* of the Ari and witchcraft. This explanation of the analogy, after all, does not answer the central question: why is it wrong to pray with the Ari's *kavanot* if a person is not 'fit'?

The answer to this question arises from the analogy itself: reciting kabbalistic formulas that do not help a person cleave to God is like reciting witchcraft formulas directed to supernatural forces and heavenly ministers in an attempt to utilize their help while remaining disengaged from God. If using *kavanot* prevents a person from cleaving to God, clearly he is not turning to God in his prayer, but to a panoply of forces, *partzufim* and spiritual worlds – an activity analogous to turning to the heavenly ministers, stars and constellations. And thus such prayer is witchcraft. But if a person incorporates the *kavanot* of the Ari into his prayer so that they lead him to cleave to God, that is not witchcraft but prayer. R. Nachman's attitude toward *kavanot* is repeated in his view of melody. When a person is engaged in the mystical dimension of cleaving to God, the use of melody is no longer regarded as witchcraft and an act of the 'masters of the name,' but is transformed into part of the worlds of praying and cleaving to God.

7. The Doctrine of Melody: Summation and Intermediate Conclusions

R. Nachman combines different mystical approaches: some see melody as a means of attaining emotional arousal that can lead to divine inspiration and prophecy, and others are magical traditions regarding the character and power of music and melody.[114]

R. Nachman's teachings and talks on the topic of melody may be classified into those in which the mystical stratum is dominant[115] and those in which the magical effect of melody is central.[116] However, even when one strain is dominant, at times one can also find traces of the other perspective and its influences.[117]

I contend that we may see in R. Nachman's emphasis on the mystical characteristics of melody and of the *Chapter of Song* a continuation and development of the foundations that were laid in the kabbalah of R. Moshe Cordovero, and which are not found in the kabbalah of the Ari. This thesis accords with the general picture of the characteristics of Hasidism in regard to its predecessors. Whereas the kabbalah of the Ari emphasizes the doctrine of divinity and focuses on describing the supernal worlds and the intradivine dynamics, Hasidism emphasizes the knowledge of man, the understanding of the dynamics of his inner soul and of how a man might come to cleave to God. This goal has no more in common with the directives in R. Moshe Cordovero's kabbalah, whose root is in the prophetic kabbalah, than it does with the directives in the Ari's kabbalah.

From the topic that we are examining we may conclude that Hasidism interpreted processes and ideas that were essentially relevant to the magical tradition in a way that emphasized their psychological and mystical association. And just as the relocation of kabbalistic terms and descriptions of divine processes to the study of man did not erase their original meaning as the

Torah of divinity, so too the shifting of magical terms to the mystical and inner realm did not erase their relevance to the magical realm.

It is possible to see R. Nachman's doctrine of melody as a view of the mystical-magical model that Idel defines as the central model of Hasidic mysticism,[118] although R. Nachman's specific manner of combining the mystical and magical components is entirely unique. R. Nachman does not discuss two distinct phases, the first mystical and the second magical, nor a process of mystical 'racing out' and magical 'return.' Rather, in his description, the magical activity that affects the world is itself the mystical activity. The mystical activity is not just a prior condition for the existence of the magical stratum, but is itself the magical activity.

For R. Nachman, magic and mysticism are not opposites that can co-exist, despite the contradiction and tensions between them.[119] Rather, they are two perspectives on the same world. The magical influence on grasses is profoundly linked to the mystical experience of hearing the holy melody; moreover, hearing the song is itself a 'magical act,' just as it is a 'mystical act.'[120] The rich traditions surrounding melody, whether regarding its magical characteristics, or its mystical properties, are woven, in R. Nachman's doctrine of melody, into one tapestry, whose various components are blended seamlessly together. This view of the world, in which distinctions between mysticism and magic are foreign, can be seen as a continuation of the mystical-magical world view of the Baal Shem Tov.[121]

Conclusion of Part I: The Sequence of Vayihi Miketz

Before continuing the analysis of *Vayihi Miketz*, let us review what we have learned so far. R. Nachman posits the unification of '*Hashem, Elokim,*' the constant awareness of God and constant cleaving to the upper world as a general goal of religious service. The unification of God's name and awareness must be a person's constant mindset aimed at uncovering the holiness and divinity in the world.

R. Nachman offers two ontological images to depict holiness in the world, within which a person shapes the nature of his turning to holiness and strives to cleave to God. The first image represents a framework of emanation from the Infinite One to the physical world, in which the act of God is described as God constricting Himself within His physical garments. The second image represents holiness as existing in the form of sparks scattered throughout the world.

Congruent with these ontological models, R. Nachman constructs three behaviors with which to reach and cling to holiness. The first is interpreting divine hints; the second is raising divine sparks; and the third is engaging in melody, which relies on the two prior models.

The doctrine of melody that R. Nachman develops in *Vayihi Miketz* does not deal with the magical strata of melody, but focuses solely on its mystical strata: revealing spirituality, experiencing goodness and joy, and constructing melody that leads a person to a holy spirit and prophecy.

Part II: States of Nocturnal Consciousness: Sleep, Dream and Wakefulness (Hitbodedut)

In the life of the Bratslav Hasid and mystic, night is the central time for spiritual activity and experience.[122] Hidden in the night are possibilities to reach states of consciousness that would be difficult, if not impossible, to attain during the day. R. Nachman describes the unique quality of night on a number of occasions, both in terms of his teaching practices, his behavior and regarding the centrality of 'night' in religious practice that is still very much alive in Bratslav communities today.[123]

Nocturnal religious practice is understood to apply to three specific areas: unconscious activity during sleep, activity in the state of consciousness unique to a dream state, and activity within a waking consciousness that takes place specifically during the night hours.

I. Sleep as a Part of the Second Behavioral Model: Raising Sparks

The night is an important time for spiritual experience not only for the mystic who is awake, but also for the common man sleeping soundly in bed. In the second model of conduct described by R. Nachman, we saw that even a person who lacks the intellect with which to inquire into the presence of holiness in the world and to understand divine hints participates in an unconscious process of raising sparks during sleep.[124] As I have pointed out, R. Nachman's words are based on the assertion in the kabbalah of the Ari, that the process of raising sparks takes place during sleep.[125] R. Nachman explains: 'This is because sleep is the aspect of causing one's thought to cling to the world-to-come in general ... the aspect of "*Hashem, Elokim*"... for during the time of sleep the soul rises to the world-to-come.'[126]

The assertion that the soul rises to the world-to-come during sleep is based on the Talmudic and kabbalistic tradition, according to which sleep is a taste of death, when the soul rises to the upper world. Awaking is the soul's return from the supernal world; thus when a person awakens he recites the blessing 'Who returns souls to dead corpses.'[127]

R. Nachman sees in the rising of the soul during sleep a specific instance of the process of 'the unification of "*Hashem, Elokim*",' which he discusses throughout *Vayihi Miketz*. This unification, in which a person's soul participates, does not occur at his initiative, nor is it dependent upon his will. It involves the raising of sparks and a renewed connection of 'low holiness' with the' supernal world' – but in contrasting R. Nachman's first example, this encounter does not require meaningful speech or the awareness of divine hints.

The definition of sleep as 'the aspect of causing one's thought to cleave to the upper world in general' apparently encompasses a radical shift in the meaning of the concept, 'cleaving with one's thought.' The topic of cleaving to the transcendent with one's thought has a long history in kabbalah and in Hasidism. The various approaches to the cleaving of thought share the idea that it is a conscious mental activity process – 'thought.'[128] But R. Nachman describes this 'cleaving of thought' as occurring during sleep, a time in which man apparently rests from his thoughts, including thoughts of cleaving to God. And thus R. Nachman broadens the scope of 'cleaving of thought' to include even states in which a person is unconscious of his environment. This is made particularly clear by the fact that Hasidic thinkers typically cited sleep as a time when a person must interrupt cleaving to God, since then he cannot continue contemplating and cleaving to God.[129]

We will see further along that it was clear to R. Nachman too that sleep is a time when cleaving to God in thought is interrupted. But R. Nachman argues that nevertheless, in a certain sense, a person continues to cleave to God in his sleep. This cleaving takes place when the soul rises during sleep, even though the person has not prepared himself for it. The concept of the ascent of the soul can also refer to a conscious and volitional occurrence, but R. Nachman is dealing with a different type of ascent of the soul: that which occurs every night independent of a person's will and conscious awareness. In that sense, night and sleep are a time of mystical activity – contact with and literal cleaving to holiness and the supernal world – that takes place even though the person is unaware of the occurrences of his soul.

1. Melody, Sleep and the Babylonian Talmud

At the beginning of Chapter 1 we discussed the connection linking melody, prophecy and madness, and cited the teaching *Akrukta*, in which R. Nachman describes melody as drawing its power from the same place that the prophets draw their prophecy: 'for he takes the melody from the same place from which the prophets draw.'[130] We will now see that in *Akrukta*, as well, where the connection between melody and prophecy is clear, R. Nachman links the components of service via melody – i.e., extracting the good spirit and judging others favorably – with night:

Behold, when a person hears melody from a wicked musician, it is harmful to his worship of the Creator. But when he hears melody from a kosher and worthy musician, then that is good for him [...] And the rectification that makes it possible for him to hear melody from anyone is to learn at night the oral Torah – i.e., Talmud, which is the aspect of night. As we find in the midrash, when Moses was on the mountain for forty days and forty nights, he did not know when it was day and when it was night. But when he learned the written Torah, he knew that it was day and when he learned the oral Torah, he knew that it was night. So we see that the oral Torah is the aspect of night. And as our sages of blessed memory have said, on the verse, '"In the dark places He placed me" – that is the Babylonian Talmud.' And the verse states, 'And the darkness He called night.' That is to say, by learning Talmud, a person rectifies the six rings in the larynx, from which the voice comes. And that is the meaning of 'Arise, sing in the night.' That is to say, that singing should rise – i.e., via the night, which is Talmud. [...] And this explains the sequence in the mishnah, 'Make for yourself a teacher, and acquire for yourself a companion, and judge everyone favorably.' This is because, as a result of hearing melody ..., a person rectifies the makeup of his sovereignty. And then, when he rectifies the aspect of his sovereignty and is able to rule over all that he desires, and is able to kill one person and give life to another, and he finds that then the world would be destroyed. Considering such an eventuality, the Mishnah states, 'And judge every individual favorably' – that one must judge every individual favorably. This is because the Holy One, blessed be He, does not desire the destruction of the world, 'not for chaos did he create it; for habitation did he form it.'[131]

R. Nachman describes 'night' literally as a time when it is appropriate to learn Talmud in order to rectify the capability of melody, and also as a symbol of the nature of that learning.

As in *Likutei Moharan* II 63, R. Nachman here too connects the ability to sing melodies with sovereignty and ruling. But in contrast to *Likutei Moharan* II 63, which discusses the useful purposes that can result from knowing melodies, R. Nachman here discusses the possibility of destruction concealed within this ability: 'and so the world would be destroyed.' The danger inherent in making improper use of the power of melody necessitates linking melody to judging others favorably, so that the melody will indeed raise the good and not the evil spirit, and maintain the existence of created beings rather than lead to the destruction of the world.

2. Sleep as an Aspect of Learning

Why is learning Talmud 'the aspect of night' and the aspect of 'dark places,'
and what can we learn from this about R. Nachman's view of night? In
Akrukta, R. Nachman offers no explanation, but makes do with providing a
basis to his linkage of learning and night by homiletically citing proof texts
from verses and midrashim. In the teaching *Ashrei Ha'am*[132] though
R. Nachman offers a somewhat broader explanation of the connection
between learning Talmud and night, between learning the simple meaning
of Torah and sleep and faith:

> And renewing the intelligence, i.e., renewing the soul, comes about
> through sleep […] As the holy Zohar teaches,[133] 'They are new every
> morning, great is your faithfulness.'[134] This is because when the
> mind grows weary, it is renewed as a result of sleep, as we can see with
> our own senses. And that is why we recite the blessing, 'He who gives
> the weary strength,' for they were at first weary and now they have
> been strengthened. And during sleep, the 'mind – i.e., the soul –
> enters into faith, the aspect of "they are new every morning," etc.,
> as the holy Zohar states.'[135] And there are a number of aspects of
> sleep. There is physical sleep, which gives rest to the mind. There is
> also the aspect of learning, which is also called sleeping in
> comparison with cleaving to the Creator. And that is learning the
> simple meaning of the Torah, which is the aspect of sleep.[136] As our
> sages of blessed memory state, '"You have placed me in the dark
> places" – that is the Babylonian Talmud.'[137] And that is the aspect
> of faith, as the verse states, 'And your faithfulness in the nights.'[138]
> 'And the darkness He called night.'[139] And when a person constantly
> cleaves to the service of the Creator, and his mind grows weary
> because of his great cleaving to God, he should at that time learn the
> simple Torah. And when he learns the simple meaning of the Torah,
> then his mind – i.e., his soul – enters into faith, in the aspect of 'they
> are new every morning,' and is renewed and regains strength after
> their weariness. And that is the aspect of *pashta, munach, zarka*.[140]
> This is because the simple meaning (*pashta*) of the Torah, which is
> the aspect of 'and our faithfulness in the nights,' gives rest (*munach*)
> to the mind, so that the mind is renewed, as it was previously […]
> And the principal mind that one receives, come through faith… And
> that is the aspect of night. As the verse states, 'And your faithfulness
> in the nights.' And it is the aspect of the simple meaning of the
> Torah. As the verse states, 'You have placed me in the dark places,'
> etc. And a verse states, 'And the dark he called night.'

R. Nachman uses sleep to describe various states of consciousness in which the 'mind' is inactive and the 'intellect' remains at rest. Sleep is a time in which 'a person's "mind" – i.e., his soul – enters into faith.' During night and sleep the 'mind' is absent, not in the sense of being totally nullified, but of being in a state of quiescence. And as we saw in Chapter 1, when the mind and the intellect descend from their central place in a person's consciousness, the imaginative faculty ascends, accompanied by faith. In that state, the slumbering 'mind' is immersed in faith, leading to a renewal of the mind.

When a person is asleep, his mind is inactive and he is completely unconscious of his surroundings. In that state he enters 'into faith,' insofar as his soul rises and clings to the world-to-come. As we saw in *Vayihi Mikeitz*, the ascent of the soul to the supernal world is the aspect of cleaving and faith, even though the person remains unconscious.[141]

And in regard to spiritual sleep, learning the simple meaning of Torah, which is identified here with learning the Babylonian Talmud, is called 'the aspect of sleep.' This statement is grounded in the idea that the waking state and sleep are opposites that parallel the measure of a person's cleaving to God. Constant thinking about God and remembering holiness is defined as wakefulness and awareness, while forgetting God and the supernal world is a state of being unaware and not awake, defined as sleep. Precisely because learning demands intellectual effort and focus, it prevents a person from cleaving to and focusing on God; when a person's thoughts are involved with learning, he cannot at the same time keep God and the supernal world in mind. Thus R. Nachman defines the time of learning as a time of forgetting and sleep.[142]

It is possible that R. Nachman's association of sleep with learning particularly the Oral Torah rather than the written Torah derives from the fact that when a person learns the written Torah, he maintains an ongoing awareness that he is reading the words of the living God – the presence of God in the written Torah is manifest, dominant and omnipresent, and leaves no room for forgetting. Conversely, in the Oral Torah, God's presence is not so direct and He is not mentioned at every turn, leading a person immersed in a Talmudic passage to forget the world and its Creator. And thus, learning is the aspect of sleep in relation to cleaving to God.

3. Business Activities in the Aspect of Sleep

In addition to the distinction between spiritual sleep and physical sleep, R. Nachman in *Ashrei Ha'am* discusses an additional aspect of sleep: faithful business dealings.[143] Business activities are another example of an activity that demands attention, and apparently, therefore, contradicts the state of cleaving to God. When a person engages in business faithfully, he is immersed in learning the laws of money and his constant thoughts about how to conduct his business in accordance with faithfulness and halakhah comprise an aspect of learning Torah. In this way, a person deeply involved in business has a state of consciousness parallel to that of someone who is learning the Oral Torah, which is defined as 'the aspect of sleep' in relation to thinking about God. On the other hand, as stated above, this aspect of sleep also contains within an ascent of the soul to the world-to-come; the process involving this type of unconscious cleaving to God occurs both during Torah learning and during faithful business endeavors.

Since learning the simple meaning of the Torah and engaging in faithful business transactions are an aspect of sleep, we may conclude that they too, like sleep, possess within a spontaneous ascent of sparks and the unification of '*Hashem, Elokim.*'

> And that is the meaning of the verse, 'Fortunate are the people that know the trumpet blast.' That is the aspect of raising the eleven ingredients of the incense, which are embedded within the gentiles and the lands that surround *faithful business practices, to which sparks are attached.* And that is the meaning of 'that know the trumpet] blast.' 'That know' – 'know' has the meaning of connecting. 'Trumpet blast' – 'blast' is related to the word for shattering, *for the sparks come from the shattering of the vessels.* 'Hashem, in the light of your face will they go out.' That is *the aspect of business.* As the verse states, 'Rejoice, Zevulun, when you go out.'[144] *That is to say, when a person engages in business dealings faithfully, in order to bring his soul into the aspect of 'They are new every morning, great is your faithfulness,' in order to receive from the light of the divine countenance a renewed mind, a renewed soul, then as a result all of the sparks rise via the eleven ingredients of the incense.*[145]

We see clearly that all of these aspects of sleep relate to the model of raising sparks, a model that R. Nachman here augments with an ensemble of components from the Lurianic model: raising sparks in sleep,[146] raising sparks in business,[147] the danger of being grasped by the *kelipott* (husks) precisely during the raising of the sparks[148] and the connection between the sparks and the eleven incense ingredients.[149] All these Lurianic components serve as a conceptual and structural base for R. Nachman's teaching.

The mystical nocturnal activity that takes place during sleep belongs to the model of the second manner of conducting oneself in regard to the presence of holiness in the world – a model of how the common person participates in the great work of 'the unification of "*Hashem, Elokim*".' This unification is accomplished by means of processes that raise sparks relating to a person even if he is unaware of them and lacks the necessary ability to mentally investigate the 'divine hints' and 'unifications.'

II. *The Night of the Third Model:* Hitbodedut, *Melody and Inspiration*

Parallel to developing the model of raising sparks in sleep, R. Nachman develops an additional 'night' activity performed in a waking state of consciousness. Its express goal is to arrive at mystical experiences and attainments, and its preferred time is the night.

At the end of *Likutei Moharan* 54, R. Nachman describes the night as the optimal time for the service of melody. He describes a broad ensemble of spiritual activities with a mystical goal that are linked to melody and are meant to be performed at night. Night is the principal time for *hitbodedut,* searching for good points, extracting the good spirit from the evil spirit and constructing melody. These actions transform the night into a fitting time for cleaving to the world-to-come. And of the various parts of the night, the best time for awakening and melody is midnight:

> And that is the aspect of 'I will recollect my melody at night, with my heart shall I speak, and my spirit shall search.'[150] During the night, which is the time for the depositing of spirits, the aspect of 'in Your hand will I entrust my spirit,' that is the time to extract the good spirit from the midst of the evil spirit – i.e., for that is the principal time for *hitbodedut,* for a person to engage in *hitbodedut* by isolating himself with his Maker and expressing his speech before Hashem, be He blessed, speaking with his heart and seeking the good spirit – i.e., the good points that are still within him, in order to extract them from the evil spirit. This is the aspect of melody [...], and as a result this person's memory is guarded [...] That is to say, as a result of this a person merits recalling his ultimate purpose in the world-to-come and he thinks constantly of his end and causes his thoughts to cling to the world-to-come constantly, all of which is the aspect of 'memory'[...] And that is 'at night,' for the principal extraction of the good spirit takes place at night, for that is the time of depositing spirits [...] And that is the aspect of arising at midnight. This is because a harp was suspended over David's bed, and when midnight arrived, it would play melody of itself (as our sages of blessed memory state – *Berachot* 3b). That is to say, at midnight the aspect of the melody of holiness, which is drawn from the harp of David, which is the aspect of extracting the good spirit, etc., is awakened [...] And so that is the proper time to grow stronger in the service of Hashem, to arise at that time in order to engage in the service of Hashem, in order to express one's speech before Him, be He blessed. This is because that midnight is the principal opportunity for extracting

> the good spirit from the bad, via the aspect of melody played
> upon an instrument […], which is the aspect of the harp of David,
> which plays at that time […] And understand these words well to
> put them into practice.

Here R. Nachman develops, to a limited extent, his understanding of why
the night is conducive to the service of melody and his description of the
connection between arising at midnight[151] and melody. The citation of both
the Talmudic story about David rising at midnight to sing and play music
and the Tanakhic story about David the musician who composed joyful
melodies – when, 'as a result, prophecy rested upon the prophets, as in the
verse, "Take for me a musician"'[152] – makes clear the mystical intent of
hitbodedut, rising at midnight and melody, which are intended to act
together to bring a person to divine inspiration and prophecy.

   Here, too, R. Nachman describes the uniqueness of the night as the
time of 'depositing of spirits, the aspect of "in your hand I entrust my
spirit",' an apparent allusion to the rising of the soul that occurs at night.
The rising of the soul fits well into the framework of the model of raising
sparks, for when the soul rises, it raises with it all of the sparks with which
it is associated. In the framework of the present description of serving
God in the waking state, however, when the soul remains on earth below,
it is not clear how the night, as a time of the rising of the soul and the
depositing of souls in God's hand, is connected with the ability of a person
who is awake to make melody and extract the good spirit from the bad.

   In this teaching, R. Nachman does not develop this topic, which
remains indistinct and germinal. Elsewhere, however, he expands this
discussion and explains how night, a time for sleep and a time for the soul
to rise, is relevant as well to those who remain awake, and why the night is
the optimal time for mystical attainments even when a person is awake and
conscious.

1. 'Sleep, Sweet and Good'
In *Tiku Emunah*, examined in Chapter 1, while discussing the imaginative
faculty, R. Nachman speaks of sleep as a time when the intellect is absent.
The absence of the intellect is presented in that context as positive and
desirable.[153] And out of this positive view of sleep as a time when the
rational mind (*da'at*) is absent, a person is called upon to bring himself of
his own initiative to a state of 'casting away his rational mind (*da'at*),' and
come to the aspect of sleep.[154]

   Faith is dependent upon the imaginative faculty, whose intensive
activity occurs precisely when the rational mind is absent. The types of
consciousness most conducive to the positive activity of the imaginative

faculty are sleep, dreams and other states of mind that a person activates when he casts away all cleverness and intellect from his consciousness; at this point his imaginative faculty takes center stage in his consciousness, and with its aid he can attain mystical experiences on various levels of contact with the holy. A person can reach spiritual attainments in a dream, in prophecy and via melody that he could not reach by remaining in the daily consciousness of rational mind and intelligence. Only the transition to a night-consciousness, with the absence of intellect and the ascent of the imagination, make their attainment possible.

We see, therefore, that when R. Nachman describes the service of melody as a service of the night, he presents it as existing particularly when a person is in those states of consciousness characterized by the absence of the rational mind, states in which a person's actions and attainments are characterized by faith. Melody, together with the other components of nocturnal service – *hitbodedut*, prayer/speech with one's Maker and raising the good spirit – are all in the aspect of 'and your faithfulness in the nights.'

2. On the Mystical Nature of the Service of Hitbodedut[155]
Hitbodedut provides the general framework for the ensemble of religious practices at night performed in a waking state. It is difficult to exaggerate the importance of *hitbodedut* in the eyes of R. Nachman[156] and in the world of Bratslav Hasidim. Indeed, the *hitbodedut* service is one of the defining characteristics of Bratslav Hasidism, both for R. Nachman[157] and for his Hasidim to this day.[158] The nature of Bratslavian *hitbodedut* and its connection to the night is explicated in the teaching, *Haneior Balailah*. This teaching was delivered at the beginning of 5563 (1802), about two years before *Likutei Moharan* 54, *Vayihi Miketz*, was delivered.

> But to attain this, to be absorbed into one's root – i.e., to return to God and to be absorbed into the oneness of Hashem, be He blessed, who is the Necessary Existent – can only be achieved via self-nullification, when a person nullifies himself entirely, until he is absorbed into God's oneness, be He blessed. And it is only possible to come to that self-nullification via *hitbodedut*, for when a person engages in *hitbodedut* and expresses his speech privately to his maker, as a result he is able to nullify all of his lusts and evil traits, until he nullifies all of his physicality and is absorbed into his root [...] Know that the essence of self-nullification, when a person nullifies his being and becomes nothing and is absorbed into the oneness of Hashem, be He blessed, comes only through *hitbodedut*.[159]

R. Nachman clearly describes absorption into God[160] as the central goal of *hitbodedut.* The path to that goal passes through an initial stage of nullifying one's lusts and evil traits, and a second stage in which a person nullifies his physicality, arriving at total self-annihilation. This comprises the key and necessary condition for being absorbed into God.[161] This process can take place solely through *hitbodedut. Hitbodedut* is thus a long process with various stages, whose goal is the complete extinguishing of self-awareness, as a preparation to cleaving to and being absorbed into God.

In their description of the nature of Bratslavian prayer and of the service of *hitbodedut,* Weiss and Green focus on the first stage of *hitbodedut,* in which a person 'speaks at length in private with his Maker.' Weiss completely ignores the climactic end of this talk, which clearly depicts a state of mystical unification, writing: 'We find that the Bratslavian life of prayer coalesces into a new concept of "private discussion with one's Maker" – prayer is an aspect of speech between one individual and another, not an occasion for the ecstasy of the nullification of being.'[162]

Yet R. Nachman's words are clear: 'his speech in private with his maker' is the path and means whereby a person 'merits to nullify all of his physicality and to be absorbed into his root.' R. Nachman explicitly mentions what Weiss calls the 'ecstasy of the nullification of being' as the patent goal of *hitbodedut.* 'Nullifying one's being and becoming nothing and being absorbed into the oneness of Hashem, be He blessed, comes only via *hitbodedut.*'[163] Prayer in *hitbodedut* is a golden opportunity and the most appropriate time, according to R. Nachman, to attain such a nullification of being.

In his book *The Tormented Master,* Green accepts the general portrait of R. Nachman and of R. Nachman's world as presented by Weiss. Green is aware of R. Nachman's mystical side and also of the existence of the mystical in the service of *hitbodedut.*[164] Nevertheless, when Green engages in a lengthy discussion of *hitbodedut,*[165] he describes only its initial stages, the 'outpouring of the soul,' and completely ignores its mystical aspect. Green even concludes from his discussion of *hitbodedut* that there is something daring in the Bratslavian service of *hitbodedut* insofar as it comes from the recognition 'that such a life of an inner openness and of a person's speech with his maker are in a certain aspect all that is truly important.'[166]

Mendel Feikazh has noted that in a number of central teachings on the topic of *hitbodedut* R. Nachman describes speech between a person and God as no more than a means of coming to the desired goal – a goal certainly even more 'truly important' than the path that R. Nachman offers as leading to it – of mystical unity.[167]

Weiss and Green's focus on the first part of the service of *hitbodedut* divorced from its purpose and from how it fits into the framework of the entire process has led to a mistaken concept about Bratslavian prayer. This concept has had critical ramifications in regard to the Weiss and Green's principal claims about the place of mysticism in the world of R. Nachman and the principal characteristics of his spiritual world.

There is a puzzling question, which does not cast doubt on the existence and centrality of the mystical goal in prayer, in *hitbodedut* and in a cluster of Bratslavian values, but which relates to the specific nature of cleaving to God and the longed-for mystical unification. Is absorption into God to be understood as a clear-cut case of total *unio mystica*, or is it perhaps to be understood as a unification in which a person, despite the nullification of his physical being, remains distinct from God even in the course of his absorption?[168] But regarding the centrality of the mystical goal in prayer/speech and in *hitbodedut*, R. Nachman is explicit here and elsewhere, leaving no room for doubt that in his eyes the mystical experience is the paramount goal of the religious man, a goal that he can and must achieve.

Nevertheless, this does not suffice to reject Green and Weiss's understanding of 'speech between oneself and one's maker' as a unique component in Bratslavian prayer, a component deserving of analysis. Furthermore, even though in *Haneior Balailah* and elsewhere R. Nachman describes speech as a means of arriving at mystical unification, other teachings imply that speech has inherent value.[169] I will again point out, however, that even if we recognize the character of speech as personal, in which 'a person speaks before Hashem, blessed be He, as a man speaks to his friend,'[170] still the higher stage in *hitbodedut* is of mystical union and the 'ecstasy of nullification of being.'

I will now proceed to examine the possibility that prayer, whose nature is clearly that of dialogue and is at its core communication between two separate and independent beings, is itself part of the preparation for mystical experience.

3. Prayer of Supplication and Mystical Prayer
R. Nachman's words about prayer as speech fit with his words in praise of supplicatory prayer for even the most minor and incidental matters:

> I heard from one of R. Nachman's followers that once our Rebbe, may his memory be for a blessing, spoke with him regarding clothing, and told him that a person must pray for everything – i.e., if his garment is torn and he needs a new garment, he should pray to Hashem, be He blessed, to give him a garment to wear. And so also in anything similar, whether great or small – for everything he should accustom himself to pray constantly to Hashem, be He blessed, for everything that he lacks, even though the principal thing is to pray for the principal thing – i.e., to be able to serve

Hashem, be He blessed, to merit to come close to God, be He blessed – nevertheless, one must pray for this as well.[171]

These words directly contradict the outlook of the Maggid of Mezeritch's school, which calls upon a person to pray 'only for the Shechinah' and to refrain from praying for personal needs. The dismissal of prayer for one's personal needs was precipitated by the goal of creating prayer that leads to cleaving to God and to mystical experience.[172]

Joseph Weiss, and to a lesser degree Arthur Green, deduce from this that prayer for one's needs contradicts the nature of the mystical quest:[173]

> The requirement for a person at prayer to strip himself of his being, of his literal 'I,' of his personal needs, is a typical mystical requirement. Supplicatory prayer inspired by difficult circumstances is not ideal mystical prayer. So we learn that the mystical school within Hasidism presents the nullification of the identity of the person praying from a number of perspectives: both in the extinguishing of personal consciousness and in the extinguishing of the personal nature of the request. If one prays only to repair the imperfection of the Shechinah and prayer itself is divinity, then that is a closed circle and not a means of creating a relationship between speaker and listener. On the other hand, the life of prayer that is found in Bratslav is always in the aspect of supplication and imploring … [174]

However, to reiterate, although this presentation of two polar opposites is quite logical, it does not correspond to the mystical world of R. Nachman. Although R. Nachman instructs a person to pray for his personal needs, even the most minor ones, he still proffers mystical unification and absorption in God as the purpose of prayer:[175] 'And for us that is the essence of the goal – that prayer should be incorporated into the oneness of God, be He blessed, in the aspect of "He is your praise and He is your God" – that prayer and Hashem, be He blessed, are one, as it were. And that is truly the essence of the goal.'[176]

There is no clearer way to state that 'prayer itself is divinity.' In light of these words, one cannot say that prayer is 'constantly in the aspect of supplication and imploring.' Indeed, for R. Nachman, 'truly the essence of the goal' of prayer and the goal of a person generally is absorption into God's oneness.

There are many paths to mysticism: some people seize upon joy as their principal instrument to attain inspiration; others emphasize suffering and weeping as a means of attaining visions and revelation; for some, music provides the means and evocation for inspiration; for others, tranquility and silence provide the proper background; others still make use of different techniques at different times.

Nevertheless, there is no doubt that the particular nature of any path influences the ultimate character of the outcome. And thus, there is great significance in the difference between R. Nachman's directive that a person pray for his needs, and the dismissal of such prayer in the teachings of the Maggid of Mezeritch's school, even if this distinction does not eradicate the two's shared mystical goal.

When we attempt to characterize R. Nachman's view of prayer as opposed to the view held by those schools influenced by the Maggid of Mezerich, which denigrate supplication, it is possible to suggest that Weiss's distinction between the 'Hasidism of faith' of R. Nachman and the 'Hasidism of mysticism' of the Maggid of Mezeritch be replaced by a distinction between the 'mysticism of faith' of R. Nachman and the 'mysticism of knowledge' of the Maggid of Mezeritch. And, regarding the school of the Maggid, we are not speaking of engaging in divine concepts in the philosophical sense, nor in intellectual activity in the style of the *kavanot* of the Ari; nevertheless, mystical activity is connected to the world of *da'at* and *mochin*. A person is advised, as a path to cleaving to God and attaining mystical experience, to concentrate his thought on the divine immanence and focus entirely on the idea that 'there is no place empty of Him' and that 'the whole earth is filled with His glory,' and as a result come to self-annihilation and make contact with the divinity that 'fills all worlds.'[177] One aid to walking on this path is focusing on letters and their meaning,[178] a way of serving God in which a person's rational mind and intellect play a principal role.

On the other hand, as we saw in the previous chapters, R. Nachman states that even a person who has attained insights and possesses a formidable intellect must, when he comes to any service of God, cast away his intellect and those attainments; precisely this will enable him to cling to God as the path to cleaving to God does not pass through the rational mind. Rather, it requires the renunciation of the rational mind, total self-dedication and service of God, aided by simple acts of worship and simple prayer.

4. Speech, Crying Out, Great Weeping: the Ecstasy of Suffering as a means to Attain Self-Nullification and Mystical Unification

When a person engages in speech with his maker under the appropriate conditions of time and place and fulfills other conditions, such as nullification of his physicality and willingness to give up his life, this can lead to an outburst of great weeping and cleaving to God that involves unification with and absorption into God.

The service of *hitbodedut* in the Bratslavian sense is similar to 'casting away one's intellect;' it is not the service of God with one's rational mind. As we will see further on, the setting of the time, place and forum appropriate for *hitbodedut* are intended to reinforce a person's disengagement from his rational mind and a normal state of consciousness so that he may pass to a different state of consciousness of absorption into God.

Even though supplicatory speech between a person and his maker originates in troubles and sufferings, it strengthens the feeling that enables him to come to be enveloped by God, like a son pleading before his father.

Praying about the hardship and difficulty of existence can bring a person to a state of suffering,[179] crying out,[180] and vigorous weeping; this in turn can lead to a person being ecstatically carried away in pain and suffering, dissociating from himself and from his rational mind; from here a pathway opens for him to a state of consciousness of self-nullification and complete absorption into God.

It is important to emphasize that at the end of the spiritual process that a person goes through during *hitbodedut* he emerges from his state of suffering and comes to joy. The process, which makes use of suffering and weeping as a tool to intensify feeling and acts as a means to help one enter the ecstatic state, does not end with suffering and depression. Even the ecstasy of the outcries and weeping are only an intermediary phase toward the stage containing joy and inspiration – 'after a broken heart comes joy.'[181] Moreover, the criterion by which to measure whether a person has experienced suffering and a broken heart, which are positive phenomena, rather than depression and bitterness, which are negative phenomena, is the ability of this stage to lead him to the following stage, which is joy. 'And that is a sign that tells us if this person had a broken heart: if he comes afterwards to joy.'[182]

R. Nachman locates this process of being carried along by suffering to absorption and nullification into God not only in the context of the service of *hitbodedut*. A clear description of the various stages in this spiritual process is found in his teaching, *Vayomer Boaz El Ruth*:

> For via a person's sufferings, he comes to the aspect of self-nulli-
> fication … . And afterwards, even though he has returned from
> that self-nullification, nevertheless, by means of the residue that
> remains of that nullification, a renewal of the Torah is brought
> about. This is because by means of that self-nullification, in which
> he had been nullified to the ultimate, and realized that all of his
> sufferings are very great favors, as a result of that he was filled with
> joy.[183]

Here R. Nachman states clearly that sufferings comprise a motivating force that leads a person to the aspect of self-nullification. And at that time, those sufferings are eradicated: 'at the time of nullification, when one is nullified to the ultimate … then one's sufferings are truly nullified.'[184] In the third stage, that of returning from self-nullification, not only are those sufferings eliminated, but with the strength that comes from the residue of the state of nullification a person comes to joy.

We are to similarly understand the processes of *hitbodedut*. A person expresses his sufferings and troubles, and precisely out of that personal, painful speech can be drawn, along with his suffering, to self-nullification and absorption into God.

Now I wish to return to my claim that the nature of the service of Bratslavian *hitbodedut* does not focus on the intellect, but involves casting away the rational mind. To support this contention, I will deal briefly with a number of additional components in the *hitbodedut* service – time, place, weeping and nullification of self to the point of death – and in the specific meaning that R. Nachman grants these.

The Time

> But the essence of *hitbodedut* is attained at night, when the world is freed of the trouble of this world. This is because during the day people are pursuing this world, which bemuses and confuses a person so that he cannot cling to and be absorbed into Hashem, be He blessed. And even if he himself is not encumbered by the world, nevertheless, since everyone else is then encumbered by the world and is at that time pursuing the vanities of this world, it is difficult at that time for him to attain self-nullification.[185]

The consciousness of the day is a disordered state of mind, not because of any specific thought or disturbance, but because people in the world are disordered and confused. Even if a person is engaged in *hitbodedut*, even if he is not involved in any particular this-worldly affair and is apparently undisturbed and tranquil, during the daytime hours his consciousness grows disturbed and confused, and he cannot disengage himself from his physical affairs and nullify himself. The consciousness of night, in contrast, is characterized by a calm rational mind and by the ability to disconnect oneself from one's ties to the physical world, and as a result to arrive at a nullification of being.

Sichot Haran quotes a pleasing parable of R. Nachman that illustrates the difference between these states of consciousness:

> I heard that R. Nachman said: Certainly there are kosher people who do not engage in *hitbodedut*. But I call them confused. And

suddenly when the messiah comes and calls them, they will be disoriented and confused. But we will be silent, like a person after sleep, whose mind (*da'at*) is at rest and well-settled. So will our mind (*da'at*) be settled and at rest, without any disorder and confusion.[186]

Hitbodedut is therefore meant to produce a person with a consciousness marked by a calm and settled mind; this is the key to disengaging one's thought from its ties to this world until one attains self-annihilation, which makes mystical unification possible.

The Place

In *Haneior Balailah,* R. Nachman points out the ability of *hitbodedut* to help a person attain a state of self-nullification:

> And it is also necessary that *hitbodedut* be done in a special place: outside the city, in a lone area, in a place where people do not go. This is because in a place where people go during the day as they pursue the things of this world, even though they are not going there now, that too disturbs one's *hitbodedut,* and a person cannot nullify himself and be incorporated into God, blessed be He. Thus, he must go by himself in the night-time on a lone path in a place where there are no people. He must go there and engage in *hitbodedut,* turning his heart and rational mind from all the affairs of this world and nullifying everything, until he merits to truly attain the aspect of nullification.[187]

Here, in *Haneior Balailah,* the designation of place is made in a negative manner. Elsewhere, however, R. Nachman presents 'outside the city' in a positive sense too: 'I found a written manuscript of the comrades in which it is written that R. Nachman stated that it is better that the *hitbodedut* occur outside the city in a place of grasses, because the grasses help the heart to awaken.'[188]

As we have seen, the awakening of the heart that occurs outside the city amidst the grasses is connected directly to the song of the grasses, both in the *Chapter of Song* and in R. Nachman's doctrine of melody:

> And our Rebbe, of blessed memory, told his Hasid: 'Go for a walk with me.' And he went with him outside town, and he walked amidst the grasses. And our Rebbe, of blessed memory, said, 'If you merited to hear the voice of the songs and praises of the grasses, how each blade of grass expresses song to Hashem, be He blessed,

without ulterior motive and without any foreign thoughts and without expecting any payment of reward, how fine and pleasant it is when we hear their song and it is very good to serve Hashem with fear in their midst.'[189]

The place for *hitbodedut* is defined on the basis of two central criteria: distance from people and their tumult, and the proximity to the grasses. It appears that these two criteria characterize the two stages of *hitbodedut* and its two basic components. Whereas the first criterion is intended to eradicate the tumult of the world and create silence, the second is intended to enable hearing the melody. This is possible only if a person is in a state of tranquility and has a settled mind. Whereas the first criterion applies to an array of ways to serve God, such as nullifying lust, nullifying one's physicality, and gaining equanimity and self-annihilation, the second involves inspiration and holy spirit, symbolized by melody and song.

Song and melody in this context are not only the means of gaining inspiration, joy and an exalted spirit; R. Nachman uses them to describe the image of inspiration itself, the revelation of holiness implicit within the world. This refers not to the prophetic disciples playing upon the harp and violin,[190] but to the song of the grasses and the elevation of melody, which is the good spirit and the spirit of holiness.[191]

In his book, *Shiur Komah* R. Moshe Cordovero describes the *hitbodedut* that the prophetic students engaged in:

> The students of prophecy would prepare themselves for prophecy, for which they required joy. As the verse states, '"Bring me a musician" – and when the musician played, etc.' And they would engage in *hitbodedut*. In accordance with their knowledge, they would engage in *hitbodedut* to attain the wondrous levels and the stripping away of their physicality and the strengthening of their intellect over their bodies, until the physical was left behind and they did not sense it at all, but were aware only of all their comprehension of Torah discourses and the structure of those supernal levels. And they would engage in *hitbodedut* and be stripped of physicality and rise upwards. And this constitutes a person's preparation that he carries out. The other factor is the preparation of the place, as in 'When I leave the city, I will stretch out my hands to Hashem,' and as in 'And I went out to the valley.'[192]

Here a rich collection of components and phases on the path of preparing oneself for prophecy is presented: joy, melody, *hitbodedut,* stripping away the physical, and the choice of a proper place, characterized by actions like leaving the city and going to the valley. This agglomeration is astonishingly similar to the components that we find in R. Nachman's teachings. It goes without saying that this parallel does not diminish the unique character of Bratslavian *hitbodedut* and melody, which are very different from that described by R. Moshe Cordovero. But this parallel of so many details offers additional testimony as to the continuity of the kabbalistic traditions that have a mystical-prophetic goal – from the kabbalah of R. Moshe Cordovero to the world of R. Nachman of Bratslav.[193]

Vigorous Weeping

> Regarding *hitbodedut* and speech between a person and his maker, the recital of *Psalms* and supplications, it is very good when a person merits to recite these with a truly whole heart, until he merits to weep before Hashem, be He blessed, like a son weeping before his father. But, R. Nachman, said that when a person recites supplications and pleadings with the conscious goal of weeping, that intent is not good. And this also confuses his mind, because as a result he cannot recite the supplications with a whole heart, with wholeness. This is because during the time of reciting supplications and pleadings a person must remove all sorts of superficial thoughts that are in this world, and only turn his mind to the words that he is speaking before Hashem, be He blessed, as a man speaking to his colleague. And then his heart will easily be spontaneously aroused, until he comes to vigorous weeping. But when he thinks about and anticipates crying, then he succeeds in neither praying nor weeping, because his recital of prayer is itself confused as a result of this anticipation [...] This is because the fact that he is thinking of and anticipating weeping is itself the aspect of a foreign thought that confuses his intent, so that as a result he is unable to pay sufficient attention to what he is saying. The principal thing is to recite the words in truth before Hashem, be He blessed, without any other thoughts at all [...] And if a person merits to truly weep, how good; and if not, not – but he should not confound his recital of prayers for the sake of weeping.[194]

It is possible to see this 'vigorous weeping' as a final goal, as attaining a particular way of standing before God, an inherently desirable ideal. However, it is more likely that this weeping serves as a means of entering the 'ecstasy of suffering' that leads to mystical experience. And as R. Nachman stated, 'By means of sufferings, a person comes to the aspect of nullification.'[195] Weeping apparently plays a central role in this mystical praxis employed by many mystics in Jewish mysticism[196] and in the Hasidic world in particular.

R. Nachman describes weeping as a necessary means not only to attainments gained in *hitbodedut*, but also to achieving novel Torah insights: 'A person who wishes to create new Torah insights of substance must first cry.'[197] This is not a figure of speech but a practice in which R. Nachman himself engaged.

> When R. Nachman spoke this teaching [...] that before creating new Torah thoughts it is necessary to cry. He said then of himself that every time he creates new Torah insights he first cries. At that time we ourselves saw this with our own eyes, for at that time he delivered the teaching *Vayomer Boaz El Rut*, on Friday evening, the holy Sabbath, in the summer of 5566 (1806). Also before that he taught the teaching *Da Sheyesh Arich Anpin Diklipah*, etc. (*Likutei Moharan* 242). And on the Thursday before that he wept before us, and on the Sabbath afterwards he told the matter (mentioned above) on the verse, 'I have mingled my drink with weeping.' And there is much to tell in this regard.[198]

Total Self-Dedication – Unto Death

Hitbodedut takes place at night, since the night is the aspect of sleep, and sleep is like death,[199] when the soul rises to the world-to-come. Similarly, the service of *hitbodedut* includes a state in which a person 'nullifies his being and becomes nothing.'[200] Taking nullification as far as it can go may lead to a nullification of existence – unto death.[201] R. Nachman, who is aware of this danger, sees it as an essential part of the state of *hitbodedut*:

> R. Nachman said that the essence of completely realized *hitbodedut* and speech between a person and his maker is that a person expresses his speech so much before Hashem, blessed be He, that he comes very close to having his soul leave, heaven forbid, so that he almost dies, heaven forbid, coming to the point that his soul is connected to his body by no more than a hair, due to the power of his genuine suffering and his yearning and longing for Hashem, be He blessed. As our sages state, 'A person's prayer is heard only if he places his soul in his hand.' (*Taanit* 8)[202]

R. Nachman does not caution against this danger, but encourages a person to tread upon the threshold of death and come within a hairsbreadth of his soul leaving his body. R. Yitzchak of Acco discusses the danger of death integral to *hitbodedut*, warning the reader that it is not proper to act in this fashion.[203] Similarly, *Tzavaat Haribash* warns: 'when a person wants to be in *hitbodedut,* he must have a colleague with him; but a person alone is in danger; rather, there should be two people in one room, each engaging in *hitbodedut* with the Creator, be He blessed.'[204] In contrast, R. Nachman tells his Hasidism that the service of *hitbodedut* is complete only when a person comes to a state in which he 'is very close to having his soul leave,' due to the intensity of his suffering and anguish. As already noted, this is an excellent example of the ecstasy of suffering, for R. Nachman explicitly directs his Hasidim to be swept up into suffering, pain and yearning, with a forcefulness leading to ecstatic states in which the soul disconnects from the body to the point of endangering one's life.

While R. Nachman frequently adds the phrase, 'heaven forbid,' he ultimately does call for coming to a state verging upon death. The danger of death that accompanies *hitbodedut* is connected to the ultimate nullification, in an attempt to achieve contact with the Infinite One. And as R. Nachman explicitly states elsewhere: 'And as a result of prayer with total self-dedication, a person nullifies all of his physicality so that there is no boundary, so that, there being no boundary, he can attain the Torah of the future, which is not finite, nor grasped within the finite.'[205]

The attestation of utter self-sacrifice as a necessary condition for the speech of *hitbodedut* teaches that the essence of *hitbodedut* is not contained within speech between a person and his maker; rather, *hitbodedut* is seen as a way to enter extreme mystical states of the nullification of being and absorption into God, which threaten the very being of the person as a separate identity.[206] Defining 'the essence of *hitbodedut*' as a state in which a person's 'soul is very close to leaving,' and refraining from the mitigating methods cited in *Tzavaat Haribash,* indicate to what degree Weiss's description of prayer as 'remaining always on the level of speech between two individual beings'[207] is far from properly construing the 'essence of *hitbodedut*' and Bratslavian prayer.

For R. Nachman the speech between a person and his maker also serves as a way of attaining other mystical states of cleaving to God – i.e., those that lead to states of inspired speech. Instances of prophesying, in which 'the Shechinah speaks from the throat' of the *zaddik,* were common in Hasidism, and were part of the mystical experience of inspiration that transforms a person into a medium for the Shechinah, which speaks from his throat.[208] These states are described by R. Nachman in a number of places.[209] But what is important to us now is R. Nachman's testimony that he himself reached such states as a result of his 'supplications and imploring' and speech before God:

He told us that it was his way to recite a great many supplications and imploring before Hashem, be He blessed, as he sat at the table at the third Sabbath meal in his room alone. And he engaged in a great deal of speech to Hashem, be He blessed, until he began to speak Torah spontaneously, without any design at all. And he listened to the words of this Torah that were coming from his mouth, and he saw that they were matters that were excellent and worthy of being communicated. 'And they are the things that I taught at times following the Sabbath, after *havdalah.*' That is to say, those words came from the Torah that he spontaneously recited at the third Sabbath meal ...[210]

This does not refer to a request that is answered at a later stage, but to an uninterrupted process beginning with supplications and imploring and proceeding in an unconscious and undirected manner to spontaneously spoken Torah, occuring of itself: 'until he began to speak Torah spontaneously, without any design at all.'

An example of the most extreme application of R. Nachman's directive to attain, through *hitbodedut,* a state bordering on death is found in the following story from *Chayei Moharan*:

R. Nachman, of blessed memory, directed one of his greatest students, when that man was a youth, that during *hitbodedut* he should speak a great deal and in detail to all the limbs of his body, and explain to them that all of the lusts of the body are vanity, for the end of every man is to die, and the body will be brought to the grave and all of his limbs will decay, etc., and the like. And this man engaged in this practice for a length of time. And afterwards he spoke with our Rebbe, of blessed memory, and complained to him that his body was not heeding and feeling any of his words and his arguments with his body. Our Rebbe, of blessed memory, told him, 'Be strong in this matter and do not weaken from engaging in it, and you will see afterwards what will result from these words.' And the man heeded R. Nachman's counsel and fulfilled his words until he merited afterwards that every limb with which he spoke in detail was drawn after his words to such a degree that his life-force literally left it and it remained without any force and feeling whatsoever. And he experienced this with his senses in regard to his outer limbs, such as his fingers and toes and the like, until, in regard to his inner organs, on which the life-force depends, such as the heart and the like, he had to restrain his words a great deal so that the life-force wouldn't leave him literally, may the Compassionate One preserve us. And I heard that one time this man spoke with people close to him on the theme of how this world is nothing, and he questioned the purpose of all matters of the body, etc. And in the midst of his words he fainted and began to expire (in Yiddish: he was faint). And he had to make great efforts until he came back and his life-force awoke in him. And he said then that he merited via the holiness of our Rebbe, of blessed memory, to attain such a level that every time he reminded himself strongly of the fear of punishment and the goal of all the matters of this world, then he felt as though all of his limbs, even his little toe, literally, were already lying in the grave and rotting and etc., until he needed great strength to retain his life-force within himself, so that his soul would not leave him literally, may the Compassionate One preserve us.[211]

This example does not comprise all the complexity and subtlety that we noticed when discussing R. Nachman's words on the service of *hitbodedut*, the elevation of the good spirit, and melody. Nevertheless, this story shows us clearly the practical usage of *hitbodedut,* and the extreme states of consciousness to which the service of Bratslavian *hitbodedut* can and is expected to lead.[212]

A brief comparison with a passage from Maimonides underscores from another vantage point the unique nature of Bratslavian *hitbodedut* and of the psycho-physiological state of the breakdown of the faculty of the body attendant to it. Maimonides too cites *hitbodedut* as service preparatory for prophecy,[213] and he too describes in this regard the loss of sensation and the breakdown of the physical faculty that takes place during the prophetic experience: 'and all of them, when they prophesy, their limbs shake and their bodily power body falters, and their thoughts grow wild and their mind remains empty so that it is free to understand what it sees.'[214]

But in complete contrast to R. Nachman, who sees the role of the states of night, sleep and *hitbodedut* as leading to a nullification of the physical so that a person will be able 'to cast away his intellect' and empty his consciousness of ordinary and rational mind so as to allow room for faith and prophecy, according to Maimonides the breakdown of the bodily structure has an opposite function: its goal is to create a state in which an area of consciousness is entirely free to focus on the activity of the mind occurring during prophecy.

Regarding the service of *hitbodedut* and treading upon the threshold of death as a way of coming to cleave to God, there were apparently fundamental experiences in R. Nachman's childhood that had an influence well into his adult life:

In the village of Usyatin, near the town of Medvedivke, lived the father-in-law of R. Nachman, of blessed memory, where R. Nachman spent his formative years. A large river flows there upon whose banks grow a very great amount of reeds and grasses. It was the holy custom of our master, our teacher and our rabbi, that righteous and holy man of blessed memory, to occasionally take a small boat and sail with it alone into that river [...], even though he could not steer the boat well. Nevertheless, he would sail with it beyond the reeds to where he could no longer be seen. And there he did what he did in the service of Hashem, be He blessed, in prayer and *hitbodedut* – fortunate is he. And so he truly merited what he merited, as we may see clearly from his holy books regarding that boat (which has been mentioned above) – because he went with the boat into the river and he did not know how to guide the boat, and when he went into the river far from the dry land and had no idea what to do, for the boat was moving along and he almost sank, heaven forbid, he then cried out to Hashem, be He blessed, and raised his hands to Him properly (and also the same thing happened when he was hanging by his hands on the wall in Tiberias, when he wanted to flee from the plague, may the Compassionate One protect us, etc., and saw beneath him the Sea of Galilee, and he almost, almost fell – as is described elsewhere in the story of his journey to the land of Israel – then he too cried out in his heart to Hashem, be He blessed, in a suitable manner). And he would tell this regularly because he wished to place in our hearts the awareness that every individual must cry out in such a way to Hashem, be He blessed, and raise his heart to God, be He blessed, as though he is in the middle of the sea, hanging by a hair, and a storm wind is raging to the heart of the heavens so that no one knows what to do and there is almost no time to cry out. But in truth, a person certainly has no counsel and escape except to raise his eyes and his heart to Hashem, be He blessed. Thus, it is necessary at every moment to engage in *hitbodedut* and cry out to Hashem, be He blessed, for man is in great danger in this world, as everyone knows in his soul. And understand these words well.[215]

R. Nachman would repeatedly tell his Hasidism this story in order to teach them the way of cleaving to God and the mystical absorption into God. That way is the path of *hitbodedut* – of crying out as one stands at the threshold of death, as one feels that one's life is hanging by a thread: 'the essence of the nullification, when a person nullifies his being and becomes nothing, and is absorbed into the oneness of Hashem, be He blessed, is attained by nothing else than by means of *hitbodedut*.'[216]

R. Nachman, who used such drastic measures as *hitbodedut* in the middle of a flowing river in order to come to states of self-sacrifice, sees it proper to bequeath to his Hasidim the service of the nullification of one's being until one comes close to death as a vital component in the service of *hitbodedut*. As an adult, R. Nachman no longer advises people to volitionally enter into life-threatening situations, but 'makes do' with advising them to expose themselves to life-threatening danger caused by the force of *hitbodedut* itself.[217]

Weiss's contention that in his youth R. Nachman overcame death by using the idea of the sanctification of God's name and in his adulthood by using the idea of the depths of sacrifice, addresses only a fraction of R. Nachman's many attitudes toward death and to the states that border upon death, attitudes from which it is possible to feel not only an 'awesome fear,'[218] but also to hear a certain ring of longing and to feel some of the captivating scent of 'the sweet seduction' of mystical death.[219]

Green's words that a 'sick fascination with death and the inner conflict with it' stand at the center of R. Nachman's interest in death,[220] also fail, in my mind, to grasp the process that occurs upon the threshold of death for R. Nachman, as well as for many other mystics. Setting aside the mystical components in R. Nachman's world and ignoring his unceasing yearning for mystical unification with God[221] has led these scholars to see R. Nachman's attraction to death as an isolated factor in itself, and to avoid seeing that it comprises a vital step in the mystical process of attaining unification with God. Green's description of a yearning for God as 'a sick fascination with death' is an extreme and unjustified reductionism.

III. On the Place of Cleaving to God in the Thought of R. Nachman

Green contends that in contrast to the general spirit within Hasidism, which posits cleaving to God as the central goal in a person's religious life and minimizes the importance of kabbalistic 'rectification,' thus neutralizing the messianic tension that such 'rectification' engendered, 'R. Nachman dismissed cleaving to God and brought the "rectification" back to its former place.'[222]

Green combines his idea of this dismissal of cleaving to God with a description of R. Nachman's view of the world as 'a place in which sin is considered to be a heavy burden and in which God stands from afar,' in consequence of which 'it is not a comfortable place to develop the concept of cleaving to God.'[223] Thus, Green argues, that 'we should not be at all surprised to find that the Hasidic ideal of cleaving to God does not get much attention in R. Nachman's writings.'[224]

Green's observation regarding cleaving to God is not isolated, but serves as a basis for a complete thesis[225] explaining R. Nachman's uniqueness and originality in the Hasidic world. It also describes a messianic fervor that held sway in Bratslav, which, according to Green, led to 'a way of life that was eschatological at its core, that stands as a sign of a vision of the end of days ... a living and active messianism whose like was not known beforehand in the Hasidic camp.'[226] All of this is in consequence of R. Nachman's putative rejection of cleaving to God and his restoring the kabbalistic 'rectification.'

In the last three chapters, we have clearly seen not only that mystical experience and mystical ideal exists in R. Nachman's teachings, something that Green himself discusses, rather that it is the central and dominant place of cleaving to God and mystical unification in R. Nachman's thought and in the framework of the behaviors in which he directed his Hasidim to engage. Although R. Nachman refers to constant thought on God and contact with holiness as 'unification,' 'recalling constantly,' 'causing one's thought to cling,' 'melody' and so forth, there is no doubt that these are all various aspects and branches of cleaving to God, the central goal in R. Nachman's world.

It is impossible to continue to accept the overall picture that Green has drawn of R. Nachman's world, a picture based on the rejection of the idea of cleaving to God and the diminishment of its importance. This picture leads to mistaken notions of R. Nachman's view of prayer, *hitbodedut*, the attraction to death, the concept of faith, and messianic tension as well as other components in R. Nachman's world to be discussed further on.

In this chapter, we have seen that the service of *hitbodedut*, whose centrality even Green attests to, and which is one of the most characteristic elements of Bratslav Hasidism,[227] presents a decidedly mystical world view and an attempt to shape a way of life that is entirely, from its goal to its smallest details, directed toward mystical cleaving to God. In light of all this, it is impossible to continue to argue that what Green calls 'a religious way of life in which *hitbodedut* stands at its existential center'[228] is characterized by a rejection of cleaving to God. It is certainly not feasible to construct an entire interpretive structure of R. Nachman's thought on the basis of this putative rejection of cleaving to God. R. Nachman of Bratslav was firmly ensconced in the camp of Hasidism and a full partner in establishing cleaving to God as the most important of religious values. Cleaving to God was the goal and challenge of each individual on his level, whether through faith or through prophecy.[229]

The absence of rational mind is seen here too as a basic component in the Bratslavian mystical experience, and appears not only in teachings of a clearly theoretical nature, discussed at length in previous chapters, but also in actual behaviors that R. Nachman required of his Hasidim, and which have come to represent the Bratslavian way of worship: *hitbodedut* and melody.

Notes

1 See *Likutei Moharan* II 120.

2 *Isaiah* 66:1.

3 *Tzavaat HaRibash*, 1, sections 2–3; ibid., 1–3, section 1–10.

4 *Likutei Moharan* I 54:8.

5 *Yemei Moharant*, Part II, 17, 145.

6 *Yemei Moharant*, Part I, 74, 104–105.

7 Quoted by Shtil, *Psicholog*, 57–58. Ibid., 105–108, 188–193. See also idem, *Chidat Ha'energiah Hanafshit*, 193–195.

8 *Likutei Moharan* I 54.

9 Jonathan Shtil has termed this 'a dialogical act' – i.e., a man's daily life expresses his dialogue with Hashem. Shtil, *Psicholog*, 93.

10 *Alim Litrufah*, letter 394, 344.

11 *Psalms* 96:3.

12 *Deuteronomy* 10:21.

13 *Sichot Haran*, 52, 37.

14 *Shivchei Haran* 10, 6.

15 *Lamentations* 2:18.

16 *Likutei Moharan* II 5:2.

17 *Psalms* 52:25.

18 *Likutei Moharan* II 5:2.

19 See Idel, *'Yofyah shel Ishah,'* especially 320–324.

20 *Likutei Moharan* I 54 and 64. See Idel, *Hachasidut*, 164–174. see Scholem, *Pirkei Yesod*, 104–108, 207–209; Tishbi, *Torat Hara*, 52–61. See Idel, *'Musag hatzimtzum,'* 112–159.

21 See Tishbi, *Torat Hara*, 17.

22 Tishbi, *Torat Hara*, 131–132.

23 See Tishbi, *Torat Hara*, particularly 21–61, 123–134.

24 See *Avot* 4:3.

25 Tishbi, *Torat Hara*, 127.

26 See Jacobs, *'The Uplifting of Sparks in Later Jewish Mysticism,'* 99–126 and particularly 116–117, 122–123. Ibid., 124–125.

27 See Meroz, *'Milikutei Efraim Pantzeiri,'* 211–257 and particularly 237–242.

28 Tishbi, *Torat Hara*, 130.

29 R. Chaim Vital, *Shaar Hakavanot, Derushei Halailah, Derush* 4, 348.

30 Ibid. *Inyan Derushei Halailah, Derush* 3, 343 and onward.

31 *Derushei Halailah*, in particular *Derushim* 3, 4 and 8.

32 See Weiss, *'The Kavvanoth of Prayer in Early Hasidism,'* 95–125; Shatz-Oppenheimer, *Hachasidut K'mistikah*, 129–147; Etkes, *Baal Hashem*, 139–140; Idel, *Hachasidut*, 267–278. See Kallus, 'The Relation of the Baal Shem Tov to the Practice of Lurrianic Kavvanot in Light of his Comments on the Siddur Rahkov,' 151–167. *Tzavaat Haribash*, section 23, 4.

33 Ibid.

34 *Likutei Moharan* I 54:6.

35 *Likutei Moharan* I 2.

36 *Likutei Moharan* I 54:6.

37 Ibid.

38 See Tishbi, *Torat Hara*, 123–124.

39 *Proverbs* 30:4.

40 *Ezekiel* 47:3.

41 *Likutei Moharan* I 54:6.

42 *Chayei Moharan, Maalat Torato*, 1. See Shtil, *Psicholog*, 34, 51–52.

43 *Sichot Moharan*, 273,169. For more on the revivifying power of melody, see *Chayei Moharan*, 'Maalat Torato,' 1 (340), 240–241 and '*Sichot Hashyachot L'torot*,' 10, 10–11.

44 *Likutei Halachot, Hilchot Pesach* 7:22. See Buber, *HaOr Haganuz*, 287–288.

45 *Likutei Halachot, Orach Chaim, Hilchot Succah, halachah* 6; *Likutei Halachot, Even Ha'ezer, Hilchot Ishut, halachah* 4. *Likutei Moharan* II 31

46 V'emunah zo tefillah,' *Likutei Moharan* II 19.

47 *Genesis* 2:5.

48 *Genesis* 24:63.

49 *Likutei Moharan* II 11.

50 *Deuteronomy* 11:17.

51 *Sichot Haran*, 98, 73; Green, *Tormented Master*,182.

52 See Tishbi, *Torat Hara*, 127–128.

53 *Genesis* 43:11.

54 *Isaiah* 24:16.

55 *Song of Songs* 2:12.

56 *Daniel* 4.

57 Beit-Aryeh, *Perek Shirah*; Moshe Idel, '*Hapeirush Hamagi*,' 33–62.

58 Yitzchak Abarbanel, *Peirush al Neviim Rishonim*, 715, 475. See Idel, '*Hapeirush Hamagi*,' 44.

59 *Derashot al Hatorah*, 83b. See Beit-Aryeh, *Perek Shirah*, 16–18.

60 See Beit-Aryeh, *Perek Shirah*, Part I, Introduction I, 1–88.

61 Ibid., and Idel, '*Hapeirush Hamagi*.'

62 *Ilmah Rabati*, 86–987.

63 *Likutei Moharan* II 63.

64 *Genesis* 2:5.

65 *Likutei Moharan* II 63.

66 *Likutei Moharan* I 54:6.

67 *Shiur Komah, Torah*, chapter 22, 32–33; and see Beit–Aryeh, *Perek Shirah*, 25–29.

68 *Chagigah* 3a.

69 Ben Shlomo, *Torat Ha'Elokut*, 303–304.

70 Beit-Aryeh, *Perek Shirah*, 30–32.

71 Handwritten manuscript, Jerusalem, *Kovez B'kabalat Ha'ari*, copied in Italy in the seventeenth century, *Beit Haseforim Hal'umi V'ha'unifersitai* 8 939, 147b–148a. Description of the handwritten manuscript in the Scholem catalogue, *kitvei yad b'kabbalah*, Jerusalem 690, number 77, 131–132. See the printing by Beit-Aryeh, 30.

72 Beit-Aryeh, *Perek Shirah*, 321.

73 Ibid.

74 Ibid., 31, 44 and note 195.

75 Chaim David Azulai, *Sefer Shem Hagedolim, Chelek Seforim, maarechet* 80, section 147.

76 See Idel, *Hachasidut*, 405–424; idem., '*Yofyah shel isha*,' 317–334, and particularly 330–334. For more on the influence of R. Moshe Cordovero on Hasidism, see Zak, '*Iyun B'hashpa'at*,' 229–246.

77 *Shivchei Habesht*, 298–300.

78 See Beit-Aryeh, *Perek Shirah*, 33.

79 *Maggid Devarav L'yaakov*, 2.

80 *Kerem Yisrael*,11a.

81 *Yalkut Shimoni, Tehillim, remez* 889, 970.

82 *Tzavat Haribash*, 90, 16; see Weiss, '*Reishit Tz'michatah*,' 88–103; Tishbi and Dan, '*Chasidut*,' 784–788. And see Idel, '*Yofyah Shel Isha*,' 320–324.

83 Weiss, '*Reishit Tz'michatah*,' 88–103.

84 See Weiss, *Mechkarim*, '*Yachaso Shel R. Levi Yitzchak Miberditshev L'R. Nachman*,' 36–41; Green, *Tormented Master*, 115–118.

85 R. Levi Yitzchak Miberditzev, *Kedushat Levi*, Part II, *Kedushah sh'niyah*, 456–457.

86 See Idel, '*Hapeirush Hamagi*,' 60–62; see Idel, 'Conceptualizations of Music in Jewish Mysticism,' 183–184; R. Shabtai of Rashkov, '*Seder K'viat Hatorah*,' section 86, in *Hanhagot Zaddikim*, volume 1, 368.

87 *Hagigah* 2a (my emphases. Z.M.).

88 As we saw above in regard to R. Moshe Cordovero.

89 *Sichot Moharan*, 273, 169. And see *Chayei Moharan, 'Maalat Torato*,' 1 (34), 240–241 and *Sichot Hashyachot L'torot*, 10, 10–11.

90 *Likutei Moharan* I 27:8

91 See Gris, *Sifrut Hahanhagut*, 103–148.

92 Ibid., 231–247, particularly 233; See also ibid., '*B'chinat Hanhagot L'umat Torot Eitzel R. Nachman MiBratslav*,' 249–275. For another view of *Sefer Hamidot*, see Green, *Tormented Master*, 63–68; and also note 94 on 380.

93 *Sefer Hamidot, 'Yeshuah*,' 2 8, 229.

94 *Likutei Moharan* II 1:9. This teaching was delivered on Rosh Hashanah 5569 (1808) in Bratslav.

95 See Green, *Tormented Master*, 226 and 426, note 27.

96 See Green, 226–236; Arend, '*Harefuah*,' 44–53. Regarding R. Nachman's view of this 'special power' – *segulah* – see also Levin–Katz, '*Segulot V'eitzot*,' 348–370.

97 See *Sefer Hamidot, 'Refuah'* 1, 502; and *Likutei Moharan* I 258; *Likutei Moharan* II 5:1 and 3; Green, 226–236.

98 *Isaiah* 38:50.

99 *Berachot* 10b.

100 *Genesis* 24:63.

101 *Likutei Moharan* II 1:11.

102 *Tiku Emunah, Likutei Moharan* II 5:1; *Taanit* 8; *Shabbat* 31.

103 *Likutei Moharan* II 1:13.

104 Ibid.

105 Ibid.

106 *Likutei Moharan* II 67. *Sichot Haran*, 53, 43.

107 See Scholem, '*Demuto Hahistorit*,' 291–296. See *Chayei Moharan, Sichot Hashayachim*

L'torato 45; and also Levin-Katz, *'Segulot V'eitzot.'*

108 See Green, *Tormented Master*, 227; Arend, *'Harefuah;'* and also Levin-Katz, *'Segulot V'eitzot.'*

109 See Green, 226–236; Arend, *'Harefuah.'*

110 *Likutei Moharan* 54:6.

111 *Deuteronomy* 18:9.

112 *Shabbat* 75a; *Rosh Hashanah* 24b.

113 *Likutei Moharan* II 120.

114 *Sefer Hamidot*, and *Likutei Moharan* I 27:8.

115 Such as *Likutei Moharan* I 54; *Sichot Moharan* 273, 169; *Sichot Haran*, 273, 115–116.

116 *Likutei Moharan* I, 27, 8; *Likutei Moharan* II 63; *Sefer Hamidot*, *'Yeshuah,'* section 28, 129.

117 Such as in *Likutei Moharan* II 63.

118 Idel, *Hachasidut*, particularly 66–261.

119 See Underhill, *Mysticism*, 149–164. See also Idel, *'Al Kavanat Shmoneh Esrei,'* 25.

120 *Likutei Moharan* II, 63.

121 Particularly in section 8.

122 See Idel, *'Nachtliche Kabbalisten;'* see Magid, 'Conjugal Union, Mourning and Talmud Tora in R. Isaac Luria's Tikkun Hazot,' XVI–XVII.

123 Shtil, *Psicholog*, 28.

124 *Likutei Moharan* I 54:3.

125 See Tishbi, *Torat Hara*, 130. Magid, 'Conjugal Union,' XXVIII–XXXVII.

126 *Likutei Moharan* I 54:3.

127 *Berachot* 60b. And see also Tishbi, *Torat Hara*, 130.

128 See Idel, *Hebetim Chadashim*, 53–76, and particularly, 64–67. See also Fechter, *'Tefisat Had'veikut,'* 51–121; Etkes, *Baal Hashem*, 123–129; Elior, *'Rik Ubesht,'* in particular the section, *'Machshevet Ha'adam V'zikatah Lik'ulat Hashechinah,'* 689–696; and the section, *'Avodah B'gashiyut,'* 702–704.

129 *Tzavaat Haribash*, section 29, 8.

130 *Likutei Moharan* I 3.

131 *Isaiah* 45:18.

132 *Likutei Moharan* I 35.

133 Zohar *Bereishit*, 19a; ibid. *Vayakhel*, 213b.

134 *Lamentations* 3:23.

135 *Shaar Hakavanot, Inyan Derushei Halaylah, Derush* 3, 343.

136 Zohar *Pinchas* 244b.

137 *Sanhedrin* 24a; *Tzavaat Haribash*, 29, 8.

138 *Psalms* 92:3.

139 *Genesis* 1:5.

140 Three of the Torah's cantillation marks.

141 *Vayihi Mikeitz* 3.

142 *Tzavaat Haribash*, section 29, 8. See Weiss, *'Talmud Torah Bereishit,'* 615–618; idem., *'Talmud Torah L'shitat,'* 151–159; Shatz-Oppenheimer, *Hachasidut B'mistika*, 157–167; Etkes, *Yachid B'doro*, 166–172.

143 *Ecclesiastes* 7:23.

144 *Deuteronomy* 33:18.

145 *Likutei Moharan* I 35:10. (My emphasis Z.M.)

146 Tishbi, *Torat Hara*, 130.

147 *Meor Einayim, Matot,* 207; R. Simchah Bunim of Peshischa, *Kol M'vaser,* 1, *Vayeitzei,* 56.

148 Tishbi, *Torat Hara,* 126–130.

149 Ibid., 83.

150 *Psalms* 77:7.

151 See Mark, *Shigaon v'daat,* 325–337.

152 *Likutei Moharan* I 54:6.

153 *Likutei Moharan* II 5.

154 Ibid.

155 See Idel, '*Hitbodedut: On Solitude in Jewish Mysticism.'* See idem, '*Hitbonenut K'rikuz B'kabalah;*' idem., '*Hitbodedut K'rikuz B'filosofia,*' Klein-Breslavi, '*Nevuah Kesem V'chalom,*' 23–68; *Tzavaat Haribash,* section 82, 26; ibid., section 8, 2a. See also *Keter Shem Tov,* section 167, 42. And also see Gris, *Sifrut Hahanhagot, 'Hitbodedut ud'veikut,'* 222–224.

156 *Likutei Moharan* II 25; *Sichot Haran,* 154, 111. And see also *Likutei Moharan* II, 95–101; *Sichot Haran,* sections 227–234, 148–152. In *Chayei Moharan,* sections 436–443, 282–286. *Hishtapchut Hanefesh.* See also Green, *Tormented Master,* 142–145.

157 *Sichot Haran,* Section 228, 148–149; In *Likutei Moharan* II 93.

158 See, for instance, Shtil, *Psicholog,* 166–172. See another interesting example in the historical novel, *Beit Mashber* by Der Nistar.

159 *Likutei Moharan* I 52.

160 See Idel, '*Universalization and Integration;*' see Elior, *Torat Achdut Hahafachim,* 51–53, 171–175.

161 See Idel, '*Hitbodedut K'rikuz B'kabbalah,'* 46–47, 64, 66–67, and on page 74 note 244; idem, '*Hitbodedut K'rikuz B'filosofiah,'* 46–49, 54–55 and elsewhere; *Igrot R. Chaim Chika Mei'amdur* at the beginning of *Chaim V'chesed,* 18. See also Schatz-Openheimer, *Hachasidut B'mistikah,* 290–300.

162 Weiss, *Mechkarim,* 93.

163 *Likutei Moharan* I 52.

164 Green, *Tormented Master,* 157.

165 Ibid., 142–145.

166 Ibid.,144.

167 Feikazh, *'Zaddik,'*160–161.

168 See Idel, 'Universalization and Integration,' 45–447.

169 *Likutei Moharan* II 95–101.

170 *Likutei Moharan* II 95 and 99; *See also Chayei Moharan, 'Maalat Hahitbodedut,'* 3 (439), 293.

171 *Sichot Haran, 'Midabber Mimaalat Hahitbodedut,'* section 233, 151.

172 See Shatz-Oppenheimer, *Hachasidut K'mistikah,* 78–95; Weiss, *Studies in Eastern European Jewish Mysticism,* 69–83.

173 Weiss, see the quotation further on; Green, *Tormented Master,* 64–65.

174 Weiss, *Mechkarim,* 93.

175 And see Fiekazh, '*Zaddik,'* 160–161.

176 *Likutei Moharan* I 19; and also *Likutei Moharan* I 22:9.

177 *M'vaser Tzedek,* 8, 2–3.

178 *Shmuah Tovah* 73, b. See Idel, *Hachasidut*, 284–315; Etkes, *Baal Hashem*, 158–160. And see also Dan, 'The Language of the Mystical Prayer.'

179 *Likutei Moharan* II 99.

180 *Sichot Haran* section 32,19; *Likutei Moharan* I 21:7–8; *Likutei Moharan* I 37:6. *Ohr Ha'emet* 15b–16a. See Idel, *Hachasidut*, 324–450.

181 *Sichot Haran*, Section 45, 28.

182 Ibid.

183 *Likutei Moharan* I 65:4.

184 Ibid.

185 *Likutei Moharan* I 52.

186 *Sichot Haran*, *Midaber Mimaalt Hahitbodedut*, Section 228, 148–149.

187 *Likutei Moharan* I 52.

188 *Sichot Haran*, *Midaber Mimaalat Hahitbodedut*, Section 227; *Chayei Moharan*, 'Yigiato V'tirchato B'avodat Hashem,' 230; See *Sichot Moharan* 65 and 275.

189 *Shivchei Haran* and *Sichot Haran*, 'Yegiyato V'tirchato B'avodat Hashem,' 163.

190 Maimonides, *Mishnah Torah, Hilchot Yesodei Hatorah* 7:8.

191 Idem., *Hilchot Yesodei Hatorah* 7:8; R. Moshe Cordovero, *Shiur Komah*, Jerusalem (726), 60; R. Chaim Vital, *Shaarei Kedushah*. Part IV, gate 2, 5.

192 *Shiur Komah*, 50.

193 See Idel, '*Hitbodedut K'rikuz B'kabblaah*,' 68–75; Idel, 'Universalization and Integration,' 38.

194 *Likutei Moharan* II 95. And in *Likutei Moharan* II 100.

195 Ibid. 65:4. See above, in the section, 'Speech, Outcry and Great Weeping,' and also further on in the section, 'Total Self-Dedication – Unto Death.' *Likutei Moharan* II 99.

196 Idel, *Hebetim Chadashim*, 93–105. See Lisky, *Ecstasy*, 168–170.

197 *Likutei Moharan* I 262.

198 *Chayei Moharan*, 'Sichot Hashychim L'hatorot,' 31, 30–31. And see also *Shivchei Haran* 8, 5.

199 *Berachot* 57b.

200 *Likutei Moharan* I 52.

201 Idel, *Hachasidut*, 233–238; *Keter Shem Tov* 121,16a; Etkes, *Baal Shem*, 141. See Idel, *R. Menachem Rekanti*, part I, 142–160; Fishbane, *The Kiss of God*, 36–37, 40.

202 *Likutei Moharan* II 99.

203 *Otzar Chaim*, handwritten manuscript Moscow–Ginsberg 775, 138a; handwritten manuscript Oxford 1911, 149b. Printed in Idel, '*Hitbodedut K'rikuz B'kabbalah*,' 50–51 and note 84.

204 *Tzavaat Haribash*, section 63, 10b; ibid., section 35, 6a; and see also *Likutei Yekarim*, section 2, 1a; ibid., section 31, 5ab.

205 *Likutei Moharan* I 15.

206 *Likutei Moharan* I 193.

207 Weiss, *Mechkarim*, 93.

208 See examples in Shatz-Oppenheimer, *Hachasidut Bi'mistikah*, 110–121.

209 *Sichot Haran* 52, 37; *Berachot* 5:5. And see also *Likutei Moharan* I 99. And see Idel, *Hachasidut*, 425–526.

210 *Chayei Moharan*, 'Maalat Torato Us'farav Hakedoshim,' 47(386), 260.

211 *Chayei Moharan,* '*Maalat Hahitbodedut,*' 6 (442), 295–296.

212 *Sichot Haran,* section 164, 116–117.

213 Maimonides, *Mishnah Torah, Hilchot Yesodei Hatorah,* 7, 8.

214 Idem., *halachah* 5. And see also above, Chapter 5, Part II, Section 1, *Joy and Faith.*

215 *Sichot Haran,* 117, 82.

216 *Likutei Moharan* I 52.

217 *Likutei Moharan* II 99.

218 Weiss, *Mechkarim,* 172–178.

219 *Likutei Moharan* I 52.; *Anochi; Likutei Moharan* I 4:9. See above, Chapter 6, Part I, Section 1.

220 See Weiss, *Mechkarim,*173.

221 See ibid., note 12.

222 Green, *Tormented Master,* 46.

223 Ibid., 312–328.

224 Ibid., 179.

225 Ibid.

226 Ibid., 178.

227 In Green's words, ibid., 179.

228 Ibid., and see 176–182.

229 Ibid., 142.

230 As Green himself defines the Bratslavian life. See ibid., 145.

231 See above, Chapter 5, Part II.

FOUR Silence and Melody Facing the Void:
      On the Place of the Mystic Melody in the
      Confrontation with Heresy in the Writings of
      R. Nachman of Bratslav

The topic of the void is undoubtedly one of the most fascinating and important subjects in the thought of R. Nachman of Bratslav, and the teaching 'Go to Pharaoh,'[1] which focuses upon the issue of *tzimtzum* (withdrawal) and the *halal ha-panui* (the void), has engaged many scholars.[2] Hillel Zeitlin already spoke of 'the great value that R. Nachman ascribed to the subject of the void, to which he continually returned.'[3] Weiss considered this teaching to be the ontological basis for the central place occupied by the topic of the question in R. Nachman's thought, and as a foundation for the paradoxical nature of Bratslavian belief.[4] Arthur Green, who has dealt extensively with this teaching,[5] describes it as 'perhaps the most important single statement of Nachman's thoughts on the themes of faith, doubt, and reason.'[6]

Weiss finds in this teaching a clear expression of R. Nachman's existentialist conceptions that, he claims, starkly contrast the world of mysticism, and even of Hasidism.[7] Green, although conscious of R. Nachman's 'mystical side,'[8] argues that 'the definition of faith emerging from his teaching on the void seems to be one that perforce must reject mysticism as the basis of religion.'[9] Since, however, Green is aware of the presence of mysticism in R. Nachman's world, he offers three different explanations for the coexistence of these opposites.[10]

This chapter will demonstrate that mysticism occupies an important place in Teaching 64. Without comprehending the place accorded to mysticism in this teaching we cannot understand the task that R. Nachman assigns to the *zaddik* in the struggle with heresy and with the questions that have no answer. The concept of faith that emerges from Teaching 64 corresponds closely to the concept of faith as expressed by R. Nachman in other texts; not only does this concept not reject mysticism, it places it in a system with mystical experience at its apex, and in which even faith itself has a distinct mystical cast, its existence dependent upon the prophetical spirit.[11]

Since Teaching 64 has already been discussed at length by Weiss and Green, I shall concentrate on the elements in this teaching not examined in these earlier studies, and whose absence led to a faulty understanding of the main principles of R. Nachman's teachings.

1. Two Models of Creation – Tzimtzum *and the Breaking of the Vessels*
Two important kabbalistic symbols that relate to the process of Creation lie
at the foundation of this teaching: the concept of *tzimtzum* and the subsequent
void, and that of the breaking of the vessels.[12] R. Nachman uses these symbols
in tandem as two models that, despite their different descriptions of reality,
do not negate each other, but rather exist parallel to one another.[13] Each
ontological model has differing epistemological and existential consequences, and one must identify to which of the two ontological models
one's situation belongs, and thereby derive the manner for contending with
it. This teaching relates primarily to the model of *tzimtzum* and the void, with
which R. Nachman begins the teaching:

> When Hashem, be He blessed, wished to create the world, there was
> no place in which to create it, for everything was infinite. He
> therefore constricted the light to the sides, and via this constriction
> (*tzimtzum*) a void was formed. And inside this void, all the 'days' and
> 'measures' came to be, which are the creation of the world. Now this
> void was essential for Creation, for without the void, there would
> have been no room for the world to exist. And this constriction of
> the void is incomprehensible and will remain so until the end of
> time.
>
>   This is because two contradictory statements must be made in
> its regard: being and non-being. On the one hand, the void comes
> about through constriction – God, as it were, constricted His divinity
> from there. Thus, God is not there. Were that not to be the case, this
> would not be a void but all would be the Infinite One and there
> would be absolutely no room for Creation. Yet in a deeper sense,
> divinity surely does exist there, for nothing exists without [God's]
> life-force.[14]

R. Nachman's teaching of *tzimtzum,* which comes to wrestle with the problem
of the absolute divine totality, on the one hand, and, on the other, the
existence of the world including man as an entity separate from God, is not
presented as a response that results in understanding and perception, but
as a paradoxical statement that, more than resolving the tension, defines its
poles and acknowledges our ability to resolve the problem 'only in the
future.'

    Along with the model of *tzimtzum* and the void, R. Nachman presents the
breaking of the vessels as another method of contending with the question
of existence apart from God, a way that leads to a different attitude toward
situations and realities from which God is seemingly absent. Teaching 64 then
shifts from ontological descriptions of the reality of God and the world to a

reliance upon these depictions to explain the presence of various types of heresy, determining the nature of the response from within this hypothesis:

> Know that there are two types of heresy. There is one heresy which is derived from 'extraneous' wisdom. Of this heresy our sages said: 'Know what to answer the heretic.'[15] In other words, [the claims of] this heresy may be answered, for they come from 'extraneous' wisdom, which comes from waste materials deriving from the level of the shattering of the vessels. Because the light was too bright, the vessels were shattered, and thus the husks came into being (as is known). Extraneous wisdoms are derived from there – i.e., from the shattering of the vessels, the leftover waste-matter of the holy. Just as a human being produces certain bodily wastes – such as nails, hair, sweat, and the like – so does the holy have its own wastes, from which extraneous wisdom, including magic, is derived.
>
> For this reason, if a person falls into that sort of heresy – although he must flee and save himself from it – still, whoever has fallen into it can find a way to be saved from there, for he can find Hashem, be He blessed, there, if he looks for Him and seeks Him out there. Since all of these [extraneous wisdoms] are derived from the shattered vessels, a number of sparks of holiness are there and a number of fallen [divine] letters are there. And so a person can find divinity and intellect there, in order to resolve the questions that result from the sort of heresy that comes from extraneous wisdoms, which result from the wastes of the shattering of the vessels. This is because divine vitality exists there – that is, intellect and the letters that were broken and fell there. Consequently, there is an answer to that heresy. Therefore, [our sages teach in this regard]: 'Know what to answer the heretic.'[16]

The breaking of the vessels created a reality in which heretical conclusions emerge from various wisdoms, but profound study enables uncovering the divine spark, the 'mind' and the letters that are concealed in them and vitalize them. Man must therefore examine those forms of wisdom in order to reveal the divine 'mind' and speech that exist within them. The *tzimtzum*, in contrast, brought about another type of heresy.[17]

The *tzimtzum* created a reality in which man cannot find any divine letter or spark. In terms of human perception, God is absent from the void, which even indicates that there is no God.[18] Consequently, in his search for the divine spark, man must not sink into a place where it cannot be found. Furthermore, man is 'forbidden' to find speech and language in the void, for then the void would cease to be. Accordingly, the only way to relate to such heresies and the existence of the void is by means of faith. There is no wisdom, no intellect, and no speech capable of providing an answer to this difficult reality that indicates that there is no God; man must therefore be aided by faith, independent of the intellect and these wisdoms, to transcend the void. At this point in the teaching, man is called upon to completely desist from engagement with these wisdoms, to divert his attention from them, and to 'transcend' further, without looking back.

This portrayal of reality and its necessary consequences harmonizes with additional teachings of R. Nachman that pertain to the obligation to cast off 'mind' and act on the basis of faith. This depiction provides the ontological background for the divine service of casting off the intellect, which explains that since man lives in a world created within the void from which the intellect is absent, it follows that in certain instances the intellect, language, and speech are irrelevant for worship and perception of and contact with God.[19]

At this point, R. Nachman hedges his previous assertions, stating that certain people are obligated to engage with the wisdoms and heresies that come from the void.

> But know that if there is a great *zaddik* who is the aspect of Moses, he in fact is obligated to study those words of heresy. And even though it is impossible to answer them, nevertheless, by means of his study of them, he raises from there a number of souls that had fallen and sunken into that heresy. This is because those confusing issues and challenging questions of that heresy that comes from the void are in the aspect of silence, since no intellect or letters [of speech] can answer them.[20]

The *zaddik* who has the quality of Moses may neither flee nor avert his eyes from the void. He must stand before the emptiness and engage with it. This engagement by the *zaddik* is effected in silence, and not by speech. The *zaddik* makes no use of 'mind' and wisdom in his attempt to provide an answer and resolve the heresies, since 'no intellect or language can resolve them;' it is therefore incumbent upon him 'only to believe and be silent there.'[21]

2. What Is Absent from the Void?

What is the significance of this silence?[22] And, what characterizes the *zaddik*, who 'has the quality of Moses,' which enables him to correctly contend with the void? In order to answer these questions, R. Nachman adds an explanation about *tzimtzum*, which adds a certain hue to the nature of the void, and therefore to the manner that R. Nachman proposes for coping with it:

Creation came about by means of speech. As the verse states, 'By the word of God were the heavens created, and all their hosts by the breath of his mouth.'[23] And speech contains wisdom, for the totality of speech consists solely of sounds that come from the five sections of the mouth. And through the divine speech all matters of all creation came into being. As the verse states, 'You made them all with wisdom.'[24] Speech is the boundary of all matters, for He bound His wisdom within the letters, for some letters form a group that is a boundary for one entity, and another group of letters form the boundary for another entity. But in the void, which surrounds all words and which is vacated of everything, as it were, there is no speech – not even wisdom without letters. Thus, the confusing issues that come from there are in the aspect of silence.

Therefore, we find[25] in regard to Moses, that, when he asked of the death of Rabbi Akiva, 'Is this Torah, and is this its reward?,' he received the response, 'Silence! Thus did it arise in the divine thought.' That is to say, you must be silent and not request an answer and solution to this problem, for thus did it arise in the divine thought, which transcends speech. Therefore, you must be silent in regard to this question, for it is in the aspect of having 'arisen in the divine thought,' which no speech can answer. Similarly, those challenges and confusing issues that come from the void, which has no speech and intellect, are in the aspect of silence. One must only believe and be silent there. Thus, it is forbidden to enter and study the words of heresy and the confusing issues, except for a *zaddik* who is the aspect of Moses. This is because Moses is the aspect of silence, the aspect of having been called 'difficult of speech.'[26] – the aspect of silence, which transcends speech.

And so the *zaddik* who is the aspect of Moses, the aspect of silence, can study these confusing words, which are the aspect of silence, and is indeed obligated to study them, in order to raise the souls that fell there.[27]

R. Nachman repeatedly stresses that silence results from the absence from the void of intellect, letters (language) and speech. The absence of these levels and expressions of the divine wisdom means that silence cannot be used to find God; from this we could therefore conclude the negation of His existence. Silence results then from our confronting the void that lacks speech, which is identified in this and other teachings with the manifestation of wisdom and knowledge.[28]

R. Nachman's emphasis considerably mitigates the meaning of God's absence from the void. He focuses the emptiness of the void to emptiness from 'mind,' language and speech, thereby opening a window to another kind of presence of God. This is implied later in the teaching, when R. Nachman argues that the void is the realm of 'the highest thought, that which is beyond language,' that is to say: there is no speech in the void, but thought does exist there.

This explanation, focusing on the emptiness of the void in the realm of wisdom and speech, corresponds closely to the course of the argument delineated by R. Nachman in the passage quoted above, a course that necessarily leads to the problematic argument of the fact of *tzimtzum* and the creation of the void. God had to withdraw Himself in order to enable the creation of the cosmos. All of Creation, R. Nachman stresses, was created by speech, an expression of the divine wisdom. Therefore, in order to enable Creation, God had to form a void lacking the divine wisdom and speech, creating an empty space in which the ten Sayings would be uttered and the world would be created by the Word of the Lord. This path consequently leads to the conclusion that wisdom and speech, specifically, are absent from the void.

R. Nachman's explanation for his example relating to Moses brings this idea into clear focus. Moses also was faced with a situation of no speech, in which he had to be silent. But Moses, too, did not confront a void lacking all divine presence; he rather faced a reality containing divine thought, but lacking divine speech:

> Therefore, we find in regard to Moses that, when he asked of the death of Rabbi Akiva, 'Is this Torah, and is this its reward?,' he received the response, 'Silence! Thus did it arise in the divine thought.' That is to say, you must be silent and not request an answer and solution to this problem, for thus did it arise in the divine thought, which transcends speech. Therefore, you must be silent in regard to this question, for it is in the aspect of having 'arisen in the divine thought,' which no speech can answer.[29]

Thought is a level that exceeds speech; not an image that merely expresses a negative vacuum, it is rather a metaphor for a phase that precedes and transcends speech, and for this reason is beyond human comprehension. Humans, including Moses, cannot 'answer' a place in which there is no speech with speech – only with silence.

The teaching, 'Know that Stories,'[30]similarly uses the concept of silence. There too R. Nachman is occupied with silence, using the expression, 'be silent, thus is the highest thought.' This teaching clearly indicates that 'silence' relates to the positive ability of coming into contact with the divine, even in a place where there is no speech, and not to standing before the empty space that is totally devoid of any divine reality. As R. Nachman formulates:

> [Man] can ascend to the world of mind, that is called the ascent of
> the words, for mind is extremely exalted, and whoever seeks to
> enter the world of mind must be silent; and even if he speaks a
> proper speaking then, he loses the mind, for mind is very exalted,
> that even proper speech causes its loss. This is 'be silent, thus is the
> highest thought,' for in order to ascend to the mind, one must be
> silent.[31]

In the teaching 'For From Compassion I Shall Lead You'[32] R. Nachman is concerned, in a different context, with the place and the role of silence, once again using the narrative of Moses and R. Akiva. Although the place and role of silence differ in this teaching from those in the teaching of 'Go to Pharaoh,' R. Nachman nevertheless maintains the principle that 'silence' refers specifically to absence from speech; the expression 'be silent, thus is the highest thought' teaches that there is 'mind' here, and only speech is absent.

This silence then does not attest to a state devoid of all insight and knowledge. On the contrary, specifically because Moses possessed the answer, attained the concealed letters, and 'the answer to this objection already rose in his mind,' he was forbidden to utter this answer, but was ordered to 'be silent.' The danger lies in the likelihood that Moses would reveal the existing answer – hidden and on the level of thought – in his speaking, and at that very moment a question more forceful than the first would enter his mind. R. Nachman emphasizes: 'The Lord, may He be blessed, accordingly told him to be silent regarding the answer.' The silence is not in the question, but in the answer. This answer falls under the category of silence, since it may not be spoken, and must remain the personal possession of the individual, who may not reveal it to another.[33]

It should be stressed that the silence in the teaching of 'For From Compassion' is essentially different from the silence of Teaching 64, since the silence in the face of the void lacks intellect, language and answer, but even though the parameters of the image have shifted, the basic principle is still preserved. The silence of 'For From Compassion' is silence from speech, and does not attest to the individual's muteness of thought. As we will see below, the silence in the teaching of 'Go to Pharaoh' does not indicate muteness of melody and song.

3. Silence and Melody

Returning to Teaching 64, R. Nachman stresses that the void's lack of speech is the basis and preparation for the next phase in the course he takes, in which he argues that it is impossible to find God in the void with speech or with intellect, and the questions will always remain. It is possible, however, to find God by means of silence and melody, and thereby negate the questions and the heresies.

R. Nachman continues to develop the theme of silence that relates to the thought that is above speech, and that connects silence to the knowledge of the melody. Only the *zaddik*, such as Moses, who has knowledge of silence, similarly knows the melody. Melody, parallel to silence, is the correct response in the face of a reality that lacks language and speech. R. Nachman stresses that the same *zaddik*, assigned the task of engaging the heresies coming from the void, also knows not only silence but also the secret of the melody. Melody is the instrument and sole means by which the *zaddik* can act to elevate the souls that have descended into the heresies of the void:

> And know that by the melody of the *zaddik*, who is of the aspect of Moses, he elevates the souls from this heresy of the void into which they descended.[34]

The role of the melody in the elevation of the souls parallels the task assigned it by R. Nachman in the elevation of the holy sparks and the 'good points.'[35] In the teaching 'And It Came to Pass at the End' R. Nachman maintains that there are situations in which we can find mind and speech, which are the divine allusions in everything; while in other situations, such as the absence of the intellect and mind, where speech and the allusion are not to be found, we must follow the path of melody.[36]

Teaching 64 depicts the confrontation with the void, an encounter that cannot be enacted by a search for the allusions and speech, since these are absent from the void. In such situations, the average man must 'be silent and believe,' while the *zaddik* is assigned the task not only of being silent and believing but also of making melody. Through melody, he expresses contact with the divine, even in a place without language and speech.

R. Nachman provides an expansive explanation for the action and importance of melody:

> For know that every wisdom in the world has a special song and melody, that is the song unique to this wisdom, and this wisdom is derived from this melody: 'Sing a hymn [*maskil*, from the same root as *sekhel* - intellect],'[37] for each wisdom has its melody and song. Even the heretical wisdom has a melody and song unique to this wisdom of heresy; this is the meaning of what our masters, of blessed memory, said: 'But what of Aher [Elisha ben Avuyah] – Greek song did not cease from his mouth, and when he arose from the study

hall, several heretical books fell from his [lap].'[38] One is dependent upon the other; because this song did not cease from his mouth, the heretical books would fall from him, because this song was unique to this heresy and apostasy to which he subscribed. Consequently, every wisdom, according to its aspect and level, similarly has its own special melody that belongs to it. And, likewise, [when going] from one level to another, it is the nature of the wisdom on the higher level to possess a song and melody that are also higher, in accordance with its quality.

The conception presented in this teaching is close to that which views the melody as the life-force of everything, an idea that R. Nachman raised and developed in *Likkutei Moharan, Tanina* (Part II), Teaching 63, *Kamma* (Part I) and Teaching 27.[39] In this teaching, the role of the melody to provide vitality is not limited to vegetation and the peoples of the world, it also vitalizes all the wisdoms, including the wisdom of heresy. Here as well, as for plant life and the non-Jewish nations, R. Nachman argues that the individual who knows the melody of the wisdom is capable of contending with it.

R. Nachman further claims that even in places where man cannot attain wisdom, he is capable of coming in contact with the melody. This statement also applies to the wisdom that encompasses the void and vitalizes it. The melody by means of which the *zaddik* contends with the heresy from the void belongs to the belief that is above all the wisdoms and heresies, higher even than the heresy from the void. The *zaddik*, who knows the melody of belief devoid of intellect and understanding, since he relates to 'the light of *'Eyn Sof* itself' that encompasses and vitalizes even the void, is capable of confronting the void, aided by the melody and belief. Although 'the wisdom that is present in the light of *'Eyn Sof* cannot be understood,' its 'song and melody' may be understood by the *zaddik* who is 'of the aspect of Moses.'

This conception is portrayed in a circular structure: every created being and wisdom has a melody and wisdom that are higher than it, that encompass and vitalize it, and by force of which 'this wisdom is derived.' Thus, it is possible to ascend from one wisdom to another, from one level to the next, until one reaches the beginning of Creation. In this beginning of Creation are the highest levels of wisdom and creation; these are encompassed only by 'the light of *'Eyn Sof*.' The light of *'Eyn Sof* also contains wisdom, but since 'it can neither be known nor understood,' man witnesses the creation of a void that lacks wisdom, and obviously the light of *'Eyn Sof*. He is only capable of understanding the aspect of belief and 'the special melody of belief' that is 'higher than all;' this melody cancels the heresy from the void; the souls that descend into it are enabled to ascend by means of this melody.

I have discussed extensively the mystical nature of the knowledge of the melody in R. Nachman's thought,[40] and will mention only a few of my conclusions here. The ability to hear the melody and the song is the ability to come in contact with the nonverbal plane of the spirituality and sanctity inherent in the world. Song and melody express the festive and spiritual strata of the reality not manifest in prose and defying verbal formulation. Man is mandated to hear the singing and the melody of the herbs and to 'know to play melody,' that is, to know to raise and give voice to those melodies that he hears. The melody comprises the exposure and ascent of the good spirit, the divinely inspired spirit, and is a necessary level and step in the acceptance of the prophetic spirit. By expressing the melodies of joy, a person can attain belief, *devekut* (adherence to God), the spirit of divine inspiration, and prophecy. This understanding well suits the description of melody as a way to attain 'the light of *'Eyn Sof*,' while the intellect, wisdom, and speech cannot serve as a vehicle for the attainment of the 'light of *'Eyn Sof* itself.'

R. Nachman therefore postulates that only the mystic *zaddik*, who is of the aspect of Moses, the greatest of the mystics, who knows both the secret of silence from the speech of the intellect, and the secret of the mystical melody of belief in 'the light of *'Eyn Sof*,' is capable of engaging the heresy that comes from the void, contending with it, and elevating the souls fallen into its depths.

The person who worships exclusively through wisdom and speech is incapable of contending with the void that lacks any intellect or language. Only one who has acquired the ability of silence and the casting off of the intellect on the one hand and, on the other, 'knows melody,'[41] is able to believe and to play the melody of the presence of 'the light of *'Eyn Sof*' when faced with the void.

The belief required in confronting the void has two components: silence and melody. Silence is the relinquishing of the intellect, and parallels the 'casting off of the intellect.' This topic is brought into clearer focus and is confirmed by the wording of a manuscript by R. Nachman: 'For this reason, we are called *'Ivrim*, for we cast off all wisdoms and adhere solely to the Lord, may He be blessed, by belief alone.'[42] Just, however, as the labor of casting off the intellect is merely an interim stage towards mystical perception,[43] here, too, silence from speech and the casting off of the wisdoms constitute the stage of renouncing the perception of intellect and language, a stage at which the *zaddik* is to construct the melody and the song. The aspect of Moses is not restricted to silence; it also comprises melody, the mystical ability to come in contact with 'the light of *'Eyn Sof*,' even when the latter is not manifested in intellect, language, and speech. The belief of the *zaddik* who is of the aspect of Moses is depicted as a mystical ability to know or come in contact with 'the light of *'Eyn Sof*,' in a way different from that of wisdom and intellect. Engagement with the void and its dangers is incumbent only upon the one who possesses the skill and level of belief and of silence, and who knows the melody that exists in the contact with 'the light of *'Eyn Sof* itself,' in which there is no speech, lying beyond the realm of understanding and wisdom. The highest phase in this belief is characterized by melody and song, and not by silence. The silence is only partial, and consists of the silence of casting off the intellect, but even within this silence man sings.

For the present, this singing is among the skills and from the special belief of the *zaddik* of the aspect of Moses, but in the future this belief and song will be shared by all:

> In the future, when all the peoples will be made pure of speech, so that they all invoke the Lord by name,[44] and all will believe in Him, may He be blessed, then the verse shall be fulfilled: 'Come and look down [*tashuri*] from Amana's peak'[45] – specifically, 'from Amana's peak,' that is, of the aspect of this supreme belief [*emunah*], that is the apex of all the beliefs; and this is specifically '*tashuri*,' that is, the melody and the song that belong to this apex of belief [i.e., R. Nachman connects *tashuri* with the word *shir*, song]. The aspect of the song of this supreme belief can be understood only by the *zaddik* of his generation, who is of the aspect of Moses, who is at this level of belief, that is of the aspect of silence, the aspect of 'be silent, for thus it is in the highest thought,' that is, it is still above speech. For Moses is of the aspects of silence, which is the meaning of 'Then Moses sang [*yashir*- the future tense].'[46] Our Sages, of blessed memory, said: 'It was not said '*shar*'' [the simple past], but "*yashir*" [the future tense; used in the verse as the past].'[47] This demonstrates that [the belief in] resurrection is from the Torah, since Moses will sing in the future, as well; this is so, because all the singings, whether in this world or whether in the future, are only by Moses, who is of the aspects of silence, who merited the song that belongs to the supreme belief that is above all, where all the songs are included, for all are derived from this. This is as Rashi interpreted: '"*yashir*" – the [letter] *yud* was written on account of his thought [to do so]'. That is to say, the aspects of 'for thus it is in the highest thought,' the aspects of Moses, the aspects of silence. Consequently, by the making of melody by the *zaddik* who is of the aspect of Moses, all the souls that fell into this heresy of the void ascend and come forth, since his making melody is of the aspect of 'the apex of belief,' that is, the supreme belief that ascends above all, for by this making of melody and belief, all the heresies are nullified, and all the melodies are nullified and included within this melody, that is above all, and from which all melodies are derived.[48]

This is the closing note of the teaching of 'Go to Pharaoh,' and is also the picture of belief that emerges from the entire teaching. This is not the belief of silence and muteness facing the void, nor should we overstate the chilling and tormented colors of this silence. This silence, coming from the wise utterances, enables the melody of belief, the all-inclusive and highest melody, to ascend and be heard. Not only the still and tortured, small voice, but also the sounds of song and melody burst forth from the world of Bratslav belief.

Teaching 64 places the image of the mystic at center stage. Only the mystic who knows the melody of 'the light of *'Eyn Sof*' is permitted and required to engage the void. This teaching, like R. Nachman's thought in its entirety, presents a world that is centered around mysticism and the mystic. Mysticism is the goal, and it is specifically the mystic who is entrusted with the task of raising up even the souls that have fallen into the depths of the void – souls that fell because they lacked the mystical skills required to safely enter and exit engagement with the void.

4. The Beggar with a Speech Defect

A study of the beggar with a speech defect in the story 'The Seven Beggars' supports the interpretation presented above regarding the relationship between silence and melody. In Teaching 64 R. Nachman explains that the description of Moses as 'hesitant of speech' is actually a complimentary depiction:

> Moses was a silent one, whom Scripture describes as 'hesitant of speech.'[49] This refers to that silence which is beyond speech.

Moses belongs to the world of silence that is above speech, and what seems to be a defect is actually something sublime. This idea closely corresponds to the character of the third *betler* (beggar) among the seven beggars, who also suffered from a 'speech defect.'[50]

It transpires that the beggar with a speech defect knows melody, and is 'a wonderful orator and speaker,' whose marvelous melodies and songs include all the wisdoms. The reader realizes that R. Nachman uses the image of the beggar to sketch the character of the *zaddik* of the aspect of Moses who is portrayed in Teaching 64. The speech defect of the *zaddik* is liable to be deceptive, and indeed did mislead important scholars who saw the silence of the *zaddik* but did not hear his singing.[51] A profound understanding of his silence teaches, however, that the *zaddik* is not at all silent; rather, his mouth is full of songs and melodies. Being of the aspect of silence and defective of speech is limited to the realm of speech, and ensues from the fact that the utterances of this world are not whole, since they do not express the praise of the Lord.[52]

Expressed differently, it may be said that the *zaddik* remains silent from speaking, since such talk is devoid of the Lord, but, in contrast, knows how to sing and play wondrous melodies that exceed and encompass all the wisdoms and melodies. Obviously, the praise of the Lord emanates from his melodies.

Despite the central role the subject of the melody plays in the confrontation with the void, it is absent from the studies of Weiss, Green and Magid, who discuss Teaching 64 and the void extensively. Weiss, who extensively examined the meaning of silence and its different strata, completely ignores the topic of the melody, even though he writes at length in different places about Teaching 64 and the void.[53]

Green also provides a lengthy analysis of Teaching 64, but halts with the passage describing the silence of the *zaddik*, and makes no mention of the critical place and role of melody.[54] In the continuation of his argument, when discussing the existence of R. Nachman's 'mystical side,' Green writes: 'In his teaching concerning the void, Nachman gives the impression that the goal of the *maqqifin*-process is reached only by the silent and paradoxical assertion of the *zaddiq*. At the very end of that teaching, however, in a passage we have not quoted, Nachman offers a hint that the entire process is illusory.'[55] But as we have already clearly seen, the theme of the melody is stated explicitly, and not by allusion, in the middle of this teaching, explaining the manner in which the *zaddik* who engages the heresies raises the souls that have fallen into the void. Even without hints, the silence of the *zaddik* is interrupted by melodies and song, constituting the way in which he relates to the 'light of *'Eyn Sof* itself,' and serving as the instrument for confronting the void and elevating the fallen souls.

Magid, as well, offers a comprehensive explanation for the significance in R. Nachman's thought of God's absence from the void, relying on the first part of Teaching 64 that relates to the void and silence, while disregarding the second part of the teaching that raises the topic of the melody. Magid also explains additional sources in R. Nachman's writings in light of this understanding of Teaching 64, while disregarding the central place of mysticism and melody in the *zaddik*'s world.[56]

The melody and its significance apparently could not be incorporated in the interpretation given by Weiss and Green to the subject of silence and the void, a subject that is the cornerstone of their comprehensive interpretation of R. Nachman's thought and world. Only the repression of the melody enabled them to construct a complete interpretation for the Bratslav belief, depicted as the polar opposite of, or different from, the mystical world. Weiss and Green do not view the complete context of Bratslav faith and the silence of the *zaddik* correctly. The dark existential colors that painted R. Nachman's world prevented them from seeing belief as part of the divine service of melody, and the elevation of the good and joyful spirit that leads to prophecy; the darkness concealed from these scholars the prophetic-mystical nature of the Bratslav belief and of Teaching 64, 'Go to Pharaoh.'[57]

This neglect is puzzling, since Hillel Zeitlin had already noted the important role of melody in regard to the void:[58] 'and how does he remove them from there? [...] Only by his song.'[59] Zeitlin's statement fits with his general perception of R. Nachman's thought and the important place occupied by melody and song in this world.[60]

Not surprisingly, Zeitlin, who had paid attention to the importance of the melody, also more correctly defined the essence of the Bratslav belief: 'And what is the power of the belief, what is the core of its essence, content, and foundation in the soul [...]? R. Nachman replies to this question that belief comes neither from the mind nor from the heart, but rather from the power of imagination in the soul,'[61] adding that 'belief [...] has its source in the prophetic imagination.'[62]

Zeitlin was also aware that the inability to understand God, of which R. Nachman speaks, relates to the way of the mind and wisdom, while, in contrast, the way of the power of imagination in belief, in prophecy, and in song enables us to attain some understanding of Him: 'The divinity cannot in any manner be understood with the mind, but, rather, by means of the imaginative force, that is pure and unblemished, man is able to portray in some fashion the sublime divine matters.'[63]

Zeitlin's description of R. Nachman's spiritual world is undoubtedly much more accurate, despite his poetic rather than scholarly writing style and despite the absence in his depictions of conceptualizations such as mysticism or existentialism.

Zeitlin did not expand his description of R. Nachman's mysticism, nor did he relate to issues such as the nature of the *unio mystica* and the means by which it can be attained. Notwithstanding these omissions, both his definitions and descriptions of Bratslav belief, along with his choice of examples and quotations, more accurately represent the world of R. Nachman than do the later scholarly studies.[64]

5. R. Nathan in Likkutei Halakhot on Tzimtzum and the Void

Support for the interpretation of the teaching of the void presented above is to be found in the writings of R. Nathan of Nemirov, whose commentary on and development of the teaching of the void allude to many of the points raised. R. Nathan's understanding of *tzimtzum* and the void and their consequences for man's service of the Lord that entails the casting off of reason is explained briefly below:

The beginning of the root of the Creation cannot be understood with the intellect. For it is from this [inability] that all the questions [of the heresies] arise, and it certainly is impossible to comprehend it, since the beginning of the root of Creation is derived from the departure of reason, that is of the aspect of the void, that is the beginning of *tzimtzum* that is of the aspect of the root of imagination, that is the departure of reason, and all that remains is its *reshimu* [residue], that is of the aspect of the root of the imaginative power, by this *reshimu.* Man has the ability to be strengthened with perfect faith if he so desires, but if he seeks to examine and understand, he will undoubtedly fall with none to support him, for it cannot be comprehended, since reason has departed from there. It is only by force of the *reshimu* that remains, that is of the aspect of the root of the imaginative power, that he has the strength to belief with perfect faith in the truth, for the Lord, may He be blessed, left this ability in the *reshimu* that remained after the *tzimtzum.* This *reshimu* has the ability to strengthen the faith of whoever so desires, and this is the essence of the root of choice, that is enrooted in belief, that is the foundation of all the commandments, as it is written: 'All Your commandments are *emunah* [literally, belief],' and as it is written [Makkot 24a], 'Habakkuk came and based them all on one [principle]: "the righteous shall live by his faith" [Hab. 2:4].' This is the source of all the names, appellations, titles, and praises of the Lord, may He be blessed, for they all are of the aspect of holy imaginative power, as our master, of blessed memory, wrote in his teachings, at the end of the verse 'for our feast day' [Ps: 81:4], see there. He explains there that all the praises and descriptions by which we praise and describe Him, may He be blessed, they all are of the aspect of the imagination, for in the innermost part of the intellect, the Lord, may He be blessed, is stripped of all the praises and titles, see there. For the Lord, may He be blessed, is above all the names, appellations, and titles, as is known. If there had been no *tzimtzum,* there would not have been any Creation, and He, may He be blessed, could not have been called by any name. It was only out of His love and His compassion, that He desired to be beneficent to other than Himself, He withdrew Himself, as it were, until the light of reason departed and made room for the creation of the worlds; all that remained there was His *reshimu.* This is of the aspect of the power of imagination, which is the power of belief, that is, the ability of man to believe in this truth. In this manner all the attributes and all Creation came into being, and in this manner He gave us permission to call Him by those names, appellations, titles, and praises. It was there that the count and the number began, for before one, what can you count?, as is known.[65]

This passage is based on the assumed analogy between man's state of awareness and the processes that occur within it, on the one hand, and the structure of the world and the process of Creation, on the other. The process of *tzimtzum* clearly relates to reason: 'He withdrew Himself, as it were, until the light of reason departed and made room for the creation of the worlds.' This approach enables constructing the analogy between the act of *tzimtzum* at the beginning of the Creation and the process of the 'departure of reason,' an expression used by R. Nachman to describe man's state of awareness.[66]

The imagination is the force that enables man to act, even when reason has departed. Moreover, when reason departs the imagination ascends and replaces it. Belief also acts by force of the imagination, and therefore, the time of belief occurs when reason has departed. The power of imagination remaining with a person when reason and mind have departed was paralleled, according to R. Nathan, at the time of Creation. The departure of the light of reason to the sides did not leave a totally empty void; it rather retained the root of the imaginative force and the residue of the light of reason, so that man's service in the face of these questions is a response to their ontology. The imaginative force within man, expressed in belief, relates to the root of the imaginative force in the Creation.[67]

All worship of the Lord, based on praises, appellations, and titles, is possible only by the departure of reason. The domination of man's awareness by reason would prevent him from uttering any praise or address with a title in prayer and thanksgiving: 'in the innermost part of the intellect, the Lord, may He be blessed, is stripped of all the praises and titles.' This situation is parallel to Creation, which was entirely dependent upon the departure of reason and was based upon the root of the imagination in order to enable the limited manifestation of God and the possibility of man to address God with title and praise.

The place of this divine worship by the casting off of reason is therefore anchored in the Kabbalistic-Hasidic ontology and in the doctrine of the void and *tzimtzum*. R. Nathan's passage is formulated much more strongly than R. Nachman's teaching, since the former states that the casting aside of reason is not the labor of man; God Himself also engages in an act of the 'departure of reason.' God withdraws the 'light of reason' to enable the Creation and in order to create man as capable of addressing God, praying to Him, and praising Him. We see, therefore, that God also has states of the 'departure of reason.' Accordingly, the act required of man to cast aside his reason and enter a state of departure of reason is an echo, and response, by man to the action taken by God in causing His reason to depart from the void.

The acts of madness performed by man in his love of God[68] are a response
to the divine madness expressed in the Creation of the world and His desire
for worship by man.

Notes

1 *Likkutei Moharan, 'Kamma'* I: 64.
2 For *tzimtzum* in Hasidism, see Shatz-Oppenheimer, *Hachasidut K'mistkah*, 121–128; Ross, '*Shnei Perushim l'Torat Hatzimtzum*,' 153–69; Idel, *Hachasidut*, 89–95. For *tzimtzum* in Lurian Kabbalah, see Scholem, *Pirkei Yesod*, 104–108, 207–209. For the historical context of the emergence of the concept of *tzimtzum*, see: idem, *Major Trends in Jewish Mysticism*; Tishbi, *Torat Hara*, 2–61. For a different interpretation, see: Idel, '*Musag Hatzimtzum*.'
3 Zeitlin, *R. Nachman M'Bratslav*.
4 Weiss, 'The Question in the Teaching of R. Nachman,' *Mechkarim*, 109–49, particularly 121–41.
5 Green, *Tormented Master*, particularly 311–317.
6 Green, *Tormented Master*, 311.
7 Weiss, 'The Hasidism of Mysticism and the Hasidism of Belief,' *Mechkarim*, 87–95.
8 Green, *Tormented Master*, 318–319.
9 Ibid., 317.
10 Ibid., 322–330.
11 See Mark, *Shigaon V'daat*, 69–74; See also Fechter, '*L'sugiat Haemunah*,' 105–134.
12 See above, note 1. See also Scholem, *Major Trends in Jewish Mysticism*, 265–268 and Tishbi's *Torat Hara*.
13 *Likkutei Moharan* I: 54.
14 *Likkutei Moharan* I: 64:1
15 Avot 2:12.
16 *Likkutei Moharan* I: 64:2
17 *Likkutei Moharan* I: 64:2
18 Additional Teachings from the Manuscripts of Our Holy Master, of Blessed Memory on Teaching I: 64, *Likkutei Moharan*; see below, note 47.
19 R. Nachman of Cheryn, *Parpera'ot le-Hochmah* 1:9; R. Nathan, *Likkutei Halakhot, Orach Hayyim*, 4:17.
20 *Likkutei Moharan* I: 64:3
21 *Likkutei Moharan* II: 5:2.
22 See: M. Chalamish, '*Al Hashtika*', 79–89.
23 *Psalms* 33:6.
24 *Psalms* 104:24.
25 BT *Menahot* 29b.
26 *Exodus* 4:10.
27 *Likkutei Moharan* I: 64:3
28 *Likkutei Moharan* I: 43; *Likkutei Moharan* I: 46; and similarly *Likkutei Moharan* I: 56; II: 5.
29 *Likkutei Moharan* I: 64:3

30 *Likkutei Moharan* I: 234.

31 Ibid.

32 *Likkutei Moharan* II: 7.

33 Weiss, *Mechkarim,* 137, 138–139.

34 *Likkutei Moharan* I: 64:4.

35 See Mark, *Shigaon V'daat,* chap. 7, part 1, section 6, 149–57.

36 Ibid.

37 *Psalms* 47:8.

38 BT *Hagigah* 15b.

39 See Mark, *Shigaon V'daat,* 157–159.

40 Mark, *Shigaon V'daat,* chaps. 5–7, 62–208.

41 *Likkutei Moharan* I: 54:6.

42 *Likkutei Moharan* (ms.), 'Additional Teachings from the Manuscripts of Our Holy
    Master, of Blessed Memory' (page 3, column a – my pagination). For these teachings
    from R. Nachman's mss., see Weiss, *Mechkarim,* 190–191 note 6 and editor's note there.

43 See Mark, *Shigaon V'daat,* 74–84.

44 Based on *Zephaniah* 3:9.

45 *Cant.* 4:8.

46 *Exodus* 15:1.

47 BT *Sanhedrin* 91b.

48 *Likkutei Moharan* I: 64:5.

49 *Exodus* 4:10.

50 *Rabbi Nachman's Stories,* trans. A. Kaplan , 383–384.

51 See below.

52 See *Likkutei Moharan* I: 45; 56.

53 Weiss, 'The Question in the Teaching of R. Nachman,' *Mechkarim* 109–49. For silence,
    see 139–141.

54 Green, *Tormented Master,* 311–317.

55 Ibid., 318–319.

56 Magid, 'Through the Void.'

57 *Likkutei Moharan* II: 8:7; *Likkutei Moharan* II: 8:8. I discussed these issues extensively in
    Shigaon V'daat, chaps. 5, 7.

58 Zeitlin, *R. Nachman M'Bratslav,* 12–15.

59 Ibid., 15.

60 Zeitlin, *R. Nachman M'Bratslav,* 16–21; and similarly in idem, *Al Gvul Shnei Olamot.*

61 Zeitlin, *R. Nachman M'Bratslav,* 22.

62 Ibid., 23.

63 Ibid., 22–24.

64 M. Fechter, 'L'sugiat Haemunah.'

65 *Likkutei Halakhot, Orah Hayyim,* 4:17.

66 See Mark, *Shigaon V'daat,* 74–84.

67 I have not found any parallel to this is the writings of R. Nachman himself, but this
    fully expresses the inner logic of his teaching.

68 *Likkutei Moharan* II: 5:15.; see: Mark, *Shigaon V'daat,* 74–84 and 298–314.

FIVE

The Land of Imagination

The analysis of the aspect of 'the land of Israel' and of 'the path to the land of Israel' in this chapter extends the discussion about the status of the rational mind and imagination in R. Nachman's teachings.

A number of academics have addressed, from various points of view, R. Nachman's journey to the land of Israel; the forthcoming discussion does not purport to review all the findings of these academics,[1] nor all of the explanations which R. Nachman himself provides.[2] While I will address some of these interpretations, the focus of my discussion is uncovering a new perspective on the journey to the land of Israel, which academics have hitherto left unaddressed, in order to further spell out the acute difference of the place occupied by the rational mind and imagination in the world of R. Nachman.

I. 'The Aspect of the Land of Israel'

In order to appreciate R. Nachman's words at the beginning of his teaching *Tiku Tochachah*,[3] sections of which I have previously discussed in this work,[4] we must revisit the assumptions and constructs that R. Nachman employs as he introduces and explains the 'aspect of the land of Israel.'

R. Nachman links prophecy, faith and the imaginative faculty, a topic already discussed at length in Chapter 1. We saw that both faith and prophecy are activities that operate in deep connection with the imaginative faculty and depend upon its proper functioning. R. Nachman stresses the activity of the imagination and its necessary vitality for the existence of faith, particularly in those areas that intellect does not reach. The prophecy of which R. Nachman speaks is not only biblical prophecy, which no longer exists; he refers as well to the spirit of holiness that even today rests upon 'a true leader.'[5] And he associates these three components – faith, prophecy and the imaginative faculty – with the creation of the world.[6] The creation of the world is not a subject for intellectual comprehension but rather for faith, which functions with the assistance of the imaginative faculty. A person who reaches conclusions about the question of creation on the basis of intellectual reasoning will come to heresy, for 'it is impossible to understand this with the intellect.'

An important motif that R. Nachman adds to the list of subjects that he discusses is that of kindness:

> For I said, 'The world is built on kindness'[7] – comes about via faith,
> in the aspect of 'To tell in the morning your kindness and your faith-
> fulness in the nights.' (*Psalms* 92:3) [...] 'Great is your faithfulness'
> – i.e., faith. Through this, the world will be renewed.[8]

The creation of the world in the past and its renewal in the future depends
upon the gathering together of acts of kindness, which are dependent upon
faith, which in turn is dependent upon the imaginative faculty.

Here, R. Nachman does not explain the connection between faith and
kindness, but makes do with bringing biblical proof texts. Elsewhere, however,
he does expand on this topic.[9] In the following section, R. Nachman develops
the exposition that associates the right of the nation of Israel to its land with
God's creation of the world:

> And when the world will be renewed in the future, then the world
> will function via wonders – that is to say, through Providence alone,
> which is the aspect of wonders – and not in a natural fashion. This
> is because the renewal of the world in the future reflects the aspect
> of the land of Israel. This is because the essence of the land of
> Israel comes about by means of the aspect of 'The might of his deeds
> did he tell his nation,' etc.[10] And this is as Rashi comments on the
> verse, 'In the beginning, God created the heavens and the earth.'
> Rashi comments 'that for this reason God began the Torah with the
> words, "In the beginning" – because of "the might of his deeds did
> he tell his nation, to give them an inheritance of the nations." That
> is to say, it is so that the nations of the world will not say to the Jewish
> people, "You are thieves, etc." Therefore, God began with "In the
> beginning," for He, be He blessed, created it,' etc. Thus, the essence
> of the land of Israel comes about by means of the might of God's
> deeds – which is to say, when people know that Hashem, be He
> blessed, created the world. And in the future, the Holy One, blessed
> be He, will renew the entire world completely in this aspect of the
> land of Israel. This is because it will then become apparent that
> Hashem, be He blessed, created everything. And then the entire
> world will be renewed in the aspect of the land of Israel. And the
> essential holiness of the land of Israel lies in the fact that God's
> Providence rest upon it constantly, in the aspect of, 'Constantly the
> eyes of Hashem your God are on it, from the beginning of the year
> and to the end of the year.'[11] And in the future, when God renews
> the entire world, entirely in the aspect of the land of Israel, then He
> will deal with the entire world entirely by means of providence
> alone, as He now does with the land of Israel. And then nature will

be nullified entirely, and the world will function in accord with providence only, which is the aspect of wonders, and not in accordance with nature.[12]

The aspect of the land of Israel is an existence that does not accord with the way of nature; it is an existence supervised by God in a revealed and miraculous fashion and not bound by the laws of creation. The land of Israel is associated with faith in the creation of the world – faith that God created the world and nature, and that He is not a part of that natural framework. A person who believes in creation believes as well that providence by means of miracles and wonders is possible, and that the existence of a reality in which 'nature will be nullified entirely' is attainable. In contrast, a person who conducts himself in accord with his limited intellect denies the creation of the world; and he denies the existence of providence and miracles, which are the quality of the land of Israel, 'since it is impossible to understand this with the intellect,' but 'only by means of faith.'

Melody and song, which represent the revelation of divinity that exists in the world,[13] are also renewed in the present-day land of Israel and will be renewed throughout the world in the future days to come.

> And then a new song will be aroused, in the aspect of 'Sing to Hashem a new song, for He has done wonders.'[14] That is a reference to the song that will be aroused in the future, which is the melody of providence, the aspect of wonders. This is because at that time the world will function by means of providence and wonders. This is because there is a melody in the aspect of the way of nature, which is the aspect of 'The heavens tell the glory of God and the work of His hands does the heaven express.'[15] This is the aspect of the melody and song of the way of nature, of the attributes of the heavens – that is to say, the aspect of the songs and praises that praise Hashem, be He blessed, for His guidance of the present, who guides the world in accordance with the way of nature. But in the future a new song will be awakened, in the aspect of wonders, the aspect of providence, for then God will guide the world through providence only. And this new song that will be awoken in the future, which is the aspect of a song that is simple, doubled, tripled, quadrupled, which, as applied to the Tetragrammaton, adds up to 72, the aspect of kindness, [*chesed*, 'kindness,' has the numerical value of 72]. Via that will come the renewal of the world in the future days, the aspect of 'the world will be built with kindness.'[16] [...] And as a result, prophecy will spread. And as a result of prophecy we will attain faith. And with faith the world will be renewed in the future days.

> And the renewal of the world is in the aspect of the land of Israel –
> i.e., in the aspect of the providence that is experienced in the land
> of Israel. And then the tune of providence and wonders will be
> awoken.[17]

Just as the world was made new when it was created, so will it be renewed in the future days. Then, once again, 'the world will be built on kindness.' But this time, the entire world will be conducted in the aspect of the land of Israel. The song that the world will sing to its God will be entirely different than today's song. It will no longer be a song of nature with its rules, but a new song of faith, providence and prophecy.

II. The Way to the Land of the Imagination

Clearly, attaining the land of Israel demands something beyond a consciousness constructed of intellect and rational mind. It demands a consciousness based on the imaginative faculty. We can thus understand why the path to the land of Israel necessitates 'casting away the intellect' and removing the ordinary mind, for when a person's consciousness is stripped of its rational presence, the activity of his imaginative faculty is able to come to the fore. Since the consciousness associated with the land of Israel is based upon the imaginative faculty, faith and prophecy, and since the essence of their activity takes place where intellect ceases to exist,[18] the condition for entering the land of Israel – in the spiritual sense of 'the aspect of the land of Israel' – is a person's readiness and ability to renounce his intellect in order to make it possible for his imaginative faculty to rise and blossom.

This understanding sheds a new light on R. Nachman's strange behavior on his journey to the land of Israel, and imparts additional meaning to states of forgetting, R. Nachman's protestations that 'I don't know' and the acts of foolishness in which R. Nachman indulged on his way to the land of Israel.

The way to the land of Israel is a preparatory and transitional stage before coming to a consciousness absent of ordinary mind. 'Consciousness is drawn after one's deeds.' Acts of foolishness and childishness express a readiness to renounce the intellect and enter a state of consciousness free of rational mind. And such actions are also, indeed mainly, the practice that helps a person enter into that state of consciousness. States of forgetting and 'I do not know' are the fruit of a process of removing the rational mind. In that realm, 'the intellect ceases to exist.' The 'way' to the land of Israel is an intermediary stage that prepares the aspect of the land of Israel and is not identical to the aspect of the land of Israel.[19] Inspiration and illumi-nation exist in the land of Israel. These are made possible with a consciousness other than that of the rational mind, a consciousness capable of sensing, via the imaginative faculty, the reality that exists within the land of Israel, which is entirely different from that outside it.[20]

This presents another perspective on the liminal character[21] of the way to the land of Israel, which I shall discuss extensively in the coming chapter.[22] The person on this path has left behind the consciousness associated with the lands outside the land of Israel and the framework of serving God that such a consciousness entails. However, he has not yet entered the consciousness of the land of Israel – neither its self-evident providence nor the service of God that derives from that providence. In other words, since forgetfulness envelopes the song that characterizes the lands outside the land of Israel, and the song of Zion and the melody of providence are not yet heard, this man remains silent. He 'has no words now,'[23] and 'he does not even know a melody.'[24]

'The aspect of the land of Israel' exists not only in the physical land of Israel. And it goes without saying that not only R. Nachman's journey to the land of Israel constituted the way to the land of Israel. Every time that R. Nachman wished to attain a new insight, higher than his present under-standing and rational mind – a new insight that would be the aspect of faith and the aspect of the land of Israel – he had to pass through a transitional phase in which his ordinary mind was absent, so as to create a consciousness empty of rational mind, and to employ the imaginative faculty to gain new insights. Additionally, following his journey to the land of Israel and after having attained high levels of inspiration, in order to attain new insights in the aspect of the land of Israel, he had to again pass through the aspect of the way to the land of Israel, which entailed again a descent involving the absence of the ordinary mind and the rational mind and entering into states of 'I do not know.' [25]

R. Nachman's actual journey to the land of Israel had a defining role in that it created an archetype for all those states of existence that are identical with the aspect of simplicity and of 'I do not know' that accom-panied R. Nachman throughout his life. Successfully dealing with the diffi-culties of the way to the land of Israel, the self-sacrifice, and (no less important) the successful conclusion of the journey, in which R. Nachman attained what he had wished for – all of these endowed meaning to all those difficult states of being that are 'the aspect of the way to the land of Israel.' They gave R. Nachman the power to deal with descents of that nature – an ability that he required until his final days.[26]

III. The Doctrine of Descriptions of God

In the continuation of the teaching at hand, R. Nachman posits the doctrine of descriptions of God or divinity, at the core of which is a discussion on the place of the imagination and intellect in descriptions of God:

> In the aspect of 'And with a compass he gives its form.'[27] 'Gives its form [*toar*]' – i.e., descriptions and praises of God, which exist in the aspect of the imaginative faculty. This is because all of the descriptions and praises with which we think of God, be He blessed, are in the aspect of the imagination. This is because in the inner part of the intellect, God, be He blessed, is stripped entirely of all praises and descriptions. Thus, all of the praises and descriptions are necessarily in the aspect of the imagination. And so when the imagination is refined and rectified, then it is possible to arrange praises and descriptions of God, be He blessed. But when the imagination is not rectified, then we have no knowledge whatsoever of how to describe God, be He blessed, as it were, with praises and descriptions, because all praises and descriptions of God are in the aspect of the imagination. And that is the aspect of a holiday – [*chag*] – the aspect of 'a compass' – *mechugah* – 'he will be described.' And in this way faith, which is the aspect of Rosh Hashanah, is rectified, because the essence of Rosh Hashanah is that it constitutes the renewal of the world, because in Tishrei the world was created, which is dependent upon faith… And by means of rectifying the imagination and faith – which is rectified by means of prophecy, the aspect of 'on the concealed day of our celebration' – in this way, we attain the aspect of the renewal of the world, the aspect of 'a new song.'[28]

The philosophical doctrine of the descriptions of God has been entirely transformed. R. Nachman agrees that, intellectually speaking, one cannot describe or praise God, since God is completely intangible. But in opposition to the philosophical position, R. Nachman does not conclude that one should renounce or diminish such praises and descriptions. Nor does he believe that they should be explained as negative descriptions, or as descriptions of action. On the contrary, he suggests that we see in the praises of God a positive activity of the imaginative faculty, which, although not entirely attuned to 'the inner being of the intellect,' nevertheless has its legitimate place and role. If turning to God with descriptions and praise is performed as an intellectual act, then it is fundamentally flawed and ends up reifying God. But if it is an action of the functioning imaginative faculty, influenced by and functioning with the faculty of prophecy, then it is a positive, rectified and refined activity.

Descriptions and praises of God are a holiday (*chag*); they are a Rosh Hashanah, which is the holiday that involves faith in the creation of the world, the aspect of 'today is the birthday of the world.' Belief in the Creator of the world is not necessitated by the intellect, whose existence is not bound to the laws of nature. This is because, by definition, belief in God sees in law, in nature and in intellect a creation that was brought about at a certain time, and which will change and be renewed in the future days. This is a localized and specific creation, which is not the totality of being, but rather a specific conduit of existence, limited to itself. But man does not have to limit himself solely to the channel of the intellect and rational mind. And thus he can, and must, act with the aid of his imaginative faculty, in order to describe and praise the Creator.

It is important to note that in this teaching the intellect's assertion that 'God, be He blessed, is completely stripped of all praises and descriptions' is not presented as an error and is not completely denied. Still, it seems that although this knowledge possessed by the inner aspect of the intellect is accepted by R. Nachman as having value, a person is obligated to believe in God, to prophesy and to arrange praises and descriptions of God with the aid of the imagination. These praises and descriptions of God need rectification and refinement, which must come from the faculty of prophecy. They need rectification and refinement since there is a true problem in praising and describing God.

In a sense, not only is praising God an error, but it constitutes the sin of reifying and insulting God, Who is not disposed to any description. But it is precisely the clear consciousness of that fact and the shifting of all religious activity of this type from the horizon of the rational mind to that of the imagination that clears it of reification and makes it theologically acceptable. That which the imagination may imagine, the intellect may not think. R. Nachman does not argue that the faculty of the imagination makes it clear that God is not tangible. But rather, that although God is intangible, a person may imagine Him with his praises and his descriptions, if these praises and descriptions are engaged in by a rectified and refined imaginative faculty that possesses a dimension of prophecy.

The praises and descriptions of God are relevant to that realm of awareness that occurs 'in the place where intellect ceases' – in that realm where the imagination acts. Thus, R. Nachman does not claim a comprehensive split between intellect and imagination. He is certainly not prepared to recognize the rational mind as the supreme judge or as the criterion determining the acceptability of spiritual insights or important religious practices occuring outside of its boundaries. On the other hand, R. Nachman does not falsify the intellect or claim that it presents a distorted image of reality and the world. His mitigated argument claims that just as intellect has its place, so does imagination – and the latter is autonomous and free of the chains of the intellect and rational mind. This is where prophecy, the place for faith and praising God, occurs.

In another discussion of the doctrine of the descriptions of God, R. Nachman associates it with clapping and the land of Israel.

> That is the aspect of clapping hands together, because in this way we gaze at the image of Hashem. This is because the image of Hashem – i.e., the ways that we imagine Him – i.e., 'compassionate' and 'gracious' and other names and images by which we refer to Him – all of these images were revealed by the prophets. And the prophets – that is the aspect of the speech of prayer, as in the phrase, 'expression of the lips.' And when we express with our lips these representations and images, as we clap hands, then the verse, 'By the hand of the prophets shall I be imagined,'[29] is fulfilled. This is because the prophets are the words and the hands are the hands of the prophets. And then the imagination is revealed, in the aspect of 'And in the hand of the prophets I will be imagined.' And then 'And the image of Hashem he will see'[30] is fulfilled. Also, clapping hands is the aspect of 'and the hands of man beneath their wings,'[31] for the wings are the words, in the aspect of 'and a being with wings tells a matter.'[32]

Against the background of the assumption that prayer possesses a prophetic nature, 'and prophets – that is the aspect of the speech of prayer' (an axiom that R. Nachman expands on and buttresses elsewhere), R. Nachman makes a fascinating claim regarding the prophetic process occuring in prayer and the place of the imaginative faculty in prophecy during prayer.

The beginning of the process is in the prophets, who gaze upon the 'image of Hashem,' with the aid of the imagination. 'The image of Hashem,' which the prophets experience as a vision and an image, is translated into words, into descriptions and praises such as '"compassionate" and "gracious" and other names by which we refer to Him.' A person praying reconstructs the words of the prophets that were spoken in a state of prophecy because all of the names, descriptions and praises – 'all of those images the prophets revealed.' Now, when a person is at prayer, an opposite process occurs, and the word precedes the imagination. The person prays and recites the visions of prophecy, 'and then the imagination is revealed … "And the image of Hashem he will see" is fulfilled.'

R. Nachman, consistent with his approach, sees not only prophetic images and visions as the result of the imaginative faculty, but claims that at its core religious language – names and descriptions of God – also comprises the activities of the imaginative faculty. The intellect denies the possibility of describing God, of giving Him a name and praising Him, since according to 'the inner part of the intellect, God, be He blessed, is entirely unrelated to all praises and descriptions.' The intellect leads to a silence that eschews all praise.[33] Only the imagination, freed of the chains of the intellect, enables the expression of the praises of God. These descriptions and praises of God are images and fragments of representations, not statements of the rational mind. Prayer and songs of praise to God do not derive from the philosophers,[34] but from prophecy. Using the power of prophecy, a person can pray, attempting with his prayer to reconstruct the prophetic experience.

IV. Clapping Hands

Clapping hands in prayerful fervor was a wide-spread Hasidic custom;[35] however, the additional importance attributed to clapping in Bratslav, both in theoretical terms[36] and in practical application (the liberal use of clapping during prayer and in *hitbodedut*) is an exceptional phenomenon.

In the teaching under discussion, the role of the hands and clapping is described as aiding the revelation of the prophetic imagination and envisioning therewith the image of Hashem. Prophecy and a vision of the image of Hashem are not only inner spiritual processes dependent upon a person's intentions and thoughts, for his limbs and deeds also play an active role in the prophetic process. His lips and hands, his speech and clapping, are a part of that process, both because they comprise part of the preparatory practice for prophecy and because they act as a medium for the appearance of the *Shechinah*. Speech, the 'expression of the lips,' is both the fruit of man's initiative and a creation of God, Who sends that speech to a person's lips. And as R. Nachman states in *Tiku Memshalah*: 'Via prophecy, prayer is made perfect, for prayer is the aspect of "He creates the expression of the lips,"[37] which is the aspect of prophecy.'[38] The hands too serve as a tool under God's control to send His visions to one's imaginative power. As the verse states, 'And in the hand of the prophets shall I be imagined.'

Passing, when praying, from the technical action of moving lips to speech in which the imaginative vision of the image of Hashem is revealed is aided by clapping: 'for the wings are the speech' with which a person is raised and elevated. And the 'hands' have the power to move and awaken the wings – 'and the hands of a man under their wings.'[39]

> And that is the meaning of 'and by the hand of the prophets will I be imagined.' By means of the hands, by means of clapping, the words are spoken on 'holy land' […] How can you merit having your

prayer in the atmosphere of the land of Israel? [...] That is to say, the aspect of clapping. By means of clapping, one's prayer is in the atmosphere of the land of Israel [...] And as a result of clapping a person lives in the atmosphere of the land of Israel.[40]

The land of Israel is the place where imagination, prophecy and faith are awakened.[41] Clapping in prayer can arouse one's imagination and create a sort of enclave of the aspect of the land of Israel. This enclave maintains a breadth of imagination and prophecy that encompasses the person at prayer and helps him arrive at a prayer that is the aspect of prophecy.

R. Nachman's identification of prayer with faith and his explanation of that identification further elucidate why 'prayer is in the atmosphere of the land of Israel.' In *Ikar Hatachlit*, which addresses the question of whether the man's ultimate purpose is faith or intellectual service with intelligence and inquiry, R. Nachman writes, '... and faith – that is prayer ... this is because prayer changes nature, and the wisdoms and inquiries, which are in accord with nature, are nullified.'[42] The quality of prayer is a proclamation of faith in the aspect of the land of Israel, and a rebellion against and denial of the rule of nature and of the intellectual outlook derived from it. Prayer is request, imploring and faith that indeed 'the world acts solely in accordance with providence, which is the aspect of wonders, and not in the way of nature.'[43] Therefore, prayer itself is 'the melody of providence,' which is the melody and song of the land of Israel.

Summation

R. Nachman's foolish and childish acts, statements of 'I do not know,' and forgetting, which he experienced on the way to the land of Israel were refined and moderated until they became the path that he advised for the Bratslavian service of God – not only for the *zaddik* but for his Hasidim too. The model of coming to a place where intellect ceases to exist as a result of a person having 'cast away his intellect,' with the goal of afterwards attaining insights beyond his normal understanding and rational mind, becomes an archetype for all worship and spiritual progress in Bratslavian worship.[44]

Casting away the intellect is necessary if one is to come to insights that Moses in his lifetime did not attain, 'why the righteous suffer and the wicked enjoy well-being.' As Yehudah Liebes has stated,[45] and as we will see further on,[46] R. Nachman argues that Moses (like the Baal Shem Tov) was not able to descend to the ultimate degree of smallness – descent that is a vital stage and necessary condition to entering the land of Israel – and therefore did not succeed in entering the land. This is because Moses in his lifetime, as the figure most identified with the rational mind, was unable to remove his rational mind, and thus lacked the fortitude of his own will to forget the Torah of Moses and return to the state before the Torah of Moses had been given. As a result, Moses did not succeed in his desire and prayer to enter the land of Israel.

We saw in this chapter that the meaning of the entrance into the land is the insight to divine providence and the entering into a state of consciousness, which is also reality, in which the righteous man enjoys well-being and the wicked person suffers.

R. Nachman's elucidations on the nature of the land of Israel, the way to the land of Israel, the failure of Moses to enter the land and on his own success in entering it are finely woven into a tapestry of the totality of R. Nachman's thought and the central role of the tension between rational mind and imagination in Bratslav Hasidism. The aspect of 'the way to the land of Israel' and the aspect of 'the land of Israel' accompany Bratslavian life in the regular service of God. These include prayer with clapping that creates 'the atmosphere of the land of Israel' via an understanding that the states of descent, loss, illumination and Torah comprise a phase that is 'the way to the land of Israel,' and dramatic and exceptional worship, necessitating self-sacrifice and preparedness 'to do things that appear like madness,' which constitute *a priori* conditions for attaining a level that transcends the level of Moses.

Notes

1 Buber, '*Tzaddik Ba La'aaretz*;' Rapaport, '*Shnei Mekorot*;' Rapoport-Albert, '*Katnut*;' Shvid, '*Chazarah L'artiyutah Shel Eretz Yisrael*;' Green, *Tormented Master*, 69–95; Idel, '*Al Eretz Yisrael*'; Goshen, '*Eretz Israel B'haguto*'; Rose, 'Erez Israel in the Theology and Experience of Rabbi Nahman of Bratzlav;' Verman, 'Aliyah and Yeridah – The Journeys of the Besht and R. Nachman to Israel.' Other sources are found in the collection *Bibliographia*, Part 11, R. *Nachman v'eretz Yisrael*, 172–177.

2 *Chayei Moharan, Nesiyato L'eretz Yisrael*, 5 (133), 130. See Green, *Tormented Master*, 83–95.

3 *Likutei Moharan* II 8. The teaching *Tiku Tochacha* was delivered in the last month of R. Nachman's life, at the beginning of 5571 (1811).

4 In Chapter 1, Part III.

5 *Likutei Moharan* II 8:8.

6 *Likutei Moharan* II 8:8.

7 *Psalms* 89:3.

8 *Likutei Moharan* II 8:9.

9 In *Likutei Moharan* II 78; see Liebes, '*Hatikun Hak'lali*,' 15.

10 *Psalms* 111:6.

11 *Deuteronomy* 11:12.

12 *Likutei Moharan* II 8:10.

13 See above, Chapter 3, Part I; sections 6–7; and also Chapter 4, particularly section 3.

14 *Psalms* 98:1.

15 *Psalms* 19:2.

16 *Psalms* 89:3.

17 *Likutei Moharan* II 8:10.

18 Ibid., 7.

19 See Liebes, *'Hatikun Hak'lali,'* 215–216; Goshen, *'Eretz Yisrael B'hagoto,'* 288, and note 52.

20 *Likutei Moharan* II 116.

21 See Van Gennep, *The Rites of Passage,* 93–111; Turner, 'Variations on a Theme of Liminality.'

22 See further on Chapter 6, section 6.

23 *Chayei Moharan, N'siyato L'eretz Yisrael* 19 (147), 137–138.

24 *Chayei Moharan, Maalat Torato* 2 (341), 242–243.

25 *Shivchei Haran, 'Seder Han'siyah Shelo L'eretz Yisrael,'* note 33, 626–634.

26 *Sichot Haran,* (153), 108–109.

27 *Isaiah* 44:13.

28 *Likutei Moharan* II 8, end of 12.

29 *Hosea* 12:11.

30 *Numbers* 12:8.

31 *Ezekiel* 1:8.

32 *Ecclesiastes* 10:20.

33 See Maimonides, *Guide of the Perplexed,* Part 1, 59.

34 Ibid.

35 *Noam Elimelech, Shemini,* 301; *'Shever Posh'im,'* in Wilenski, *Hasidim Umitnagdim,* Volume II, 129 and 159; *Degel Machaneh Efraim, Parshat Noach,* beginning with *'Vayihi,'* 10.

36 See *Likutei Moharan* I 10, 44, 46, 212; see Goshen, *'Eretz Yisrael B'haguto,'* 281–289.

37 *Isaiah* 57:19.

38 *Likutei Moharan* II 1:8; *Likutei Moharan* I 10; see Naeh, *'Borei Niv Sefatam'* and also Wolfish, 'Hatefilah Hashegurahet.'

39 *Likutei Moharan* I 45.

40 *Likutei Moharan* I 44; *Chayei Moharan,* Makom Leidato, 12 (115), 116.

41 *Likutei Moharan* I 44.

42 *Likutei Moharan* II 19.

43 *Likutei Moharan* II 8:10.

44 *Likutei Moharan* II 5. And see Chapter 5, Part III.

45 Liebes, *'Hatikun Hak'lali,'* 212–216.

46 Chapter 6, section 4

SIX

'Smallness' and 'Greatness' and their Roots in the Kabbalah of the Ari

Introduction

One of the most fascinating topics associated with the absence of the ordinary (*mochin*) and rational mind (*da'at*) is that of 'smallness.' The inability to speak words of Torah, 'forgetting' and behaving like a child and fool, are some of the phenomena that R. Nachman associates with the state of 'smallness.' This topic is moreover intimately connected to R. Nachman's journey to the land of Israel, in the course of which he acted in a variety of strange ways – playing children's games, acting like a fool and more generally, engaging in behavior that disgraced him – which he referred to as 'matters of "smallness".'[1]

Before I place 'smallness' in the framework of R. Nachman's overall understanding of the function of the *rational mind* and *madness* in serving God, I shall first discuss the concepts of 'smallness' and 'greatness' of mind (*mochin*) as they appear in the kabbalah of the Ari, which will serve as a backdrop and provide a basis for understanding R. Nachman's unique approach to this topic.

Recognizing the Lurianic roots of these concepts contributes to a better understanding of the mysterious episode of R. Nachman's journey to the land of Israel. Knowing R. Nachman's relationship with Lurianic kabbalah helps to disclose fundamental elements, hidden until now, which serve as the structural basis of R. Nachman's overall thought and the status he accords acts of foolishness and 'smallness' in the framework of religious worship.

The terms 'smallness' and 'greatness' are often used in Hasidic tradition to describe various internal-spiritual states, of the *zaddik* in particular and of man in general. Often 'greatness' describes a person's state when cleaving to God (a state with various levels), whereas 'smallness' refers to a person's state when he feels distance from God and is not immersed in cleaving to Him.

Although these states of being occur for every individual (each on his own level), the principal focus of engagement with these ideas in Hasidism is in the world of the *zaddik*, for often his state of being indicates that of his generation or is at least influenced by it. States of 'smallness' are described as times of 'the descent of the *zaddik*' from the level of consciousness of 'greatness' to a consciousness of 'smallness.'

The Hasidic masters enumerate three principal reasons for times of 'smallness:'

1. Not even a great person is able to cleave to God continuously. He must relax his intensity in order to continue to exist in the physical world. States of 'smallness' provide rest and renewal of strength before an impending ascent.

2. The descent of the *zaddik* enables him to come close to simple people ('the common man') for the sake of their advancement and ascent. In this sense, he is obligated to descend of his own volition to a state of 'smallness' in order to raise up the masses.

3. The descent of the *zaddik* to a state of 'smallness' is due to his generation, whose spiritual condition affects his own spiritual world. In such an instance, the *zaddik's* descent occurs against his will and not volitionally. The *zaddik's* 'smallness' is expressed in his actions, which are like those of a normal person not disposed to cleaving to God – i.e., engagement in everyday speech, in business and in other mundane affairs. Only at the time of his descent can the *zaddik* come in contact with the members of his community, for while cleaving to God, the *zaddik* is engaged exclusively with his God.[2]

Gershom Scholem states that the Hasidic use of the concepts of 'smallness' and 'greatness' represent a completely novel redaction of the kabbalah of the Ari. Whereas in the kabbalah of the Ari, the terms 'smallness' and 'greatness' refer to *processes* and *states* within the divine structure – the 'supernal *partzufim*' – Hasidism transformed these concepts into apperceptions that apply to the condition of a being human, and, more precisely, according to the degree to which one cleaves to God.[3] 'The Baal Shem Tov transfers these concepts to the realm of the human and gives new meaning to theosophical ideas.'[4] Scholem sees this transformation as part of a broader orientation of Hasidism, which places 'a new emphasis on psychology instead of theosophy.'[5]

Isaiah Tishbi was the first to state that one may find roots of the idea that states of 'smallness' and 'greatness' refer to the human world in the kabbalah of the Ari. Tishbi cites examples[6] demonstrating the idea that the *zaddik's* states of 'smallness' and 'greatness' dependent upon the state of his generation may be found in the kabbalah of the Ari.

Mordecai Fechter[7] has developed an approach to demonstrate that analysis reveals the place of 'consciousness of "smallness"' in the framework of the *sefirot* to be a process and state of being within the *partzuf* of *Zeir Anpin*. And out of an understanding of the connection between *Zeir Anpin* and that which occurs in the human world, we also see a connection between the states of 'smallness' in *Zeir Anpin* and the states of 'smallness' in the human world.

Fechter comes to the unequivocal conclusion that the use of 'smallness' and 'greatness' to describe human states of being 'in later conceptualizations of "smallness" and "greatness" not only is not to be defined as an innovation, as Gershom Scholem defines it, but even to describe it as an "interpretation" is inaccurate. At most, it is possible to see it as providing greater emphasis on Lurianic motifs to which R. Haim Vital had already given expression in his writings.'

Fechter shows Hasidic statements, which Scholem as well as those who follow in his footsteps quote as unprecedented innovations of Hasidism, to be found in the kabbalah of the Ari. In Fechter's view the kabbalah of the Ari contains both the concept that 'in all things exist "smallness" and "greatness"'[8] and the view that there are even states of 'smallness' and 'greatness' in the historical realm (e.g., the exile as a state of 'smallness') so that people can influence situations, including historical situations, by performing mitzvot and engaging in prayer. Similarly, it is possible to find in the kabbalah of the Ari the assertion that a person can bring himself to a state of 'smallness' by engaging in behaviors that involve danger and adversaries; for 'smallness' is to be found in the qualities represented by the divine name, Elokim – the trait of judgment.[9]

Yehudah Liebes, in an even more radical move, asserts that not only 'the psychological meaning of consciousness of "smallness," which Scholem considers to be an innovation of the Hasidim, is already to be found in the kabbalah of the Ari, but that 'this meaning is even more important than the one referring to the supernal *partzufim.* The principal focus of the kabbalah of the Ari is on the psychological plane. That is what stands at the foundation of the ontological mythos that we are used to relating to as the essence of the kabbalah of the Ari.'[10]

Moshe Idel claims that the Hasidic interpretation of the terms 'smallness' and 'greatness' and, more generally, Hasidism's psychological interpretation of the framework of the *sefirot* and kabbalistic structures, was not created *ex nihilo* and is not a Hasidic innovation, but rather a change in emphasis and a dominance of a preferred interpretation. This view was indeed incidental to the kabbalah of the Ari, but it played a central and important role in kabbalistic streams that preceded the kabbalah of the Ari. In Hasidism, the psychological interpretation became the principal means of understanding kabalistic concepts and a primary tool in explaining the existential-religious meaning of the framework of kabbalistic concepts.[11]

It seems to me that a short and precise definition of the relationship between the innovation of the Baal Shem Tov and the kabbalah of the Ari was formulated by R. Nachman of Bratslav, a definition relevant as well to the topic of 'smallness:'

R. Nachman spoke with me about the innovations of the Baal Shem Tov, of blessed memory, who revealed new things in the world. This

is because the *narrative* of the Baal Shem Tov, of blessed memory, is
a new thing that had not been previously revealed. Only in the
writings of the Ari, of blessed memory, may something of the like be
found in a few places.[12]

There is no doubt that the Baal Shem Tov revealed new things. Although one
may find something of the character of his words also in the writings of the
Ari, in the Ari these are found only 'in a few places,' and only 'of the like.'
For the Baal Shem Tov, though, these matters are of central importance; they
are developed and given a sharp and clearly delineated form that they did
not previously possess. Therefore, says R. Nachman, despite the precedence
of the kabbalah of the Ari, it is still possible to maintain that the Baal Shem
Tov constructed and revealed a complete and new 'narrative' without
precedent in the world.

On a number of occasions, R. Nachman deals with the relationship
between his teachings and 'the ways of kabbalah of the Ari,'[13] and states that
his teachings comprise a commentary on the kabbalah of the Ari,
mentioning, in particular, *Etz Chaim* and *Pri Etz Chaim.*[14]

It is clear from R. Nachman's words that his intention is not to offer 'a
simple interpretation,' but to develop matters to the point of creating new
teachings that contribute to an understanding of the kabbalah of the Ari. It
is also clear that R. Nachman consciously emphasized the human existential-
ethical aspect of the Ari's teachings. The tension that lies between relating
to the writings of the Ari as authoritative texts, and engaging in free development which goes beyond the bounds of the original source material
appears as well in the following conversation:

> R. Nachman said those who look into his works who have some intel-
> ligence may think that the ways of the kabbalah of the Ari, of blessed
> memory, and similar teachings, are alluded to as well in
> R. Nachman's works. And they consider this as a positive quality of
> R. Nachman's works – that they reach that far. However, they do not
> know that the opposite is the case. To the contrary, the kabbalistic
> ways of the earlier authorities, of blessed memory, are included in
> R. Nachman's words. And R. Nachman did not explicitly conclude
> his statement, but his intention was manifestly clear. That is to say,
> what he has in mind in the essence of his teaching is exceedingly
> high, and the holy words of the Ari, [*et al.*] are incorporated as well
> into the words of his teaching.[15]

Although R. Nachman takes care not to explicitly conclude his words, in the
end he proclaims that his teaching includes the elements found also in the

kabbalah of the Ari. His teaching though continues to rise 'exceedingly high,' so that it attains places and heights to which even the teaching of the Ari did not arrive.[16]

And indeed, as we shall see, R. Nachman's teachings on 'smallness' constitute a foundational tangent to the kabbalah of the Ari, though this is not to say that he forces the Ari's terms and descriptions of structures into completely transformed content.

In this sense, it is possible to see R. Nachman's teachings as a commentary on the Ari's writings. It is untenable to argue, however, that R. Nachman's teachings provide only an accentuation and emphasis of existent Lurianic motifs. Rather, R. Nachman's teachings present a process that builds and develops new directions in the kabbalah of the Ari, at which the Ari only hints, or a development of ideas that arise in the Ari's writings but are insufficiently cultivated to establish an approach and lead to conclusions. R. Nachman takes these seeds of thought, develops them and causes them to bear beautiful blossoms and fruit.

In a number of places where R. Nachman discusses topics related to 'smallness,' he directs the reader to the Ari and his writings, and not only against a background of shared concepts. R. Nachman's explicit references to the Ari's writings show that his development of kabbalistic materials was created not only via Hasidic conduits and intermediaries who preceded him, although he was certainly influenced by them as well, but in direct contact with the Lurianic corpus, which led R. Nachman to fields and topics not dealt with by other Hasidic thinkers.

The work that follows does not purport to offer a 'correct' explanation of the kabbalah of the Ari, but attempts to identify the materials that occupied R. Nachman when he developed the concept of 'smallness.' I also intend to examine the degree to which R. Nachman remained 'faithful' in his interpretation and dialogue with the kabbalah of the Ari and what remains of the original meanings of Lurianic terms and structural descriptions after R. Nachman uses them to explain various internal states that he experienced. In particular, I aim to examine whether consideration of the kabbalistic background of R. Nachman's teachings can contribute to an additional understanding of R. Nachman's view of 'smallness' and 'the journey to the land of Israel.'

I. A Minor is not obligated in Mitzvot

Ada Rapoport-Albert points out that R. Nachman describes states of 'smallness' as not only a descent to the plane of existence of simple people, but as an experiment in a 'life without rules,' in which people violate the law.[17] In *Likutei*

Moharan II 78, R. Nachman speaks of 'the way of simplicity of the *zaddik*, which is a state of separation from the Torah,' explaining that in this state the *zaddik* is 'of the aspect of the existence of the world before the receiving of the Torah.' This state is described by R. Nachman as analogous to 'the path to the land of Israel.'

Indeed, in the description of R. Nachman's journey to the land of Israel R. Nachman speculates a number of times about serving God without Torah and mitzvot, corresponding to the patriarchs' worship of God prior to the giving of the Torah.[18] A life without the Sabbath and holidays and without the ability to keep any mitzvah is a life without Torah and mitzvot, and thus necessarily a life in violation of the Torah. The patriarchs kept the mitzvot in a spiritual manner that did not include the physical performance of the mitzvot as they are known today. On the way to the land of Israel, R. Nachman gained the ability to engage in the service of God without keeping the Torah and mitzvot in their simple halachic sense.

In *Shaar Hamitzvot, Vayichi,* R. Chaim Vital describes the core of the spiritual change that a mourner undergoes and the halachic ramifications resulting from the state of mourning and their meaning:

> In regard to that which is relevant to the mourner, himself, and the change that he undergoes during his days of mourning [...] And behold, the loss that the mourner suffers is the following: It is known that all souls are dependent upon Supernal Man, *Zeir Anpin.* And every soul possesses 248 limbs and is called 'perfect man.' And in that aspect, in *Zeir Anpin* upon which the soul of the mourner depends, the aspect of the 'image of the *mochin* of Abba and Imma' rises. And all that remains in the aspect of *Zeir Anpin* on which the mourner's soul depends is the aspect of the *mochin* of 'smallness,' which is the time of 'nursing' [...] This is because the *mochin* of 'greatness' are called 'the life of the king.' And when they rise, death remains, heaven forbid. That is the aspect of the *mochin* of 'smallness' of the divine name Elokim, from which the *kelipot* (husks), which are called death, nurse. And since the mourner's relative died, that indicates that also on the level of the mourner's root above [...] the *mochin* of 'greatness' have been entirely removed from the mourner's root and have returned to the days of the *mochin* of 'smallness' – Elokim.[19]

The basic assumption is that the death of a person's relative indicates that a change has taken place in the mourner's spiritual root in the supernal world. The 'change that occurs to a person during his days of mourning'[20] is the removal of the *mochin* of 'greatness' and the return to the days of the *mochin* of 'smallness.'

R. Yosef Karo's *Shulchan Aruch* states in regard to the halachot of mourning:

> If a person has suffered the death of a relative over whom he is obligated to mourn before the burial [...] And he does not recite the blessing over bread nor the grace after meals, and no one recites a blessing on his behalf. And people do not include him to join them in beginning the grace after meals. Even if he eats with others who do recite the grace after meals, he does not answer amen after them. And he is freed of the obligation of the mitzvot stated in the Torah, and even if he does not need to engage in attending to the deceased person.[21]

An *onen*, a person whose as yet unburied dead lies before him, is not obligated 'by any of the mitzvot stated in the Torah.' But at the moment a person buries his dead, the designation of *onen* ceases and he is obligated by the laws pertaining to the *avel*. Regarding the first day of mourning, the halachah states that 'it is forbidden to put on *tefillin* on the first day.'[22] This is so even in regard to an *avel* – even after the mourner has buried his dead. The mitzvah of *tefillin* is unique in that not only is the mourner not obligated to put on *tefillin*, but on the first day he may not do so even if he so desires.

In *Shaar Hamitzvot* 'the removal of the *tefillin*' is explained as referring to the removal of the *mochin* of 'greatness' and a return to the *mochin* of 'smallness,' which occurs at the time of mourning. R. Chaim Vital emphasizes the difference between the *onen* and *avel*. He explains the 'removal of the *tefillin*' in that the mourner is 'a complete *onen*' on the first day and exists with a 'smallness' of *mochin*. Thus, R. Chaim Vital forges a direct link between the state of *mochin* of 'smallness' and the halachic status of the *onen*, 'who is freed of all the mitzvot stated in the Torah.'

This correspondence between *mochin* of 'smallness' and the *onen* is not stated explicitly, for R. Chaim Vital is dealing solely with *tefillin* and with its connection to *da'at* and to the *mochin* of 'greatness.' But the link between *mochin* of 'smallness' and the *onen* is R. Chaim Vital's presumable conclusion, for he explains that the complete *onen* is placed in a state of *mochin* of 'smallness.'

Broadening the explanation of the state of 'smallness' so that it explicates the status of the *onen* (besides the explanation of why the mourner is prohibited to put on *tefillin*) may be inferred from R. Chaim Vital's explicit linking of *tefillin* with *mochin* of 'greatness.' That explanation raises the question of why the *onen* is forbidden to wear *tefillin* and not only freed of the obligation of wearing *tefillin*.

The conclusion of R. Chaim Vital's words, where he draws an analogy between the mourner and the child – 'and this also explains why the child is free of the obligation to put on *tefillin*' – proves this approach.

A child is free of all the mitzvot presented in the Torah, not only from the mitzvah of *tefillin*. Moreover, 'if a child knows how to take proper care of his *tefillin*, his father gets *tefillin* for him in order to train him to keep mitzvot.'[23] And that is the custom. A child begins to put on *tefillin* some time before he comes of age, not because he is obligated to do so, being free of the obligation to perform mitzvot, but because of his father's obligation to educate him.

Certainly therefore, the parallel between the child and the *onen* does not rest upon the prohibition to put on *tefillin*, for the child is not prohibited from putting on *tefillin*. The analogy must then be based on the freedom of these two classes of people from the obligation of keeping all the mitzvot stated in the Torah, a status due to the fact that both of them are in a state of *mochin* of 'smallness.'

This may explain what R. Nachman meant when he linked the secret of his entry to the land of Israel (which was in the aspect of 'smallness' and involved attaining an existence lacking the obligation to keep the Torah and mitzvot) with 'the secret *kavanot* of *tefillin*.'

Shivchei Haran tells us that 'one of the great sages who was considered to be very important in the land of Israel and outside the land of Israel ... and who was also one of the masters of kabbalah,' begged R. Nachman to explain to him 'with which point of the points of the land of Israel did your eminence of your Torah enter the land.' R. Nachman initially refused to explain, but after the great sage begged him to at least reveal some insight from his teachings, R. Nachman turned to him with a question: 'Do you know the secret of the *kavanot* of the *tefillin*? ... And since you do not know the secret of the *kavanot* of *tefillin*, you do not know the secret of the four directions of the land of Israel.'[24]

In light of our knowledge of the descent to 'smallness' and R. Nachman's attainment of the level of serving God without Torah and mitzvot as part of the journey to the land of Israel, it is reasonable to see in R. Nachman's words an allusion to the words of R. Chaim Vital quoted earlier. It is also possible that there is here an allusion to additional perspectives of R. Chaim Vital regarding matters of 'smallness' and *tefillin*, with which we shall deal further along.

II. 'And He was a Youth' – 'Smallness' as Making Oneself Foolish and Engaging in Childish Acts

One of the strange phenomena associated with R. Nachman's descent into 'smallness' on his journey to the land of Israel was his practice of engaging in playful and foolish actions.

> For in Istanbul, R. Nachman would engage in all sorts of acts of
> 'smallness.' And he would go barefoot and without a belt and
> without his hat, and he dressed only in the lining that he had from
> some garment. And he went in the marketplace in the manner of
> children who run about in the marketplace and play. And he
> engaged in make-believe wars as children do. And they would call
> one person by the name of France and another by another name,
> and they engaged in war. And it literally involved war strategies. And
> in Istanbul, R. Nachman engaged in these matters of 'smallness' a
> very great deal.[25] Before R. Nachman came to the land of Israel, he
> experienced great sufferings and great obstacles – so many that it is
> impossible to explain and tell about them. And in Istanbul he threw
> himself into an incredible state of 'smallness,' to an unimaginable
> degree. And he dressed in a torn garment and he went barefoot and
> without his hat. And he went outside, and he went about like one
> of the most worthless of people, and engaged in many similar
> insignificant matters of 'smallness' for a period of time. And he
> engaged in war games with others, in the manner of children who
> play with each other, etc., and similarly he played other games and
> engaged in other acts of 'smallness' – something that is impossible
> to explain and tell.[26]

Although the concept of 'smallness' is regularly used in Hasidism,
R. Nachman's usage of this term is not otherwise found there. 'Smallness' is
generally associated with a group of clear characteristics: sadness and
depression, passivity and the subduing of a person's faculties, this serving as
a period of relaxation and rest from cleaving to God.[27]

But in R. Nachman's words we find states of 'smallness' that are not states
of rest or associated with depression. On the contrary, they are marked by
lively activity and happiness. R. Nachman runs about in the marketplace, acts
mischievously and plays war games with children, in all their strategic details.
This is hardly a state of depression and passivity. To the contrary, it is an
explosion of joy, frolicking and playfulness. This is not the 'smallness' due to
the connection between a *zaddik* and his Hasidim, or because of his
engagement in mundane matters and his congregation's needs. For
R. Nachman, the concept of 'smallness' has the meaning of 'childishness.'
And thus, the descent into 'smallness' is expressed in behavior that characterizes youth and children. According to R. Nachman's view, the state of
'smallness' has a regressive quality, in which a person reverts to previous stages
of his development.

A basis for this view of 'smallness' may be found in the writings of R. Chaim Vital. In a number of places, he writes that when Joseph is in a state of 'smallness' of *mochin*, he is called a 'youth.' A special importance inheres in this comment, since Joseph represents the trait of the *zaddik*; therefore, Joseph's qualities are understood as being relevant to the world of the *zaddik* in the Hasidic sense.[28] Moreover, in R. Chaim Vital*'s Likutei Torah* and *Shaar Hapesukin* the connection between Joseph and *zaddikim* is explicit.[29]

In these works, before R. Chaim Vital begins his discussion of Joseph's states of 'smallness' and 'greatness,' he first notes that *zaddikim* too have states of 'smallness' and 'greatness.' Joseph is cited as an example of the *zaddik*, the aspect of *yesod*, who remains a *zaddik* even when he is in a state of 'smallness,' as well as when he is in a state of 'greatness.' Important for our purposes is the assertion that when the *zaddik* Joseph is found in *mochin* of 'smallness,' he is called 'small youth.'

Standing behind these teachings is the verse, 'These are the generations of Jacob: Joseph, who was seventeen years old, was grazing the flock with his brothers. And he was a youth together with the sons of Bilhah and with the sons of Zilpah, the wives of his father. And Joseph brought their evil report to their father.'[30] And the Talmudic sages expound, '"And he was a youth" – i.e., he engaged in youthful acts.'[31]

In accordance with this Talmudic exposition, the expression, 'and he was a youth,' is not meant to indicate Joseph's age, mentioned explicitly at the beginning of the verse, but to characterize his behavior. This aspect of Joseph is that of 'smallness:' 'And behold, at the time that Joseph only possessed the aspect of the *yesod* of *Zeir* in the aspect of those *mochin* of "smallness" that descended there, then he is called "small youth".'

From these quotations, we may understand that the *zaddik's* states of 'smallness' are those in which he returns in some sense to being a child or youth. The state of 'smallness' involves the removal of the *mochin* of 'greatness' and a return to the *mochin* of 'smallness.' And the state of the *mochin* of 'and he was a youth' affects his deeds – he 'engages in acts of youth.' R. Nachman's deeds of 'smallness' 'as the way of youth,' who play and act foolishly, may therefore be seen as a realization of the description of the *zaddik's* state of 'smallness' as described in the kabbalah of the Ari.

It is possible that the passageway in R. Nachman's doctrine that leads from 'youth' to acts of foolishness relies consciously or not on the fact that *naar* – 'youth' – is homonymous with the Yiddish term *narish*, meaning 'engaging in acts of foolishness, stupidity and madness.'[32] And we find in the language of R. Nachman himself the expression *narish* used to describe deeds of foolishness and madness in which a person is obligated to engage in order to attain joy. And thus testifies R. Natan:

For in a number of places our rebbe, of blessed memory, delivered a number of important exhortations to the effect that a person must accustom himself to be happy always. And we find in his holy words, that it is possible to be joyful only with foolish matters, by making oneself like a fool and making oneself happy with foolish matters [...] And the essence of joy can come only via matters of foolishness, as I heard from the mouth of R. Nachman, of blessed memory, who said these words: '*Se hat a panim az men mer nit freilich zein nar mit narish makhn zich* – it seems that a person can only be happy if he engages in foolish deeds.'[33]

III. 'Smallness' and Forgetting – 'Smallness' and 'I Do Not Know'

R. Nachman conditions the phenomenon of forgetting on *mochin* of 'smallness': 'also, the essence of forgetting comes from the *mochin* of "smallness" … "And your Torah have I not forgotten" – for forgetting is *mochin* of "smallness," the aspect of Elokim. And when judgments are ameliorated (as above), then a person is in *mochin* of "greatness," and he does not experience forgetting.'[34]

A link between states of 'smallness' and forgetting arises as well from an analysis of occurrences in which R. Nachman himself was stricken with forgetting. In a number of places, we find descriptions in which R. Nachman forgets his Torah and proclaims 'I do not know' in relation to events that he associates with 'the journey to the land of Israel.'[35] R. Nachman defines this journey as involving a descent into 'smallness of smallness.'[36]

In *Yemei Moharanat*, R. Natan describes how R. Nachman taught *Likutei Moharan* II 78 – a teaching that deals with the *zaddik*'s state of simplicity and with the connection of this state to the land of Israel:

On *Shabbat Nachamu*, a number of guests gathered with R. Nachman for that Sabbath (the one just mentioned). And R. Nachman came in from his room to the house where they were eating. And he made kiddush on the wine with faint strength, because he was already very weak, for it was close to his passing.

And he sat at the table after he made kiddush, before he washed his hands for the meal, and he began to speak with the people. He said: 'Why have people come here? I now know nothing at all! When I teach Torah, it is certainly worthwhile coming to me. But now, when in truth I know nothing at all, for I am now a completely simple man (called *prostik* in Yiddish) and I don't know anything at all, and so why have people come?'

And R. Nachman spoke at some length in this talk about the fact that he is at present completely *prostik* and truly knows nothing at all. And he said that he revives himself only with the fact that he had journeyed to the land of Israel. And he spoke at some length of this as well, until, from the midst of that holy talk, in which he told that he knows nothing at all, and that he is completely *prostik* and that he revives himself only with his journey to the land of Israel, in the midst of these words, he began to speak, until he revealed to us the wondrous teaching of how via the path of the journey to the land of Israel, the *zaddik* revives himself at the time of his being simple, etc.

But it is impossible to explain this entire matter in writing – how this teaching was revealed and drawn forth, truly *ex nihilo*. This is because at first R. Nachman truly did not know anything, because every time that he said that he does not know, he truly did not know anything at all, as he once made an oath to this effect by making reference to the holy Sabbath. And he said the following, '*Do shver ich by Shabbos* – I swear by the Sabbath,' regarding this matter that he does not know anything at all.[37]

R. Natan here associates the states of 'simplicity' and 'I do not know' with the journey to the land of Israel, which was accompanied by states of 'smallness of smallness'[38] (a combination of concepts that he mentions elsewhere too[39]).

R. Nachman's 'I do not know' is not a lack of knowledge and understanding of something that he had never before known, but a state of forgetting, a loss of memory and concealment of insights and teachings that he had already known and attained.

R. Nachman said that the fact that he is not able to teach Torah at times is something particularly novel – 'that I have already developed and prepared a number of great new insights, but in the midst of that I forget everything and I do not remember anything, and I do not know anything at all, of any book in the world, and I do not even know any melody. Instead, everything, indeed everything, is forgotten and hidden from me. And that is truly a great wonder.' I heard of this matter from R. Nachman's holy mouth a number of times, for it is usual for him – that a number of times he says, 'Now I do not know anything, nothing at all,' although in the previous hour he had revealed wondrous and awesome insights.[40]

R. Nachman's fear of total forgetting and the sufferings that accompany the states of 'I do not know' are clearly expressed in a dream that he had in Kislev 5570 (1808):

I said to him, 'Give me the book.' And he gave it to me and I took it, but I did not know anything, not even how to hold the book. And I opened the book and I did not know anything in it, and it appeared to me like another language and like another script, because I did not know anything in it at all. And I experienced great suffering because of this.[41]

In *Etz Chaim, Shaar Mochin Dekatnut*, we find the following:

And behold, the entire faculty of forgetting is drawn to a person from these *mochin* of 'smallness.' And when a person can draw them down via his deeds below, by drawing forth *mochin* of 'greatness' and pushing away Elokim of 'smallness' and removing them from *Zeir Anpin* altogether, then he will have a wondrous memory in Torah and will understand all of the secrets of the Torah. This is because every act of remembering is in the male. However, the Elokim of 'smallness' impedes the illumination of the male in the secret of 'remember.' And indeed, a person who draws them down as well from the female to *beriah* will certainly not experience any forgetting, and the secrets of the Torah will be revealed to him in their rectified state.[42]

Here too, the influence of the *mochin* of 'smallness' on the human plane, on an individual person, is clearly described. On the one hand, R. Chaim Vital describes a person's personal merit in succeeding to push away the 'smallness' by means of *mochin* of 'greatness.' And on the other hand, he describes forgetfulness and loss of secrets of the Torah as deriving from the state of 'smallness.'[43] Further on, we will see that other sources in the Lurianic kabbalah present forgetting the Torah as a result of *mochin* of 'smallness' as something occuring to the *zaddik* not because of his personal spiritual state but because of the state and sins of his generation.

IV. 'Smallness' and the Land of Israel

R. Nachman claims that a condition for attaining the 'greatness of greatness' that may be received from the land of Israel is the ability to descend to the 'smallness of smallness.'

And I heard in the name of our Rebbe, of blessed memory, that he said that before coming to 'greatness' it is necessary to first fall to 'smallness.' And the land of Israel is 'greatness of greatness.'

Therefore, it is necessary to first fall to the 'smallness of smallness.' And thus the Baal Shem Tov, of blessed memory, was not able to come to the land of Israel, because he could not descend to that 'smallness.' But R. Nachman, of blessed memory, merited to come to the land of Israel by means of the extraordinary 'smallness' to which he descended with his great wisdom, to an incredible 'smallness,' a 'smallness of smallness,' until he merited to come to the land of Israel, which is the 'greatness of greatness.' And as for the prodigious insight that he attained in the land of Israel – if all of the seas were ink, etc., it would not suffice to explain something that was never before heard or seen – a person who merited by means of his entry to the land of Israel such an incredible, mighty and supernal attainment as that of R. Nachman, until he rose to an extremely high status and level.[44]

As we saw above, R. Nachman indeed acted in this manner on his way to the land of Israel, deliberately lowering himself to states of 'smallness,' both by means of acts of youthful foolishness and by intentionally entering into situations that would result in him being treated with contempt and anger.[45]

The Baal Shem Tov did not succeed in entering the land of Israel because of his inability to contend with the descent to the state of 'smallness of smallness.' And indeed, in a number of versions recounting the Baal Shem Tov's attempt to go to the land of Israel,[46] we learn that when arriving in Istanbul he underwent a 'falling of the *mochin*'[47] and was immersed in 'smallness.' His daughter Edel saw that 'the spirit of her father had left him, because he was in a state of "smallness," lying down in the study hall like one of the common people, and his spirit of holiness and all of the great levels that he had possessed left him.'[48] In another version of the story, the Baal Shem Tov 'forgot the secrets of the Torah and the *kavanot* and he became like a regular person.'[49] In a version cited by R. Yitzchak Izak Safrin of Kamarna, we find that the Baal Shem Tov experienced a state very similar to the description found in R. Nachman's dream of excommunication and forgetting: 'and all of his levels were taken away from him, even his Torah and prayer, so that he did not even know how to say "Blessed" from the siddur, for he did not understand the letters.'[50] According to the version cited in *Edat Zaddikim*, the Baal Shem Tov said, 'I do not know anything now; my power has been taken from me.'[51] These states of being resemble closely the states of forgetting and 'smallness' experienced by R. Nachman, and comprise a part of the journey to the land of Israel.[52] R. Nachman, who succeeded in dealing with the 'smallness' and simplicity of the journey to the land of Israel, would later revive himself in difficult moments in which he experienced states of simplicity and 'I do not know' with the power of that journey to the land of Israel.[53]

Another foremost personality, who did not succeed in fulfilling his desire to enter the land of Israel, was Moses. In *Likutei Moharan* 78, dealing with the times when the *zaddik* acts like 'a simple man, literally,' a mode of behavior intimately connected with the conduct of 'smallness,'[54] R. Nachman correlates the journey to the land of Israel with the behavior of simplicity and with the aspect in which the world existed before the receiving of the Torah. He claims that even Moses requested to enter the land of Israel via this aspect, but does not explain why this request was denied. Since, however, we know that Moses did not enter the land, we also know that Moses failed in his attempt to enter into the aspect of 'smallness' and simplicity on the way to the land of Israel.[55]

It is instructive to note that the writings of R. Chaim Vital also associate the failure of Moses to enter the land of Israel with his descent to 'smallness of smallness' – i.e., to the aspect of 'fetal existence.' Moses, unlike R. Nachman of Bratslav in a later generation, was not able to deal with this state of 'smallness' and thus did not succeed in entering the land of Israel.

In *Shaar Hapesukim*, the verse, 'And Hashem grew angry at me for your sake' is explained as dealing with states of 'smallness.' The verse is part of the speech of Moses describing his prayers and requests that God allow him to enter the land of Israel and see the good land. These requests were denied and he did not merit entering the land of Israel. R. Chaim Vital explains the rejection of his request by analyzing the words, 'And Hashem grew angry at me for your sake and did not listen to me.'[56]

Moses returns to 'smallness' and to a state of 'fetal existence,'[57] and thus forgets the illuminations and knowledge of the halachot that he attained beforehand, when he had been in a state of *mochin* of 'greatness.' This return to the aspect of 'fetal existence' did not occur of his initiative and desire, but rather against his will, caused by the sins of his generation. This, the context teaches, is why Moses did not succeed in entering the land of Israel.

We learn in another of R. Chaim Vital's teachings, which does not deal with the topic of entering the land of Israel, that Moses feared being involved in states of 'smallness.' Rather than contend with such a state, he ran and fled from it:

And that is the secret of Moses our teacher, peace be upon him, the Rabbi of the prophets. As the verse states of him, 'And Moses fled from before it.' And the reason is that the topic of the staff that turned into a snake is the aspect of the 'smallness' of *Zeir Anpin*, which is called 'snake,' as written in *Etz Chaim*.[58] And as he dealt with that exposition he was afraid, 'and he fled from before it.' And thus, this secret needs to be hidden, whether because of its intrinsic nature or whether because we do not know its truth – not even a fragment of a mustard seed of that exposition.[59]

The secret of 'smallness' is thus revealed to be a threatening secret, one with which even Moses could not contend and from which he fled. The state of 'smallness' and 'fetal existence' to which Moses returned against his will cost Moses dearly, causing him to lose and forget his spiritual illuminations and knowledge of halachot. It is impossible to exaggerate the difficulty that Moses, father of the prophets and giver of the Torah, experienced in returning to 'smallness' and to 'fetal existence,' bereft of prophecy and Torah. The conclusion we must draw, therefore, is that the secret of 'smallness' must be hidden and not dealt with and that a person should flee from it as from before a snake.

Yehudah Liebes notes that in *Sod Shevi'i shel Pesach*,[60] the Ari refers to R. Shimon ben Yochai as a figure analogous to Moses, for he too feared an encounter with the secret of 'smallness.'[61]

We thus learn that all four central figures whom R. Nachman saw as his spiritual predecessors – Moses, R. Shimon bar Yochai, the Ari and the Baal Shem Tov[62] – failed in their encounter with 'smallness.' Despite this, R. Nachman was determined to succeed where they had failed. And indeed, he was not afraid to descend to 'smallness of smallness,' with utter dedication of heart and mind; he was also able to return from there alive and attain all that he wished,[63] even though he too paid a heavy price.

V. 'Smallness' and Death

R. Nachman viewed his ability to contend with the descent to 'smallness of smallness' on his journey to the land of Israel as the factor that saved him from death. The attempt to go to the land of Israel was freighted with the penalty of death, a penalty that R. Nachman escaped because of his descent to 'smallness' and the accompanying shame, which was a sort of substitute for death.

We understand that, R. Nachman, of blessed memory, purposefully allowed himself to be abused with all sorts of insults. And he said to his companion that these insults would be a great favor for him in going and in returning. This is because the great power of the great obstacles that he experienced as he went to the land of Israel is impossible to imagine and evaluate and describe. And it was possible for R. Nachman to come to the land of Israel only by means of this 'smallness.' And we heard afterwards from his mouth explicitly that if he had not experienced these insults and this 'smallness,' he would not have been able to come to the land of Israel by any means. And he said that he saw that he must remain there in Istanbul – i.e., that he must die there, but his 'smallness' and the insults that he suffered saved him, because before one comes to the land of Israel, etc. ...[64]

Not only was R. Nachman condemned to death as a result of his journey to the land of Israel, but, as we shall see, one of his daughters was too; she was not saved.

When R. Nachman came from Kaminetz, one of his daughters passed away, peace be upon her. R. Nachman said, 'I lost one like this, and another one of mine like this may die, heaven forbid, because of one movement that I make, for there is a difference in me between what I was before I was in Kaminetz and what I was after I was there, may Hashem save us.' [65]

R. Nachman's journey to Kaminetz was the first step on his journey to the land of Israel. In *Chayei Moharan*, in the chapter, 'His Journey to the Land of Israel,' R. Natan tells of R. Nachman's journey to Kaminetz. Similarly, the booklet, *Seder Han'siyah Shelo L'eretz Yisrael*, presents R. Nachman's journey to Kaminetz as an introduction to and beginning of the story of his journey to the land of Israel. R. Nachman himself explicitly connected the two trips: 'And our rebbe, of blessed memory, said that whoever knows why the land of Israel was first in the hands of Canaan and only afterwards came into the hands of Israel knows why he first went to Kaminetz and only afterwards to the land of Israel.'[66] R. Nachman saw the journey to Kaminetz as part of the process of going to the land of Israel. And thus his daughter's death was part of the price that R. Nachman paid in his first steps to the land of Israel.

We saw above that R. Nachman noted that the Baal Shem Tov failed to enter the land of Israel since, unlike R. Nachman, the Baal Shem Tov 'was not able to descend into such a state of "smallness".' Stories about the Baal Shem Tov's attempt to enter the land of Israel recount that as he sailed from Istanbul to the land of Israel the sea began to storm and all the people on the ship, including the Baal Shem Tov, were in danger of dying. Only the Baal Shem Tov's proclamation that he was returning home and not proceeding to the land of Israel calmed the storm and made possible their safe return home. Thus, the journey to the land of Israel – whether of the Baal Shem Tov or R. Nachman – was associated with the danger of death, for them and for members of their families. But whereas R. Nachman knew that he had lost his daughter because of his journey yet continued on his way, at the moment that the Baal Shem Tov heard the outcries of his daughter Edel drowning in the sea, he said, 'Master of worlds, I am returning home.'[67]

In the context of the danger of death associated with an attempt to attain 'smallness' on the way to the land of Israel, also the kabbalah of the Ari describes the figure of Moses as someone who attempted to go to the land of Israel but who died at its threshold.

> We can also expound, in accord with that which we have already learned regarding the verse, 'My beloved went down to his garden' that when Hashem, be He blessed, takes the *zaddikim* from this world, they become a garment for Him, so that He is like a fetus within them and clothed within them. And that is the meaning of the phrase, 'And Hashem was angry me for your sake' – because due to your sin I was gathered from the world before my time – *vayitaber,* 'He was angry,' can be read as 'He was inserted into a fetal existence – *ibur.*'[68]

Despite his requests and prayers to enter the land of Israel, Moses was gathered from the world before his time, due to the sins of his generation. The Baal Shem Tov understood the danger of death; he returned home and was thus saved. R. Nachman is the only one who succeeded in descending to an extraordinary state of 'smallness' so as to enter the land of Israel whole and to return from it whole.

In a section from *Shaar Hamitzvot*, which deals with mourning,[69] R. Chaim Vital describes a close connection between death and the *mochin* of 'smallness': 'for the *mochin* of "greatness" are called "the life of the king" and when they are removed there remains death, heaven forbid, which is the aspect of *mochin* of "smallness" of the name Elokim, because from there is the "nursing" of the husks, which are called death.' This phrasing clearly expresses the view that death is a consequence of the return to a *mochin* of 'smallness.' And indeed, engaging in the secrets of 'smallness' is presented as a great danger that can lead to a person's death or to the death of a family member. Even the Ari was punished because he dealt with the secret of 'smallness:'[70]

> And indeed, his union is one of 'smallness.' And that is the secret mentioned in the Zohar (*B'shalach,* 52b) regarding the secret of the splitting of the Red Sea. And R. Shimon bar Yochai, peace upon him, said in regard to that, 'Do not ask about that word and do not test Hashem your God' – precisely so. And this matter is a very, very deep secret, so much so that a person almost puts himself in danger by writing about it – and how much more if he speaks of it. And under-

stand. Know that every place that the supernal 'smallness' is aroused, those are powerful judgments. And even if a person engages in the most supernal 'greatness' of all, or if he involves himself in any area of all the expositions of supernal *atzilut*, he is not in as great a danger as a person who engages in the secret of 'smallness.' That is because it is over there that the external forces take hold, as is known to those who know the hidden wisdom and who understand knowledge. Therefore, when a person deals with them, the external forces are aroused and make mention of this person's sins and he is caught in the net, heaven forbid. And so every time that my master, of blessed memory, dealt with any exposition on 'smallness' he was punished, as occurred for my many sins, since I begged him to reveal this deep secret to me, as is known, etc. And I should not expand on this, since my eyes overflow with tears like a flowing river. And even Moses our teacher, peace be upon him – when he came upon the secret of 'smallness,' which is the secret of the staff that turned into a snake, what is written of him? 'And Moses fled from before it.' And these matters are deep.[71]

Here we see again that dealing with 'smallness' is dangerous and difficult: Moses descended to 'smallness' not of his own will, consequently forgetting his illuminations and knowledge of halachot. Although he fled from the 'smallness,' he nevertheless passed away before his time. The Ari, of his own volition or in answer to the pleadings of R. Chaim Vital, dared to deal with and reveal the secrets of 'smallness,' and he too was punished for as long as he involved himself with it.[72]

The Ari lost his son because he involved himself in the secret of 'smallness.' And as Yehudah Liebes shows, the Ari himself passed away because he revealed the secrets of *trein urzilin d'ailata*, which are connected to the secret of 'smallness.'[73] Learning about and dealing with 'smallness' leads a person to a state of 'smallness;'[74] this arouses the judgements associated with the divine name Elokim so that the *mochin* of 'greatness' leave, resulting in the person's death.

R. Nachman was well-aware of these sources, and offered an analogy between himself and the Ari:[75]

One time a grandchild of R. Nachman, of blessed memory, was ill and bedridden with smallpox, may the Merciful One save us. And R. Nachman lamented to me that he suffered from this a great deal. And he told me then that there are ways of Hashem that cannot be understood. For instance, we find that in the case of the Ari, of blessed memory, one son passed away, and the Ari said that he passed away because of the secret that he revealed to his student, R. Chaim Vital, of blessed memory. And in truth the Ari had to reveal this secret to R. Chaim Vital, because R. Chaim Vital begged him a great deal to do so, and when R. Chaim Vital begged him, he had to reveal it to him. This is because the Ari said that he had come to the world solely to rectify the soul of R. Chaim Vital, of blessed memory, and so he was forced from heaven to reveal the secret to him. Nevertheless, he was punished as a result ... And that is 'the ways of Hashem,' which are impossible to understand with intellect in any way. And what may be understood from R. Nachman's words in regard to himself is that all of his suffering and pain and the suffering of his children, may they live, was solely due to the fact that he involved himself with us in order to bring us close to Hashem, be He blessed. And although he was forced to do so, because certainly Hashem, be He blessed, desires this, because Hashem, be He blessed, 'thinks thoughts so that none may be distanced from Him,' yet nevertheless R. Nachman suffered a great deal as a result of this, because that is 'the ways of Hashem' [...] And R. Nachman would come and tell me of the great suffering that he experienced due to the fact that his grand-child was ill (as mentioned above). And he said that he wished that he himself could be sick in place of the child (mentioned above). And he said that he felt all of the groans (*kretzin* in Yiddish) of the baby in his heart, etc. Afterwards, he said, 'But the following will be accounted to me for the good – [i.e.,] that when another person has an illness in his house and brings me a *pidyon* or asks me to pray for him, I also experience the same amount of suffering, literally'...

Also, when one of R. Nachman's followers would drift away, heaven forbid, R. Nachman said, 'I experience suffering literally in my heart,' just like that mentioned above. And he told then of a person who had left him at that time. And he said that he experienced all the suffering mentioned above because of that person. Again, I heard from one of R. Nachman's followers that he too heard from our Rebbe, of blessed memory, about this matter at the time that R. Nachman's small son, Shlomo Efraim, of blessed memory, passed away – i.e., that R. Nachman said that he experienced sufferings for our sake. He said, 'Is it not the case that the Ari, of blessed memory, only revealed one secret yet he was punished? How much more in my case, since I have revealed so many secrets as these to you.'[76]

R. Nachman is well-aware of the price of dealing with 'smallness' and of the attempt to travel to the land of Israel, both because of the loss of illumina-tions and attainments and because of the danger of death. Similarly,

R. Nachman is aware of Moses's attempt to avoid dealing with 'smallness' and of the price that the Ari paid; he also recalls and mentions the failure of the Baal Shem Tov to descend to 'smallness.' But despite all this, R. Nachman decides to descend to 'smallness of smallness' in an attempt to arrive at the end of the journey, to the land of Israel, and there to attain 'greatness of greatness.'[77]

VI. From Particulars to the Totality: The Return to 'Smallness' as a New Birth

This is an appropriate place to move from a detailed discussion of the various phenomena of 'smallness' to an analysis of the complete cluster of characteristics deemed 'smallness' that R. Nachman developed from the kabbalah of the Ari. 'Smallness' is characterized as a period or state at the border of a normal, adult and mature existence. The descent into 'smallness' in essence entails a return to the initial stages of the development of life, and includes – terminologically and in terms of content – a return to the fetal state ('a second gestation'), which is to be understood not only as a *pre-mochin* and *pre-da'at* existence but even as one that is pre-life. The relationship between 'smallness' and death is due to the qualitative similarity between them. 'Smallness' and, even more explicitly, the fetal state, are by definition especially close to the initial point of life, and in this sense are also close to the point of the end of existence. If the dynamic of returning to 'smallness,' 'nursing' and 'fetal existence' is not halted at the proper place, the next stage is death and lack of life, in a pre-fetal, pre-life state.

'Fetal existence' and 'smallness' serve as links of connectivity between life and death, between absolute lack of *da'at* and *mochin* of 'greatness.' And so we find these states at the opposite end of the spectrum of life as well – not only at the beginning of life, but also at its end. The mourner, whose relative's death indicates that death has touched him at his core, falls into a state of 'smallness.' The on-going process of life and the touch of death imprint themselves via the absence of *da'at* and the fall into *mochin* of 'smallness.' These characterize the passageway between life and death, between lack of *da'at* and *mochin* of 'greatness.' This imagery linking old age and childhood may be seen in actual human life: old age is accompanied by forgetting and the loss of Torah and spiritual illumination. Even in the area of basic psychological functioning, an old person is like a child.[78]

The child and mourner experience their own versions of the absence of *da'at* and the existence of a realm bordering between life and death. The danger involved in a descent into 'smallness' is thus due not only to having ignored the dictum, 'The honor of Hashem is to hide a matter' and having dealt with problematical aspects of divinity, aspects best served by silence and concealment,[79] but because the state of 'smallness' borders between life and death.[80]

The above description serves also as the background to explaining why a child and an *onen* are both freed of the obligation to perform mitzvot. Their states of 'smallness' are understood to be liminal states,[81] which by their nature free one of the obligation to adhere to 'Torah and mitzvot.' This freedom may be understood by taking into account two qualities that characterize the child and the *onen*. The first is the lack of *da'at* – 'a fool is freed of all mitzvot.'[82] And the second is the closeness to death – 'with the dead is my freedom' (since when a person dies he is freed of the obligation to keep the Torah and mitzvot[83]). These statements assume that the framework of Torah and mitzvot is relevant only to a particular manner of life and to a particular consciousness – one that is mature and possesses knowledge.[84]

The ambivalence about falling to a state of 'smallness' is highlighted when we account for the cyclical nature of the processes of 'smallness' and 'greatness' in the kabbalah of the Ari. The absence of *mochin* of 'greatness,' an absence resulting in forgetfulness and a loss of the knowledge of halachot that characterize the consciousness of 'smallness,' constitutes a step down the ladder of growth and spiritual development and a loss of the attainments gained until that point. On the other hand, the return to 'smallness' is 'a second fetal existence' and 'a fetal existence of the *mochin*;' it is not only a return to a previous state but it aims at advancing a person to a fuller *mochin* and to a more complete 'greatness.' This is not a fortuitous event, but the proper step occurring at the proper time. Therefore, 'smallness' should not be understood as a negative regression, but as a functional and desirable stage of the dynamic, expressed well by the Hasidic axiom, 'descent for the sake of ascent.'[85] 'Smallness' comes for the purpose of the 'greatness' that will arrive after it.[86] Only by a return to 'smallness' and a second 'fetal existence' can the divine framework and the individual develop to a higher level of 'greatness.' 'Smallness' is a step backward, but it is precisely from that step that one can rise, with great agility and might, to 'greatness' and to 'greatness of greatness.'[87]

The descent to 'smallness' and the ascent from it is to be described as a process of death and rebirth. The purpose is the rebirth, which leads to another life and other attainments. But in order to come to this goal a person must nullify his present existence and nature; he must renounce his attainments and levels, remove them and begin afresh. He must pass anew through 'a second fetal existence,' 'birth'[88] and 'smallness.'[89] The more radical the implied change, the more sharply delineated the present nullification of a person's nature and the new beginning must be.

> Before one comes to 'greatness,' one must first fall to 'smallness.'
> And the land of Israel is 'greatness of greatness.' Therefore, it is
> necessary to fall at first to 'smallness of smallness' [...] And
> R. Nachman, of blessed memory, merited to come to the land of
> Israel by means of the exceeding 'smallness' to which he descended
> in his great wisdom, to an extraordinary 'smallness,' 'smallness of
> smallness,' until he merited to come to the land of Israel, which is
> 'greatness of greatness.' [90]

Only a radical metamorphosis can enable a person to come to the *mochin* of
'greatness of greatness,' associated with the land of Israel. And that begins
with a nullification of the existent, a nullification of the *mochin*, the removal
of *da'at* and a descent to 'smallness of smallness' of the *mochin*. That is the
condition that makes it possible for a new creation and new *mochin* to
blossom and grow.[91]

In this instance, the descent to 'smallness' does not occur against the
person's will (unlike the narratives of the Baal Shem Tov and of Moses
falling into a state of 'smallness'). It is an active, planned deed of one who
knows that the depth of the necessary descent accords with the height of the
desired insight.

The Lurianic mythology, which describes the divine drama of descent to
a second 'fetal existence' and to 'smallness' of the *mochin* in order to attain
rebirth, was transformed by R. Nachman into a mythos that explains and gives
meaning not only to his dramatic journey to the land of Israel, including his
descent to 'smallness of smallness' and ascent to 'greatness of greatness,' but
also explains the spiritual life and daily states of descent and ascent. Moreover,
we see clearly that for R. Nachman the myth became an ethos, and the
mythic image of 'second fetal existence' and 'rebirth' explains not only the
spiritual existence and dynamic, but also ranks a person's values and goals.
'Rebirth' and making a completely new beginning comprise one of the
central ways of being in Bratslav Hasidism. The great value placed on the new
and renewal in Bratslav – an exceptional phenomenon in a community of
tradition[92] – relies in great measure upon the mythos of rebirth, in which the
preliminary stage that makes rebirth possible is the descent to 'smallness' and
the return to the fetal state.

> When a person falls from his level, he should know that this was
> initiated from heaven, because [in the] distancing is the beginning
> of coming close. Therefore, this person fell in order that he will
> awaken yet more to come close to Hashem, be He blessed. And
> R. Nachman's advice is that a person in this situation should begin
> anew and enter the service of Hashem as though he had never yet

begun at all. And that is a great principle in serving Hashem – that one must literally every day begin anew.[93]

R. Nachman's directive not to attempt to return to one's place from before the fall and not to attempt to improve and perfect one's previous level, but rather 'every day to begin anew' is to be understood in accordance with the axiom that the descent is 'the beginning of coming close to God' and an essential stage in coming close to God in that it is a 'second fetal existence' that make rebirth possible. In this sense, a person's spiritual stature is not built consecutively, brick by brick; rather, every day a person falls to 'smallness' and begins his way from nothingness. Every day, a person is in the aspect of the 'dead' and is born anew. The behaviors in which R. Nachman directed his Hasidim to engage were shaped in accordance with his way in the service of God:

> And R. Nachman would regularly begin every time anew – i.e., when he fell from his level on occasion, he did not give up on himself because of that but said that he would begin anew, as though he had not yet begun at all to enter into the service of God, be He blessed, and that only now was he beginning anew. And so every single time he would always regularly begin anew. And at times even within one day, he would fall from his service of God and he would begin anew, and so a number of times in that one day.[94]

R. Nachman emphasizes and explains his directive not to attempt to rectify that which already exists, but rather to start again from the beginning: 'for the main thing is the beginning (as above). Therefore, a person must begin every time anew, because perhaps his previous beginning was not proper. This is because everything functions in accord with the beginning. Therefore, he must begin each time anew.'[95]

The formulation of these words makes it clear that the topic of beginning anew refers not only to a new freshness and energy, but in essence to the beginning point, the point of zero. This return involves the nullification and forgetting of everything that has been attained from the beginning until now, for only by nullifying that which exists currently is it possible to create a new man who can arrive at insights and new attainments and levels; this is not possible if a person attempts to continue and progress from his present point and state even if that involves energy and new strength. The assumption is that a new spiritual level comprises a new man, a new manner of existence, which necessitates an actual metamorphosis, one made possible solely by means of a return to the zero point, to the point of beginning,[96] from which everything is renewed: 'fetal existence,' 'nursing' and 'greatness.'[97]

R. Nachman's stages of 'I do not know' and the periods in which he 'forgot all the past' are described here as part of his efforts to attain 'divine inspiration' by means of beginning anew. 'Beginning' anew means the erasure of all the insights and levels that had been attained until that moment, and an entrance into a state of 'I do not know,' like a person who has not yet begun at all, like a child and youth at the beginning of his way. [98]

The phase of 'I do not know' is presented here as a second stage, that which follows R. Nachman's decision to initiate a renewed beginning: 'afterwards, he began again anew and he forgot all the past, as though he had not yet begun at all, and he returned and began anew.'[99]

Elsewhere, we find as a part of the description of R. Nachman's journey to the land of Israel the claim that the passage from level to level passes through 'smallness' and the absence of *mochin*.[100]

The stage of 'smallness' is not only a point of theoretical nothingness that exists in the blink of an eye in the passage from one form of existence to another. Rather, it is a stage that comes into actuality, and that is expressed in the consciousness and behavior of a completely simple person or of a foolishly behaving youth. The danger in 'smallness' is that the person who descends to this state is liable to remain in it if he is not cognizant and does not gather his strength to start a renewed beginning, despite the difficulty and his habituation.

The following quotation demonstrates the centrality that this model of 'fetal existence,' 'birth' and '*mochin*' attained in R. Nachman's teachings as a model describing a process in which a person 'conceals himself' in the stage of 'fetal existence' and is afterwards transformed into a 'new creature:'

> And behold, everything in holiness possesses three features: 'fetal existence,' 'nursing' and '*mochin*.' This is because every time that something is in potential it is called 'fetal existence' (because it is hidden in it. And when it comes from potential to actuality, it is called) 'birth' and 'nursing.' And when the matter has spread forth to effect a necessary action, then it is called '*mochin*.' And when a person learns Torah he must possess these three things (as above). This is because when a person sits down to learn Torah and places his thought and heart in the Torah and hides himself within it, he is said to be a 'fetus,' because he hides in it like a fetus in the womb of its mother. And when he learns the Torah and understands it, that is called 'birth and nursing.' As the verse states, 'Her breasts will satisfy you at every moment.'[101] And afterwards, when he infers one matter from another and has a desire to generate an original insight, that is called '*mochin*' [...] And when he learns in this manner, that is congruent with complete repentance. And he connects the letters

and the combinations that are in his portion from the totality of the worlds to their root and to their place. And he becomes a new creature. And then his *da'at* is complete.[102]

R. Nachman claims that this model of concealment and rebirth is not only a local model that explains a particular phenomenon, but an archetypal model that represents 'everything in holiness.' He cites one example from learning Torah: a person must, he states, learn in such a manner, that at first he hides and is nullified in the Torah and returns to a state of existing in potential and not in actuality, as the stage of fetal existence. Afterwards the stage of learning and understanding arrives, which parallels birth and nursing. And only the last stage, in which a person creates original Torah thoughts, is the stage of *mochin* (of 'greatness').

What is important in this teaching is that it is not presented as an explanation and a description solely of an existent phenomenon, but as a directive and the presentation of a goal. There are also other ways to learn, understand and to be original, but R. Nachman says that 'to learn in this way is congruent with complete repentance.' This constitutes a clear value judgment, one that teaches that the model of the 'fetal existence' and 'birth' that occur in a person's consciousness is not a model that describes only what exists, but also what is desirable. According to R. Nachman, it is desirable in that when a person learns Torah he first conceals himself as a result of which he can become 'a new creature' and attains 'complete repentance,' since he is not the same person he had been before, and only then does he merit to attain 'complete *da'at.*'[103]

We will conclude with another quotation, in which R. Nachman defines the concealment of the *mochin* as the aspect of 'fetal existence,' and the renewal of the *mochin* as the aspect of 'birth:'

> And at times the *mochin* and the divine life-force are hidden, in the aspect of 'fetal existence.' And then 'it is good for a person to cry out,' whether in prayer or in Torah, when his *mochin* are concealed, for that concealment – i.e., that 'fetal existence' – is in the aspect of 'the Rock who has borne you, you have forgotten.'[104] [...] And with a person's outcry in his prayer and in his Torah, when his *mochin* are absent, he is in the aspect of 'fetal existence' – those outcries are the aspect of the outcry of the woman giving birth [...] And the revelation is the aspect of 'birth.'[105]

It is good for a person to cry out when this is a part of the process and pain of 'fetal existence' and 'birth.' Revelation, like 'fetal existence,' is not easy. And at times a person feels that 'and there is no strength for birth,' and he cries out in his pain, whether in prayer or in Torah, and thus this is appropriate for him until he there comes the revelation and the birth arrives.

Summation and Conclusion

Hasidism in general emphasized and developed the human dimension of the concepts of 'smallness' and 'greatness.' Although this dimension existed in the kabbalah of the Ari, there it was not the focus of discussion – and it was certainly not revealed and explicated.[106] The customary Hasidic understanding of the concepts of 'smallness' and 'greatness' associates them with states of closeness and distance, cleaving to God and the cessation of cleaving to God. The descent into 'smallness' is explained as a necessity resulting from the tension that results from cleaving to God, both for the sake of the *zaddik* himself, who as a human being cannot live in a constant tension of cleaving to God, and in order for the *zaddik* to be able to descend in order to deal with the concerns of his Hasidim and with various mundane affairs.

R. Nachman developed the topic of 'smallness' and 'greatness' in a unique and unusual manner. He fortified and developed the topics of forgetting, loss of illumination and death that are associated with 'smallness' – a development that must be understood against the background of the kabbalah of the Ari no less than against the background of Hasidic thought in matters of 'smallness' that preceded R. Nachman. He granted the state of 'smallness' a meaning more dramatic than relaxation from cleaving to God. In R. Nachman's view, 'smallness' is not a descent and relaxation from cleaving to God that the *zaddik* makes use of in order to speak with his Hasidim and elevate them. On the contrary, in times of 'smallness' and states of 'I do not know,' R. Nachman feels that he has no Torah to transmit to his Hasidim, and that there is nothing that he can give them – so that there is no reason that they should come to him.[107]

For R. Nachman, in states of 'smallness,' not only is there no cleaving to God, but even Torah, counsel and advice are concealed from the *zaddik*, so that he possesses no words to speak with his Hasidim and no advice with which to guide them on the way of God.[108] But alongside this intensification of 'smallness,' R. Nachman develops as well a perspective on the entire process of 'smallness' and 'greatness' as a complete and positive process, one that expresses development and not regression. This intentional fall or descent is the course of his soul on its path of continual renewal which must characterize the life of every person. The descent facilitates a new beginning and a new birth, through which person can arrive at what was previously impossible for him. And indeed we find that when R. Nachman was immersed in states of 'I do not know,' in which he was not even fit to speak with his Hasidim, he consoled himself that his life was characterized by constant renewal: '… this is my entire consolation is that I bear in mind that in the world of truth, they will all need me, and they will all yearn to hear the original innovations that I create at every time and at every minute. What am I? Only what my soul creates.'[109]

R. Nachman's self-definition, which comes to the fore in difficult moments, when he has no words and does not succeed in acting as a *zaddik* who is supposed to bring his Hasidim close to him and speak with them, is presented as part of the explanation of R. Nachman's uniqueness, in contrast to the other *zaddikim* and as an answer to the question, 'What am I?' And the clear answer is: 'Only what my soul creates' – 'and I create at every moment and every minute.' This constant creativity is R. Nachman's self-definition and provides R. Nachman the explanation and the reason for his states of 'I do not know' and 'I have no words.'[110]

When we combine the well-known Bratslavian axiom, 'It is known that before a person goes from level to level, it is necessary that there be a descent before the ascent, etc., and then he requires matters of "smallness" in order to be a completely simple man etc.,'[111] with R. Nachman's famous statement, 'I am constantly progressing from level to level; if I thought that I am now standing where I had been an hour ago, I would have absolutely no desire to be in this world,'[112] we can understand to what degree matters of 'smallness' played a central role not only in R. Nachman's thought and theory, but also in his self-understanding and in the dynamics of renewal that constituted the breath of his nostrils and the meaning of his life.[113]

It would be a considerable misapprehension to define R. Nachman's states of 'smallness' as a descent into pollution.[114] They are rather, as the Bratslavian expression has it, a descent into 'smallness' that is a descent into simplicity and into 'I do not know.' This is because a state of 'smallness' is not sin or pollution. Rather, it is an aspect of childhood free of sin and pollution, even should the child transgress. Nor should descent into 'smallness' be described as a moral undertaking whose purpose is to rescue a person from becoming arrogant or as a state meant to protect him from harm caused by heavenly forces that oppose his desire to rush up the mountain of spirituality. Rather, 'smallness' constitutes a part of the process of renewal and rebirth.

We may see in 'smallness' and in R. Nachman's journey to the land of Israel an attempt to attain an existence denuded of law.[115] This return to 'smallness' is comparable to an experience of renewal that possesses the character of childhood, of small children, who are not obligated by any of the mitzvot of the Torah, rather than being comparable to the character of the unlawful lives of completely wicked people.[116] Experience of the state of 'smallness' is an experience of a liminal existence, where the norms and mitzvot do not pertain, rather than a state in which a person obligated to abide by the law presumptuously violates it.[117]

It is important to note that R. Nachman's placing of the cyclical model of death and rebirth at the very core of the processes attendant on the absence of *mochin*, 'second fetal existence' and 'greatness' of the *mochin* is not an imposition of alien concepts and external models on Lurianic phraseology and images. On the contrary, R. Nachman's description constitutes a return to the most original and simple meaning of concepts such as 'second fetal existence,' 'nursing' and 'greatness' in the Lurianic writings. R. Nachman's interpretation shows his close attention and readiness to accept the manner and phraseology that describes these processes in their Lurianic source.[118]

There is no doubt in my mind that there is a need for a searching examination of the similarities that exist between the descriptions of the processes of death and rebirth as found in ancient cultures, as well as in their Christian incarnation – in the mythology of a messiah who dies and is resurrected – and (on the other hand) in the description of the world of divinity as presented by the kabbalah of the Ari, which also speaks of the cycle of death and rebirth. A formulation such as 'For the *mochin* of "greatness" are called "the life of the king," and in their absence death remains, heaven forbid, which is the aspect of the *mochin* of "smallness" of the name Elokim'[119] underscores the need to engage in a comparative analysis with the theme of the death of the king/god and his rebirth in other cultures, both in the realm of mythos and in the realm of rituals derived from it.[120]

Notes

1   *Shivchei Haran*, '*Seder Hanesiyah Shelo L'eretz Yisrael*,' 12,: 27–28. See Rapoport–Albert, '*Katnut*,' 7–33; Liebes, '*Hatikun Hak'lali*,' particularly 207–219; Green, *Tormented Master*, 74–76; Ankori, *Meromei R'ki'im*, 1–38.

2   Scholem, '*Deveikut*,' 342–345; see Shatz-Oppenheimer, '*L'mahuto Shel Hazaddik*,' 359; Rapoport-Albert, '*Katnut*,' 7; Dan and Tishbi, '*Chasidut*,' 783, 802; Etkes, *Baal Hashem*, 142.

3   Scholem, '*Deveikut*,' 342–345.

4   Ibid., 342.

5   Scholem, *Major Trends in Jewish Mysticism*, 340.

6   Tishbi, '*Hara'ayon Ham'shichi*,' 14–15, note 77.

7   Fechter, '*L'virur Hamusagim*,' 171–210

8   *Shaar Hakavanot*, part 2, '*Inyan Sefirat Ha'omer*,' 188. And see Scholem, *Major Trends in Jewish Mysticism*, 342.

9   Fechter, *L'virur Hamusagim*, 171–210

10   Liebes, '*Trein Urzilin*,' 146 and 114–115.

11   Idel, *HaChasidut*, 88–90, 407–424.

12 *Chayei Moharan, 'Gadlut Noraot Hasagato,'* 40 (280), 219.

13 See *Chayei Moharan, 'Maalat Torato,'* 325 (364), 252. See *Sichot Haran*, 128, 88–89. And similarly, see *Chayei Moharan, 'Maalat Torato,'* 26 (365), 252–253.

14 *Chayei Moharan, 'Maalat Torato Us'farav Hak'doshim,'* 23 (362), 251. Ibid., 24 [363], 252.

15 Ibid., 27 (365), 252–253.

16 See Rapoport-Albert, '*Katnut*,' 27–28, note 9; *Chayei Moharan, 'Avodat Hashem,'* 78 (521), 330. *Sichot Haran*, 2647, 167; *Likutei Moharan* II 105.

17 Rapoport-Albert, '*Katnut*,' 8–17.

18 *Shivchei Haran, 'Seder Han'siah Shelo L'eretz Yisrael,'* 22, 50–51; *Chayei Moharan, 'Nesiyato L'eretz Yisrael,'* 14 (142), 135.

19 *Shaar Hamitzvot, Vayichi*, 23.

20 *Shaar Hamitzvot, Vayichi*, 23–24.

21 *Shulchan Aruch, Yoreh Deah*, 341:1.

22 Ibid., 380:1.

23 Maimonides, *Mishnah Torah, Hilchot Tefillin, Halachah* 13.

24 *Shivchei Haran, 'Seder Han'siyah Shelo L'eretz Yisrael,'* 31: 59–61.

25 *Shivchei Haran, 'Seder Han'siah Shelo L'eretz Yisrael,'* 12: 27–28.

26 *Chayei Moharan,' Ne'siyato L'eretz Yisrael,* 11 (139), 136.

27 Scholem, '*Deveikut*,' 342–343. *Tzavaat Haribash*, 129: 46; similarly, see *Keter Shem Tov*, 366: 54a and 54b. See, for instance, *Keter Shem Tov*, 37: 6a and 6b; ibid., 77: 10a; ibid., 366: 54a and 54b; *Tzavaat Haribash*, 135: 25.

28 See *Likutei Moharan* I 10,19, 34, 72, 211; *Likutei Moharan* II 67; *Likutei Torah* (R. Chaim Vital), *Vayeshev, Vayihi Achar Had'varim Ha'eilah*, 102–103.

29 *Likutei Torah* (R. Chaim Vital), *Vayeshev, Vayihi Achar Had'varim Ha'eilah*, 102–103.

30 *Genesis* 37:2.

31 *Bereishit Rabbah* vol. IV, 84:7, 15.

32 Joseph Guri and Shaul Friedman, *Milon Yddi-Ivri-Angli Katzar*, Jerusalem 5754.

33 *Likutei Hilchot, Orach Chaim, Hilchot Nesiat Kapayim*, 4:5.

34 *Likutei Moharan* I 46.

35 See Rapoport-Albert, '*Katnut*.'

36 *Chayei Moharan, 'Nesiyato L'eretz Yisrael,'* 12:140.

37 *Yemei Moharanat*, part I, 51: 74–75.

38 Rapoport-Albert, '*Katnut*.'

39 *Sichot Haran*, 153:108–110: *Chayei Moharan, 'Nesiyato Vishivato B'uman,'* 31 (215), 83.

40 *Chayei Moharan, 'Maalat Torato,'* 2 (341), 242–243.

41 *Chayei Moharan, 'Sipurim Chadashim,'* 11 (91), 87. See Weiss, *Mechkarim*, 42–57.

42 *Etz Chaim*, part 1, *Heichal Zeir Anpin, Shaar Mochin Dekatnut*, chapter 3, 314.

43 Fechter, '*L'virur Hamusagim*,' 201–202.

44 *Chayei Moharan, 'Nisiyato L'eretz Yisrael,'* 12 (140), 134.

45 Ibid., 11 (139), 133.

46 See Nigal, *Hasiporeth Hachasidith*, 280–292 and 285.

47 *Sipurim Chasidi'im, Sefer Maaseh Zaddikim*, 31.

48 Ibid., 30; and [see] also there, '*V'lamad V'hitpalel B'katnut Hamochin*.'

49 *Sipurei Yaakov*, section 34, 107–110.

50 *Netiv Mitzvotechah, Shvil Ha'emunah*, 1, 4a; See Nigal, *Hasiporeth Hachasidith*, 283, note 14. *Shivchei Habesht Biyiddish*, chapter 62, 25, side b; and 26a.

51 *Edat Zaddikim*, section 3, 24.

52 *Shivchei Haran, Seder Haneiyah*, 13: 31; *Likutei Moharan* II, 78; See Rapoport-Albert, *'Katnut,'* and particularly 13–14; *Sipurim Hasidiim*, 30; *Netiv Mitzvotecha, Shvil Ha'emunah*, 1, 4a.

53 See regarding this Rapoport-Albert, *'Katnut,'* 27, note 9; Liebes, *'Hatikun Hak'lali,'* 212–216; Mundstein, *'Al Hatikun Haklali,'* 199, note 9; Liebes, *'Magamot B'cheker Hachasidut,'* 226.

54 *Shivchei Haran, 'Seder Han'siah Shelo L'eretz Yisrael'* 13: 31.

55 See Liebes, *'Hatikun Hak'lali,'* 212–216; Goshen, *'Eretz Yisrael B'haguto,'* 288 and note 52.

56 *Deuteronomy* 3:23-29.; *Shaar Hapesukim, V'etchanan*, section 3, 194

57 *Etz Chaim*, 1, *Heichal Zeir Anpin, Shaar Hamochin*, chapter 1, 283; regarding this, see Fechter, *'L'virur Hamusagim,'* 174–175 and notes 13, 19.

58 See Liebes, *'Trein Urzilin,'* 128–130.

59 *Shaar Hakavanot*, part 2, *Derushei Hapesach, Derush* 12: 187.

60 Ibid., 12: 186.

61 Liebes, *'Trein Urzilin,'* 146–147.

62 *Chayei Moharan, 'Gedulat Noraot Hasagato,'* 39 (279), 218–219. See Feikazh, *Chasiduth Bratslav*, 12–16; Green, *Tormented Master*, 124–126; Liebes, *'Hatikun Hak'lali,'* 2–3; Verman, *'Aliyah and Yeridah – The Journeys of the Besht and R. Nahman to Israel,'* 163.

63 *Chayei Moharan, 'Nesiyato L'eretz Yisrael,'* 6 (134), 131.

64 *Shivchei Haran, 'Seder Han'siyah Shelo L'eretz Yisrael,'* 10: 27–28; ibid., *Seder Hanesiah Shelo L'eretz Yisrael*, 29: 58–59. And see Rapoport–Albert, *'Katnut,'* 9–13.

65 *Chayei Moharan, 'N'siyato L'eretz Yisrael,'* 3 (131), 129.

66 *Shivchei Haran, 'Seder Han'siah,'* 2: 21.

67 *Netiv Mitzvotech, 'Shvil Ha'emunah,'* 1, 4a.

68 *Shaar Hapesukim, V'etchanan*, section 3, 194.

69 Ibid., 300.

70 See the essay of Liebes, *'Trein Urzilin,'* particularly 113–118.

71 *Arba Meiot, 'Sod Hashem Eilata,'* 46.

72 *Shaar Hakavanot, 'Inyan Sefirat Ha'omer,'* Derush 12:187.

73 Ibid.

74 See Liebes, *'Trein Urzilin'*, particularly 145.

75 Ibid., 146, note 300.

76 *Sichot Haran*, 189: 130–131. See *Chayei Moharan, 'Nesiyato L'lemberg,'* 3 (169), 154–155; and 11 (177),158.

77 There is a tradition that claims that the Baal Shem Tov's commentary on *Psalms* 107, a commentary entitled *Sefer Katan* (regarding which see Shatz-Oppenheimer, *Hachasidut B'mistikah, 'Peirusho Shel Habaal Shem Tov Lit'hillim'* 107; *Mithos V'rithmos Shel Yeridah L'shaul,'* 193–223) was written as a response to [his] experiences in Istanbul and during the storm at sea on his journey to the land of Israel. Markos, *Keset Hasofer*, 8a. And see also idem, *Hahasidut*, 316. See also Shatz-Oppenheimer, *Hahasidut B'mistikah*, 198–199 and 213; Nigal, *Hasiporet Hahasidit*, 290, note 35; Verman, *'Aliyah and Yeridah – The Journeys of the Besht and R. Nahman to Israel,'* 167, note 15.

78 *Likutei Moharan* I 37; *Midrash Tanchuma* (*Pekudei*, 3: 401).

79   Such as Liebes mentions in this regard in the kabbalah of the Ari (*Trein Urzalin,*' 129.)

80   See Weiss, *Mechkarim,* 'Koah Hamoshech Shel Hag'vul,' 96–108.

81   See Van Gennep, *The Rites of Passage,* 93–111; Turner, 'Variations on a Theme of Liminality,' 36–51: 311–373.

82   *Tzidkat Hazaddik,* 146.

83   *Shabbat* 30a.

84   *Ketonet Passim, Behar,* 18.

85   See Arthur Green, *Tormented Master,* 73–76; and also Verman, 'Aliyah and Yeridah – The Journeys of the Besht and R. Nahman to Israel.'

86   Fechter, *'L'virur Hamusagim,'* 172–184.

87   See Idel, *Messianic Mystics,* 309–314.

88   *Etz Chaim,* part 2, *Heichal Zeir Anpin,* 'Shaar Hapartzufim', *Derush* 3, 94; *Shaar Hakavanot,* 'Derushei Hapesach,' *Derush* 2, 150.

89   Elior, *'Hazikah Hametaforit.'*

90   *Chayei Moharan,* 'N'siyato L'eretz Yisrael,' 12 (140), 134.

91   *Chesed L'avraham, Maayan* 3, *Nahar* 12; and see *Chalamish,* 'Kavim L'ha'arechtah,' 228.

92   See *Chayei Moharan,* 'Avodat Hashem,' 78 (521), 330; *Sichot Haran,* 245: 157; *Likutei Moharan* I, 76, 78l;156; ibid. II 97,105; *Chayei Moharan,* 'Gadlut Gedulat Noraot Hasagato,' 3 (243), 204. See *Chayei Moharan,* 'N'siyato Vishivato B'uman,' 10 (194), 167. See *Sichot Haran,* 267:167.

93   *Likutei Moharan* I 261. And see also *Sichot Haran,* 48: 39–31; ibid., 51: 34–35.

94   *Shivchei Haran,* section 6, 4.

95   *Likutei Moharan* I 62. *Chayei Moharan,* 'Maalat Hahitbodedut,' 1 (437), 292.

96   See Elior, *Cheirut Al Halachot,* 150–164, and 154–191; Yakovson, *Torat Hachasidut,* 36–43, 86–94.

97   See *Likutei Moharan,* I 105.

98   *Shivchei Haran,* 'Seder Han'siyah Shelo L'eretz Yisrael,' 33: 63.

99   *Chayei Moharan,* 'Maalat Torato,' 18 (357), 248–249. *Chayei Moharan,* 'Avodat Hashem,' 36 (479), 313–314; *Bava Metzia* 85a.

100 *Shivchei Haran,* 'Seder Han'siah Shelo La'aretz Yisrael,' 13: 31.

101 Proverbs 5:19.

102 *Likutei Moharan* I 105. Similarly, see *Likutei Moharan* I 21:7–8.

103 *Chayei Moharan,* 'Sichot Hashaychim L'hatgorot,' 37: 33.

104 Deuteronomy 32:18.

105 *Likutei Moharan* I 21:7.

106 See R. Elior's essay, *'Hazikah Hametaforit.'*

107 *Sichot Haran,* 153:108–109.

108 *Likutei Moharan* II 78.

109 *Chayei Moharan,* 'N'siyato L'eretz Yisrael,' 19 (147), 137–138.

110 *Sichot Haran,* 154:111. *Chayei Moharan,* 'Gedulat Noraot Hasagato,' 7 (247), 206; *Chayei Moharan,* 'Maalat Torato Us'farav Hakedoshim,' 42 (381), 258. See *Chayei Moharan,* 'Gedulat Noraot Hasagato,' 49 (289), 224; *Chayei Moharan,* 'Maalat Torato Us'farav Hakedoshim' 37 (375) 256; *Chayei Moharan,* 'Gedulat Noraot Hasagato,' 40, (280), 219. *Chayei Moharan,* 'Inyan Hamachloket Sh'alav,' 1 (392), 264.

111 *Shivchei Haran,* 'Seder Han'siyah Shelo L'eretz Yisrael,' 13:31.

112 *Chayei Moharan*, '*Inyan Hamachloket Sh'alav*,' 10 (401), 268. Ibid., '*L'hitrachek Meichakirut Ul'hichazek B'emunah*,' 9, (415), 280; *Chayei Moharan*, '*Gedulat Noraot Hasagato*,' 3 (243), 259.

113 *Chayei Moharan*, '*Maalat Torato Us'farav Hakedoshim*,' 46 (384), 259.

114 See Green, *Tormented Master*, 76–77.

115 Rapoport-Albert, '*Katnut*,' 8.

116 Ibid.

117 See Idel, *Kitvei R. Avraham Abulafia*, 269–274.

118 Mark, '*Al Matzavei Katnut V'gadlut*,' 77–80.

119 *Shaar Hamitzvot, Vayichi*, 23.

120 Liebes, '*Trein Urzilin*,' 126. See Frazer, *The Golden Bough*, 324–384; Eliade, *Hamythos Shel Hashivah Hanitzchit*.

SEVEN

The Ultimate Purpose of Knowing is that
We Do Not Know

Introduction

The axiom, 'The ultimate knowledge is that we do not know'[1] is an important topic in R. Nachman's thought, relevant to his views on the presence or absence of the rational mind (*da'at*) in regard to human existence in general, and more specifically, to individual spiritual attainments and the service of God. This axiom was apparently dear to R. Nachman's heart, for he refers to it frequently in his talks with his Hasidim,[2] and also discussed it in his formal expositions.[3]

Explication of this topic will enable us to address an additional aspect of R. Nachman's approach to the rational mind (*da'at*), in which he instructs on the positive role played by the intellect in the service of God and how the rational mind (*da'at*) may serve as a means of cleaving to God. In the course of this discussion, I will address the question of how this position accords with the sum of R. Nachman's thought as presented so far.

Academic scholars maintain a range of views on the nature of the state for which R. Nachman yearned, that of 'not knowing.' Arthur Green explains it to be a state of doubt, of questioning the tenets of faith, a phase in an ongoing dialectical process between faith and doubt. This understanding of ultimate knowledge leads Green to the conclusion that, according to R. Nachman, 'a person is obligated to cry out to God and ask of Him that his faith be shaken.'[4] On the other hand, Ada Rapoport-Albert states unequivocally that 'R. Nachman's intent was the mystical knowledge of God – i.e., merging with Him – which he saw as an continual process, as rising ever higher upon the levels of an impossible knowledge.'[5] Ron Margolin follows in Rapoport-Albert's footsteps and affirms the mystical character of that knowledge from other sources.[6]

Understanding the manner in which R. Nachman employs the concept of 'not knowing' is greatly dependent on the degree to which we can associate it with other of R. Nachman's concepts. A central question is whether the concept of 'that we do not know' is identical with R. Nachman's 'I do not know,' the latter being a component in his state of 'smallness' and descent.[7] Another question concerns the relationship between 'ultimate knowledge' and the states of lack (of *da'at*), absence of *mochin* and loss of self-consciousness that R. Nachman spoke of at length. Further on, I will show that a failure to distinguish between these various concepts has caused confusion in the understanding of R Nachman's teachings.

I shall first address the question of whether the meaning of 'that we do not know' is identical to R. Nachman's state of 'I do not know.' Afterwards, I shall consider the manner in which these matters fit into the whole of R. Nachman's thought and their relationship with other concepts of 'not-knowing' employed elsewhere. Within this framework, I shall discuss the various proposals presented in the academic literature regarding 'ultimate knowledge.' Finally, other perspectives on this topic will be mentioned in the course of the following chapter, *The Story of the Humble King*.

I. *'That We Do Not Know' and 'I Do Not Know'*

Ada Rapoport-Albert in her essay *Katnut, Peshitut, V'eino Yodea Shel R Nachman MiBratslav*[8] argues that at a certain stage a change took place in R. Nachman's attitude toward states of 'smallness' and 'I do not know.' From describing these states as a descent from cleaving to God and as distance from God, states in which the *zaddik* is unable to teach Torah and is sometimes unable to pray, R. Nachman came to describe them as an exalted goal to which a person must strive.[9]

According to Rapoport-Albert, this shift in R. Nachman's attitude toward states of 'I do not know' occurred when it grew manifest to him 'that in truth R. Nachman's "I do not know" is in itself the highest attainment of all, for the attainment of not-knowing is the ultimate knowing, the optimal knowing.'[10] Rapoport-Albert identifies the 'not knowing' described in association with R. Nachman's states of smallness as being part of the not-knowing described in the phrase, 'The ultimate knowledge is that we do not know.'[11] She notes that these are two antitheses that apparently cannot be reconciled, for states of 'smallness' are states of distance from God and from Torah, the antithesis to states of cleaving to God, which constitutes the *zaddik's* desire, objective and ambition. Prior to this shift of attitude, states of smallness were understood by R. Nachman as a preparatory stage for imminent greatness, but at that time the two were defined as opposite poles, and it was clear that one served as a means to attain the other; thus, that they possessed separate characters posed no problem. But after this shift in perspective, the not-knowing itself became described as the *zaddik's* goal and supernal attainment. Rapoport-Albert does not resolve this difficulty, appearing to relate to this problem with a certain degree of tolerance, since paradox is an outstanding characteristic of R. Nachman's world.

Rapoport-Albert arrives at identification of 'the ultimate knowledge' with the state of 'I do not know' based on an analysis of a passage in *Seder*

Han'siyah Shelo L'eretz Yisrael, a passage that she understands as constituting a bridge between the two concepts. And she quotes as follows:

> And R. Nachman said explicitly of himself that although his Torah is a very great innovation, his 'I do not know' is an even greater innovation. That is the topic that was discussed above – that it was always his way to say that now he does not know anything at all. And in regard to the statement that 'the ultimate knowledge is that we do not know,' R. Nachman spoke with us briefly a few times about how every field of knowledge possesses this ultimate purpose. And so, although we merit to come to that ultimate awareness that we do not know, nevertheless, that is still not the ultimate goal, for that is not yet an attainment of the ultimate knowledge, outside of this particular field of knowledge. And so we must, afterwards, toil in order to attain a higher goal, to attain the level of the ultimate not-knowing, on a higher state of knowing. And so on forever. Thus we never know anything at all. But nevertheless R. Nachman had not yet even begun to attain the ultimate goal [...] And this matter is deep and very, very hidden. And there is more about this matter that I heard once following Passover, and that will be explained elsewhere, God willing.

Rapoport-Albert writes of this passage: 'In the passage before us, the paradox of the identification of the two opposite ends of the ladder with each other is clear: the descent to the bottom of the ladder is not only a track that prepares the *zaddik* for ascent, of an independent and separate character, but in itself, as well, it is the ascent to a higher level.'

Indeed, this passage apparently discusses the interchangeability of R. Nachman's 'I do not know' and 'the ultimate knowledge is that we do not know.' However, further examination of the quote itself reveals that matters are not that simple. Rapoport-Albert has joined together two separate passages: the end of section 33 and the whole of section 35. These sections are separated in the original by section 34, which is elided by Rapoport-Albert, its place marked with four dots.[12] The 'I do not know' in passage 33 does not refer to 'the ultimate knowledge.' After that, section 34 discusses R. Nachman's untiring efforts in his worship of God and in his constant ascent from level to level. Only section 35 mentions the topic of 'the ultimate knowledge is that we do not know.' The original text makes no connection between 'I do not know' and 'the ultimate knowledge.'

One may speculate in support of Rapoport-Albert's contention that mention of the topic of 'ultimate knowledge' in *Seder Han'siyah Shelo L'eretz Yisrael* must be significant and thus indicates a connection of some sort between 'I do not know' and 'ultimate knowledge.' Even so, however, it is possible that section 34, which deals with R. Nachman's efforts to rise from level to level, is the connecting link between the two topics, as it tells of R. Nachman's efforts to raise himself from states of 'I do not know' and also of his constant ascension from ultimate knowledge to an even higher ultimate knowledge.

But even if there is a further connection between these two topics, certainly we must take care to distinguish between the existence of a relationship of some kind that links two states and two concepts and the claim that they are identical to each other, particularly when these two different states stand at opposite ends of the spectrum of spiritual states that a person can experience. And simply referring to such a presumed identity as a 'paradox' or an 'extreme paradox' does not suffice to clarify the matter, if the description is not accompanied by an explanation.

Besides the necessity of defining the parameters of the possible connection between these two topics, it should be recalled that it is not R. Nachman who conflates these topics but R. Natan. It is possible that R. Natan, in his desire to soften any negative impression of R. Nachman's strange deeds associated with 'smallness,' juxtaposed them with the topic of ultimate knowledge in the hope that as a result R. Nachman's states of not-knowing would be accepted *in toto* as indicating his greatness, when seen as a vital component of his path to his goal.

There is another source, in *Chayei Moharan,* that apparently indicates a link between states of 'smallness' and 'not knowing,' and 'the ultimate knowledge is that we do not know:'

> After a long time, in the summer of 5570 (1810), when R. Nachman traveled to Uman, he again told a little of the topic [...] and said that we know nothing – i.e., that we know nothing, nothing at all. And he spoke at length about the greatness of the Creator, be He blessed, which is impossible to explain. And he said that we do not know [...] And I asked him: 'Have you not already spoken of this, of the fact that 'the ultimate knowledge is that we do not know'? And you already explained all this – that although we attain the knowledge that we do not know, nevertheless, we still do not know anything. And you said that it already seems to you that you have attained this ultimate goal, etc.' ... R. Nachman replied, 'Who knows in regard to which field of knowledge that ultimate knowledge was involved with?' That is to say, because then too, at the time that he told us this, after Passover, he did not attain the aspect of 'we do not know' literally, but rather only in regard to some particular field of knowledge – i.e., in regard to that field of knowledge, he attained

'the ultimate knowledge is that we do not know.' And his meaning
was that there is a knowledge higher than knowledge, an attainment
higher than attainment, higher and higher. And for each field of
knowledge and attainment, higher and higher, the ultimate goal is
that we do not know. And he said then that even from the time that
he had left Bratslav until now (which had taken place that day and
only a few hours before, because at that time he had only traveled
about three *parsaot*) he again does not know. That is to say, during
this time he attained the aspect of 'he does not know.' And understand these words, because they are extremely deep and high and
exalted words. Fortunate is the child of woman who merited such
attainments, to the truly ultimate extent. And see above regarding
this that in this matter, in the aspect of 'I do not know,' R. Nachman
was an extremely extraordinary innovation, as we heard from his
holy mouth.[13]

In analyzing this passage we must distinguish between R. Nachman's words
transmitted to us here and R. Natan's added explanation. R. Nachman's
words that 'again he does not know' are not connected here to 'states of
smallness' and the 'I do not know' associated with them.[14] Rather, here
R. Nachman describes a different state – the attainment of the ultimate
knowledge that we do not know, something he achieved on this journey. Only
the words of R. Natan, who at the end refers the reader to the aspect of 'I do
not know,' forge a connection between the state of 'I do not know,' which is
discussed in other contexts and regarding which it is said that R. Nachman
was a great innovator, and the idea that 'the ultimate knowledge is that we
do not know,' the topic of this talk. It is difficult to guess what R. Natan is
alluding to in this reference, but it appears that he wished to say that
R. Nachman's states of non-knowing constitute a deep topic with many
aspects, incorporating both 'the ultimate knowledge is that we do not know'
and the 'I do not know' of the states of smallness. If R. Natan's intent is to
forge an identification between these states, it is clear that this identification
is R. Natan's, and is not hinted at in R. Nachman's words. In addition,
Rapoport-Albert claims that from this passage it is not clear how the
attainment of the level of 'the ultimate knowledge is that we do not know'
is connected with R. Nachman's descents into states of smallness, which
involved the loss of the ability to teach Torah and a strong sense of distance
from God.[15] One can discern from this section that an ongoing process that
changes from hour to hour is being discussed; R. Nachman adds and tells us
that even on that very trip he merited a deeper attainment of 'the ultimate
knowledge is that we do not know.' His words do not imply any connection
whatsoever between 'states of descent' and 'smallness.' This assertion is

validated, states Rapoport-Albert, by our awareness that on that journey R. Nachman was not immersed in a state of 'I do not know.' She notes that even at other times, when we know that R. Nachman experienced a state of 'I do not know,' including those occasions that occurred at the end of his life, there is nothing to connect that state to the idea that the 'ultimate knowledge is that we do not know.'[16]

Nevertheless, Rapoport-Albert does not withdraw her identification of R. Nachman's 'I do not know' with 'the ultimate knowledge is that we do not know.' And she concludes her essay with the assertion that 'in a later period, around 5563 [1803] and soon before his settling in Bratslav, there was added to R. Nachman's "I do not know" a new dimension – that it was also his highest attainment ... The experience that was at first a distant but threatening possibility gradually became an obligation, an initiative and an intermediary, and was finally transformed into an exalted goal and a high attainment in itself.'[17]

As stated above, there is no reason to posit the presence of paradoxes over and above those that R. Nachman himself specifically mentioned; nor is there reason to connect two such disparate states, which R. Nachman himself did not link together, and which cannot possibly be linked together. I find no testimony in R. Nachman's writings that suggest that a change in his attitude to 'smallness' and 'I do not know' occurred. It seems, rather, that until his last days R. Nachman saw in 'I do not know' and in 'smallness' a stage of descent and distance from God and, though a condition for ascent, renewal and rebirth, not in itself that desired attainment and exalted goal. This is in contrast to the 'not-knowing' associated with 'the ultimate knowledge' that characterizes unifying states of consciousness associated with various processes and leading to completely different realms.

Now that we have more clearly defined the parameter of 'not-knowing,' which is 'the ultimate knowing,' and we have distinguished it from states of 'smallness' and the 'I do not know' associated with them, we can turn to the nature of 'ultimate knowledge' and its various levels.

II. Wondrous and Very Awesome

Examining the various contexts of R. Nachman's use of the statement, 'the ultimate knowledge is that we do not know,' shows that it is understood as referring to a general state with more than one goal and implication. In *Likutei Moharan*, this statement is cited as one component in a train of thought that describes a process leading to the mystical experience, whereas in his talks R. Nachman returns a number of times to the topic of 'ultimate knowledge' as a unit with independent and self-contained meaning. The latter may be seen in the sections quoted above from *Chayei Moharan* and

Shivchei Haran. There these matters are cited briefly, for the basic intent is to praise R. Nachman and his life. *Sichot Haran* 3, on the other hand, presents R. Nachman's words on this topic more fully:

> R. Nachman expounded a great deal on the greatness of the Creator, blessed be His name. And it is impossible to explain this in writing. And he said that there is no measure to the greatness of the Creator, be He blessed, for awesome things are done in the world, wondrous and very awesome, and we do not know anything – i.e., we still possess no knowledge at all, not at all. And also that idea cited earlier that 'the ultimate knowledge is that we do not know' – i.e., this is also pertinent to each individual field of knowledge – i.e., that even when we arrive at the ultimate understanding of a field of knowledge – i.e., 'that we do not know' – nevertheless, that is still not the ultimate goal, for this particular ultimate goal is so only in regard to that particular field of knowledge. But in regard to a field of knowledge higher than itself, a person has not even begun in that arena at all. And so does this matter proceed, higher and higher. Thus, we never know anything at all, not at all. Yet nevertheless, that 'not knowing' is not the ultimate goal, because a person has still not yet begun at all to know the fields of knowledge above that particular field of knowledge, of which he has attained the awareness that 'the ultimate knowledge is that we do not know,' etc.

'The ultimate knowledge is that we do not know' is cited here as part of a description of man's position in the presence of the Creator's greatness. The greatness of the Creator is not something that can be explained in writing; it is greatness without measure, and man stands before it as in the presence of something wondrous and awesome, something that cannot be known and comprehended.

R. Nachman adds that a person should not think that arriving at an awareness that his standing before the Creator and creation means that he is standing in the presence of something wondrous and awesome, something that he cannot know, means that he has come to the pinnacle of understanding the Creator and to the ultimate knowledge of Him. This not-knowing is merely a temporary peak and goal, for a person must climb to new attainments and new fields of knowledge, whose endpoints and pinnacles are much higher. From those pinnacles we experience more intensely the wondrous and awesome matters of the Creator. The end that this person has come to is merely the ultimate in a particular field of knowledge and a particular understanding that he had previously been familiar with – but 'that is still not the final ultimate goal.'[18]

The knowledge 'that we do not know' is thus the awareness of the exalted nature of the incomprehensible divine. Standing in the presence of that exalted Being is different than standing in the presence of power, wisdom or beauty that impresses a person and that even fills him with admiration, but which still can be understood and absorbed by his consciousness. 'Elevated' and 'wondrous,'[19] in contrast, denote matters that a person is not able to incorporate into himself and know. Still, the nature of the sense of that exalted Being is positive, and does not merely denote a denial of comprehension. A person experiences in a positive fashion the presence of that which in its essence goes beyond his understanding. As a result he remains astonished before it, filled with wonder and, in a certain sense, yearning and longing, for he feels that which he cannot feel and he experiences that which he is unfit to experience and make the best use of.[20]

R. Nachman is dealing here with the basic human condition of a person in the presence of God and with a basic religious consciousness, built upon an appropriate religious stance of a person before the exalted God, Whom man does not understand and cannot know. Ultimate knowledge is not only theoretical knowledge of the exalted nature of God. It is the material that shapes and the fuel that burns, feeding the most basic religious experience: that of standing before the exalted God and His holiness. According to R. Nachman, a person is called upon to sustain and intensify the feeling of awed wonder, applied to new insights and fields of knowledge, and in this way to constantly deepen and enrich the awareness that 'we do not know.' The purpose of learning and knowledge is not to construct theology, and not to come to an encompassing knowledge of the doctrine of divinity. Its goal is realized precisely at the point that a person has used all of his knowledge, has come to its end, and feels anew and with great intensity that he is standing before a wondrous, awesome and elevated 'we do not know.' There are some who will see in this experience of 'we do not know' the essence and unique nature of holiness and of religious feeling.[21]

In contrast to Arthur Green's claim,[22] these talks of R. Nachman do not in any way involve a dialectic between faith and doubt. And 'not-knowing' does not indicate denial of God or doubt as to His existence, but in this context characterizes the unknown nature of religious knowledge. And thus not only are the 'we do not know at all' and the idea that the ultimate purpose is that 'we do not know,' as revealed in the presence of the extra-ordinary greatness of God, not an expression of the 'absence of God from the realm of existence,'[23] but they are God's fingerprints in the world; they serve as a very important window to the sense of the presence of God in the world and to the sense of comprehending Him.[24]

The assertion of Ada Rapoport-Albert and, after her, of Ron Margolin, that in regard to ultimate knowledge 'it is clear that R. Nachman's intent is that of a mystical knowledge of God – i.e., of merging with Him,'[25] is correct in regard to R. Nachman's expositions in *Likutei Moharan*. It does not, however, deal with the manner in which R. Nachman uses the phrase, 'the ultimate knowledge is that we do not know' in his talks. In the sources that we have seen until this point, the axiom that 'the ultimate knowledge is that we do not know' describes a person's basic and primary stance in the presence of God more than it does the mystical experience. As we will see further on, the basic experience of standing before an unknowable and elevated Being can develop into a mystical experience; this, however, is by no means an inevitable development. R. Nachman's words praising the greatness of God, the ultimate knowledge of Whom is lack of knowledge, refer to the broad range of religious feeling and of stages of consciousness based on this awareness and experience, and do not necessarily involve merging with God or attaining mystical knowledge of God.

Other possibilities of religious experience based upon the foundation of the inner state of 'we do not know' and theoretical reflection that grounds them in a more general religious perspective may be found in the three teachings in *Likutei Moharan*, in which R. Nachman discusses the phrase, 'the ultimate knowledge is that we do not know.'

III. Al Yedei Tikun Habrit[26]

R. Nachman's teaching *Al Yedei Tikun* is short, and seems more like an initial introduction to a number of concepts than a complete and finished teaching. In this teaching, R. Nachman devotes only a few words to 'ultimate knowledge.' However, it is possible to find in these words terms and ideas that he develops in other teachings.

> And the holiness of the Sabbath – that is the aspect of the ultimate knowledge. And the ultimate knowledge is that we do not know. And thus, the Sabbath is called 'the ultimate goal of heaven and earth.' And this ultimate goal is the aspect of, 'I said that I will be wise, but it is far from me'[27] – i.e., that is the essence of a person's wisdom: to realize that wisdom is far from him. And that ultimate goal is the essence of 'place' – i.e., the aspect of the Place of the world – i.e., God – the ultimate Being Who encompasses the entire world, which was created with wisdom. As the verse states, 'You made all of them with wisdom.'[28] And that is the aspect of 'a person who makes a set place for his prayer,'[29] for that is the essence of the place, in the aspect of 'no man may leave his place on the seventh day.'[30]

The ultimate goal of the creation of heaven and earth lies beyond the boundaries of heaven and earth, because by virtue of its being their goal, it stands as something beyond them. Heaven and earth function within the framework of wisdom, for they were created with wisdom, whereas the 'ultimate goal' is not a part of creation and thus transcends wisdom. Since, in the end, the ultimate goal of the world and wisdom stand beyond heaven and earth, wisdom itself, when used entirely, directs a person to its ultimate goal, which exists beyond itself. And thus the ultimate goal of knowledge and wisdom is to be found in a place where wisdom and knowledge do not exist.

R. Nachman describes the ultimate goal as 'encompassing the entire world, which was created with wisdom.' R. Nachman's words are fundamental to the broader development of the terms 'encompassing' and 'inner,' in his teaching *Ki M'rachamam.* A description of the ultimate goal as an encompassing entity that transcends all creation and is higher than 'wisdom' is developed in the teachings *Emz'uta D'Alma* and *Ki M'rachamam,* in which the 'ultimate knowledge' refers to an attainment higher than the *sefirah* of *chochmah,* wisdom – an attainment connected to *keter,* crown, which exists in the light of the Infinite One, and which encompasses the *sefirah* of *chochmah.*

In *Ki M'rachamam* R. Nachman describes the axiom, 'the ultimate knowledge is that we do not know' as referring to an insight gained outside the boundaries of time: 'and there, there is no time, for that is the aspect of transcending time.' And in the teaching *Al Yidei Tikun,* ultimate knowledge is described as being outside the boundaries of space, so that attaining it necessitates going out to the place of the place, the place of the world, which encompasses the world. Ultimate knowledge is thus an attainment that transcends time and place, and thus cannot be understood by a wisdom that acts within the framework of the creation of heaven and earth, of time and place.

We can gain a more precise understanding of these matters only by studying R. Nachman's other teachings that deal at greater length with the topic of the ultimate knowledge.

IV. Emtz'uta D'Alma[31]

The teaching *Emtz'uta D'alma* addresses the possibility of attaining the light of the Infinite One, although the intellect cannot grasp it:

> Know that there is a light that is higher than *nefesh, ruach* and *neshamah.* And this is the light of the Infinite One. And although the intellect does not attain it, nevertheless, thought races to pursue it. And by means of that pursuit, the intellect attains it, in the aspect

of 'arriving, yet not arriving' – for in truth, it is impossible to attain,
for it is higher than *nefesh, ruach* and *neshamah.*[32]

This teaching is based upon kabbalistic concepts and terms taken from a
variety of sources; its central structure, however, is based upon the Zohar
(*Noach* 65a), which deals with the dynamics of the world of the *sefirot,* and in
particular with the effort of the *sefirah* of *chochmah* ('thought') to cling to its
source, which is the Infinite One, *Keter,* the Supernal Will. Even the
description of spiritual attainment on the level of 'arriving, yet not arriving'
is based on this passage from the Zohar, which explains the parameters of the
contact of 'thought' with the light of the Infinite One.[33]

Ada Rapoport-Albert states that R. Nachman 're-directs the pursuit after
divine light from the realm of the *sefirot* to the human realm,' using the
Zoharic terms and structure as a basis for a free exposition that is not faithful
to every nuance of that Zoharic model.[34]

The dynamic that leads to spiritual attainment is activity within the
realm of thought and intellect, so much so that R. Nachman even describes
the outcome with the words, 'the intellect attains the spiritual goal.'
Nevertheless, ultimately that attainment is described as breaking beyond the
boundaries of what the intellect can attain. The phrase, 'arrives, yet does not
arrive,' expresses this double meaning, as it attempts to simultaneously
portray two opposites: the claim that there is an attainment, yet the continued
claim that the matter remains beyond the boundaries of attainment.

Also, as R. Nachman teaches in the framework of the desired and positive
activity of the intellect, intellect should not be allowed to act alone but
should be linked together with 'faith:'

> And the essence of the blessing that pours down from the hands is
> intellect [...] And it is necessary to draw faith into the blessing of the
> intellect, because one should not rely on the intellect itself, as is
> known. And that is the aspect of 'A man of faith is rich in blessings,'[35]
> and the aspect of 'And his hands were faith,'[36] and the aspect of 'And
> the kingship of Israel will rise in your hand'[37] – i.e., a person draws
> faith into the blessing of the hands. And that is the aspect of 'And
> I will build for him a faithful house.'[38] And that is the aspect of 'Your
> faithfulness is in the community of the holy ones.'[39] 'Holy' is the
> aspect of *mochin.* And this is the aspect of the concept that '*chochmah,*
> *binah* and *daat* of *asiah* are made from *malchut* of *yetzirah.*'[40]

R. Nachman's lack of faith in the intellect and its ability are apparent in this
passage, for – 'as it is known' – it is impossible to rely on the intellect in itself.
Chochmah, binah and *daat* are problematical, and one must see to it that they

too are drawn into faith. It is interesting to note that, according to R. Nachman, the inner nature of the blessing of the intellect expresses itself not in the intellect's power of breaking forth and engaging in original thought, but rather in its power of self-restraint and calm mindfulness:

> And in the inner being of blessings, which is the subtlety of the blessings, exists the organizing and arranging principle of the intellect, which is the aspect of *keter*, blessed. This is the aspect of 'And I will be with you, and I will bless you.'[41] *Keter* is the language of waiting, as in the verse, 'Await – *k'tar* – for me a little.'[42] This is because when we ask a person something related to intellect, he says, 'Wait until I consider the matter.' And there too one needs faith, in the aspect of 'wondrous faithfulness' (see Tikun 70). And that is the aspect of the concept that *keter* of *asiyah* is made from the inner being of *chesed, gevurah, tiferet* and from the inner being of *malchut* of *yetzirah*. And so do the worlds rise up until *atzilut*, higher and higher.

R. Nachman again states that even though the intellect possesses the faculty of arranging and organizing, which is the intellect's inner blessing, 'there too one requires faith.' This faculty is called *keter*, which, as is known, stands at the top of the ladder of the *sefirot*, or even higher than the *sefirot*, so that no intermediary grade stands between it and the Infinite One.[43] The activity of this faculty, which is in a state of tension with and in opposition to the tendency of the *mochin* to pursue and attain the light of the Infinite One, creates the 'palace' and 'vessel,' and that in turn enables a person to 'arrive, yet not arrive' at the light of the Infinite One:

> And when a person acts and rectifies the arranging and organizing principle, which is *keter*, correctly, and the *mochin* race to attain the light of the Infinite One, and *keter* stops the intellect in order to put the intellect in the proper arrangement, and as a result of the pursuit and the hindrance of that pursuit, then the *mochin* strike the arranging and organizing principle, and palaces are made for the light of the Infinite One, still nevertheless, He is not known and not knowable, as is stated in the Zohar (*Noach* 65a): 'And due to that curtain and the pursuit of that thought, it arrives, yet does not arrive.' 'That curtain' – that is the organizing and arranging principle, which is the aspect of *keter*, which is spread out like a curtain between the emanated and the Emanator. 'And nine palaces are made, which are not lights, nor *ruach*, nor *neshamah*. And no one can understand them, cleave to them or know them.'[44]

There is no doubt that R. Nachman is describing a comprehension that is not intellectual but mystical, a contact with the light of the Infinite One, which is defined principally in a negative fashion: 'not known and unknowable.' This knowing, yet not knowing, this attaining yet not attaining, is the ultimate knowledge and the highest attainment that a human being can reach:

> And know that this is the ultimate knowledge, for the ultimate knowledge is that we do not know. And that is the aspect of 'And satisfy your soul with bright clarity,'[45] for those lights are bright clarity, which are higher than the *sefirot.*[46] Fortunate is the person who merits to have his thought pursue and come to these attainments, even though it is not possible for the intellect to attain them, for one cannot cling to them nor know them.[47]

The complex nature of the religious experience of 'the ultimate knowledge is that we do not know' – which includes on the one hand a chasmal distance and on the other a feeling of the wondrous presence of God – is underscored in this teaching. The religious state, which is sustained by the gulf separating man from God (as described in *Sichot Haran*) is developed into an experience of not only a strong feeling of God's presence, but even of contact with God. Although this is a weak contact, one of 'arriving, yet not arriving,' it is still a way of cleaving to and making contact with the light of the Infinite One.

R. Natan adds his own explanation to this section of *Emtz'uta D'alma* regarding the function of the hindering force. R. Natan states that 'if there were no hindrance (as mentioned above) at all, and there was nothing to stop the *mochin* from their pursuit and chase, the *mochin* would be nullified completely, because the person would be nullified out of existence.'[48] This danger constitutes a link joining the topic of 'arriving, yet not arriving' with that of 'racing outward and returning.'[49] And a prayer that R. Natan composed on the basis of this teaching states:

> And draw onto me, the light of the holiness of the power of the organizing and arranging principle of the *mochin*, which is supernal *keter*. And may I merit in this way not to go beyond the proper border, heaven forbid. But may I merit that my thought will pursue and reach the light of the Infinite One, 'running outward and returning,' in the aspect of 'arriving, yet not arriving,' in the aspect of 'pursuing, yet holding back,' by means of the faculty of the organizing and the arranging principle that stops the *mochin* – in truth and with complete faith.[50]

There is a strong phenomenological basis for the parallel that R. Natan forges between the mystical state described in 'we do not know,' which exists in the aspect of 'arriving, yet not arriving,' and the mystical experience involved in self-nullification, which is attained by means of 'racing forward and returning,' as we may see by comparing the two models as they appear in R. Nachman's teachings.[51]

The state of 'we do not know' parallels 'and no man knew;' and 'arrives, yet does not arrive' parallels 'racing out and returning.' Apparently R. Natan understood that just as R. Nachman sees in the state of cleaving to the light of the Infinite One, as described in *Anochi*, danger to the mystic's life, a danger from which he must protect himself, so does this danger of 'being nullified out of existence' exist as well in the mystical state described in *Emtz'uta D'alma*.

However, despite the striking similarity between these two states of cleaving to the light of the Infinite One, characterized by 'not knowing,' we must be careful not to equate the various *means* of mysticism described in these sources with each other. Whereas in *Anochi* and other sources the way to mystical unification passes through 'casting away the intellect' and the 'absence of the *mochin*' (as we earlier described at length),[52] here a different model is presented. Although it proclaims, 'For one should not rely upon the intellect itself, as is known,' in the end it creates a way to serve God with the various faculties of the intellect and thought, and it calls upon a person to allow these to fully play themselves out in a way that will lead him to attain that which is higher than they are.

The mystical attainment under discussion is distinguished from other models of mystical attainments described in that, although it too is defined as 'that which we do not know' and as an attainment that transcends '*chochmah, binah* and *da'at*,' this particular *via mystica* passes through the realm of intellectual activity. The 'palace' of this attainment is built out of the struggle between the thought that pursues the light of the Infinite One and the restraint imposed by the faculty of the arranging and organizing principle, which is the inner blessing of the thought itself, and which knows the limits of the intellect's attainments.

'The ultimate knowledge is that we do not know' is thus an independent model for the service of God, at whose summit mystical attainment is to be found. This model at its highest levels unites with the path of mysticism that passes through the rational mind (*da'at*), but it goes beyond that, passing beyond rational mind (*da'at*), via the intellect, to that which 'the intellect does not attain.' This model presents a more positive relationship to the aid provided by intellect and the rational mind (*da'at*) in serving God than appears in R. Nachman's other models of the service of God that we have heretofore seen.[53]

It is appropriate to note that regarding this of R. Nachman's models, which is based on a certain understanding of the dynamics of the thought process, we can find kabbalistic sources in addition to those to which R. Nachman alludes (and which we have already noted). I am referring to those kabbalistic perspectives that see *keter* as associated with 'cessation of thought' – i.e., that realm in which thought is transformed into nothingness, a *sefirah* that indicates the place where human understanding comes to an end.[54]

Despite the tension between these various models presented by R. Nachman, I see no reason to attempt to reconcile them – in particular, when we clearly recognize that they all came from the same shepherd, are members of the same family, and that they all see 'non-knowledge' as constituting the most manifest characteristic of the peak of religious attainment.

The investigation into *Emtz'uta* is concluded for the present with a brief but fascinating testimony regarding R. Nachman's experience of the state of 'arriving, yet not arriving,' as cited in *Chayei Moharan*: 'To record the story of "arriving, yet not arriving." R. Nachman was dancing, as Ch. was playing music. And at that point R. Nachman sensed R. Shimon bar Yochai, at the time that R. Nachman was in the aspect of "arriving," and he did not hear Ch. playing music at all. And afterwards, when R. Nachman returned, in the aspect of "yet not arriving," then he heard the music a little.'[55]

There are many unclear details in this testimony, which raises fascinating questions: do we have here a testimony to R. Nachman's mystical experience, in which 'he sensed R. Shimon bar Yochai'? And what does it mean that he 'sensed' R. Shimon bar Yochai? Is this a mystical vision, in which R. Nachman saw R. Shimon bar Yochai, or did R. Nachman perhaps experience a unity with R. Shimon bar Yochai and felt himself to be R. Shimon bar Yochai? Is this the experience that inspired R. Nachman's self-concept as the continuation of R. Shimon bar Yochai and the incarnation of his soul, or is it perhaps a visionary actualization of such a self-awareness that preceded it?[56]

In any case, we see that this is a captivating testimony about a mystical experience that takes place during a dance – an experience in which R. Nachman enters into a state of consciousness at whose pinnacle, at the level of 'arriving,' he is disengaged from his environment and does not at all hear Ch., who is playing next to him on a musical instrument; and that even when he returns to a state of 'not arriving,' his hearing still remains weak.

It would be difficult to rely too much on this brief description, but it certainly contains enough material to serve as additional testimony to the fact that R. Nachman's mystical teachings and descriptions of various states of consciousness, as found in his writings, are not merely speculative thought but are rooted as well in his personal mystical experiences.

V. Ki M'rachamam[57]

The teaching *Ki Merachamam* contains R. Nachman's most trenchant phrases in praise of the rational mind (*da'at*): 'for the essence of a person is his mind (*da'at*), and a person who does not have *da'at* ... is not referred to by the name of man at all, but is the aspect of an animal in human form.'[58] And, 'a person who lacks a 'rational mind' is no human being at all.'[59]

These statements are surprising, since they come from the mouth of one of the greatest contesters of philosophy and rationalism, and arouse astonishment in light of all that we have seen of R. Nachman's attitude toward states of absence of 'rational intelligence,' and because of the importance that R. Nachman attributes to 'casting away the intellect' in religious worship.

These statements in praise of the rational mind are related to other sources in R. Nachman's teachings in which we find the praise of intellect and its centrality in a person's religious life. A more precise reading of these sources shows that the particular meaning that R. Nachman gives these terms, the manner in which one uses the intellect and mind and the limitations that R. Nachman delineates for them, make it possible for him to combine them as positive elements into the tapestry of his thought. We saw an example of this above, in *Emtz'uta D'alma*, and an even clearer example is to be found in *Ki M'rachamam*.

1. The Illumination of the Rational Function (Da'at)

R. Nachman explains the nature of the rational function that defines man as man in the following terms: 'And Moses our teacher ... opened for us the light of knowledge (*da'at*). As it is written, "You have been shown in order that you may know that Hashem, He is God"[60] – for Moses opened knowledge (*da'at*) and revealed to us that there is a God who rules the world.'[61]

Beyond the definition of *da'at* as knowing that 'there is a God,' we learn that this knowledge does not rely upon inquiry and philosophy, but on tradition and the revelation that Moses passed on to the Jewish people. In R. Nachman's words in the continuation of this passage, the specific nature of this knowledge receives additional clarification:

> for the main thing is to set up generations of human beings, precisely, and not species of animals and wild beasts in the image of man. Therefore, as long as knowledge (*da'at*) does not shine within people and they do not know and sense the divinity of God, be He blessed, and His monarchy, they are not within the genus of human beings, since they do not possess the *da'at* to know Hashem, such knowledge (*da'at*) being the essential definition of a human being.[62]

Knowledge is an illumination combined with feeling: 'they know and sense the divinity of God, be He blessed.' A person who knows and senses the existence of God cannot violate God's will. And therefore sin must be explained as the outcome of a state in which a person loses his *da'at* and his sense of God's divinity: 'and in truth, from where do sins come, heaven forbid? That only occurs when a person lacks knowledge (*da'at*), for "a person only commits a sin if a spirit of foolishness has entered into him".'[63]

We see therefore that the knowledge (*da'at*) of which R. Nachman speaks is not theological doctrine or philosophical elucidation, but an internalization of the awareness of the existence of God, to such a degree that it grows palpable.

Another key element in understanding the nature of the illumination of *da'at* that R. Nachman discusses in this teaching is his description of the ultimate knowledge as 'not knowing.'[64] Here it grows clear that the essential and ultimate point in the knowledge of God, which is 'the essence of the definition of man,' is not hidden in the knowledge itself, but in the ability of that knowledge to lead a person to a state of 'not knowing.'

In order to understand the meaning of the lack of knowledge described in this teaching, we must look at the broader scheme, which addresses the topic of the 'encompassing influences,' a discussion that includes the statement regarding 'ultimate knowledge.' This topic of encompassing influences deals with the structure of consciousness and the process of learning and attainment:[65]

> For that which a person understands and attains with his intellect, is the inner aspect, insofar as that intellectual knowledge enters his intellect. But that which cannot enter his intellect – that which he cannot understand – is the aspect of the encompassing influence.[66] And there are a number of aspects of the encompassing influence. This is because although one thing may encompass another, in relation to a third state superior to itself it is the aspect of inner being. And so upward and upwards. And there is an intellect that is the aspect of an encompassing influence to this one. Yet to another, this intellect is even lower than the aspect of inner being, since the latter is on a much higher aspect than it is.[67] And when a person engages in speaking with people and he places his *da'at* in them, his *moach* is emptied of the intellect and *da'at* that it had until then possessed. Then, as a result, the encompassing intellect enters into him. This is because as a result of his intellect being emptied as a result of his placing his *da'at* into his fellow man, as a result of that the encompassing influence entered into him. And he comes to understand the aspect of that encompassing intellect

– i.e., he understands that which he was not able to initially understand [...][68]

These passages describe a process of attainment that is shaped like a ladder
arranged in such a fashion that a person can climb it in a graduated fashion,
rung after rung, insofar as the difference between rungs is one of degree and
not of essence. In the continuation of this teaching, it grows clear that the
encompassing influences of the 'sage of the generation' have an entirely
different character, and attaining them requires a different consciousness –
or, at the least, an exceptional state of consciousness. When this process
occurs and the encompassing influences of the 'sage of the generation'
enter within a person, he attains the ultimate knowledge.[69]

The encompassing influences of the 'sage of the generation' are the
aspect of the world-to-come, the world-to-come being distinguished from this
world in that the former is an existence without time, and as a result is
distinguished by a consciousness removed from time. The activity of this
world, which turns upon the axle of time, has in a sense a parallel in the
world-to-come. But that parallel is not of a chronological order, but rather
turns upon an axle based on the qualitative distinctions that exist between
the character of the attainments.

Another qualitative difference can apparently be derived from the
previous distinction: on the level of the aspect of the world-to-come,
attainment and learning are not a part of a progress toward any goal. They
are not a part of a process of change occurring within a person and bringing
him forward from one state to another, the latter superior to the first. Rather,
they are a delight and pleasure that are not a part of a framework that
possesses a teleology and goal. Such an attainment, which does not occur
along the axle of time, is without end and without beginning, a constant
delight and pleasure whose goal is innate, possessing no extrinsic encompassing influences.

Even though this state of consciousness is described as an aspect of the
world-to-come, this is not a description of the future that cannot be brought
into being in this world. Rather, it is a description of a state of consciousness
that, although 'not of this world,' can exist for and be actualized by the 'sage
of the generation' even while he is immersed within this world. The encompassing influences of the rabbi of the generation are the ultimate encompassing influences that can possibly be reached, and they are the ultimate goal
in the knowledge of God.[70]

The highest attainment, the ultimate knowledge whose attainment is the
aspect of the delight of the world-to-come, is defined solely by the negative
'that we do not know.' Also, the wealth of positive descriptions with which
R. Nachman crowns and praises 'the ultimate knowledge' do not reveal the

content of that knowledge and that attainment of which he speaks, but only testify that they are unattainable and unknowable. The query, 'what,'[71] sums up the nature of that knowledge, which is also described as 'hidden,' 'concealed,' 'set aside from the eye of all,' the aspect of 'what have you seen, what have you felt?'

In addition, R. Nachman explains the term *keter*, which denotes the first emanation or the first *sefirah*, as expressing the unattainable nature of that *sefirah*. *Keter* means 'encompassing' – signifying, in the term that R. Nachman created, an unattainable attainment.[72] In addition, R. Nachman's characterization of 'attainment' as 'delight,' as the aspect of *keter* and as the aspect of 'do not know,' are to be understood as indicating activity without cause and effect, activity that cannot be explained and understood.[73] This perspective has roots in the kabbalah of R. Moshe Cordovero, who writes:

> This chapter is meant to caution you not to destroy the barrier and enter a place of danger. And do not think about what precedes *keter* [...] Just as we cannot know Him, we cannot know His delights before creation, and even after creation we cannot understand creation from the aspect of created elements as God's activities, as we will explain – how much more, then, can we not know whether God's existence itself had pleasure or delight. Rather, the ultimate of all is that we do not know Him.[74]

Whereas R. Moshe Cordovero attributes 'delight' to God, for R. Nachman the delight belongs to man. Either way, we see that the delight is hidden and not comprehended, and that 'just as we cannot know Him, we cannot know His delight.' And this connects with the idea that 'the ultimate of everything is that we cannot know Him,' which appears to be a variation of the saying, 'the ultimate knowledge is that we do not know.'

All of R. Nachman's descriptions do not reveal anything, not even in part, of the knowledge that is the ultimate knowledge, that which is 'higher than everything.' But it is precisely here that the gist of his words are found: the character of that highest attainment is the intensified contact with the unattainable, with the unknowable, regarding which, all that a person can know is that it is beyond the limits of this world and its concepts and belongs rather to 'the aspect of the world-to-come.' The 'not known' is indeed the highest attainment of a man in coming to God, understanding that he is a 'God who hides himself,'[75] 'hidden and concealed and set aside from the eye of all.'

The meaning of the saying, 'The ultimate knowledge is that we do not know,' in this context is consistent with its meaning in R. Nachman's talks, which unreservedly praise God's greatness. The ultimate purpose of the process of learning and attainment is to intensify and deepen the sense of exaltation in the presence of God's holiness and oneness, which exceed all the concepts of this world. But this teaching adds an additional layer to the comprehension of God's exaltedness, a layer made possible only via the nullification of the boundaries of normal human consciousness. It is possible for a person to break out of time-contained consciousness and to come to a consciousness free of the flow of time. But even in this non-normative state of consciousness, the attainment that a person reaches is only a higher level of the exaltedness of God and His nature as 'hidden and concealed and set aside from the eye of all.' This teaching thus describes an additional spiritual state of being and consciousness that comes to its realization in the statement, 'The ultimate knowledge is that we do not know.'

In the continuation of this teaching, R. Nachman qualifies his words. The first qualification concerns the various spiritual needs of human beings, and the *zaddik's* obligation to align his words with those who hear his teaching. Therefore, even though the highest level is an attainment of the aspect of 'what,' there are situations in which the *zaddik* must communicate to his Hasidim not the exalted aspect of God and the yawning gap between man and God; on the contrary, he must communicate the presence of God in the world and His closeness to man:

> For there are those who dwell above and those who dwell below – i.e., the supernal world and the lower world, the aspect of heaven and earth. And the *zaddik* must show those who dwell above that they do not know anything of the knowledge of God, be He blessed. And this is the aspect of the attainment of 'what,' the aspect of 'What have you seen, what have you felt,' the aspect of 'Where is the place of His glory?' And contrarily, he must show those who dwell below that, to the contrary, 'The entire earth is filled with His glory.' This is because there are those who dwell in the dust, those who are human beings who lie in the lowest level, and to whom it appears that they are very far from God, be He blessed. And the *zaddik* must rouse them and awaken them, in the aspect of 'Awaken and sing, dwellers in the dust,'[76] and reveal to them that Hashem is with them, and that they are close to Him, be He blessed, for 'the entire world is filled with His glory.'[77] And he must strengthen them and encourage them, so that they do not despair of themselves, heaven forbid, for they are still together with Hashem, be He blessed, and close to Him, for 'the entire world is filled with His glory' […] God grasps and maintains the supernal world in the aspect of 'what,' the aspect of 'Where is the place of His glory,' and He maintains the lower world in the aspect of 'The entire world is filled with His glory.'[78]

The second qualification concerns the world of the *zaddik* and the danger that threatens him when he deals with the encompassing influences that transcend time.

> Also, that sage of the generation must know which encompassing influences he must draw down and which encompassing influences he must not draw down. And thus there are matters that may not be revealed before his students. This is because if he reveals those things, the other encompassing influences will enter his intellect … And at times he should not receive those encompassing influences […] Similarly, in regard to attainments, there are things that it is forbidden to reveal, for if he reveals this answer to a student, a new encompassing influence will enter into him, as a result of which the question will be stronger and broader than it had been at first, until he might enter into the realm of attainments, encompassing influences, that transcend time, so that time does not suffice to explain the questions and the answers to be found there, since they are higher than time.[79]

It transpires, therefore, that R. Nachman's previous description of how the encompassing influences of the 'sage of the generation' enter within refers to an optimal occurrence, regarding which R. Nachman says, 'Fortunate is the one who merits.' On the other hand, there is also the possibility that this 'sage of the generation' will himself be entangled in the encompassing influences that he is incapable of absorbing. This occurs when encompassing influences that transcend time enter within him, but his consciousness does not extend beyond its normal limits and instead continues to function within the framework of time. This draws the sage into an unending chain of questions and answers that time does not suffice to explain. A person must guard himself against such encompassing influences by means of self-restraint and silence.

> And that is the aspect of that which our sages, of blessed memory, said: 'When Moses arose on high, he found the Holy One, blessed be, He tying crowns onto the letters. 'Moses told Him, "Master of the world! Who is stopping you from adding crowns to more letters?" 'He said to him: "In the future, someone will stand, and Akiva ben Yosef is his name, who will expound mountains upon mountains of halachot upon each point".' 'He said to Him, "Master of the world! It is fitting that the Torah be given through him".' 'He said to him, "Silence! This has arisen in my thought".'[80] But this seems to create a difficulty. Why did Hashem, be He blessed, tell Moses to be silent,

etc.? Hadn't Moses already expressed his question? And why would this silence be acceptable, since he had already issued Him a challenge? But the answer is that as soon as Moses issued his challenge, an answer to the question fell into his mind. But if he would have expressed that answer, another encompassing influence would have entered into him, and he would have come to a stronger and more encompassing question than the first. Thus, God told him, 'Silence,' in regard to that answer – i.e., he should be silent and not reveal the answer, in order not to come to a question stronger than the first one – i.e., that as soon as the inner intellect is revealed, then a new intellectual item arises in one's thought, for another encompassing influence enters within. And thus it is necessary to be silent, in order not to come to encompassing influences that one may not attain [...] And that is: 'Be silent, thus arose in my thought.'[81]

In Chapter 4, *Silence and Melody Facing the Void*, I dealt with this passage and with the place of silence in other contexts as well. The silence in this passage is described as a state different to and alternative to the state of 'the ultimate knowledge is that we do not know.' Whereas 'the ultimate knowledge is that we do not know' describes a state in which the encompassing influences of the sage of the generation enter inward and he merits to attain the aspect of 'what,' which is the aspect of the world-to-come, here R. Nachman describes a state in which the sage must renounce the internalization of encompassing influences that are beyond time, and instead remain silent and stay in his present state of knowledge and with the answer that he presently possesses.

In complete opposition to the words of Joseph Weiss, who sees in the directive 'Be silent,' as it appears in this teaching, an expression of the goal of 'grasping and taking a stance within the question,' and 'an expression of the religious preference of remaining within a question and not within the answer,'[82] and who has developed an entire theory regarding the nature of Bratslavian faith that prefers remaining in a state of doubt,[83] R. Nachman's express directive is not to come to doubt but to remain in a state of knowledge. 'To be silent regarding the answer' does not mean to remain with a question without knowing the answer, but to remain with an answer in one's thought and not to reveal it to one's student. The sage remains silent lest, by stating the answer, a space within him will be left vacant and encompassing influences and new questions with which he cannot contend will come down, so that he is liable to remain immersed in the question. The religious Bratslavian preference that arises from this teaching is the opposite of Weiss's claims, for it states that a person should remain with an answer and not with a question.[84]

Arthur Green follows in Weiss's footsteps and argues that the desired goal of 'that we do not know' is coming to an inner state of questioning, doubt and raising challenges to faith. This leads Green to the fascinating, although clearly incorrect, conclusion that according to R. Nachman 'a person is obligated to cry out to God and ask Him to shake his faith.'[85] But as we have seen, and in opposition to Green's words, the state of 'not knowing' as it appears in *Sichot Haran* expresses the religious position of belief as a person faces the awesome wonders of God, Who is exalted beyond his understanding. In *Emtz'uta D'alma*, the state of not knowing expresses a state of attaining the light of the Infinite One that transcends knowledge (*da'at*). And in *Ki M'rachamam*, the state of not knowing expresses a comprehension higher than time, the delight of the world-to-come. All of the sources that we have thus far examined testify clearly that the concept of the 'ultimate knowledge is that we do not know' has nothing to do with heresy and doubt, and certainly has nothing to do with prayer to God to shake one's faith.

The state into which the sage falls should he internalize encompassing influences that transcend time while he is unable to absorb them is entirely different to the sage of the generation's attainment of 'not knowing.' In this situation, he is liable to be drawn into a chain of questions and answers that time will not suffice to complete. In this state it is indeed possible that these questions will lead to doubt and a shaken faith; however, this should not be mistaken for the attainment of the ultimate knowledge.

A third state that R. Nachman describes in this teaching is silence. Silence, remaining with an answer and knowledge, and not revealing them, is the proper way to act if it is impossible to attain the ultimate knowledge.

We must point out R. Nachman's different attitude to each of these three states that we have mentioned. The first, 'The ultimate knowledge is that we do not know,' is a desirable and positive state, of which R. Nachman says: 'Fortunate is the one who merits to attain them.'[86] The second, the chain of questions, doubts and answers, is an undesirable state presented as a danger than one must avoid, and against which R. Nachman cautions. Silence is the third state, which, on the one hand, is a renunciation of the attainment of 'not knowing,' but, on the other, is preferable to the second state of questions and answers that time cannot contain. A failure to distinguish between these various states has led Green to link them all together: the 'ultimate knowledge that we do not know,' 'the state of doubt and challenge,' and silence.

In the following quotation, taken from the continuation of the teaching under discussion, Green sees proof of the idea that 'the inability to attain one's spiritual goals that the *zaddik* has shown to the believer is, practically speaking, like the absence of God'[87] and like heresy. But this proof too is built upon an imprecise understanding of the various states of which R. Nachman speaks:

And it is necessary to blend the worlds: supernal into the lowly, and the lowly into the supernal, so that the son is composed of the aspect of student, and also the student is composed of the aspect of son, in order that they should both possess fear of God. This is because of the nature of the son – who is the aspect of the attainment of 'what,' the aspect of 'what have you seen,' etc., and if so, he will have no fear at all, since he does not see the glory of God, be He blessed, at all.[88] And thus it is necessary that the son be composed of the aspect of student, to show the aspect of the son as well a little of the attainment of the aspect of the student – i.e., the aspect of 'the entire world is filled with His glory,' so that he should possess fear. And also the student, whose attainment is the aspect of 'the entire world is filled with His glory' – as a result of that, he can be nullified out of existence, and thus it is necessary to show him a little of the attainment of the aspect of the son – i.e., the aspect of 'what' – so that he will not be nullified out of existence, and that he will possess fear.[89]

Green reads this passage as presenting two types of faith: one, 'the ultimate knowledge is that we do not know,' which is 'a state of continuous negation, dangerously close to complete disbelief,'[90] whereas the second faith is 'a simple faith' of 'a simple person.'[91] Green explains the danger of 'being nullified out of existence' as resulting from the person being completely stunned by the presence of God.'[92] And further on Green explains this danger by saying that when this new consciousness is attained by simple Hasidim, it will afflict them with insanity.[93] To my mind, this reading errs both in understanding the two types of spiritual attainment and the dangers associated with them.

R. Nachman is dealing with a state in which a believer sees nothing of the glory of God. This is not speaking of 'an absence of God' or a disbelief in Him, but of a feeling of distance from God that comes from a person's growing awareness of his inability to see God and comprehend Him. At a certain stage, this distance is liable to create not longing and a feeling of exaltation but rather disengagement. In this state, continued emphasis on the distance from God ceases to be a vector that intensifies a person's religious experience and instead acts to develop the feeling that God is so distant, unseen and unattainable that He is irrelevant to his life. This is the state that leads to a nullification of a person's fear of God. This danger characterizes the perspectives that emphasize the divine transcendence.[94]

On the other hand, the intensification of a sense of the existence of God in the world, that 'the entire world is filled with His glory,' can lead to states of consciousness of 'nullification out of existence' and mystical unification with the divine All. The topic of 'nullification out of existence' that is associated with 'self-annihilation' is well-known and dealt with at length, both in general and in Jewish mysticism, and in particular has received extensive treatment in the framework of research into Hasidism.[95] This topic is associated with exalted mystical peaks and states of oneness with God. And in the words of the Maggid of Mezeritch: 'And there is unity with the Holy One, blessed be He, until a person is nullified out of existence – and then he is called "man".'[96] R. Nachman himself expresses a number of attitudes regarding the danger that lies at the doorway of the mystic – i.e., that the mystical experience will lead to the mystic's 'nullification out of existence,' to the point of the cessation of life.[97] Often the danger of 'nullification out of existence' is associated with mystical approaches that emphasize divine immanence, the concept that 'there is no place empty of God and that the entire world is filled with His glory.'[98] This danger of being nullified out of existence has absolutely nothing to do with the 'simple faith' of 'a simple person'[99] and with a concern for the mental well-being of simple Hasidim.

2. The Illumination of Will

After R. Nachman explains that every aspect needs a little of its companion so that it will not to lead to undesirable spiritual realms, he adds that this combination prepares a person to attain 'the illumination of will.'[100] The characterization of the supernal encompassing influence, which is *keter*, as 'the illumination of will,' is obviously based on the kabbalistic perspectives that associate *keter* with will, which is itself a term for the first *sefirah* or for that emanation which is higher than the *sefirot* of *chochmah*, *binah* and *da'at*.[101] In this too, R. Nachman forges an equivalence between the will that relates to the world of divinity and the will of man and his desires.

It is clear from R. Nachman's words that the ultimate knowledge, which has been defined until now solely in terms of negation, as 'not knowing' and as the aspect of 'what,' as that 'which is hidden and concealed and set aside from the eye of all,' is 'the illumination of the will' – the illumination that is absent of 'any knowledge' and any intellect. We may go a step further and say that, accordingly, it is possible to restate the axiom to read, 'The ultimate knowledge is the will.' Thus, even this teaching of R. Nachman, which begins with far-reaching proclamations in praise of *da'at*, places at the head of the ladder of spiritual attainments and as the level that is 'higher than all' the attainment characterized by a radical lack of *da'at*, in which a person 'does not at all know what he wants.'

The model of the concept that 'the ultimate knowledge is that we do not know' described in *Ki Merachamam*, presently under discussion, is similar to the model that we saw in *Emtz'uta D'alma*. The proposed path to come to the desired state of 'not knowing,' is based upon the dynamic of learning and the development of knowledge (*da'at*), and not upon 'casting away the intellect.'

R. Nachman here describes a complex process, parts of which are built upon learning and activity clearly relating to the realm of knowledge; however, at a certain stage, that activity itself creates a state of absence of knowledge (*da'at*). The dynamic of encompassing and inner influences, which is constructed upon the idea that a person teaches and speaks with people, as a result of which 'his brain is emptied of the intellect and *da'at* that he had possessed,'[102] clearing a place for a new encompassing influence, acts as an intellectual process as long as there still exist encompassing influences of intellect and *da'at* that can enter into the mind. But as soon as we come to supernal encompassing influences, although the process of emptying the mind of intellect and *da'at* occurs, new intellect and *da'at* do not enter in their place, as a result of which the person remains absent of *da'at* and *mochin*. The dynamic of the encompassing and inner influences, of 'to teach' and 'to learn,' is transformed at the end of an intermediary process into the emptying of intellect and *da'at*. In this sense, there is a parallel here to the service of God via the casting away of the intellect and to states of absence of *mochin*. If the person emptied of *da'at* is 'a mighty man' – i.e., a strong person, not a *schlimazel* (who lacks decisiveness and who has a weak will) – he will remain with the 'illumination of will' that is higher than everything, the content of this illumination being longing and yearning and pining for God, without any *da'at* and lacking all intellect.

As stated, the basic model is shared by *Ki M'rachamem* and *Emtz'uta D'alma*. But in other teachings as well R. Nachman makes use of various perspectives regarding intellectual activity, which, when fully utilized, leads eventually to 'not knowing.' *Ki Merachamam* speaks of a progression of encompassing influences entering one's inner being, whereas *Emtz'uta D'alma* speaks of a struggle between the faculties of the intellect, between 'pursuit' and 'restraint' – a struggle that creates the possibility and arena for experience that breaks beyond the attainments of the intellect and which is in the aspect of 'not knowing.'

Until this point, we have seen that the saying, 'The ultimate knowledge is that we do not know,' serves as a label given to a number of spiritual states that end with a person being in a state of absence of knowledge. The common denominator shared by all of these states is that knowledge and learning, in their various iterations, are a means of arriving at this state of not knowing. Some states of 'not knowing' come from standing in the presence of the wonders of the Creator (as R. Nachman discusses in his talks), and some states of 'not knowing' are clearly mystical experiences, such as contact with the light of the Infinite One and the attainment of that which is higher than intellect (as described in teachings in *Likutei Moharan*). But this topic has no direct bearing on the topic of states of 'smallness' and R. Nachman's 'I do not know,' which describes states of descent and distance from God.

Additional layers in the service of God as aided by knowledge (*da'at*) and the intellect will be made clear in the coming chapter, in the course of examining R. Nachman's 'The Story of the Humble King.'

Notes

1   R. Yediah Hap'nini's *Bechinot Olam*, Chapter 13, 3–55; R. Yosef Albo's *Sefer Ha'ikarim*, *Ma'amar Sheini*, chapter 30, 194; see Rapoport-Albert, '*Katnut*,' 32–33, note 72.

2   *Shivchei Haran*, 'Seder Hanesiyah,' 35: 65.

3   See *Likutei Moharan* I 24; ibid. II 7, 83; *Chayei Moharan*, '*Sichot Hashayachot L'torot*,' 8 (67), 64; ibid., '*Gedulat*,' 42–43 (283–283), 221–222; *Sichot Haran* 3:2; *Shivchei Haran*, 'Seder Han'siah,' 35: 65.

4   *Tormented Master*, 284–290, quote on 288.

5   Rapoport-Albert, '*Katnut*,' note 72.

6   Margolin, *Ha'emunah V'hak'firah*, 152–158.

7   See above, Chapter 6, section 3, '*Katnut V'shich'chah – Katnut V'eini Yodea*.'

8   Rapoport-Albert, '*Katnut*,' 7–33.

9   Ibid., note 72.

10 Ibid., 21,172–175, 153 and note 4 there.

11 See Liebes, '*Hatikun Haklali*,' 211.

12 *Shivchei Haran*, 'Seder Han'siyah Shelo L'eretz Yisrael,' 33–35: 64–65.

13 *Chayei Moharan*, 'Gedulat Noraot Hasagato,' 43 (283), 221–222. *Chayei Moharan*, 'Sichot Hashayachot L'sipurei Maasiyot,' 8 (67), 61–65.

14 *Chayei Moharan*, 'Sichot Hashayachot L'sipurei Maasiyot,' section 8 (67), 64–65.

15 *Shivchei Haran*, 'Seder Han'siah Shelo L'eretz Yisrael,' 21: 49.

16 Ibid., 23–24.

17 Ibid., 27.

18 *Shivchei Haran*, 'Seder Han'siyah Shelo L'eretz Yisrael,' 35: 65.

19 See *Chayei Moharan*, 'Sipurim Chadashim,' 4 (84), 81; ibid., '*Gedulat Noraot*' Hasagato, 6, (246), 206; 22 (262), 211; *Sichot Haran*, 151:107.

20 See Schiller, *Al Hanisgav*, 87–99. See also Ben Shlomo's discussion on this topic in the afterword of Otto's book, *Hakedushah*, 'On the Non-Rational in the Knowledge of God and Its Relationship to the Rational,' 199–203.

21 Otto, *Hakedushah*.

22 Green, *Tormented Master*, 284–290.

23 As Green argues, ibid., 288.

24 Ibid., 286.

25 Rapoport-Albert, '*Katnut*,'note 72; Margolin, *Ha'emunah V'hak'firah*, 152–158.

26 *Likutei Moharan* II 83.

27 *Ecclesiastes* 7:23.

28 *Psalms* 104:24.

29 *Berachot* 6b.

30 *Exodus* 16:29.

31 *Likutei Moharan* I 24. Delivered in the summer of 5563 (1803).

32 Ibid., 24:1.

33 See Tishbi, *Misnat Hazohar,* part I, 176–177.

34 Rapoport-Albert, '*Katnut,*' 22–23. See also Margolin, *Ha'emunah V'hak'firah,* 156–157.

35 *Proverbs* 28:20.

36 *Exodus* 17:12.

37 *Samuel* I 24:21.

38 *Samuel* I 2:35.

39 *Psalms* 89:6.

40 *Likutei Moharan* I 24:5–6.

41 *Genesis* 26:3.

42 *Job* 36:2.

43 See Tishbi, *Mishnat Hazohar* part I, 107–111; *Chalamish, Mavo L'kabbalah,* 305–306.

44 *Likutei Moharan* I 24:8.

45 *Isaiah* 58:11.

46 See R. Moshe Cordovero, *Pardes Rimonim,* Shaar 11, 61b–65b.

47 *Likutei Moharan* I 24:8.

48 Ibid.

49 *Meor Einayim, Yitro,* 173; R. Avraham Yehoshua Heschel, *Oheiv Yisrael, 'Shekalim,'* 116.

50 *Likutei Tefilot,* part I, prayer 24.

51 *Likutei Moharan* I 4:9. *Likutei Moharan* I 65:4

52 See above, Chapter 1, Part III, 'Casting Away the Intellect' and the beginning of Chapter 2.

53 See above, Chapter 1, Part III, section 3.

54 See *Chalamish, Mavo L'kabbalah,* 103–104; and Scholem's essay, '*Sh'nei Kuntresim,*' 334.

55 *Chayei Moharan, 'Avodat Hashem,'* 163 (206): 367.

56 Feikazh, '*Chasidut Bratslav,*' 13–15; Green, *Tormented Master,* 242–246.

57 '*Ikar Shleimut Hazaddik*' in *Likutei Moharan* II 68.

58 *Likutei Moharan* II 7:2, ibid., 2.

59 Ibid.

60 *Deuteronomy* 4:35.

61 *Likutei Moharan* II 7:2.

62 Ibid., 7:4.

63 Ibid., 7:3.

64 Ibid., 7:6.

65 See Weiss, *Mechkarim,* particularly, 116–120; Green, *Tormented Master,* 284–298.

66 *Likutei Moharan* II 7:4.

67 Ibid., 5.

68 Ibid., 6.

69 *Likutei Moharan* II 7:8.

70 *Likutei Moharan* II 7:6; *Likutei Moharan* I 18:2.

71 See Liebes, '*Zohar V'eros,*' 67–68.

72 *Shaarei Orah,* Part II, 124. *Shaarei Orah,* Part II, 118. *Chalamish, Mavo L'kabbalah,* 1404.

73 *Likutei Moharan* I 18:2.

74 *Sefer Ilamah Rabati,* 6, column 2 (beginning of chapter 8). See Yosef ben Shlomo, *Torat Haelokut,* 60–61.

75 *Isaiah* 45:15.

76 *Isaiah* 26:19.

77 *Isaiah* 6:3.

78 *Likutei Moharan* II 7:7.

79 Ibid., 7:8.

80 *Menachot* 29b.

81 *Likutei Moharan* II 7:8.

82 Weiss, *Mechkarim*, 137.

83 Ibid., 138–139.

84 *Likutei Moharan* II 12.

85 Green, *Tormented Master*, 288.

86 *Likutei Moharan* I 5.

87 Green, *Tormented Master*, 297.

88 This sentence is emphasized by Green (ibid.).

89 *Likutei Moharan* I 9.

90 Green, *Tormented Master*, 298.

91 Ibid., 297–298.

92 Ibid., 298.

93 Ibid.

94 *Likutei Moharan* I 64, *Likutei Moharan* II 12.

95 Shatz-Oppenheimer, *Hachasidut K'mystika*; Elior, *Torat Ha'Elokut*, particularly chapter six, 'Ha'avodah B'vitul,' 178–243; idem, *Torat Achdut Hahafachim*, particularly 131–139; Feikazh, *Bein Idi'ologiah L'mitziut*; Weiss, *Studies in Eastern European Jewish Mysticism*, 'Via Passiva,' 137–155.

96 *Maggid Devarav L'yaakov*, 39. *Keter Shem Tov*, 292:74.

97 See also *Chayei Moharan*, 'Maalat Hamitkarvim Eilav,' 40 (330): 235–236.

98 Ibid., 297.

99 Green, *Tormented Master*, 298.

100 *Likutei Moharan* I 10

101 Zohar. See Scholem, *Pirkei Yesod*, 176 and *Shnei Luchot Habrit*, 4b. See Scholem, *Reishit Hakabalah*, 140–141; Ben Shlomo, introduction to *Shaarei Orah* of R. Yosef ben Avraham Gikitiliah, 18–19; Chalamish, *Mavo L'kabbalah*, 104.

102 *Likutei Moharan* I 10, 6

'The Story of the Humble King' – On Laughter and Foolishness in the Service of God

The structure of the concluding chapter of this book differs from that of the previous chapters. Here we will clarify the place of *da'at*, imagination and madness in religious service through a detailed analysis of R. Nachman's 'Story of the Humble King.'[1] This tale will serve as the starting point of the chapter and guide the process of the subsequent discussion, which will be supplemented with additional materials such as R. Nachman's talks and formal teachings.

The first part of the analysis of the story continues the previous chapter's discussion of 'the ultimate knowledge.' The second part will address the role played by laughter and foolishness in the story and, more generally, in the thought of R. Nachman

The Story of the Humble King

This is the story of a king, who had a sage.

The king told his sage, 'There is a king who claims on his seal that he is powerful, great, and a truthful and humble man. As for his being powerful, I know that he is powerful, because surrounding his country is the sea. And he has soldiers on ships upon the sea with *hormates* (cannon), who do not let anyone come close. And within the sea, there is (a place where people sink, called) a large *zump* (quicksand) around the country, where there is only one small path, on which only one man can travel. And *hormates* are also set up there. And when someone comes to wage war, they shoot the *hormates*, and it is impossible to come close to the country.

'But as for his claiming on his seal that he is a truthful and humble man, I do not know about that.

'So want you to bring me that king's *portret* (portrait).'

The king who gave this order had all the portraits of all the kings – 'but no king has the portrait of that other king, because he is hidden from people, because he sits behind a curtain, and he is far from the people of his own country.'

The wise man went to that county. The wise man said to himself that he must know the nature of the country. And how can he know the nature of the country? Through the *katavesh* of the country (i.e., jokes, which are called *katavesh*).[2]

This is because when one needs to know something, one must know the jokes of that thing.

This is because there are various types of jokes.

There is a person who really means to hurt his fellow with his words, and when his fellow is upset with him, he tells him, 'I am joking.' As the verse says, 'Like one who shoots firebrands,' etc., and says, "I am merely joking"!' (*Proverbs* 26:18–19).

And there is also a person who simply intends to make a joke – nevertheless, his words hurt another person.

And so there are all types of jokes.

And there are amidst all the countries a country that includes all the countries. And in that country, there is a city that includes all the cities of the entire country, which includes all the countries. And in that city is a house that includes all the houses of the entire city, which includes all the cities of the country, which includes all the countries. And within that, there is a person who is composed of the entire house, etc. And there, there is a person who makes all of the humor and jokes of the country.

So the wise man took a great deal of money with him, and he went there.

And he saw that the people were engaged in various kinds of tricks and jokes. And he understood from the jokes that the country was entirely filled with lies, from beginning to end. This is because they would make a joke of oppressing and cheating each other in business. And when a person came to lodge a claim in a *manistrat* (court), there everything was false, and the judges took bribes. And the man who lodged a complaint would go to a higher *sand* (court), but there too everything was falsehood. And they used to make an *an-shtel*[3] (humorous skit) of things.

And the wise man understood from this joking that the country was full of lies and cheating, and that there was no truth in it whatsoever.

So he went and he engaged in business in the country. And he let himself be cheated in business, and he filed a complaint in the courts. And [the judges] were all filled with lies and took bribes.

So one day, he gave them a bribe, and the next day, they claimed not to recognize him.

So he went to a higher court, and there too everything was false – until at last he came before the *senate* (the supreme court).

And there, the judges were also filled with falsehood and took bribes – until he came to the king himself.

And when he came to the king, he exclaimed, 'Over whom are you a king? That the country is filled with falsehood entirely, from beginning to end, and that there is no truth in it ....' And he began to enumerate all of the falsehoods of the country.

And when the king heard his words, he bent his ear to the curtain to hear his words, for it was astonishing to the king that there should be someone who knows about all the falsehoods of the county. And the royal ministers who heard his words grew very angry at him. But he continued to describe the falsehoods of the country.

He (the wise man, as above) exclaimed, 'And it would make sense to say that the king too is like them – that he loves falsehood like the people of his country. But from this, I see how you are a man of truth – for which reason you stay far from the people, since you cannot bear the falsehood of the country.'

And he began to praise the king exceedingly.

And the king, because he was very humble – and where his greatness was, there was his humility, for that is the way of a humble person, that the more he is praised and lauded, the smaller and more humble does he become – so because of the great praise of the wise man, who praised and lauded the king, the king came to an extreme state of humility and smallness, until he became literally nothing.

And he could not restrain himself. And he cast aside the curtain to see that wise man. 'Who is this, who knows and understands all of this?'

And the king's face was revealed, and the sage saw it. And he brought the king's portrait to his own king.

Part I. Seeking the Face of the King

I. The Face of the King

Many components of this story lead to the understanding that the search for the king's portrait is a search for the face of God, a search that concludes in 'and the king's face was revealed, and the sage saw it.' The king serves in many parables – Hasidic and earlier too – as the 'King of the universe.'[4] The 'face' is a widespread and dominant image used to describe God's revelation of Himself, and the use of the phrases 'revelation of the face' and 'hiding the face' is also widespread, as is describing closeness to, revelation of or distance from God. The use of the term 'face' in the description of God's revelation to Moses in *Exodus*[5] serves as a paradigmatic image of the revelation of God – a model, as we shall see further on, relevant to the story under consideration. In addition, the more concrete image of seeking the 'face' in the sense of seeking God may also be found in the Bible.[6]

The description of the seal of the king as 'mighty, great, a man of truth and humble,' is a variation on the phrase recited at the beginning of the *Amidah* prayer, three times a day: 'God, Who is great and mighty.' This phrase, as I shall discuss further on, has a long history in the Bible, rabbinic literature and Jewish thought.

The seal of the king as 'a man of truth' is associated with R. Chaninah's statement that 'the seal of the Holy One, blessed be He, is truth.'[7] Also, the unusual combination of might and humility is explicitly described as a divine quality: 'R. Yochanan said: Wherever you find the greatness of the Holy One, blessed be He, so there do you find His humility.'[8] In describing the response of the king to hearing himself praised, the storyteller uses the phrase, 'and in the place of his greatness, there is his humility,' which is the abbreviated paraphrase of R. Yochanan's words, referring to God.

Both the description of the king as 'hidden from human beings' and the description of the curtain that separates him from people are associated with common images referring to God, Who is hidden from the eyes of man, and to the veils separating Him from man.

The two kings in the story are one and the same king – the King of the world – for God, the King, presents man the mission of seeking His face. As the verse states, 'On Your behalf,[9] my heart said, "All of you, seek my face." And your face, Hashem, will I seek.'[10]

II. The Structure of the Story

At the starting point of this story, the might of the king, God – a 'might' and 'power' that fill the world – is not in question. The question is where the seal of truth and humility can be seen.

In the first stage of the story, the measure of the truth of the king is made clear to the sage when he sees the distance of the king from his land, so filled with falsehood. In the second stage, the measure of the king's humility grows clear from his response to praise and from the reference to his trait of truth in humbling himself: 'for that is the way of a humble person.'

The revelation of the king's face and the clarification of the measure of truth and humility are intertwined with a discovery of the paradox standing at the center of the story: although the king is a man of truth, his land is filled with falsehood. The sage only sees what occurs in the land and does not see the king; nevertheless, it is precisely because the land is filled with falsehood that he discovers that the king is a man of truth. Indeed, the paradox provides its own solution, explaining that the distance of the king from his land and the concealment of his face indicate that he is not a part of the falsehood, but its complete opposite, and thus he is far from the land. Still, although the paradox is solved, its impression remains.

This story presents an example of negative theology, in which the recognition of God is based on the distance between God and the world, and man's knowledge of God is knowledge through negation. Man only knows that God is not the world; by looking at the world, he can know what God is not. Therefore, paradoxically, a land filled with falsehood teaches about an honest king.

III. The Revelation of the Face

'And his face was revealed, and the sage saw him and he brought his portrait to the king.' What does the portrait of the king look like? What is the image of his face? In the process described in the story, the more the sage praises the king, the smaller the king grows, 'until he became literally nothing.' At this point, the king casts aside the curtain, his face is revealed, and the sage sketches him. But since we know that the king became 'literally nothing,' clearly the sage came away with a blank portrait, on which only the 'nothing' was delineated.

This point of the story combines with and supports the direction of the interpretation introduced earlier that it is impossible to see and draw the face of the king. What can be learned of the king's face comes only by way of negation; in the end, the picture remains blank. Still, it should be emphasized that this process of removing the curtain and revealing the king's face is described positively in the story as giving the sage what he seeks. The sage attains a revelation not attained by the people, a revelation without a curtain, revealing the king as 'nothing.'

We can explain the revelation of the king as 'nothing' in various ways. If we understand 'nothing' solely in the sense of emptiness, nothingness and negation, we may conclude that the king is revealed to the protagonist at the end of his search as not existing – that there is no God and no one to draw – and so the sage returns from his search for the face of the king with a blank portrait. This explanation, if true, would divulge a radical secret heresy in R. Nachman of Bratslav's story. But as appealing this interpretation may be to some, it does not concur well with R. Nachman's story, for we cannot understand the 'nothing' in the story without the Hasidic-kabbalistic context of the term 'nothing.'[11]

The exact meaning of *ayin* – 'nothingness' – is not invariant and has been interpreted differently by kabbalists across the generations. For the purpose of our discussion, I will make do with the statement that 'nothingness' serves as a term for the *sefirah* of *keter* or as a term for that which is higher than all the *sefirot*;[12] it is associated as well with the Infinite One, indicating the plane upon which God transcends all understanding and is hidden completely from the human horizon.[13]

In Hasidism, 'nothing' is a central concept, often referred to in its kabbalistic-Hasidic sense. And thus, even when this term appears in a story, one cannot relate to it solely according to its simple meaning and ignore the clear cultural context in which it was created. In that context, the revelation of 'nothing' at the top of the ladder of spiritual attainments has no connection to disbelief and heresy, but rather represents a revelation of the supreme layer in the divine framework, as it is conceptualized in kabbalistic and in Hasidic thought.[14]

Rachel Elior explicates the concepts of 'being' and 'nothingness' in the teachings of R. Nachman: 'Two opposites – "being" and "nothingness" – in the language of R. Nachman express the contradiction between the uninterrupted presence of divinity above and below, and the experience of being, and, constriction, absence, emptiness of divinity and the experience of nothingness, which leaves "being" alone to the comprehension of man.'[15]

'Nothingness' expresses the hidden divinity, which is not sensed in normative human experience. The concealment and lack of connection to that 'nothingness' causes the sense of the absence of God from the world; thus a person confronts a reality empty of divinity and, in the language of our story, the feeling of the distance of the king from his land. The more the sage of the story praises the king for his distance from the land, for not being in the world, the smaller the king becomes 'until he becomes literally nothing;' the king's distance from the world is the aspect of 'nothingness.'

The appropriate experience of 'nothingness,' however, is the revelation of the divinity hidden in being; thus, it is not only an experience of distance from God, but precisely also an experience of the revelation of God and His closeness, as described in many Hasidic sources[16] as in this story. In this story, we see that the process of praising God and describing His distance from the world leads paradoxically to an opposite end: to the revelation of His face: 'and his face was revealed,' 'and the sage saw him.' It is precisely because he understands the distance of God until He is transformed into 'nothingness' that the sage attains and sees the face of the king. This story is a revelation – but the content of that revelation is 'nothingness.' The canvas of the portrait remains blank; nevertheless, standing before the 'nothingness' is an experience of the revelation of the king's face.[17] Further on, after discussing the philosophical basis of this story, I shall comment more on the kabalistic-Hasidic context of the term 'nothingness' and its relevance to this story.

IV. The Praises of the King

I mentioned above that the seal of the king as 'mighty and great' is a variation on the familiar phrase from the *Amidah* blessing of the patriarchs, 'God, great and mighty.' This phrase, based on a biblical verse,[18] forms the basis for a number of important conversations on attributions and praise of God and on the difficulties of religious speech – beginning in the Babylonian and Jerusalem Talmud[19] and continuing, in another form by Maimonides in the Middle Ages.[20] These deliberations are directly connected to the present story.

In his deliberations on the 'doctrine of attributes,' Maimonides uses the Talmudic passage in *Berachot*[21] that deals with the phrase 'God, the great, the mighty, and the awesome' in order to illustrate the deeply problematic nature of describing God. He presents a strict view that forbids describing God with positive attributes and only allows descriptions in the negative: one may not say what God is, but only what He is not. Maimonides asserts that if making a decision were solely up to our judgment, it would be strictly forbidden to say that God is 'great, mighty and awesome,' for that statement reifies God. We may recite this phrase and others like it only when two conditions are met: first, that the phrase is found in the Torah, and second, that the Men of the Great Assembly included it in the prayer service. If not specifically instituted by the Men of the Great Assembly, it would even be forbidden to quote verses of the Torah with the intent of praising God. Maimonides depreciates not only praise and descriptions of God but even prayers of request, for a request posits that God can be 'affected' and that it is possible to influence Him to change His mind.[22]

What, then, is the knowledge of God in Maimonides' view? 'The comprehension of God means that a person realizes his inability to comprehend Him.'[23] This is very similar to the statement, 'The ultimate knowledge is that we do not know,' as discussed in the previous chapter.

Maimonides raises the question: if all that a person can know of God is a set of descriptions of negation, what is the point of learning Torah altogether? It would seem that the knowledge of the sage and of the simple man familiar with the principle that God cannot be positively described is equal. Why, then, should a person make an effort to learn Torah? Maimonides replies that a person can and must advance in his knowledge of God: the more that he learns Torah, the more he denies descriptions of God that reify Him, and the more he erases ideas in his mind about God. And thus, he removes successive amounts of dross from his understanding of God, purifying and correcting his words about God until, at the end of the process, he arrives at silence.

> And the most clear comment of all on this topic may be found in *Psalms*: 'To You, silence is praise'[24] – silence in regard to God is praise. And that represents a very great level of clarity in this matter, since everything that is said with the intent of elevating and praising God contains some degree of error in regard to Him, be He elevated, and we sense that it possesses some imperfection. And thus, silence is preferable.[25]

The end of the process of knowing God is silence from all praise and homage. This refers not only to silence of the lips but to silence of thought as well, and its purification of any reifying concepts of God.

In 'The Story of the Humble King,' R. Nachman develops a similar model of negative theology, but expresses it in a narrative form and with visual concepts. R. Nachman states that the attempt to describe and draw the image of God involves the service of negation and erasure. The person making the image must erase one line after another from the image of God, the king, until at the end of his work he comes to an empty picture, to 'nothingness.' This empty picture, which is silent, constitutes the peak of knowing the face of the king and his praise. And thus the verse states, 'Do not make for yourself a statue, any image.'[26]

In *Sefer Ha'ikarim*, R. Yosef Albo discusses the topic of divine attributes and raises anew Maimonides' question: what reason is there to attempt to know God and engage in successive descriptions of negation, if one is already aware that it is impossible to say anything about God? R. Yosef Albo answers this question by drawing a distinction between two types of negation concerning God and by emphasizing the importance of distinguishing between them; thus the value of learning and gaining clarity about each act of negation grows evident.[27] R. Yosef Albo concludes, 'And our lack of understanding does not indicate the absence of God's existence. And the ultimate that we can understand of God, may He be Blessed, is that it is impossible to understand Him. As the sage states, "The ultimate of what we know of You is that we do not know You".'[28]

This is the philosophical version of the principle, 'the ultimate knowledge is that we do not know.'[29] Intellectual and philosophical learning based upon negative theology brings a person to silence and to a knowledge pure of all dross and separate from all reification – a knowledge in which a person is aware that he does not know God. The image of God at which the philosopher gazes is empty of all intellectual and ideational images. The sage quoted by R. Yosef Albo is apparently R. Yidayah Hap'nini (Habadrashi), who states, 'The ultimate of what we know of You is that we do not know You, except that we know that You exist. That is our portion of all the toil of attaining insights and awarenesses of proper outlook, besides the understanding of a few negatives.'[30]

'The ultimate of what we know of You is that we do not know You' is also the meaning of the process described so well in 'The Story of the Humble King.' The more the sage praises the king, the smaller the king grows, so that the praises are negative attributes; they do not praise and positively describe the king, but solely describe the degree to which the king is far from the world and not of the world. The more the sage praises the king, the more the king disappears, for his praises are the erasure and negation of all the descriptions that are mistakenly applied by the people of the land to its king, by the world to the King of the world. Since there are no positive descriptions besides those whose source is in the world, as this process advances less and less remains of the king, 'until he becomes literally nothing.'

It bears emphasizing again that though the process reveals the humble king as 'nothingness,' there is no doubt that this is a process of advancement and revelation, expressing a positive experience of the revelation of the face of the king. This is underscored by a study of another of R. Nachman's short stories, 'The Story of the Menorah of Imperfections.' The question of why we engage in negative descriptions is, to my mind, part of the conceptual background of this story and provides its explanation:[31]

This is the story of a person who left his father and stayed in other lands for many days, amongst others. And after a while, he returned to his father and boasted that over there he had learned a great skill: how to make a chandelier. And the son told his father to gather all of the artisans schooled in this craft and that he would show them his ability in this craft. And his father did so. He gathered all of the artisans in this craft to show the greatness of his son, to show what he had accomplished all the days that he had been in the land of others.

And the son brought out a chandelier that he had made. But it was very ugly in the eyes of all of the artisans. And his father went to them and asked them to tell him the truth. And they were forced to tell him the truth: that it was very ugly. But the son boasted, 'Don't you see the wisdom of my craft?' But his father told him that it did not appear beautiful in the eyes of any of the artisans. The son replied, 'To the contrary. It is precisely here that I have shown my greatness, for I have shown everyone his flaw, because in this chandelier are to be found the flaws of each of the craftsmen here.

Don't you see that one artisan finds this part ugly, but finds another part very beautiful? And another artisan, to the contrary, finds the part that his colleague finds ugly to be beautiful and wondrous in his eyes, but views another part as being ugly. And the same holds true for all of them. That which is bad in the eyes of one is beautiful in the eyes of his colleague, and vice versa.

'And I made this chandelier from imperfections only, to show all of them that they have no perfection, and that each one has an imperfection – because that which is beautiful in the eyes of one is an imperfection in the eyes of his colleague. But in truth I could make it properly.

'If people would know all of the imperfections and limitations of the matter, they would know the nature of the matter, even if they had never seen it.'

The son's statement is presented in the negative, and the chandelier that he made is a negative image of a proper chandelier. It has no description and positive tangibility as a 'chandelier,' but is composed entirely of attributes of negation: it is the opposite of a proper lamp. The claim made at the end of the story indicates that the service of negation is not only the aspect of 'turning from evil,' of removing any reification of God, but has a positive aspect of 'doing good' – of knowing the nature of the matter. By the service of negation a person knows more and more clearly the nature of the matter, even if he never saw it and has neither words nor imagery to visualize it.

V. Philosophy and Kabbalah

I have stated that 'The Story of the Humble King' gives tangible literary expression to the philosophical perspectives on the theology of negation, in which the framework of philosophical thought provides an explanation for the transformation of the king into 'nothingness.' I have also argued that the concept of 'nothingness' as expressed in this story cannot be removed from its core kabbalistic-Hasidic context; thus the revelation of the king's face as 'nothingness' is to be understood not only as the negation of philosophical being but as a revelation, as the aspect of the 'nothingness' that stands at the pinnacle of the levels of divine emanation, at the head of the world of the *sefirot*.

But there would appear to be a contradiction, or at least a tension, between these two claims, for each attempts to fit the story into a different spiritual climate and a different conceptual framework. This tension, however, is not as pronounced as it may at first appear, for variations of the theology of negation are adapted by many kabbalists as well, and the point of the story – the revelation of the king as 'nothingness' – is a significant and meaningful meeting point between two central frameworks of Jewish thought – the philosophical and the kabbalistic.

The tension between the view of God as infinite and transcendental, existing beyond all insight and comprehension, and the view of God as interested in the world and in man – commanding, exercising providence and hearing prayer – as described in the biblical and rabbinic tradition, is in the background of philosophical thought in the Middle Ages and of kabbalistic thought from its inception. Many kabbalists decided categorically in favor of the philosophical view that unequivocally denies any comprehension of or ability to discuss God.[32] God is 'infinite' and concealed from all thought. We may not conclude anything about God from anything written in the Torah and expressed by the sages about Him, the Commander to Whom man turns, for all of these are statements describing the framework of the relationship between God and the world and between God and man and not statements whose object is the 'Infinite One' Himself.[33] As in the unambiguous words of *Sefer Maarecht Ha'Elokut*: 'The being of the Infinite One is not even alluded to in the Torah, in the Prophets, in the Writings, nor in the words of our sages; but the masters of worship[34] received a slight hint regarding this.'[35]

Many of the kabbalists accepted negative theology as applying to the Infinite One Himself and understood all of the Torah and kabbalistic speech as referring to the framework of the ten *sefirot*, which is only an emanation of the Infinite One.[36] The first stage in the knowledge of God is to distance Him from all reification, multiplicity and change. Only afterwards is it possible to begin to speak of kabbalistic matters – the *sefirot* and the structure of the worlds, all of which refer not to the Infinite One Himself, but only to the emanation drawn down from Him. According to these approaches, it may be said that in a sense kabbalistic discourse follows in the footsteps of philosophical discussion, which constitutes a sort of introduction to and definition of the realms of kabbalistic discussion.[37] In the words of R. Moshe Cordovero, 'And all that those who pursue divine knowledge with intellect have spoken … are correct in removing from God descriptions and attributes of activities … And we must be thankful to them for having distanced matters of physicality and the like from God.'[38]

From a kabbalistic standpoint, philosophy brought philosophical discourse to its ultimate end, reaching its peak in the concept, 'to You, silence is praise,' whereas the kabbalists keep silent regarding the Infinite One Himself, but speak about the worlds emanated from him. In the words of R. Moshe of Borgos, 'The philosophers whose wisdom you praise actually know that the place of their heads is the place of our feet.'[39] It is possible that

R. Nachman alludes to this statement when he says, 'In the place where the wisdom of philosophy ends, there begins (the wisdom of truth, which is) the wisdom of the kabbalah.'[40]

In the 'Story of the Humble King,' we see a reflection of two ideational frameworks: the philosophical and the kabbalistic. The structure and central lines of the plot can be explained in terms of the philosophical model, whereas the thrust of the story, the imagery that represents the 'nothingness,' is an axiom and image rooted in kabbalistic-Hasidic terminology.[41]

According to this, the very structure of the story illustrates R. Nachman's statement that where philosophy ends the wisdom of kabbalah begins. And even if the path of kabbalah passes through the theology of negation, it does not stop there but proceeds to an additional stage, possessing a revelation that is the goal of all those who seek the face of God.[42]

VI. From 'The Ultimate Knowledge' to Experiencing 'Nothingness': A Phenomenological Note

I do not think that in his 'Story of the Humble King' R. Nachman is attempting to present us with a congruent philosophical-kabbalistic teaching. Rather, as these systems are internalized into his world, they become a view and sense of existence in which his life and its experiences take place. These are reflected in the story and are thus imbued with literary substance of depth, grace and vivacity.

Without diminishing the importance of the conceptual map and structure of the story, which become clear when we understand its philo-sophical foundations discussed earlier, we will see that we cannot understand the meaning of the story without relating to the religious experience at its core, for we must see this story not only as a literary illustration of theological, kabbalistic and philosophical positions, but also, if not principally, as the literary expression of an inner process that peaks in the experience of the revelation of God's face.

The positive meaning that the story gives to the revelation of God as 'nothingness' is to be understood not only as relying upon kabbalistic terms of 'nothingness' and 'Infinite One,'[43] but as flowing from the ineffable human mystical experience, which forces a person to make do with descrip-tions of negation and with applying the appellation 'nothingness' to God.

William James describes the tendency of mystics, both Eastern and Western, to refer to God solely in terms of negation: 'He can be described only by "No, no!",'[44] and cites many examples of the appellation of God as 'nothingness' in various cultures. The refusal to give God any title, says James, 'is superficially negative, but in truth it comes in the service of a deeper positive.'[45] The experience of the mystic who is in touch with the infinite prevents him from giving expression to that with which he comes in contact by reference to attributes and any name with a finite nature, as these squeeze, diminish and crush his experience in consciousness or in infinite existence. The description of God as 'nothingness' in these cases does not come from harnessing philosophical terms, but best fits the nature of the mystical experience, which cannot be defined in words and positive concepts.

Rudolf Otto, in discussing the *Misterium Tremendum* (awesome mystery) at the heart of the feeling of holiness, describes the sense of mystery that comes from confrontation with the 'ultimate other,' a confrontation that inspires expressions about God such as 'beyond the world' and 'super-natural.'[46] Otto claims that in mysticism there is a stronger sense of contact with God and a radical increase in a person's sense of God's separateness and otherness, so that the contrast between God and the world and nature is trans-formed into a universal contrast between God and all existence. This feeling leads a person to refer to God as 'nothingness.' Otto emphasizes that 'together with the absolute nature of the negation and contrast, which are all that can be grasped at the moment of *mysterium,* and their extension to the point of paradox, the positive content of the "total other" also grows stronger and more powerful, rising to the peak of its emotional vitality, rising and overwhelming one's feeling, which is too much to contain.'[47]

This description closely correlates with 'The Story of the Humble King' and the sage's outburst of words of praise, which focus on the fact that God the King 'is entirely different' than the world. This process grows stronger until in the end God is revealed as being 'nothingness.' 'Nothingness' is indeed the description that best fits the sage's personal mystical and positive experience of the revelation of the face of God.

The blankness of the image of the king is precisely what symbolizes God's eminence. As Rudolph Otto states, 'Emptiness and nothingness are in truth a numinous ideogram of "the entirely other." The emptiness symbolizes the absolute height.'[48]

Accordingly, in regard to Jewish mysticism too, descriptions stated in the negative should not be seen solely as an outcome of philosophical thought, but should be understood as the mystic's natural response, his attempt to give verbal expression to his contact with 'the absolute other' – the awesome mystery that a human being cannot know. Since we know that mystics across the world, even those not subscribing to negative philosophy and theology, tend to express the subject of their mystical experience in the negative and with the appellation 'nothingness' without relying on any philosophical school of thought, we should not be surprised to learn that this occurrence, a natural part of the mystical phenomenon, has not bypassed Jewish mysticism. Therefore, when we come upon descriptions of negation and appellations of 'nothingness' in the writings of the kabbalists and Hasidim, those expressions should not be automatically attributed to a dialogue with, response to or absorption of philosophical traditions. Rather, this is to be understood first and foremost as an authentic description of mystical experience and as an inner component of the mystical language and the simplicity derived from it.

I am not denying my earlier assertion regarding the influence of philosophy and the doctrine of attributes on many kabbalists, but rather am emphasizing two points. The first is that one should not rush to assert that descriptions of the negative in a kabbalistic text necessarily indicate philosophical influence. Secondly, even when we find a kabbalistic text that adapts the language and terms of the philosophical world, it is possible that the roots of negation are native to the mystical experience itself and to the language that naturally arises from the nature of that experience, and that only at a second stage, when the description of the experiences was being formulated, did the kabbalist adapt philosophical terms. Philosophy itself, however, played no meaningful role in shaping that experience, not even in the consolidation of the mystical, reflexive contemplation.

It is difficult to decide the extent of the philosophical foundation of R. Nachman's 'The Story of the Humble King.' On the one hand, as we will see, there is reason to assume a philosophical background, not only because of a multitude of corresponding details, but also because of the structure of the story, which describes negation as preceding the revelation of the king's face. It is not the experience of the revelation of God's face that brings about the description of God's otherness and distance; on the contrary, the revelation of 'nothingness' results from the adopted activity of negation. On the other hand, the negation in the story can be seen not only as a philosophical service, but as giving expression to. an experience whose exalted nature and attendant awareness of the divine 'otherness' intensifies until arriving at last at a mystical experience of the revelation of the divine countenance.

In the previous chapter, we saw that the axiom, 'the ultimate knowledge is that we do not know,' comprises for R. Nachman both a description of man's status in the presence of the divine exalted Being and of the 'we do not know' that indicates a mystical experience without *da'at*. In 'The Story of the Humble King,' the formula 'the ultimate knowledge is that we do not know,' is not mentioned. From a structural aspect, however, it is given substance in the revelation of God as 'nothingness' – a revelation that is the ultimate knowledge and the proclamation of the negation of any ideas about God.

In R. Nachman's story, the various meanings of 'ultimate knowledge' resonate to an equal degree. Philosophical 'not-knowing' and mystical 'not-knowing,' the sense of the exalted nature and otherness of God blend together into a single vector that leads towards a mystical experience of the revelation of the face of God as 'nothingness.'

Part II. Regarding Katavish[49] and Laughter

The sage in R. Nachman's tale who wants to understand the nature of the land focuses on knowing its *katavish*, 'because when one needs to know a thing, one needs to know the *katavish* of that thing.' One can learn about a land from its laughter and mockery, thus learning through a distorting mirror. By its nature, such a mirror exaggerates existent facts. However, because of that very intensification and enlargement, images of matters are formed whose lack of feasibility is conspicuous; from the images created by this mirror, states the sage, one can learn about the nature of the land.

This learning precedes the sage's learning by way of negation, when he contrasts the land with its king. In the two instances, this learning is not direct and in the positive sense, but rather by way of reflections and in the manner of negation. The sage learns the nature of the land from its mockery and laughter, and he learns the nature of the king from the land, from which the king is distant, and from the land's characteristics, which are the opposite of the king's.

The intriguing question is the nature of the house of universal laughter that includes all the houses, cities and countries. And who is the comedian who makes all of the jokes and *katavish* of the land?

From the series of allusions that follow this story, allusions 'that we heard from the holy mouth' of R. Nachman, we may conclude that this is the Temple in Jerusalem. And this is the language of that passage:

> 'The ways of Zion are mourning' (*Lamentations* 1). Zion is the aspect of the signposts *ziunim* of all the lands, all of which meet there. As the verse states, 'When one sees ... he will build next to it a signpost' (*Ezekiel* 39:15). And that is the meaning of the words, 'Look upon Zion, the city of our gathering' (*Isaiah* 33). The acronym of this phrase is *metzachek* 'laughs' – for there, all of the signposts would gather. And whoever needed to know whether to do something or engage in some business would know the answer there. May it be God's will that it be built quickly, in our days, amen.[50]

Zion, Jerusalem is the city found at the center of the world and includes the entire world. If identifying this city with Zion seems questionable and surprising, the prayer cited at the end of this passage, 'May it be rebuilt quickly in our days, amen' removes any doubt that the Temple is the house under discussion.

In *Rimzei Maasiyot*, R. Nachman of Tcherin states explicitly that this story speaks of the Temple in Jerusalem:

> And perhaps this is the aspect of that which is explained in the above story. 'There is a land that includes all of the lands.' That is the aspect of the totality of the holiness of the community of the land of Israel. 'And in that land there is a city that includes all of the cities in that land.' That is the aspect of Zion and Jerusalem. 'And in that city is a house that includes all of the houses in that city.' That is the aspect of the Temple and the Heichal. 'And there, there is a man,' etc.[51]

Another source for this identification may be derived from the allusions that follow the story of 'The King Who Decreed Apostasy.' Those allusions refer to an image of a man composed of all the metals in the world, via which a person can rule over the entire world: 'for that corresponds to the king over Zion, the holy mountain, because all of the parts of the world are included there, etc.' In other words, Jerusalem is the place that incorporates into itself all the parts of the world.

If the Temple is the place in the story, we may reasonably infer that the man within the house is the *Kohen Gadol*. We can now appreciate the difficulty of 'explaining so much in matters of this nature,' for what conclusions may be derived from this astonishing identification? If the house is the Temple and the man is the *Kohen Gadol*, we must infer that by its nature the Temple is a dwelling place of scoffers where all of the mockery and laughter of the entire city, the land and the world are centralized and incorporated. And the *Kohen Gadol* is the great comedian and universal entertainer who stands at the head of all the acts of mockery.

Does R. Nachman grant mockery and scorn religious value, placing it within the framework of the commandments? And if not, what is the meaning of the imagery of the description of the Temple service as mockery, comedy and clowning? Before I attempt to answer this question, I shall offer a few introductory ideas.

I. Religious Ritual as Theatrical Presentation

Johann Hoyzinga's model regarding the linkage between games, theater and ritual[52] provides background to explaining these matters. Hoyzinga sees religious ritual as a type of game: just like a game, the rules of religious ritual and their meaning are determined in accordance with pre-determined principles, which give the ritual its meaning and logical basis. As in a game, the value of ritual and religious ceremony does not come from its fulfillment of any economic function or of any human, physical needs. In that sense, both games and religious deeds are superfluous. Their value and unique nature come precisely from the fact that people engage in them for their own sake and not for any other purpose. At the moment that any other purpose can explain an activity, it is no longer a religious act or a game. Games, like rituals and religious ceremonies, create a closed framework, bound in terms of place, time and the figures that take place within. Thus, an independent space is created, one disconnected from the regular life of action, one that maintains an enclave of celebration within the mundane. Also, games do not lack in religious gravity; both child and adult relate seriously to their play. In this sense, the Temple service may also be seen as a ritual, as an arrangement of activities with its own fixed codes, like the rules of games or the stage. The *Kohen* who engages in the ritual and offers the sacrifices is the prime actor in the theater of the Temple.[53]

Although Hozingah's words constitute an important contribution to understanding the imagery of the Temple as a place of play, in themselves they do not provide a sufficient explanation of the imagery of the Temple as a place of laughter and mockery. Hoyzinga emphasizes, and justifiably so, the awe and respect that characterize religious ritual. Although he sees the elements of play and theater in ritual, he stresses the profound gravity that characterizes the theater of the holy.[54] It would have been easier to understand R. Nachman's words if he had compared the Temple service to tragedy, which arouses a spirit of seriousness and respect. However, R. Nachman chose to describe the Temple as a universal center of laughter, mockery and *katavish.*

II. God's Comedians

An earlier description of the Temple as a place of laughter and mockery, which compares those who work in the Temple to comedians, may be found in the Zohar (*Vayeitzei*):[55]

> 'Your Kohanim will wear righteousness and Your pious ones will sing.' From here, we learn that a person summoned to the king should change his deeds in order to give pleasure to the king. If the king usually has regular comedians to amuse him, this person should arrange before the king comedians who are ministers and dukes. But if not, that would not be a pleasure for the king. Come, see: David invited the king and queen to rest. What did he do? He put the king's jesters in place of his ministers. And who are they? The answer

may be found in the verse, 'Your Kohanim will wear justice and Your pious ones will sing.' 'Your pious ones will sing.' The verse should have stated, 'Your Levites will sing,' since the Levites are the king's jesters. And now David, who invited the king to rest, made the Kohanim and pious men the king's jesters.[56]

In his essay, *Zohar V'eros*,[57] Yehudah Liebes discusses this midrash and how it is woven into the Zohar's tapestry of play, eros and humor. I intend to discuss this midrash as a possible source of inspiration for the comparison of the Temple service to laughter and mockery in 'The Story of the Humble King' and to see, in the context of this Zoharic midrash, the meaning and significance that inheres in R. Nachman's use of this image.

The Zohar uses the figure known to us from historical reality – the king's jester – in order to describe the Temple's activities. The *Kohanim* in their work and the Levites in their song and music give joy to the king, in a way different from the pilgrims who bring offerings and gifts. The pilgrims give God joy with a present that possesses tangible value. The *Kohanim*, on the other hand, give God joy in the same way that the court fool[58] amuses the king and gives him joy, with simple, humorous deeds that that lack value if examined in terms of utility.

The incompleteness of these deeds – the fact that they are not integrated into a framework of purposeful activity – is itself their unique quality. It is precisely the lack of functionality that arouses joy and amusement. If mockery becomes officially endorsed, it is liable to lose its value, since it becomes part of the framework of familiar and purposeful activities: the jester becomes a professional, someone 'serious,' of whom expertise and experience are expected. Therefore, the Zohar states that the mockery and jest must be invested with meaninglessness. Thus it is not the expert jester who provides the amusement but, quite to the contrary, it is the ministers, those with 'serious' professions, who amuse and jest. The meaningless deed, which shatters the framework of functionality and breaks beyond the rules of normative logic, creates an amusing occurrence and delights the king and queen.

It should be noted that this change of roles is presented in the Zohar as a one-time event. However, the description of the purpose of the Levites as jesters is not related to a particular occurrence but to their regular role, and in this the Temple is assigned the fixed function of serving as a place of jesting.

The Zoharic midrash is close to the spirit of R. Nachman's story in that it emphasizes the laughter and jesting in the Temple service. Although Hoyzinga's model relates to the enjoyment and pleasure that accompany and are an essential component of play, it does not relate sufficiently to jesting and mockery to explain their central place in both the Bratslavian tale and the Zoharic midrash. Hoyzinga emphasizes the seriousness and celebratory nature that characterize religious ritual, and presents them as one of 'two extreme spiritual dispositions at the moment of "play" – these being both "frivolity" and "intense cleaving to God".'[59] During holy play, the frame of mind is one of intensity and cleaving to God, whereas in other games the mood is one of frivolity and lightness. These words do not entirely fit with the descriptions of the Temple service in the Zohar and in R. Nachman's 'Story of the Humble King.'

Although, neither the source from the Zohar nor Hoyzinga's model can completely explain the image of the Temple service as comedy, they provide the background to my following remarks, which undertake to explain this imagery in R. Nachman's story by reference to the context of the story itself and to additional sources in R. Nachman's teachings.

III. *The Humble King – the Temple Service as Comedy*

According to R. Nachman's story, the Temple service and its religious ceremonies arouse ridicule and laughter. Like the *katavish* in the singular house of this story, which radically reflects what is occurring in the entire land, so does the Temple show what is occurring in religious service in general. The Temple represents a sharply delineated paradigm, one that is apparently even exaggerated, of the nature of religious worship in general. In the Temple, people give gifts to the elevated and infinite God; they appease His countenance with offerings of fine flour; they believe the scent of the incense to be pleasing to God; and the Levites sing to Him in order that He will, as it were, spend His time pleasantly. Can there be a greater comedy than that?

The extreme examples of the ridiculous nature of man's attempts to serve God in the Temple by means of offering oxen, sheep and two *log* of oil exhibit religious worship as a whole in its laughable aspect – for how does this attempt to appease God and serve Him differ from a person's attempts to appease Him with prayer and imploring, or from a person's hope of pleasing God by performing mitzvot? The absurd nature of the latter is not as shocking and conspicuous as the Temple service, but at the core the untenable nature of religious worship is the same, whether in the Temple or in the land.

This description fits well with the flow of R. Nachman's story, as described above in Part I. The story is based on the problematic nature of religious speech, on negative theology and on the emphasis of the distance between God and the world and between God and man. Man cannot know God and cannot visualize the image of His countenance. The only path left to a person is that of negation, which intensifies the awareness of the distance between man and God. But when taken to its logical end, philosophical thought regarding the problematic nature of religious speech, which leads to the conclusion that 'to You silence is praise' and to the blank portrait, raises an even graver problem: the nature of ritualistic speech and of the meaning of the mitzvot and of the Temple as the service of God.[60] Indeed, if praying to God and addressing Him as 'God, who is great, mighty and awesome' creates a grave theological problem of reification, how much greater, then, is the problematic nature of bringing God sacrifices, of slaughtering sheep and oxen and arranging a bombastic performance of Kohanim, Levites and the Temple. When examined in this manner, not only is the Temple service revealed to possess an exigent religious problem, but that service appears as an untenable and astonishing comedy: the divine comedy that describes God, the 'Infinite One,' changing His mind when bribed with a bullock; or the human comedy of attempting to serve the abstract God Who has no body and no form of a body with corporeal matters like sprinkling blood, offering incense and burning animal limbs.[61]

As stated above, this problem exists in all religious service that purports to be worship of God; however, the Temple is the locus, the paradigm of the flow of all religious service. Thus R. Nachman states that comedy exists everywhere: the *katavish* and *anshteln* exist wherever there is religious service, prayer, Torah learning and the performance of mitzvot. The all-inclusive comedy, though, which sharply distills all other comedies, is the comedy of the Temple. The protagonist who stars in the Temple comedy – the *Kohen Gadol* – represents, most of all, the entire human-religious comedy.

The sage of the story who sees things clearly apparently discovers the falseness that exists in the framework of the service of the king and the dimension of bribery that characterizes this service. He does not, however, stop at this stage, but understands from it how far the king is from the people of his land and how impossible it is to learn from the falsehood and the comedy taking place as the service of the king and in the name of the king about the king himself. Only the sage's service of extreme negation, which cleanses the king's portrait of all falsehood and bribery and of all attributes and names, can lead to the lowering of the curtain and to the revelation of the face of the king as nothingness.

We can now understand why 'the ministers who heard the sage's words were very angry at him,' for the ministers who work in the name of the king are now revealed to be disconnected from the source of their authority. The sage shows that the entire religious framework with its leaders, its ministers and its advisors is presenting a giant performance, all in the name of God and as the service of God that makes a joke of God and man.

It is possible that R. Nachman's concern about the anger of the 'royal ministers' of his day was one of the factors that led him to clothe his words in a story and not to explicate them in his teachings and talks, although, as we will see further on, a clear echo of these perspectives may be found in a slightly moderated tone in those sources as well.

IV. Service of God

How, therefore, is it possible according to R. Nachman to serve God with Torah learning, prayer and mitzvot? As I will show further on, we can identify in R. Nachman's words various explanations of the meaning of religious service that echo and answer the question of the problematical nature of religious service as it appears in 'The Story of the Humble King.'

In *Sichot Haran*, R. Nachman states:

> And as to serving Hashem – I do not know who can say that he serves Hashem in accordance with the greatness of the Creator, may He be blessed. If someone knows a little of God's greatness, [...], I do not know how he can say that he will serve God, may He be blessed. And no angel or *seraph* can claim that it can serve God, may He be blessed.
>
> But the main thing is the desire that one's desire be strong and powerful constantly to come close to God, [...] And although everyone wants and desires to serve God, nevertheless, not all desires are equal, and there are many differentiations within desire. Even in one person himself, at every instant and moment there are great differences between his desires.
>
> And it is axiomatic that the principal element is the desire and longings – i.e., that a person should long constantly for God, [...]. And in the midst of that, we pray and learn and do mitzvot, (although in truth, taking into account God's greatness, [...], all of these types of service are nothing; rather, everything is in the way of 'as if,' because everything is like a simple joke in comparison to God's greatness, may He be blessed – in Yiddish, *klamersht*).[62]

Whoever knows even a little of God's greatness knows that in light of His extraordinary eminence, it is impossible to say that a person, seraph or angel serves God. Whoever engages in any service of God without distinguishing between levels must know that his service is a simple joke when compared to God's stature.

No service of God is literally service of God – rather, it is all 'as though.' The only thing that has value is a person's desire to come close to God, and his desire, which cannot actually be fulfilled, to serve God.

These longings and yearnings are the important element in the service of God. Attributing independent meaning to various acts of serving God such as Torah learning, praying and mitzvot is ridiculous, foolish and laughable. Only the view of performing mitzvot as mad acts of love transforms them into something forgivable – 'love conceals all iniquities.'[63] Acts and games of love have no intrinsic value and, if judged in isolation from the love that impels them, appear as embarrassing acts of madness, without rhyme or reason. So too the value of a religious deed derives from the fact that it is the fruit of love; without desire and yearning it is simple foolishness.

Prayer, Torah learning and performing mitzvot are described in this talk as a secondary outcome of a person's desire and longings for God. When this desire intensifies, it seeks expression and a channel of communication; as a result a person keeps mitzvot, learns Torah and prays, even though he knows that there is something untenable in this. This is the import of R. Nachman's words 'that the main thing is the desire and the longings, that a person must long constantly for God, be He blessed – and in the midst of that, we pray, learn Torah and perform mitzvot.' A person must be aware that all the mitzvot that he performs are a type of performance, an 'as though,' a '*klamersht*' – a game out of love, 'a simple game' – and he must not relate to them with a seriousness they do not warrant.[64]

This talk of R. Nachman describes the routines of the religious world as based upon activity that is at its foundation and by its nature untenable. A sober gaze reveals that untenable nature and thus the grotesquery in the performance of mitzvot. Thus too in 'The Story of the Humble King,' the performance of mitzvot and the Temple service are a joke and comedy. They should, however, be approached with tolerance and understanding, for their source lies in a person's longing to pray and in an unvanquished yearning to serve God. The performance of the mitzvot is an outburst of a person's desire and love for God and should be seen more as the delights of love than as purposeful activity and 'the service of the king.'

In 'The Story of the Humble King' and the related talks we have quoted, a picture arises that sharply and pointedly portrays the inability of the rational mind (*da'at*) to explain the world of Torah and mitzvot. Only love, desire and longing, which lead a person to breach the laws of the rational mind (*da'at*), can assign reason and meaning to religious service. R. Nachman's statement does not deny religious life, but presents its non-rational basis in a stunning fashion. Whoever analyzes religious life solely with the help of his intellect and rational mind (*da'at*) will assert that it speaks of acts of foolishness and madness, which are the opposite of rationality (*da'at*) and reason. If a person would decide to act in accordance with rational mind and intellect, his rational mind would utterly uproot and undermine religious service, presenting it as a joke and as an 'as if,' *klamirsht*. The religious person, however, is not impelled solely by the power of the rational mind, but by the faculties of love, desire and yearning. The lack of rational mind is explained here not disparagingly but as being praiseworthy. The blessed lack of *da'at*, as in R. Nachman's words in his teaching, *Ki M'rachamam Yinhagam*, which deals as well with the axiom that 'the ultimate knowledge is that we do not know,' means that 'this person is able to receive … an illumination of will – i.e., that his will shall illumine him … And he yearns and longs a great deal for God, may He be blessed, with an outstanding desire, without any knowledge, so that he does not at all know what he wants.'[65]

This extraordinary desire, will and yearning for God is disconnected from any knowledge, even of knowledge regarding the object of desire and longing; it is out of that extraordinary will that a person prays, learns Torah and performs mitzvot.

V. Awareness as 'Giving Permission'

It is important to emphasize that the lack of *da'at* characterizing desire and longing for the Creator should not be identified with simplicity and lack of awareness. R. Nachman is make his Hasidim aware that all service of God is a joke and an 'as if,' a *klamirsht*, and that he is not interested in anyone remaining in a state of *simplicity*, in 'serving' God in the simple sense of the word. Believing that there is functional value to service, to prayer and to performance of mitzvot constitutes a reification and an insult to God and man. The only thing that can give a person permission to engage in the 'service of God,' is the awareness that it is all an 'as if' and that the entire essence and nature of Torah study, prayer and mitzvot inheres in the fact that they are the fruit of love and longing for God. Torah study and mitzvot have no justification and permission besides the love that breaks through the boundary and excuses all of the mitzvot. Only such a clear awareness grants a person permission to serve God with such corporealized means as Torah learning, the performance of mitzvot, the Temple service and sacrifices. This is similar to the passage that we saw in the Zohar. The humor that comes to amuse the king indeed amuses him, but only if we know that this humor is not 'serious,' that it has no function and is a joke and delight. David switches people's roles in the Temple service in order to underscore the delight and lack of functionality of the Temple service. That service is a *katavish*, and not something of intrinsic worth presented as a gift to the king.

Abandoning *da'at* for the sake of a will and desire stripped of knowledge is not, according to this, a proposal for living without awareness. On the contrary, a person must be well aware that his religious deeds lack *da'at* and logic, for only that awareness enables him to relate to them as to the main elements of the love of God, of which it is said, 'In her love you will go mad constantly,'[66] and which Rashi explains to mean, 'For the sake of her love, you make yourself mad and foolish.'[67] [68]

The teachings of R. Nachman regarding the obligation to do things that appear to be mad as part of the service of God may now be understood as a call to clarify the nature of the service of God in general. To roll in the trash and mud is a service that emphasizes and demonstrates the nature of the service of God. A person must know that every time that he 'comes to any worship' that act of worship is in the aspect of something that appears as madness because it purports to be the service of God. Thus, a person must 'cast aside all his cleverness' and perform these deeds in the aspect of 'in her love you grow mad always,' because 'for the sake of the love of Hashem it is necessary to do things that appear as madness.'

Part III. The Palace of Changes

The similarity of the service of God to jokes and comedy may also be found in the teaching, *Da Sheyesh Chadrei Torah*:

> Know that there are chambers of the Torah. And a person who attains them – when he begins to create original Torah thoughts, he enters into those chambers. And he enters from chamber to chamber, and from chamber to chamber. This is because in each single chamber there are a number of doors to other chambers. And so it is from those chambers to other chambers. And he enters and wanders through all of them. And he gathers from there very dear and beloved treasures and precious things – fortunate is his portion.[69]

The performance of the mitzvot and learning Torah as granting one access to the treasury is a well-known image,[70] but R. Nachman ascribes to it a unique meaning by describing such behavior as parenthetical to the wandering. He does not describe a goal of great importance, nor a wearying journey or ascent on a hierarchical ladder, rung after rung. Rather, he speaks of a relaxed wandering, of a free movement from chamber to chamber without a particular route and defined direction.[71] This description attributes to the service of God a subtle type of unfettered delight, not a defined track upon which a person must race, advancing as long as he is alive.[72] Further on, R. Nachman also discusses the dangers of which a person must be aware as he wanders through the chambers of the Torah.[73]

R. Nachman here gives a new, and in my view astonishing, interpretation to the meaning of 'the palaces of changes.'[74] In *Pardes Rimonim*, in the introduction to *Shaar Koh Hu Shaar Hatemurot*,[75] R. Moshe Cordovero writes: 'It is appropriate for us to know that "this corresponding to this did God make." This is because just as there is a side of holiness and purity and righteousness and straightness and a good quality of divine guidance of the world, (as I have explained), so must there also be the side of the husk, which is an unrestricted uncleanness, which is the accuser, and from whose side comes the enemy, who diverts man from the straight path to the path that is not good.'[76]

'The palaces of changes,'[77] which represent impurity and the husk, are described by R. Nachman as a person's new Torah thoughts and spiritual insights, which, although similar to and alluding to the 'true Torah,' are not themselves that 'true Torah.' This is referring not to thoughts of wickedness and lust, and apparently not even of perversity and falsehood, but to different levels of attainment. The word 'man,' the picture of a man and the wooden statue of a man are not the man himself, but are only representations. They are, however, the proper way for a person who does not know what a 'man' is to come to some understanding of man. A person who creates original Torah thoughts begins with a verbal concept and with attempts to demonstrate the true concept; but in the end, only man himself is man.

These words of R. Nachman may be interpreted as dealing with the question of the internalization of Torah and its transformation into 'the Torah of man.' Indeed, at first it seems that R. Nachman is only using the word 'man' to illustrate his point. It afterwards grows clear, however, that his example of 'man' constitutes the essence of his thesis. Original Torah thoughts and spiritual attainments are not the true Torah as long as they are not 'the Torah of man.' True attainments are not theoretical and not just the ability to depict images and worlds. All of these merely allude to the thing itself: 'man.' As long as there remains a gap between the Torah and man, a person's attainment can be described as no more than a hint of true attainment, and not the true attainment itself.

'The palaces of changes' express therefore a stage in religious attainment, in which a person gains insights that allude to the world of holiness and maintains an image of that true world. A person must be careful not to halt in these palaces, but to enter further inward, internalizing the insights until they are transformed into 'this is the Torah of man.' This explanation is fortified by the continuation of R. Nachman's lesson, which makes it clear that a person has no other way to gain insights into the Torah than to pass through the 'palaces of changes:'

And know that every man, before he attains a true attainment in the Torah, must necessarily pass through those palaces of changes. But the main thing is that it is forbidden to fool oneself, to think that one has already come to the appropriate insights, because if a person thinks that, he will remain there, heaven forbid. But when he knows that he has still not begun to enter into the true chambers of the Torah, then he will grow strong in his service of Hashem, and engage in much prayer, and beg until the gates of holiness are truly opened for him. And then he will see the difference. And even if he had performed acts of worship and fasts and self-mortifications for the sake of Hashem, be He blessed, and afterwards attained original Torah thoughts, nevertheless, he should not think that he has arrived and think that these are attainments of truth (as above), for even gaining the illusions of the palaces of changes requires acts of worship and fasting.[78]

R. Nachman calls for a person to knowingly enter the 'palaces of changes,' for that is the only way to come to the true chambers of the Torah. Moreover, it grows clear that even though the 'palaces of changes' belong to the world of illusions, they represent a high level in serving God, for in order to come to them one must engage in 'acts of service and fasts and self-mortifications.' And even after all this, a person is still immersed solely in the world of illusion of the 'palaces of changes' and not in the true world.

Although in the teachings of R. Moshe Cordovero and other kabbalistic masters one can find the claim that 'the husk exists for the sake of the fruit,'[79] in this teaching, R. Nachman does not at all deal with evil that precedes the good nor with the importance of evil and the ability to distinguish between good and evil, nor even with a person's evil inclination, which must be harnessed to the service of God. Instead, R. Nachman deals with the question of the nature of a person's spiritual Torah attainments, described as belonging to the world of illusion, to the world of 'changes.'[80] In the continuation of this lesson, R. Nachman makes this statement even more clear, to which end he makes use of an example from everyday mundane life:

And even in the desires of this world, there is an example of this. For instance, when comedians are going to present a humorous performance and comedy, first a person travels ahead of them and proclaims and describes all of the things that the comedians will do at the comedy. And although this is pleasurable to hear, nevertheless, that is not the humor itself. And also, when the public comes to the auditorium, where the comedians will perform the comedy, all of the things that they will do there are illustrated on a board. But that too is not the thing itself. And even when the audience enters, a clown stands onstage and acts like a monkey, and whatever the comedian does, he imitates him humorously. And that too is not the thing itself. But the main thing is the humor itself that is performed there.

And similarly – understand the meaning of this, because – there is a person who imagines that he has entered within, and deeply within. But he is still standing completely outside, because he has not yet begun to achieve any attainment of truth. But as for the very great *zaddik*, even though he achieves great attainments of holiness in truth, they are nevertheless not considered as anything in his eyes, because of the great intensity of his recognition of the greatness of the Creator, may He be blessed. Therefore, he works and strengthens himself constantly so that Hashem, may He be blessed, will begin to show him the light of the Torah, as though he has not begun to attain anything in his life.[81]

The emphasis in this description of the 'palaces of changes' is not on the fact of the existence of a structure parallel to goodness, but on the dimension of imitation that exists in the palaces of changes and on the attempt to impersonate the world of holiness. This description and the image of the monkey that imitates a human being[82] uses motifs found in the kabbalah of R. Moshe Cordovero, and which are discussed as well in *Shaar Heichal Hatemurot*: 'We already hinted earlier that these husks are similar in their existence to *atzilut*, like a monkey before people.'[83] 'The matter of the husks ... for they correspond to holiness, like a monkey before a person.'[84] 'We must know that the husks stand before holiness like a monkey before people. And just as a monkey standing before a person performs each act of the person mockingly, wanting to be identical to him, but he is not identical, so too, the uncleanness and the husk perform acts like the act of the holiness.'[85]

The motif of imitation is also found in the kabbalah of the Ari, but in a weaker fashion. There, emphasis is placed on the description of the parallel structure coming from 'this corresponding to this,' and less on the topic of imitation and mockery.[86]

R. Nachman's introduction to his description of original Torah thoughts and the insights that derive from the 'palaces of changes' ultimately leads him to the far-reaching conclusion that all of a person's service of God and all of his attainments are imagination and illusion. In his attainments and in his acts of worship, a person is like a clown who acts like a monkey, mockingly imitating 'an attainment that is not true.' These words apply not only to the man who does not internalize his attainments and whose his Torah is thus not 'a Torah of man,' but even to 'a very great *zaddik*' whose attainments are apparently true attainments and whose Torah is a 'Torah of man.' When that *zaddik* faces 'the great intensity of his recognition of the greatness of the

Creator, may He be blessed,' his attainments 'are not considered in his eyes as anything.'

It is clear from R. Nachman's closing words that every person is immersed unendingly in a world of changes, a world of illusion, of imitation, of 'as though.' This is true even of the *zaddik;* when he considers God's greatness, he grows aware of the fact that he is immersed in a world of changes, and that his service and attainments resemble the behavior of the clown who imitates the thing, but is not the thing itself. This point grows even clearer if we consider the conclusion concealed in R. Nachman's parable.

This parable tells of a person who describes a performance, then of the knowledge and description of the performance, and finally of the clown who imitates the comedians' deeds. All of these, states R. Nachman, are not the true thing, although they appear similar to it and describe it on various levels of congruence. What, then, is that true thing? What is 'the thing in itself'? The thing in itself is the joke that the comedian makes. And it is here, of course, that R. Nachman's acerbic barb is hidden, for even that true thing is not a true thing either, but a show, a comedy and joke about the true thing. The entire nature of the comedy is not the true thing but a mocking imitation. Whether a societal-communal comedy or a comedy of any other type, these are not true life but a show, a mockery and a joke, which at the best allude to a true life. Thus, R. Nachman's conclusion is that there is nothing true. Even that said to be true is itself a comedy and joke; and the clown who stands on the outside and imitates the comedians makes a comedy about the comedy and mocks the mockery.

According to this, the service of God is not 'the thing itself.' Any service and attainment is only a joke, a comedy and a mockery, in contrast to God's greatness. A person's religious service is by its nature only a show and an imitation of something said to be the service of God. All the religious world's a stage, and although the very great *zaddik* might not be a clown who acts like a monkey, he is at best the comedian, whose service of God is self-conscious foolishness.

The Image of the Service of God as a Game in Hasidism

This explanation of the mitzvot that makes use of the comparison to play has many parallels from the very earliest Hasidic teachings. One can see in these sources the climate and mood that blossomed into a perspective on the mitzvot as comedy and as an 'as though,' and they add an additional dimension to R. Nachman's words on this topic.

In these sources, the mitzvot and insights are often compared to children's games, particularly the games of a father with his son.[87] The

The Story of the Humble King275

Maggid of Mezeritch and his students often used the parable of a father who, in his love for his son, plays games with him. At times this parable emphasizes the descent of the father to the level of the understanding and ability of the son in order to speak and play with him. At other times, the parable emphasizes the father's joy in the actions of his son, even though they are acts of childishness and foolishness.[88] These parables contain the warning, sometimes implied and sometimes explicit, not to think that the games of the father with his son indicate the level that the father is on, 'that the father is as small as he shows himself to be before his son.'[89]

The 'doctrine of play'[90] of the Maggid of Mezeritch and of other Hasidic thinkers is intimately connected to the topic of delight and pleasure. Delight and pleasure are related both to God's activities and the joy that he derives from the service of man,[91] and to the pleasure and delight of man when he cleaves to God.[92] There is a deep connection between these two topics – the delight of God and the pleasure of man – that has not been adequately explored in the academic literature. The pleasure of man and the delight of God are at times two aspects of the state of 'love in pleasures' between God and man, describing the essence of the contact between God and man as a supernal activity that has no goal higher than itself and which justifies itself in and of itself.

Hasidic sayings about play and delight may be seen as relating to the question of whether the mitzvot are 'a supernal necessity' – i.e., needed by God.[93] The Hasidic doctrine of play grants meaning to the service of God, the performance of the mitzvot and the attempt to know God via insight and cleaving to him, without having to make use of the unsettling theurgic perspective that speaks about 'need' or 'benefit' in the service of God – neither in the case of 'benefit' for man, who would then be serving himself and not God, nor 'benefit' to God, for in attributing some 'utilitarian benefit' to God one would be insulting His perfection. Delight and pleasure add a dimension to the nature of religious service, one not dependent on theurgy or on the perspective of mitzvot as intended to perfect a person. If we analyze 'delight' in formal terms, the ascription of pleasure or delight to God is indeed to be defined as 'theurgic,' since its goal relates to the world of divinity.[94] But on the other hand, delight corresponds with no 'supernal need,' for by its very nature it is not a 'need;' rather, it is 'superfluous,' having no purpose and no goal. Delight is not part of the act of 'rectification' or raising sparks that have fallen nor of raising the Shechinah from its dust. In contrast to all these, delight does not fulfill any lack and is not a response to any suffering. Rather, it is as its name indicates: delight for its own sake. In this sense, defining the goal of worship, insight and cleaving to God as delight greatly ameliorates and refines the theological conundrum inherent in the perspective of mitzvot as 'a supernal need.'[95]

Seeing religious service and cleaving to God as the pleasure of man and the delight of God transforms the performance of mitzvot and cleaving to God into the aspect of 'love in pleasures,' delights of love and games of love between man and God. Although the definition of these as theurgy is formally justified, it is liable to miss the essence of the Hasidic process and its goal, instead attributing to that process a character that diametrically opposes its entire purpose. In this sense, it would be more correct to describe the religious viewpoint and state of being that presents delight as the peak of its religious world as reflecting an anti-theurgic goal,[96] one that comes to confute the understanding of religious worship as 'supernal need' and to deny the view of involvement in Torah and in mitzvot as a 'serious' deed that rectifies the world and God.

These words from the Hasidic teachings provide additional background to R. Nachman's description of the service of God as comedy and *katavish*. The understanding of delight as the final goal, on the one hand, and the comparison of religious worship to a children's game, on the other, are part of the spiritual climate in whose framework R. Nachman's thought developed.

But assuming such a background, the uniqueness of R. Nachman's world grows more apparent. A great gap exists between the pleasing and attractive descriptions of games of love and games engaged in by a father and his young child, on the one hand, and descriptions of the service of God as comedy and as performance, on the other. The former spiritual world is created by describing man's insights in terms of a father constricting his mind so that his son will be able to grasp and understand something of his words, whereas the latter is a religious reality formed by the presentation of every religious insight as a comedy and mockery, in comparison to true religious attainment, which is itself at heart comedy.

In 'The Story of the Humble King,' in talks on the service of God as *katavish* and as a joke, and in his teaching, *Chadrei Torah*, R. Nachman explains and describes the religious world by making use of a radical semantic and symbolic field, which creates a certain ambiguity from a moral perspective. The two parables – 'The Story of the Humble King' and the parable of the imitation of the comedic performance – could be interpreted as statements that stand at the locus where heresy and religious nihilism meet, and as agreeing with an outlook that sees in the very essence of the idea of the service of God a grotesque one, something comical that is fit to be no more than a joke and mockery.[97]

However, the context of R. Nachman's teachings and the explanatory words that accompany these talks and lessons lead us to a different reading that is more subtle and that does not deny the value of religious service nor the entry into the chambers of the Torah. It rather states that awareness of the meaning of serving God is a necessary pre-condition, one that makes that service of God possible, and that serves as a warning against mistaking the world of illusion and change for the thing itself.

In the sources we have seen, the service of God is presented as untenable, as something revealed by a sober gaze to be in the nature of a comedy and joke; however, it is something that also flows from a love of God and out of a strong desire to come close to Him. The only expression that a person can give to this elevated love is that of religious worship. Only the awareness 'that the essential thing is the desire to yearn always with a strong longing and will'[98] can permit the service of God – not as something genuine and not literally as the thing itself – rather, 'we learn as though we are learning and pray as though we are praying and perform mitzvot as though we are performing mitzvot.'[99] The service of God flows from a yearning and longing for the thing itself, which cannot be reached, so that a person is left only with taking delight in an imitation of and in a performance depicting that object yearned for unto death, yet which is so untenable as to be absurd. 'And in truth, in accordance with God's greatness, be He blessed, all of these modes of service are nothing, but everything is in the way of "as though," *klamersh*, for everything is merely like a joke when compared to God's greatness, be He blessed.'[100]

Conclusion

In light of these words, the restricted arena which R. Nachman allocates for the service of God with the help of intellect and *da'at* and his call for a person to cast away his intellect before engaging in any religious service are thus understood with greater depth and are seen as existing within a broader context. The service of God is based on desire, on love of and yearning for God, and is in constant tension with logic and intellect, which denies the legitimacy of any deed, whatever it may be, performed in the service of God. Only the absence of the mind and the casting away of *da'at*, on the one hand, and the surrender to yearning and love, on the other, make the existence of Torah and mitzvot possible. Any intellectual explanation of the Torah and the mitzvot that purports to comprehend their rationale and purpose undermines their legitimacy and transforms them into something execrable and a desecration of God's name.

Religious service is not based upon intellect and *da'at*; moreover, its entire basis and permissibility are based on a person's readiness to cast away his intellect and renounce his *da'at*. In this sense, keeping the Torah and performing the mitzvot is madness, for it demands of a person the constant readiness to act foolishly, like a clown, and 'to act and do things that appear as mad for the sake of the service of Hashem.'[101] This madness is a part of the sickness of love, 'in the aspect of "in her love you go mad constantly;" for the sake of the love of Hashem, it is necessary to do things that appear as madness.'[102] And it is only the understanding that these are 'the mad elements of love,' that give the Torah and mitzvot not their logical sense, but rather their significance, meaning and supernal value.

Notes

1   *Sefer Sipurei Maasiyot, Maaseh* 6, 63–69. Regarding this story, see Bend, *Hafunktziah Shel Ha'enigmati*; Green, *Tormented Master*, 350–356; and also idem., *Bakshu Panai*, 11–14.

2   The *Milon Yiddi-Ivri-Angli Katzar* by Yosef Guri and Shaul Ferdman (Yosef Martin, Jerusalem 5554) translates *kataves* as '*tzechok* (joke), *kundesuth* (mischievousness).' In the *Milon Yiddi-Ivri Malei* by Avak (Eliezer Barziniak) (L. Barzanyak, Paris 5699), *Kativish* is translated as '*halatzah* (jest), *mahatalah* (jest), *sechok* (joke).'

3   *Anshtelen* is translated in the Avak dictionary (ibid.) as '*amtala* (pretext), *beduta* (fabrication), *panim* (appearance), *haamadat panim* (pretense).' In the *Meshech Hanachal* edition (Jerusalem 5745) of *Sefer Sipurei Maasiyot*, *an-shtelen* is translated as 'show themselves only externally.'

4   For example, *Tzavaat Haribash*, 22, 27–28; R. Efraim of Sudilkov, *Degel Machaneh Efraim*, *'Derush L'purim,'* 129; ibid., *Parshat Tzav*, 141 and. 143; R. Shneur Zalman of Ladi, *Tanya*, part 1, chapter 31; and many other places.

5   *Exodus* 33:12–23.

6   *Psalms* 27:8; *Samuel* II 21:1.

7   *Yoma* 69b.

8   *Megillah* 31a.

9   Rashi there. Also R. Nachman in *Likutei Moharan* I 138.

10 *Psalms* 27:8.

11 Regarding the importance and meaning of the term 'nothing' in Hasidism, see Shatz-Oppenheimer, *Hahasidut K'mistikah*, in particular 22–31; Elior, *'Yesh V'Ayin,'* on 55 and 59 regarding R. Nachman; idem., *'Bein Hayeish L'Ayin,'* 167–218, particularly 192–203; and also idem., *'Kabbalat Ha'ari,'* 392–397; Yakovson, *Torat Hahasidut*, 20–43, 86–94. See Idel, *Hahasidut*, particularly 195–202; Matt, *Ayin*

12 See above, Chapter 7, section 4, which deals with the teaching *'Emtz'uta D'alma,'*

13 *Pardes Rimonim, Shaar Erkei Hakinyuim* (*Shaar* 23), in entry *Ayin*; see Scholem, *Major Trends in Jewish Mysticism*, 25.

14 Hillel Barzel's essay, *'Heitzitz Umeit,'* 15–40.

15 Elior, *'Yesh V'Ayin,'* 59 and 55.

16 Ibid., 53–74.

17 *Exodus* 33:11 and 23. And see Bond's essay, *'Hafunktziah Shel Ha-Enigmati,'* 197–198.

18 *Deuteronomy* 10:17; *Jeremiah* 32:18; *Nehemiah* 9:32.

19 PT, *Berachot* 7:3; ibid. *Megillah* 3:7; BT, *Yoma* 69b; *Berachot* 33b.

20 *Guide of the Perplexed*, part 1, chapter 59.

21 *Berachot* 33b.

22 *Guide of the Perplexed,* part 1, chapter 59 and chapters 35–36 and 54–55.

23 Ibid., part 1, 59.

24 *Psalms* 65:2.

25 Maimonides, *Guide of the Perplexed,* part 1, 59.

26 *Deuteronomy* 5:7.

27 *Sefer Ha'ikarim,* second essay, chapter 30.

28 Ibid. 97b.

29 See Zack, '*Yachaso Shel R. Shlomo,*' 290–299 and note 6.

30 *Bechinat Olam,* chapter 13, section 15, 53–55.

31 In *Sefer Sipur Maasiyot* after the thirteen stories, in the section called *Sichot Sh'acharei Hasipurim.*

32 Chalmish, *Mavo L'kabbalah,* 97–100.

33 See Scholem, *Reishit Hakabbalah,* 104–408; and idem., *Mekorot Hakabbalah,* 430–454; idem., *Pirkei Yesod,* 173; Idel, '*Demuth Ha'adam,*' 41–55.

34 I.e., the kabbalists.

35 R. Peretz ben Yitzchak of Gerondi, *Maarecht Ha'Elokut,* 22b. Also see Gottlieb, *Mechkarim B'sifrut Hakabbalah,* 293–294.

36 *Maarecht Ha'Elokut.* Also see Gottlieb, *Mechkarim B'sifrut Hakabbalah,* 576–577; Scholem, *Reishit Hakabbalah,* 148–150; Ben Shlomo, cited in R. Yosef ben Avraham Gikitiliah's *Shaarei Orah,* 12–17; Idel, '*T'arim Us'firot,*' 87–111.

37 See Scholem, *Major Trends in Jewish Mysticism,* 22–25.

38 *Shiur Komah,* 67. And see Ben Shlomo, *Torat Ha'Eelokut,* 23.

39 Quoted by Scholem, *Major Trends in Jewish Mysticism ,* 24; *Ilmah Rabati,* 7a. And see Ben Shlomo, *Torat Ha'Elokut,* 23–37.

40 *Sichot Haran,* 225, 147.

41 See Scholem, *Reishit Hakabbalah,* 104–108.

42 See Ben Shlomo, *Hayesodot Hafilosfiyim B'kabbalah.*

43 See Ben Shlomo, introduction to *Shaarei Orah,* 18, 30–33. And see Chalamish, *Mavo L'kabbalah,* 103–104. Also see Scholem's essay, '*Shnei Kuntresim,*' 334.

44 James, *Hachavayah Hadatit,* 272–273.

45 Ibid.

46 Otto, *Hakedushah,* 29–36.

47 Ibid., 34. See also Idem., *Mysticism East and West,* 185–187.

48 Otto, *Hakedushah,* 34. Raz, *Sichot Meturafot,* 74.

49 Joking and Mockery

50 *Sipurei Maasiyot,* 63.

51 *Rimzei Maasiyot, Sipurei Maasiyot,* 7.

52 Hoyzinga, *Ha'adam Ham'sachek,* 48–60.

53 Ibid., 30, 48–52.

54 Ibid., 53.

55 Zohar, Part I 148a–b. Zohar, *Mishpatim;* Zohar, Part II, 107b.

56 See as well *Zohar B'lashon Hakodesh,* Vol. 2, 307–308.

57 Liebes, '*Zohar V'eros,*' 67–111.

58 See Keiser's introduction to *Shivchei Hashtut,* 1–16.

59 Hoyzinga, *Ha'adam Hamisachek*, 55.

60 Presenting the mitzvot as no more than a way of perfecting man uproots and expropriates from them their meaning as the service of God.

61 *Guide of the Perplexed* 3:32.

62 In *Milon Yiddi-Ivri Shalem* of M. Tzanin (Tel Aviv, 754), *klampersht* is translated as *k'ilu* ('as though'). *Sichot Haran*, 51:34–35.

63 *Proverbs* 10:12.

64 *Likutei Halachot, Choshen Mishpat, Hilchot Erev, Halachah* 3, section 31.

65 *Likutei Moharan* II 7:10.

66 *Proverbs* 5:19.

67 Rashi, *Eiruvin* 54b.

68 *Likutei Moharan* II 5.

69 *Likutei Moharan* II 5.

70 Buber edition, *Mizmor* 119, beginning '*Gal Einai*'; See also *Shemot Rabbah* (Vilna), chapter 45, beginning '*Vayomer Hashem.*'

71 *Shivchei Haran*, 2:3. Similarly, see *Chayei Moharan*, '*Sichot Hashayachimn L'hatorot*,' 41:36; ibid., 50: 46; ibid., '*Sichot Shehayah Eitzel Kol Torah*,' 79: 72; *Sichot Haran*, 145: 101–102. Regarding *tiyul* in 'the palaces of faith,' see *Chayei Moharan*, '*Avodat Hashem*,' 151 (594): 360–361; ibid., '*L'hitrachek Meichakirot*,' 14 (420): 282–283.

72 See Zack, *B'shaarei Hakabbalah*, 171, 173, 190, 218, notes 25 and 296.

73 *Likutei Moharan* I 245.

74 See Shatz-Oppenheimer, *Hahasidut K'mistikah*, 22–25; Rosenberg, '*Huh U Ut'murato*,' 325–333.

75 R. Moshe Cordovero, *Pardes Rimonim*, volume 2, 53.

76 Ibid., column 3. See Tishbi, *Torat Hara*, particularly 62–72.

77 In '*Mafteichot V'simanei Hasefer*,' at the end of *Pardes Rimonim*, Gate 26 is called the gate of 'the palaces of changes,' not the gate of 'the palaces of the husks,' as it is called in the body of the text. R. Nachman also uses [the term] 'palaces of changes' in *Likutei Moharan* I 24:8.

78 First version from Buber, *Or Haganuz*, 90. Its source is noted in *Netiv Mitzvotechah*. The second source accords with *Mazkeret Shem Hag'dolim*, 91.

79 See Zack, *B'shaarei Hakabbalah*, 83–102.

80 See regarding this Elior, *Torat Ha'elokut*, 298–309, and also, as above, *Torat Achdut Hahafachim*, 181–186.

81 *Likutei Moharan* I 24:8.

82 Weiss, *Mechkarim*, 127–128. See Werblowski, 'Ape and Essence,' 318–325.

83 At the beginning of *Shaar Heichalot Haklipot*, which is *Shaar* 26, 56, column 3 and 57 column 1.

84 Ibid., Shaar 25, chap. 4, 55a.

85 ibid., chap 7, 56b–c.

86 See Tishbi, *Torat Hara*, 62; See Green, *Tormented Master*, note 7 on page 443.

87 See Rozenberg, '*R. Boruch Mikosov*,' 175–177.

88 *Likutei Amarim*, 42a. See *Maggid Devarav L'yaakov*, 9, 21, 79, 233.

89 R. Shlomo of Lutzk, *Divrat Shlomo, Terumah*, 25a.; *Amud Ha'avodah*, 77–78. See Rozenberg, '*R. Boruch Mikosov*,' 176–177.

90 *Maggid Devarav L'yaakov* 186, *piskah* 111.

91 See Shatz-Oppenheimer, *Hahasidut K'mistikah*, 32, and note 1 there, 89–91, and index, entries: *Shaashua Eloki* and *Taanug Haborei*; Idel, *HaHasidut*, 241–253; idem., '*Yofyah shel Ishah*.' Regarding *shaashua* – 'delight' – in kabbalah, see Zack, *B'shaarei Hakabbalah*, particularly 15–18, 71–82, 150–176; *Peirush Kabbali*, 34–35, in his commentary on the verse '*V'ehyeh Shaashuim Yom Yom Misacheket L'fanav B'chol Eit*.' On *shaashua* and play in the Zohar, see Liebes, '*Zohar V'eros*,' 119–167. There on page 81, note 88 are additional sources to *shaashua* in kabbalah; Yoshah, *Mitos Umetaforah*, particularly 197–200.

92 See Shatz-Oppenheimer, *Hahasidut K'mistikah*, in the index, entry *Taanug*. Also see Etkes, *Baal Hashem*, 139–144; Elior, '*Rik V'habesht*,' 695–697; Idel, *Hebetim Chadashim*, 166; see Dan and Tishbi, '*Chasidut*,' 796–797. See Idel, *Hachavayah Hamistit*, 140–143 and note 51.

93 Rosenberg, '*R. Boruch MiKosov*,' 176; idem, '*Mitos HaMitosim*,' 159–161.

94 Idel, '*Yofyah shel Ishah*,' 317–334.

95 See Rosenberg, '*R. Boruch Mikosov*,' 176; *Maggid Devarav L'yaakov*, 7: 21. And see Rosenberg, '*Mitos HaMitosim*,' 159–161.

96 See Idel, '*Yofyah shel Ishah*.'

97 *Hitgalut Zaddikim*, 167–141; Goldberg, '*Hasipur Hachasidi Sheb'fi Hazaddik*,' 151–152.

98 *Likutei Halachot, Choshen Mishpat, Hilchot Erev, Halachah* 3, section 31.

99 Ibid.

100 *Sichot Haran*, section 51.

101 *Likutei Moharan* II 5.

102 Ibid.

Bibliography

Alim Litrufah =

ר׳ נתן מנמירוב, עלים תרופה, ירושלים תשמ״א.

Amud Ha'avodah =

ר׳ ברוך מקוסוב, עמוד העבודה, יוזעפאף 1883.

Bechinot Olam =

ר׳ ידעיה הפניני, בחינות עולם, ירושלים תשי״ד.

Ben Porat Yosef =

ר׳ יעקב יוסף מפולנא, בן פורת יוסף, פיעטרקוב תרמ״ד.

Chaim V'chesed =

ר׳ חיים מאמדור, חיים וחסד, ירושלים תשי״ג.

Chayei Moharan =

חיי מוהר״ן המנוקד, ירושלים תשנ״ה.

Chesed L'Avraham =

ר׳ אברהם אזולאי, חסד לאברהם, וילנא תרל״ז.

Degel Machaneh Efraim =

ר׳ אפרים מסדילקוב, דגל מחנה אפרים, ירושלים תשנ״ד.

Derashot al Hatorah =

ר׳ יהושע אבן שועיב, דרשות על תורה, דברי פתיחה שרגא אברמסון, ירושלים תשכ״ט.

Derashot Haran =

ר׳ ברוך מקוסוב, שנים עשר דרשות הר״ן, למברג 1858.

Derech Chaim =

ר׳ יהודה בר׳ בצלאל, ספר דרך חיים, ישראל תש״ם.

Divrat Shlomo =

ר׳ שלמה מלוצק, דברת שלמה, למברג 1859.

Edat Zaddikim =

מיכאל לוי רודיקסון, עדת צדיקים, מהורת ג נגאל, ירושלים תשמ״ט.

Etz Chaim =

עץ חיים (שלושה חלקים), סדרת כתבי רבינו האר״י, ניו-יורק תשנ״ה.
ר׳ חיים ויטאל,

Hanhagath Habriut =

ר׳ משה בן מימון, הנהגת הבריאות, בתוך: כתבים רפואיים, מהדורת ז׳ מונטנר, ירושלים תשכ״ג.

Hanhagot Zaddikim =

הנהגות צדיקים, חיים שלמה רוטנברג עורך, ד כרכים, ירושלים תשמ״ה.

Hishtapchut Hanefesh =

ר׳ אלטר טפליקר, השתפכות הנפש, בני ברק (תשמ״ט).

Guide of the Perplexed =

משה בן מימון, מורה נבוכים, מהדורת יוסף קאפח, ירושלים תשל״ב.
ר׳

Hitgalut Zaddikim =

שלמה גבריאל רוזנטל, התגלות צדיקים תפארת צדיקים,
מהדורת ג׳ נגאל, ירושלים תשנ״ו.

Ilmah Rabati =

ר׳ משה קורדובירו, אילמה רבתי, ירושלים תשכ״ו.

Kedushat Levi =

ר׳ לוי יצחק מברדיצ׳וב, קדושת לוי השלם, ירושלים תשי״ח.

Kerem Yisrael =

ר׳ ראובן מאוסיטלא, כרם ישראל, לובלין תר״ץ.

Ketonet Passim =

ר׳ יעקב יוסף מפולנאה, כותונת פסים, מהדורת ג נגאל,
ירושלים תשמ״ח.

Keter Shem Tov =

מהדורת קה״ת, ברוקלין ניו-יורק 1987.

Kol M'vaser =

קול מבשר - ״ליקוטי מאמרי קודש מתוך ספרי תלמידיו
של אדמו״ר ר׳ שמחה בנים מפשיסחא, אשר הביאו בשמו. נלקט,
סודר והובא לדפוס על-ידי יהודה מנחם״ (בוים), רעננה תשנ״ה.

Likutei Amarim =

ר׳ מנחם מנדל מוויטבסק, ליקוטי אמרים, ברוקלין תשכ״ב.

Likutei Halachot =

ר׳ נתן מנמירוב, ליקוטי הלכות, ח כרכים, ירושלים תשמ״ד.

Likutei Moharan =

ליקוטי מוהר״ן, עם נוסחאות והגהות מכת״י מוהרנ״ת בהשתדלות
נתן צבי קעניג, ירושלים תשמ״ה.

Likutei Moharan =

ליקוטי מוהר״ן המנוקד, ירושלים תשנ״ד.

Likutei Tefilot =

ר׳ נתן מנמירוב, ליקוטי תפילות המנוקד, ירושלים תשמ״ט.

Maarecht Ha'Elokut =

ר׳ פרץ בן יצחק מגרונדי, מערכת האלוהות, מנטובה שי״ח.

Maggid Devarav L'Yaakov =

ר׳ דב בער ממזריץ׳, מגיד דבריו ליעקב, מהדורת רבקה
ש״ץ-אופנהיימר, ירושלים תש״ן.

Maggid Meisharim =

ר׳ יוסף קארו, מגיד מישרים, עורך יחיאל בר לב, פתח תקווה תש״ן.

Mazkeret Shem Hag'dolim =

משה חיים קלינמן, מזכרת שם הגדולים, ירושלים תשכ"ז.

Meor Einayim =

ר' מנחם נחום מטשרנוביל, מאור עינים, בני ברק תשנ"ח.

Meor Vashemesh =

ר' קלמן קלנימוס הלוי עפשטעיין, מאור ושמש, ניו יארק תשל"ו.

M'vaser Tzedek =

ר' ישׂשכר בר מזלוטשוב, מבשר צדק, ברדיטשוב תקע"ז.

Netiv Mitzvotechah =

ר' יצחק אייזיק ספרין מקומרנה, נתיב מצוותיך, לעמברג 1858.

Noam Elimelech =

ר' אלימלך מליז'נסק, נעם אלימלך, ב כרכים, מהדורת ג נגאל,
ירושלים תשל"ח.

Oheiv Israel =

ר' אברהם יהושע השיל מאפטא, ספר אוהב ישראל, בני ברק תשנ"ו.

Ohr Ha'emet =

ר' דב בער ממזריץ', אור האמת, ברוקלין תשי"ז.

Parpera'ot L'hochmah =

ר' נחמן מטשהרין, פרפראות לחכמה, ירושלים תשמ"ג.

Peirush Kabbali =

מ' חלמיש, פירוש קבלי לבראשית רבה לר' יוסף בן שלום אשכנזי,
ירושלים תשמ"ח.

Pardes Rimonim =

ר' משה קורדוביברו, פרדס רימונים, ירושלים תשכ"ב.

P'ulat Hazaddik

פעולת הצדיקו, ברוקלין, ניו-יורק תשל"ח. [חסר שם המחבר
(ר' אליעזר שיק)].

Reishit Hochmah =

ר' אליהו די וידאש, ראשית חכמה המנוקד, ג כרכים, ירושלים תשנ"ז.

Sefer Habrit =

ר' פנחס אליהו ברבי מאיר מוילנא, ספר הברית השלם,
ירושלים תש"ן.

Sefer Ha'Ikarim =

ר' יוסף אלבו, ספר העיקרים, ווארשה תר"ל.

Sefer Hakuzari =

ר' יהודה הלוי, ספר הכוזרי, תרגום: י' אבן שמואל, ירושלים תשל"ג.

Sefer Hachezyonot =

ר' חיים ויטאל, ספר החזיונות, מהדורת א"ז אשכולי ונ' בן מנחם,
ירושלים תשי"ד.

Sefer Hamidot =

ר' נחמן מברסלב, ספר המדות עם מראה מקומות, ירושלים תשנ"א.

Sefer Shem Hagedolim =

החיד"א, ספר שם הגדולים, רמת גן תשי"ד.

Shaar Hakavanot =

ר' חיים ויטאל, שער הכוונות, (שני חלקים) סדרת כתבי רבינו האר"י,
ניו-יורק תשנ"ה.

Shaar Hamitzvot =

ר' חיים ויטאל, שער הכוונות, סדרת כתבי רבינו האר"י,
ניו-יורק תשנ"ה.

Shaarei Kedushah =

ר' חיים ויטאל, שערי קדושה, ירושלים תשמ"ה.

Shaarei Orah =

ר' יוסף ג' יקטיליה, שערי אורה, מהדורת יוסף בן שלמה, ב כרכים,
ירושלים תשנ"ו.

Shiur Komah =

ר' משה קורדובירו, שעור קומה, רושלים תשכ"ו.

Shivchei HaBesht =

שבחי הבעש"ט, קארעץ תקע"ו.

Shivchei HaBesht =

שבחי הבעש"ט, מהדורת א' רובינשטין, ירושלים תשנ"ב.

Shivchei Haran =

שבחי הר"ן, ירושלים חש"ו.

Shmuah Tovah =

ר' לוי יצחק מברדיצ'ב, שמועה טובה (אמרות מהגיד ממזריץ'),
ורשא תרח"ץ.

Shnei Luchot Habrit =

ר' ישעיהו הורוביץ, שני לוחות הברית, ירושלים תשל"ה.

Sichot Haran =

שיחות הר"ן המנוקד, ירושלים תשמ"ה.

Sipurei Maasiyot =

ר' נחמן מברסלב, ספר סיפורי מעשיות המנוקד, ירושלים תשמ"ה.

Sipurim Chasidi'im =

מנחם מנדל בודק, סיפורים חסידיים, מהדורת ג' נגאל,
תל-אביב תשנ"א.

Teshuvot HaRambam =

תשובות הרמב"ם, מהדורת יהושע בלאו, ג כרכים, ירושלים
תשי"ח-תשכ"א.

Tzafnat Paaneach =

ר' יוסף טוב-עלם, צפנת פענח, קרקא תרע"ב.

Tzafnat Paaneach =

ר' יעקב יוסף מפולנאה, צפנת פענח, מהדורת ג' נגאל,
ירושלים תשמ"ט.

Tzava'at HaRibash =

הוצאת קה״ת ברוקלין, ניו-יורק תשנ״א.

Tanya =

ר׳ שניאור זלמן מלאדי, ליקוטי אמרים עם אגרת התשובה
ואגרת הקדש, כפר חב״ד תש״מ.

Tikkunei HaZohar =

תקוני הזהר, מהדורת ר׳ ראובן מרגליות, ירושלים (תש״ד).

Tzidkat Hazaddik =

ר׳ צדוק הכהן מלובלין, צדקת הצדיק, ירושלים תשמ״ז.

Yalkut Shimoni =

ילקוט שמעוני, ירושלים תש״ך.

Yemei Moharant =

ר׳ נתן מנמירוב, ימי מוהרנ״ת המנוקד, ירושלים תשמ״ב.

Yosher Divrei Emet =

ר׳ משולם פייבוש מזבאריז, יושר דברי אמת, מהדורת קהאן,
ירושלים תשנ״ח.

Zohar =

זוהר, מהדורת ר׳ ראובן מרגליות, ג כרכים, ירושלים תשמ״ד.

Zohar B'Lashon Hakodesh =

ר׳ יהודה אדרי, ספר הזוהר מנוקד בלשון הקודש, ירושלים תשנ״ח.

Secondary Sources

Ackerman, *The Philosophical Sermons of R. Zerachia Halevi,* unpublished
dissertation, Hebrew University, Jerusalem: 1999.

Ankori, *Meromei R'ki'im =*

מ׳ אנקורי, מרומי רקיעים ותחתיות שאול - מסע הנפש של רבי נחמן
מברסלב, תל-אביב תשנ״ח.

Arend, *'Harefuah' =*

א׳ ארנד, ״הרפואה במשנתו של ר׳ נחמן מברסלב״, קורות י
(תשנ״ד), עמ׳ 44-53.

Band, A.J., 'The Function of the Enigmatic in Two Hasidic Tales.' *Studies in
Jewish Mysticism.* Eds. J. Dan and F. Talmage. Cambridge Mass:1982.
185–209.

Barzel, *'Heitzitz U'meit' =*

ה׳ ברזל, ״ ׳הציץ ומת׳ המשמעות העלומה״, בקורת ופרשנות
22 (תמוז תשנ״ד), עמ׳ 15-40.

Beit-Aryeh, *Perek Shirah =*

מ׳ בית-אריה, פרק שירה, עבודת לשם קבלת תואר דוקטור
(2 כרכים), האוניברסיטה העברית, ירושלים.

Ben Shlomo, *Hayesodot Hafilosfiyim B'kabbalah*

י׳ בן שלמה, היסודות הפילוסופיים בקבלה לפי גרשם שלום, דברי
האקדמיה הלאומית למדעים, כרך שמיני,
חוברת6, ירושלים תשנ״ז.

Ben Shlomo, *Torat Ha'Elokut* =

י׳ בן שלמה, תורת האלוהות של ר׳ משה קורדובירו, ירושלים תשמ״ו.

Blidstein, '*Hasimchah B'Rambam*' =

י׳ בלידשטיין, ״השמחה במשנתו המוסרית של הרמב״ם״, אשל באר
שבע ח״ב, באר שבע תש״ם, עמ׳ 145-163.

Buber, *HaOr Haganuz* =

מ׳ בובר, האור הגנוז, ירושלים ותל-אביב תשל״מ.

Buber, '*Tzaddik Ba La'aaretz*' =

מ׳ בובר, ״צדיק בא לארץ״, בין עם לארצו, ירושלים
ותל-אביב תש״ה, עמ׳ 111-91.

Chasin, *Shirah Umythos* =

ז׳ חסין, שירה ומיתוס ביצירת דליה רביקוביץ, תל-אביב תש״ן.

Chalamish, *Netiv L'Tanya* =

מ׳ חלמיש, נתיב לתניא, תל-אביב תשמ״ח.

Chalamish, '*Kavim L'ha'arechtah*' =

מ׳ חלמיש, ״קווים להערכתה של ארץ-ישראל בספרות הקבלה״,
ארץ ישראל בהגות היהודית בימי הביניים,
מ׳ חלמיש וא׳ רביצקי (עורכים), ירושלים תשנ״א, עמ׳ 215-232.

Chalamish, *Mavo L'kabbalah* =

מ׳ חלמיש, מבוא לקבלה, ירושלים תשנ״א.

Chalamish, '*Al Hashtika*' =

מ׳ חלמיש ״על השתיקה בקבלה ובחסידות״, דת ושפה, משה חלמיש
ואסא כשר (עורכים), תל-אביב
תשמ״ב, עמ׳ 79-89.

Dan, *Al Hakedushah* =

י׳ דן, על הקדושה, ירושלים תשנ״ז.

Dan, J., 'The Language of the Mystical Prayer.' *Studies in Spirituality* 5 (1995): 40–60.

Eliade, *Hamythos Shel Hashivah Hanitzchit*

Elior, '*Bein Hayeish L'Ayin*' =

ר׳ אליאור, ״בין היש לאין - עיון בתורת הצדיק של ר׳ יעקב
יצחק, החוזה מלובלין״, בתוך ר׳ אליאור, י׳ ברטל
וח׳ שמרוק (עורכים), צדיקים ואנשי מעשה: מחקרים בחסידות
פולין, ירושלים, תשנ״ר, עמ׳ 167-218.

Elior, *Cheirut Al Halachot* =

ר׳ אליאור, חירות על הלוחות, תל-אביב תש״ס.

Elior, '*Hazikah Hametaforit.*' =

ר' אליאור, ״הזיקה המטאפורית בין האל לאדם רציפותה של
הממשות החזיונית בקבלת האר״י״, דברי הכנס
הבינלאומי לחקר תולדות המיסטיקה היהודית לזכר ג' שלום:
קבלת האר״י, מחקרי ירושלים
במחשבת ישראל, כרך י (תשנ״ב), עמ' 57-47.

Elior, '*Kabbalat Ha'ari*' =

ר' אליאור, ״קבלת האר״י, שבתאות וחסידות״, קולות רבים, ספר
הזיכרון לרבקה ש״ץ אופנהיימר, כרך ב, מחקרי ירושלים במחשבת
ישראל יג (תשנ״ו), עמ' 379-397.

Elior,'*Miziut B'mivchan Habidyon*' =

- החלום במחשבה המיסטית - חירות הפירוק והצירוף״, מגוון דעות
ר' אליאור, ״מציאות במבחן הבדיון
החלום בתרבות ישראל, ד' כרם (עורך), ירושלים תשנ״ה, עמ' 63–79.
והשקפות על

Elior, '*Rik Ubesht*' =

ר' אליאור, ״ ר' יוסף קארו ור' ישראל בעל שם טוב, מטמורפוזה
מיסטית, השראה קבלית והפנמה רוחנית״,
תרביץ סה, ד (תשנ״ו), עמ' 671-709.

Elior, *Torat Achdut Hahafachim* =

ר' אליאור, תורת אחדות ההפכים - התיאוסופיה המיסטית של
חב״ר, ירושלים תשנ״ג.

Elior, *Torat Ha'Elokut* =

ר' אליאור, תורת האלוהות בדור השני של חב״ר, ירושלים תשמ״ב.

Etkes, *Baal Hashem* =

ע' אטקס, בעל השם: הבעש״ט מאגיה, מיסטיקה, הנהגה, ירושלים
תש״ס.

Etkes, *Yachid b'doro* =

ע' אטקס, יחיד בדורו: הגאון מוילנא - דמות ודימוי, מרכז שזר,
ירושלים תשנ״ח.

Fechter, '*Tefisat Had'veikut B'tz'fat*' =

מ' פכטר, ״תפיסת הדביקות ותיאורה בספרות הדרוש והמוסר של
חכמי צפת במאה הט״ז״, מחקרי ירושלים
במחשבת ישראל ג (תשמ״ב), עמ' 51-121.

Fechter, '*L'virur Hamusagim*' =

מ' פכטר, ״לבירור המושגים ״קטנות״ ו״גדלות״ בקבלת האר״י כרקע
להבנתם במחשבת החסידות״, דברי הכנס הבינלאומי לחקר תולדות
המיסטיקה היהודית לזכר ג' שלום - קלת האר״י מחקרי ירושלים
במחשבת ישראל י (תשנ״ב), עמ' 171-210.

Fechter, 'L'sugiat Haemunah' =

מ׳ פכטר, ״לסוגיית האמונה והכפירה במשנת ר׳ נחמן מברסלב״,
דעת 45 (קיץ תש״ס), עמ׳ 134-105.

Feikazh, '*Zaddik*' =

מ׳ פייקאז׳, ׳צדיק לבני הדור החדש?!׳, תרביץ 51 (תשמ״ב),
עמ׳ 149-165.

Feikazh, *Chasidut Bratslav* =

מ׳ פייקאז׳, חסידות ברסלב: פרקים בחיי מחוללה ובכתביה,
ירושלים תשל״ב.

Feikazh, *Bein Idi'ologiah L'mitziut* =

מ׳ פייקאז׳, בין אידיאולוגיה למציאות - ענווה אין, ביטול ממציאות
ודביקות במחשבתם של ראשי החסידות, ירושלים תשנ״ד.

Fishbane, M., 'Joy and Jewish Spirituality,' *Exegetical Imagination*. Cambridge,
        Mass: 1998. 151-172.

Fishbane, M., *The Kiss of God*. Seattle and London: 1994.

Frazer, J.G., *The Golden Bough*. New York: 1960

Goldberg, '*Hasipur Hachasidi Sheb'fi Hazaddik*' =

ר׳ גולדברג, הסיפור החסידי שבפי הצדיק: בין עיצוב ספרותי למסר
אידיאי - עיון במדגם מייצג של סיפורים בהדגש על סיפורי רבי
ישראל מרוז׳ין, חיבור לשם קבלת תואר דוקטור לפילוסופיה,
האוניברסיטה העברית, ירושלים תשנ״ז.

Goshen, '*Eretz Israel B'haguto*' =

א׳ גושן, ״ארץ ישראל בהגותו של ר׳ נחמן מברסלב״, בתוך: א׳
רביצקי (עורך), ארץ ישראל בהגות היהודית
בעת החדשה, ירושלים תשנ״ח, עמ׳ 300-276.

Gottlieb, *Mechkarim B'sifrut Hakabbalah* =

א׳ גוטליב, מחקרים בספרות הקבלה, תל-אביב תשמ״ו.

Green, *Tormented Master* =

א׳י גרין, בעל היסורים - פרשת חייו של ר׳ נחמן מברסלב,
תל-אביב תשל״א.

Green, '*L'bikorato*' =

א׳י גרין, ״לביקורתו של מ׳ פייקאז׳ על ספרי ׳בעל היסורים׳״,
תרביץ נא תשמ״ב), עמ׳ 508-509.

Green, *Bakshu Panai* =

א׳י גרין, בקשו פני - קראו בשמי - אמונתו של מחפש, תל-אביב
תשנ״ז.

Gris, *Sifrut Hahanhagut* =

ז׳ גריס, ספרות ההנהגות - תולדותיה ומקומה בחיי חסידיו
של הבעש״ט, ירושלים תש״ן.

Harvey, 'Torat Hanevuah Hasintetit' =

ז' הרוי "תורת הנבואה הסינאסתטית של ריה"ל והערה על ספר
הזוהר", קולות רבים ספר הזיכרון לרבקה ש"ץ-אופנהיימר כרך
א ר' אליאור וי' דך עורכים, ירושלים תשנ"ו, עמ' 155-141.

Heller-Vilinski, '*Hitgalut Emunah Ut'vunah*' =

ש' הלר וילנסקי "התגלות אמונה ותבונה בפילוסופיה היהודית של
ימי הביניים" התגלות אמונה תבונה משה חלמיש ומשה שוורץ
(עורכים), אוניברסיטת בר-אילן, רמת-גן תשל"ו, עמ' 27-25.

Hoyzinga, *Ha'adam Hamisachek* =

י' הויזינגה, האדם המשחק - על מקור התרבות במשחק, תרגם ש'
מוהליבר, ירושלים תשמ"ד.

Idel, '*Al Eretz Yisrael*' =

מ' אידל "על ארץ ישראל במחשבה היהודית המיסטית של ימי
הביניים" בתוך: מ' חלמיש וא' רביצקי (עורכים), ארץ ישראל בהגות
היהודית בימי-הביניים, ירושלים תשנ"א, עמ' 207-206.

Idel, '*Al Kavanat Shmoneh Esrei*' =

מ' אידל, "על כוונת שמונה עשרה אצל ר' יצחק סגי-נהור, משואות
- מחקרים בספרות הקבלה ובמחשבה ישראל מוקדשים לזכרו של
פרופ' אפרים גוטליב, בעריכת מ' אורון וע' גודרייך,
ירושלים תשנ"ז, עמ' 25-52.

Idel, *Perakim B'kabbalah N'vuit* =

מ' אידל, פרקים בקבלה נבואית, ירושלים 1990.

Idel, M., 'Conceptualizations of Music in Jewish Mysticism,' *Enchanting Powers
   – Music in the World's Religion*. Ed. Lawrence E. Sullivan, Cambridge,
   Mass, 1997, 159–188.

Idel, '*Demuth Ha'adam*' =

מ' אידל, "דמות האדם שמעל הספירות", דעת4 (תשמ"ם), עמ' 41-55.

Idel, '*Dimuyim Umaasim*' =

מ' אידל, "דימויים ומעשים מיניים בקבלה", זמנים42 (תשנ"ב),
עמ' 31-39.

Idel, *Hachasidut* =

מ' אידל, החסידות: בין אקסטזה למאגיה, ירושלים ותל-אביב
תשס"א.

Idel, *Hachavayah Hamistit* =

מ' אידל, החויה המיסטית אצל אברהם אבולעפיה, ירושלים תשמ"ח.

Idel, '*Hapeirush Hamagi*' =

מ' אידל, "הפירוש המאגי והתיאורגי של המוסיקה בטקסטים יהודיים
מתקופת הרנסנס ועד החסידות", יובל - קובץ מחקרים של המרכז
לחקר המוסיקה היהודית, בעריכת י' אדלר וב' באיאר, בשיתוף
ל' שלם, ירושלים תשמ"ב, כרך ד, עמ' לג-סב.

Idel, *Hebetim Chadashim* =

מ' אידל, קבלה - היבטים חדשים ירושלים ותל־אביב תשנ"ג.

Idel, '*Hitbodedut*: On Solitude in Jewish Mysticism.' *Einsamkeit, Archaeologie der Literischen Kommunikation VI*. Eds. Aleida Assman and Jan Assman, Munchen: 2000. 189–212.

Idel, '*Hitbodedut K'rikuz B'kabbalah*' =

מ' אידל, "התבוננות כריכוז בקבלה האקסטטית וגלגוליה, דעת 14 (תשמ"ה), עמ' 35-81.

Idel, '*Hitbodedut K'rikuz B'philosophiah*' =

מ' אידל, "התבודדות כריכוז בפילוסופיה היהודית" ספר היובל לשלמה פינס ח"א, מחקרי ירושלים במחשבת ישראל ז (תשמ"ה), עמ' 39–60.

Idel, *Kitvei R. Avraham Abulafia* =

מ' אידל, כתבי ר' אברהם אבולעפיה ומשנתו, עבודה לשם קבלת תואר דוקטור, ב כרכים, ירושלים

Idel, '*Latoldoth Ha'isur lilmod kabbalah lifnei gil arbaim*' =

מ' אידל, "לתולדות האיסור ללמוד קבלה לפני גיל ארבעים" AGS Review 5 1980 עמ' א-כ.

Idel, M., *Messianic Mystics*. New Haven and London: 1998.

Idel, '*Musag Hatzimtzum*' =

מ' אידל, "על תולדות מושג 'הצמצום' בקבלה ובמחקר" דברי הכנס הבין לאומי הרביעי לחקר תולדות המיסטיקה היהודית לזכר ג' שלום - קבלת האר"י מחקרי ירושלים במחשבת ישראל (תשמ"ב), עמ' 59-112.

Idel, '*Nachtliche Kabbalisten*,' *Die Wahrheit der Traume*. G. Benedetti, E. Hornung (Hrsg), Munich, 1997: 85–117.

Idel, *R. Menachem Recanati Hamekubal* =

מ' אידל, ר' מנחם רקנאטי המקובל, כרך א, ירושלים ותל-אביב תשנ"ח.

Idel, '*Shtei Ha'arot*' =

מ' אידל, שתי הערות על ס' חרב פיפיות לר' יאיר בן שבתאי, קרית ספר נג (תשל"ח) עמ' 213-214.

Idel, '*T'arim Us'firot* =

מ' אידל, "תארים וספירות בתיאולוגיה היהודית" מחקרים בהגות היהודית, ש' הלר וילנסקי ומ' אידל עורכים, ירושלים תשמ"ט, עמ' 87-111.

Idel, '*Tefisat Hatorah*' =

מ' אידל, "תפיסת התורה בהיכלות ובקבלה", מחקרי ירושלים במחשבת ישראל א (תשמ"א) עמ' 23-84.

Idel, 'Universalization and Integration: Two Conceptions of Mystical Union in jewish Mysticism.' *Mystical Union and Monotheistic faith – an Ecumenical Dialogue*,' in Eds. Moshe Idel and Bernard McGinn. New York and London: 1988. 27–57.

Idel, *'Yofyah shel Ishah'* =

מ' אידל, "יופיה של אישה - לתולדותיה של המיסטיקה היהודית", במעגלי חסידים - קובץ מחקרים לזכרו של פרופ' מרדכי וילנסקי, ע' אטקס, ד' אסף, י' ברטל וא' ריינר עורכים, ירושלים תש"ס, עמ' 317–334.

Jacobs, L., 'The Uplifting of Sparks in later Jewish Mysticism.' *Jewish Spirituality, From the Sixteenth-Century Revival to the Present*. Ed. A. Green, Vol. 2, London: 1987. 99–126.

James, *Hachavayah Hadatit* =

ו' ג'יימס, החוויה הדתית לסוגיה - מחקר בטבע האדם, תרגם י' קופילוביץ, ירושלים תשנ"ד.

Kallus, M., 'The Relation of the Baal Shem Tov to the Practice of Lurrianic Kavvanot in Light of his Comments on the Siddur Rahkov.' *Kabbalah – Journal for the Study of Jewish Mystical Texts* 2 (1997): 151–167.

Klein-Bratslavi, *Hapeirush shel Harambam* =

ש' קליין-ברסלבי, הפירוש של הרמב"ם לסיפורים על אדם בפרשת בראשית, ירושלים תשמ"ז.

Klein-Bratslavi, *'Nevuah Kesem V'chalom'* =

ש' קליין-ברסלבי, "נבואה קסם וחלום והמונח "התבודדות" במשנת הרלב"ג", דעת 39 (תשנ"ז), עמ' 23–68.

Kreisel, *'Chacham V'navi'* =

ח' קרייסל, "חכם ונביא במשנת הרמב"ם", אשל באר שבע ג, עמ' 149–169.

Lachover, 'B'Shaar Hamigdal' =

פ' לחובר, "בשער המגדל", על גבול הישן והחדש, ירושלים תשי"א, עמ' 29–78.

Levinger, *'Al Taam Han'zirut'* =

י' לוינגר, "על טעם הנזירות במורה נבוכים", בר-אילן - קובץ העשור, רמת-גן תשכ"ז, עמ' 299–305.

Levinstein, *'Ha'arot'* =

ד' לוינשטיין, "הערות ביחס לדמותו של שאול", בית מקרא 37 (תשרי-כסלו תשנ"ב), עמ' 79–83.

Levin–Katz, *'Segulot V'eitzot'* =

י' לוין-כ"ץ, "סגולות ועצות למציאת הזיווג בכתבי ר' נחמן וגלגוליהן", שנה בשנה, מ' (תש"ס), עמ' 348–370.

Liebes, *'Hatikkun Hak'lali'* =

י' ליבס, "התיקון הכללי של ר' נחמן מברסלב ויחסו לשבתאות", ציון 45 (תש"ם), עמ' 201–245.

Liebes, '*Magamot B'cheker Hachasidut*' =

י׳ ליבס, ״מגמות בחקר חסידות ברסלב - לביקורתו של י׳ מונדשיין
על מאמרי ׳התיקון הכללי של ר׳ נחמן מברסלב ויחסו לשבתאות׳״,
ציון מז (תשמ״ב), עמ׳ 231–224.

Liebes, '*Trein Urzilin*' =

י׳ ליבס, ״׳תרין אורזילין דאילתא׳ - דרשתו הסודית של האר״י
לפני מותו״, דברי הכנס הבינלאומי לחקר תולדות המיסטיקה
היהודית לזכר ג׳ שלום: קבלת האר״י, מחקרי ירושלים במחשבת
ישראל, י (תשנ״ב), עמ׳ 113–161.

Liebes, '*Zohar V'eros*' =

י׳ ליבס, ״זוהר וארוס״, אלפיים 9 (תשנ״ד) עמ׳ 119–67.

Lasky, M., *Ecstasy*, New York: 1968.

Magid, S., 'Conjugal Union, Mourning and Talmud Tora in R. Isaac Luria's Tikkun Hazot,' *Daat* 36 (1996): xvii–xlv.

Magid, S., 'Through the Void:' The Absence of God on R. Nachamn's *Likkutei Moharan*' *Harvard Theological Review* 88 (1995): 485–519.

Markos, *Keset Hasofer* =

א׳ מרכוס, קסת הסופר, קראקא 1912,

Markos, *Hahasidut* =

א׳ מרכוס, החסידות, תרגם מ׳ שנפלד, תל-אביב תשי״ד.

Margolin, *Haemunah V'Hakefirah* =

ר׳ מרגולין, האמונה והכפירה בחסידות ברסלב על פי הספר
ליקוטי הלכות לר׳ נתן שטרנהרץ, עבודת גמר לתואר
מוסמך, אוניברסיטת חיפה 1991.

Mark, '*Al Matzavei Katnut V'gadlut*' =

צ׳ מרק, ״על מצבי קטנות וגדלות בהגותו של ר׳ נחמן מברסלב״ דעת
46 (חורף תשס״א), עמ׳ 80-45.

Mark, *Shigaon v'daat* =

צ׳ מרק, שגעון ודעת בצירת ר׳ נחמן מברסלב - על זיקת העבודה
הדתית וההתנסות המיסטית למצבי תודעה נטולי דעת, עבודת
דוקטורת האוניברסיטה העברית, ירושלים, תש״ס.

Mark, *Sipurei R. Nachman* =

צ׳ מרק, סיפורי ר׳ נחמן מברסלב - אקזיסטנציאליזם חסידי,
עבודת מ״א, אוניברסיטת בר-אילן, רמת-גן תשנ״ג.

Matt, D. C. '*Ayin* – The Concept of Nothingness in Jewish Mysticism,' in Robert K.C. Forman (ed.), *The Problem of Pure Consciousness: Mysticism and Philosophy.* New York, Oxford: 1990: 121–159.

Meroz, '*Milikutei Efraim Pantzeiri*' =

ר׳ מרוז, ״מליקוטי אפרים פאנצ׳יירי - דרשת האר״י בירושלים
וכוונות האכילה״, מחקרי ירושלים במחשבת ישראל י (תשנ״ב),
עמ׳ 257–41.

Mundstein, '*Al Hatikun Hak'lali'* =

י׳ מונדשיין, "על ׳התיקון הכללי של ר׳ נחמן מברסלב ויחסו
לשבתאות׳", ציון מז (תשמ״ב), עמ׳ 245–201.

Naeh, '*Borei Niv Sefataim'* =

ש׳ נאה, "׳בורא ניב שפתים׳ - פרק בפנומנולוגיה של התפילה על פי
משנת ברכות ד, ג; ה, ה״, תרביץ סג, ב (תשנ״ד), עמ׳ 218–185.

Nigal, *Hasiporet Hachasidit* =

ג׳ נגאל, הסיפורת החסידית - תולדותיה ונושאיה, ירושלים 1981.

Nistar, Der, *Beit Mashber* =

דר נסתר, בית משבר (רומן היסטורי), א, תרגמו: ח׳ רבינזון וש׳
נחמני, מרחביה 1947; ב, תרגם: א״ד שפיר, תל-אביב 1951.

Oppenheimer, *Hanevuah Hakeduma* =

הנבואה הקדומה = ב׳ אופנהיימר, הנבואה הקדומה בישראל,
ירושלים תשמ״ד.

Oppenheimer, '*Akdamot L'shealat Haekstaza'* =

ב׳ אופנהיימר, "אקרמות לשאלת האקסטזה הנבואית", ספר בר-אילן
כב-כג, רמת-גן תשמ״ח, עמ׳ 62–45.

Otto, *Hakedushah* =

ר׳ אוטו, הקדושה - על הלא-רציונלי באידאת האל ויחסו לרציונלי,
תרגום מ׳ רון, ירושלים תשנ״מ.

Otto, R., *Mysticism East and West*. London: 1932.

Poko, *Toldot Hashigaon* =

מ׳ פוקו, תולדות השיגעון בעידן התבונה, תרגם אהרן אמיר,
ירושלים 1972.

Rapoport, '*Shnei Mekorot'* =

ע׳ רפפורט, ׳שני מקורות לתאור נסיעתו של ר׳ נחמן מברסלב
לא״י׳, קרית ספר, 46 (תשל״א), עמ׳ 147-153.

Rapoport-Albert, A., 'Confession in the Circle of Rabbi Nahman of Bratslav,'
   Bulletin for the Institute of Jewish Studies, I, London: 1973: 65–96.

Rapoport-Albert, '*Katnut'* =

ע׳ רפפורט-אלברט, "קטנות׳, ׳פשיטות׳ ו׳איני יודע׳ של ר׳
נחמן מברסלב",

Studies in Jewish Religious and Intellectual History, Presented to A. Altmann,
Alabama, 1979.

החלק העברי, עמ׳ ז-לג

Raz, *Sichot Meturafot* =

י רז, שיחות מטורפות, מעשי זן, תל אביב 1995.

Rose, N., 'Erez Israel in the Theology and Experience of Rabbi Nahman of
   Bratzlav,' *The Journal of Hebraic Studies* 1,2 (1970): 63–84.

Rosenberg, '*Huh U Ut'murato* =

ש׳ רוזנברג, ״הוא ותמורתו יהיה קודש״, שנה בשנה 40 (תש״ס),
עמ׳ 333–325.

Rosenberg, '*Musag Ha'emunah*' =

ש׳ רוזנברג, ״מושג האמונה בהגותו של הרמב״ם וממשיכיו״, ספר
בר-אילן כב-כג (תשמ״ח), עמ׳ 351-389.

Rosenberg, '*Mitos HaMitosim*' =

ש׳ רוזנברג, ״מיתוס המיתוסים״, מדעי היהדות 38 (תשנ״ח),
עמ׳ 145–179.

Rosenberg, '*R. Boruch Mikosov*' =

ש׳ רוזנברג, ״ר׳ ברוך מקוסוב וראשיתה של החסידות״, סיני קטז
(תשנ״ה), עמ׳ קעה-קעז.

Ross, '*Shnei Perushim l'Torat Hatzimtzum*' =

ת׳ רוס, ״שני פירושים לתורת הצמצום - ר׳ חיים מוולוז׳ין ורש״ז
מלאדי״, מחקרי ירושלים במחשבת ישראל (תשמ״ב), עמ׳ 169–153.

Schatz-Oppenheimer, *Hachasidut K'mistkah* =

ר׳ ש״ץ-אופנהיימר, החסידות כמיסטיקה: יסודות קווייאטיסטיים
במחשבה החסידית במאה הי״ח, ירושלים תשכ״ח.

Schatz-Oppenheimer, '*L'mahuto Shel Hazaddik*' =

ר׳ ש״ץ-אופנהיימר ״למהותו של הצדיק״ מולד יח (1960) עמ׳ 365–378.

Schiller, *Al Hanisgav* =

פ׳ שילר, על הנשגב - שירה נאיווית וסנטימנטאל׳יסטית, תרגום ד׳
ארן, תל-אביב תשמ״ו.

Scholem, '*Demuto Hahistorit*' =

ג׳ שלום, ״דמותו ההיסטורית של הבעש״ט״, דברים בגו, תל-אביב
תשל״ו, עמ׳ 324–287.

Scholem, '*Deveikut*,' =

ג׳ שלום, ״דבקות או התקשרות אינטימית עם אלוהים בראשית
החסידות - הלכה ומעשה״, דברים בגו, תל-אביב תשל״ו, עמ׳ 350–325.
Scholem, G., *Major Trends in Jewish Mysticism*. New York: 1941.
Scholem *Pirkei Yesod* =

ג׳ שלום, פרקי יסוד בהבנת הקבלה וסמליה, תרגם י׳ בן שלמה,
ירושלים תשל״ו.

Scholem, *Reishit Hakabalah* =

ג׳ שלום, ראשית הקבלה, ירושלים ותל-אביב תש״ח.

Scholem, '*Sh'nei Kuntresim*' =

ג׳ שלום, ״שני קונטרסים לר׳ משה די-ליאון״, קובץ על יד, סדרה
חדשה, ספר ח (יה), ירושלים תשל״ו, עמ׳ 384–325.
Scholem, G., *Origins of the Kabbalah*. Ed. R.J.Z Werblowsky. Princeton: 1987.
Shochet, '*Al HaSimchah*' =

ע׳ שוחט, ״על השמחה בחסידות״, ציון טז (תשי״א), עמ׳ 43–30.

Shoham, *Yetzirah V'hitgalut* =

ג׳ שלום, יצירה והתגלות, תל אביב תשמ״ז.

Shtil, *Psicholog* =

י׳ שתיל, פסיכולוג בישיבת ברסלב מיסטיקה יהודית - הלכה
למעשה תל-אביב 1993.

Shtil, *Chidat Ha'energiah Hanafshit* =

י׳ שתיל, חידת האנרגיה הנפשית; משמעותה של האנרגיה הנפשית
בתורות-אישיות פסיכולוגיות ודתיות, תל-אביב תשנ״ו.

Shvid, *'Chazarah L'artiyutah Shel Eretz Yisrael'* =

א׳ שביד, ׳חזרה לארציותה של ארץ ישראל - ארץ ישראל במשנתו
של הרבי נחמן מברצלב׳, בספרו מולדת וארץ יעודה - ארץ ישראל
בהגות של עם ישראל, תל-אביב תשל״ט, עמ׳ 105–93.

Tishbi and Dan, *'Chasidut'* =

י׳ תשבי ו׳ דן, ערך ׳תורת החסידות וספרותה׳, האנציקלופדיה
העברית יז, ירושלים תשכ״ה, טורים 821–756.

Tishbi, *'Hara'ayon Ham'shichi'* =

י׳ תשבי, ״הרעיון המשיחי והמגמות המשיחות בצמיחת החסידות״,
ציון לב (תשכ״ז), 45–1.

Tishbi, *'Hashlamot'* =

י׳ תשבי, ״השלמות למאמרי על מקור האמרה קודשא בריך
הוא אורייתא וישראל כולא חד״, קרית ספר (תשל״ה), עמ׳ 674–668.

Tishbi, *'Kudsha brich Hu v'oraita'* =

י׳ תשבי, ״״קודשא בריך הוא ואורייתא וישראל כולא חד׳ - מקור
האמרה בפירוש אדרא רבא לרמח״ל״, קרית ספר נ (תשל״ה),
עמ׳ 492–480.

Tishbi, *Mishnat Hazohar* =

י׳ תשבי, משנת הזוהר, ירושלים תש״ט.

Tishbi, *Torat Hara* =

י׳ תשבי, תורת הרע והקליפה בקבלת האר״י, ירושלים תשנ״ב.

Turner, V., 'Variations on a Theme of Liminality,' *Secular Ritual.* Eds. Sally F. Moore and Barbara G. Myerhoff. Assen and Amsterdam: 1979. 36–51.

Underhill, A., *Mysticism: A Study in the Nature and Development of Man's Spiritual Consciousness.* New York: 1955.

Van Gennep, A. *The Rites of Passage.* London: 1960.

Verman, M., 'Aliyah and Yeridah – The Journeys of the Besht and R. Nachman to Israel.' *Approaches to Judaism in Medieval Times*, Vol. 3. Atlanta, Georgia: 1988. 159–171.

Weiss, J., 'The Kavvanoth of Prayer in Early Hasidism.' *Studies in Eastern European Jewish Mysticism.* Oxford: 1985. 95–125.

Weiss, '*Reishit Tz'michatah*'=

י' וייס, "ראשית צמיחתה של הדרך החסידית", ציון טז (תשי"א),
עמ' 105–46.

Weiss, '*Talmud Torah Bereishit*' =

י' וייס, "תלמוד תורה בראשית החסידות", הדאר לג (תשכ"ה),
עמ' 618–615.

Weiss, J., *Studies in Eastern European Jewish Mysticism*, Oxford, 1985.

Weiss, *Mechkarim* =

י' וייס, מחקרים בחסידות ברסלב, ערך וההדיר: מ' פייקאז',
ירושלים תשל"ה.

Weiss, '*Talmud Torah L'shitat*' =

י' וייס, "תלמוד תורה לשיטת ר' ישראל בעש"ט", תפארת ישראל,
ספר היובל לכבוד ר' ישראל ברודי, לונדון תשכ"ז, עמ' 159–151.

Werblowsky, 'Ape and Essence,' Geo WidFestschrift (ed.) *Ex orde Religionum*,
        Leiden, 1972. 159–171.

Werblowsky, *R. Yosef Karo* =

רי"צ ורבלובסקי, ר' יוסף קארו - בעל הלכה ומקובל, תרגם י'
צורן, ירושלים תשנ"ו.

Wilenski, *Hasidim U'mitnagdim* =

מ' וילנסקי, חסידים ומתנגדים, ב כרכים, ירושלים תש"ן.

Wolfish, '*Hatefilah Hashugeret*' =

א' וולפיש, "'התפילה השוגרת' (ברכות ד, ג; ה, ה;) - על גבול
ההשראה והאקסטזה", תרביץ סה, ב (תשנ"ו), עמ' 314–301.

Wolfson, E. R., *Circle in the Square* = E. R. Wolfson, *Circle in the Square – Studies
        in the Use of Gender in Kabbalistic Symbolism*. Albany: 1995.

Wolfson, E.R., 'Female Imaging of The Torah' = E. R. Wolfson, 'Female
        Imaging of The Torah:' From Literary Metaphor to Religious
        Symbol,' *Circle in the Square – Studies in the Use of Gender in Kabbalistic
        Symbolism*. Albany: 1995.

Wolfson, E.R., *Through a Speculum that Shines* = E. R. Wolfson, *Through a
        Speculum that Shines: Vision and Imagination in   Medieval Jewish
        Mysticism*. Princeton, NY: 1994.

Wolfson, *Pilon* =

צ' וולפסון, פילון; יסודות הפילוסופיה הדתית היהודית,
תרגם מ' מייזליש, ב כרכים, ירושלים תשל.

Yaakovson, *Torat Hahasidut* =

י' יעקובסון, תורתה של החסידות, תל-אביב תשמ"ו.

Ysif, *Sipur Ha'am Ha'ivri* =

ע' יסיף, סיפור העם העברי, ירושלים תשנ"ד.

Zack, '*Iyun B'hashpa'at*,' = B. Zack, '*Iyun B'hashpa'at* R. Moshe Cordovero al
        Hachasidut,' *Eshel Beer Sheva* 3 (1976): 288–306.

Zack, '*Yachaso Shel R. Shlomo*' =

ב׳ זק, ״יחסו של ר׳ שלמה אלקבץ לחקירה הפילוסופית״,
תשל באר-שבע א (תשל״ו), עמ׳ 306–288.

Zack, *B'shaarei Hakabbalah* =

ב׳ זק, בשערי הקבלה של ר׳ משה קורדובירו, ירושלים תשנ״ה.

Zeitlin, *R. Nachman M'Bratslav* =

ה׳ צייטלין, ר׳ נחמן מברסלב - חייו ותורתו, ורשה תר״ע.

Zeitlin, *Al Gvul Shnei Olamot* =

ה׳ צייטלין, גבול שני עולמות, תל-אביב תשנ״ז.

Index